SOUTHERN HORRORS

SOUTHERN HORRORS

Women and the Politics of Rape and Lynching

CRYSTAL N. FEIMSTER

HARVARD UNIVERSITY PRESS
Cambridge, Massachusetts, and London, England

Printed in the United States of America

First Harvard University Press paperback edition, 2011

Library of Congress Cataloging-in-Publication Data

Feimster, Crystal Nicole, 1972–
Southern horrors : women and the politics of rape and lynching / Crystal N. Feimster.
p.   cm.
ISBN 978-0-674-03562-1 (cloth: alk. paper)
ISBN 978-0-674-06185-9 (pbk.)
1. Women—Violence against—Southern States—History.   2. Women—Southern States—Social
conditions—History.   3. Southern States—Social conditions—History.   4. Rape—Southern
States—History.   5. African Americans—Southern States—History.   I. Title.
HV6250.4.W65F43 2009
364.1'34—dc22   2009013934

For
Dani and Charles

CONTENTS

Illustrations follow page 124

SOUTHERN HORRORS

INTRODUCTION:
IN BLACK AND WHITE

This is a history of two southern women, Rebecca Latimer Felton (1835–
1930) and Ida B. Wells (1862–1931), and the thousands of women who
joined their campaigns against rape and for women's rights in the late nineteenth and early twentieth centuries during the height of lynching in the
American South. Felton was born in 1835 to a prosperous slaveholding family in De Kalb, Georgia. Wells, the daughter of slaves, was born in 1862 in
Holly Springs, Mississippi. Despite differences in their age, race, class, and
status, they both, in very different contexts, took radical stances on rape and
lynching. Together, their struggles against sexual violence—Wells advocated on black women's behalf and Felton mostly fought for the protection
of poor white women—brought to southern politics the concerns of women
who historically had been excluded from debates about rape and protection.
Although both campaigned for women's safety, they confronted the problem
of lynching in completely different ways. While Wells became internation-
ally known for her radical anti-lynching crusade, it was Felton's notorious
plea to "lynch a thousand a week" that thrust her into the national spotlight.
From different sides of the color line, Felton and Wells were women's rights
pioneers who negotiated and challenged the racial and sexual politics of the
New South.

The story of these two women (and the movements they spearheaded)
begins during the early nineteenth century on the Georgia slave plantation where Felton was born, and concludes in the nation's capital in 2005,
when the 109th U.S. Congress honored Ida B. Wells-Barnett with a resolution apologizing for the Senate's failure to pass anti-lynching legislation. While the narrative is firmly fixed in the political turmoil of the late
1800s, it has deep roots in the antebellum South and the national controversy over slavery. During the decades when Rebecca Latimer was growing up and being trained as a plantation mistress and Ida Wells's parents

were coping with the harsh realities of slavery, America was rushing toward civil war with a momentum terrifying to those invested in the institution of slavery and exciting to those in bondage who believed the war might bring freedom.

The rise of the abolitionist movement and its relentless focus on the racial and sexual dynamics of slavery influenced every facet of civil and political discourse in the years leading up to war as well as the decades that followed the South's defeat. Whites and blacks, free and enslaved, male and female, all helped to bring attention to the brutal horrors of slavery. By highlighting the violent nature of that institution—from the whipping of slave children to the sexual exploitation of female slaves—abolitionists hastened the nation toward war. The following sequence of events defined the antislavery debates and set the stage for war: In 1829, David Walker, a black abolitionist, published an *Appeal* that called on slaves to resort to violence when necessary to win their freedom.[1] Nat Turner's slave rebellion in Virginia in 1831 brought urgency to the question of violence as a means of acquiring freedom. In the same year, William Lloyd Garrison published the first issue of his antislavery newspaper, the *Liberator*, and called for the immediate emancipation of all slaves. In 1833 he founded the American Anti-Slavery Society, an interracial organization that embraced women's support. Soon after, black and white women together began to organize auxiliary female antislavery societies.[2] The publication of Frederick Douglass's autobiography exposed the particular horrors of slavery for children and women, and Harriet Beecher Stowe's *Uncle Tom's Cabin* energized antislavery forces.[3] Finally, in 1859, John Brown led a raid on the federal arsenal at Harpers Ferry, Virginia, in a plan to arm slaves and bring about emancipation.

Helping to propel this radical movement against slavery were two southern white sisters, Angelina and Sarah Grimké of Charleston, South Carolina. The daughters of a prominent judge and plantation owner, they had witnessed the horrors of slavery on their family plantation. Sarah, the eldest of the two, initially expressed abolitionist sentiments after seeing a slave being whipped. Her brother's illicit relationship with a slave woman no doubt had a profound impact on her ideas about slavery as well. In 1821, Sarah left the South for Philadelphia, where she became a Quaker. Angelina joined her in 1829. In 1836, Angelina wrote her first abolitionist tract, *Appeal to the Christian Women of the South*, to encourage southern white women to join the antislavery movement.[4] She argued that white women had a common cause with female slaves. In 1838, Sarah explained in *Letters on the Equality of the Sexes,* "If amid all her degradation and ignorance, a woman desires to preserve her virtue unsullied, she is either bribed or whipped into compliance, or if she dares resist her seducer, her life by the laws of some of the slave States may be, and has actually been sacrificed to the fury of disappointed passion."[5] Denouncing southern white men who sexually exploited slave women and then allowed their offspring to grow up enslaved, the Grimkés were not typical southern white ladies. Their willingness to openly discuss the sexual behavior of white men provoked public outrage in the South. Officials in South Carolina publicly burned the pamphlet and the sisters were warned that they would be arrested if they returned home.

The Grimkés also caused an uproar in the North by lecturing publicly about the evils of slavery, making them the first women to do so outside private circles.[6] They called on white women to acknowledge their natural bond with black female slaves and provided mixed audiences with shockingly detailed descriptions of the sexual corruptions of slavery. When educator Catherine Beecher attacked them by arguing that women should restrict their activities to the domestic sphere, Angelina wrote her a series of letters staunchly defending the abolitionist cause and her right to speak publicly. When they were criticized in Congregationalist pulpits for engaging in "promiscuous conversation . . . with regard to things 'which ought not be named,'" Sarah defended women's right to the public platform: "Men and women were CREATED EQUAL," she wrote, "they are both moral and accountable beings; and whatever is *right* for man to do, is *right* for woman."[7]

The Grimkés' call for equal rights for women produced a split in the abolitionist movement. One wing, led by Garrison, moved to include women as full and equal participants in the work of converting white Americans to the moral necessity of abolishing slavery. After 1840 women served as officers and paid organizers of the American Anti-Slavery Society. A second wing insisted that the issue of women's equality needed to be kept separate from that of abolition. The split within the abolitionist movement would have long-term consequences. Nevertheless, the Grimkés' plea for the protection of black women laid the foundation for a fragile, but profound, alliance between white and black women committed to both the abolition of slavery and women's rights.

The Grimkés' courageous defense of black womanhood and their relentless insistence on equal rights created a political opening for black female abolitionists such as Sojourner Truth and Harriet A. Jacobs. Born into slavery in New York in 1797, Truth joined the abolitionist movement in the 1840s and published her autobiography, *Narrative of Sojourner Truth*, in 1850. She began speaking publicly against slavery and for women's rights; after delivering a speech in 1851 at a women's rights convention in Akron, Ohio, Truth famously emerged as an enduring "symbol" of antislavery feminism.[8] As a woman and a former slave, she represented both the horrors of black women's experiences under slavery and the limits of women's freedom. Her call for women's rights without regard to race or former status—captured in the phrase "Ar'nt I a woman?"—would serve as a mantra for black and white women well into the twentieth century.[9]

Harriet Jacobs, a slave in Edenton, North Carolina, escaped to New York in 1842 and joined the antislavery feminist movement. Her autobiography, *Incidents in the Life of a Slave Girl* (1861), is one of the best-known slave accounts of the impact of sexual violence on black women. Jacobs's autobiography left little doubt about slave women's sexual vulnerability.[10] Like the Grimké sisters, she highlighted white men's sexual exploitation of female slaves and called on white women for protection. Jacobs recounted how her master sexually harassed her: "He told me that I was made for his use and made to obey his command in every thing; that I was nothing but a slave, whose will must and should surrender to his."[11] She concluded, "There is no shadow of law to protect [slave women] from insult, from violence, or even from death; all these are inflicted by fiends who bear the shape of men."[12] Only an alliance between black and white women could ensure slave women's safety, Jacobs argued.

The vicious racial and sexual politics of slavery spilled over into the postwar South. Although the heroic efforts of female abolitionists based in the North provided a powerful example of the possibility of interracial cooperation, the great divide between black and white women in the South was not easily overcome. After the war and emancipation, new possibilities did begin to open up, but against the wider background of postwar politics, black and white women's efforts to come together across the color line in the New South remained a struggle. The Grimkés, however, had left a powerful legacy.

After the war, as white anxiety about the political, economic, and social meanings of emancipation intensified, different constituencies assembled a convergent set of racial and sexual fantasies. During the overthrow of Reconstruction, southern white men managed to flip the antebellum script of racial and sexual violence. Whereas prior to the war abolitionists had espoused a political narrative that centered on the rape of black women by white men, in the postwar years southern white men articulated a political discourse that defined rape as a crime committed by black men against white women. In constructing the image of the "black rapist," southern white men sought to challenge black men's rights as citizens while simultaneously expanding their own sexual power over both black and white women.[13] The portrayal of black men as beastly and unable to control their sexual desire served to justify the practice of lynching, segregation laws, and disfranchisement of black men.[14]

Not only did the justification of lynching as a protection for white womanhood allow for unprecedented violence against African Americans, it also served to terrorize women and place limitations on their sexual freedom and political rights. Indeed, by the 1890s, southern white men had found in the image of the "black rapist" a powerful political tool for violently maintaining white male supremacy, while also denying Africans Americans their rights as citizens. While the rape justification of mob violence never cohered with reality, it shaped southern politics into a cautionary tale for southern women. Lynching and the threat of rape served as warnings that the New South was a dangerous place for women who transgressed the narrow boundaries of race and gender. At the same time, the stories that southern white men told and used in their white supremacy campaigns served to draw attention away from their own sexual crimes against black and white women.

Studies of lynching have generally ignored how women experienced and responded to rape and lynching in the American South. Because most lynchings in the South had very little to do with the actual crime of rape, scholars have left unexplored the question of how lynching informed women's politics and anti-rape campaigns. A comparative examination of the lives of Felton and Wells provides insight into why southern black and white women asserted their presence in a sexually charged and violent public sphere and how they marshaled narratives of rape and lynching for their own political empowerment. Whether they promoted or denounced lynching, participated in lynchings, or fell victim to mob violence and rape, southern women, both black and white, forced their entry into the racial and sexual politics of the New South.

Indeed, a conjunction of shifting sexual practices, black protest, and female political mobilizations provided the conditions for the elaboration of the rape/lynch narrative. Out of this maelstrom emerged a powerful anti-rape movement led by Felton on one side and Wells on the other. While they may have differed fundamentally about the place of blacks in southern society, they were, ironically, fellow travelers on the path for women's rights. Wells's anti-lynching pamphlet, "Southern Horrors" (1892), and Felton's "Women on the Farm" (1897) lecture (which was taken as a call for and justification of lynching), manifested the same preoccupation with protection against sexual violence and forged an enduring link between the two women. As teachers, journalists, temperance women, anti-rape activists, and suffragists, they shared philosophies of women's rights that were, in many ways, rooted in the ideas and tactics of antislavery feminism. They both took to the public platform for women's rights when it was still deemed inappropriate behavior for women. They published radical tracts insisting on female protection and political rights. They both sought to rein in southern white men's sexual behavior. And they both, albeit in very different ways, laid the groundwork that would eventually allow southern black and white women to come together in the fight against lynching. Like the feminist abolitionists who came before them, Wells and Felton were outspoken and uncompromising advocates for female protection who would radically change the sexual and racial politics of the American South.

1

THE HORRORS OF WAR

In her memoir, *Country Life in Georgia in the Days of My Youth*, Rebecca Latimer Felton recounted the fear on her plantation in 1860 when rumors spread that slaves were planning an insurrection in Cartersville. Writing in the postbellum period, she linked lynching to slave insurrections and reasoned that both the threat of rape by black men and the phenomenon of southern mob violence were slavery's ugly offspring. According to Felton, the mere suggestion of a slave rebellion exposed southern white men's worst fears: the rape of their wives and daughters. "The terror of these risings," Felton wrote, "made Southern fathers and husbands desperate as to remedies. It is the secret of lynching instead of a legal remedy. It was 'born in the blood and bred in the bone,' and a resultant of domestic slavery in the Southern States."[1]

Without question, the racial and sexual politics that made lynching a dominant feature of the postbellum southern political landscape had deep roots in both the slaveholding South and the white southern imagination. This was not because southern planters made a practice of lynching slaves—they were far too valuable to destroy—but because white and black southerners understood perfectly that the institution of slavery had been built on a foundation of racial violence and sexual exploitation. The major players in the postwar drama of rape and lynching were products of this oppressive and violent antebellum past. While southern white men sought a heroic role in this drama and black men were inevitably cast as villains, white and black women often took center stage to claim both protection and independence. Former plantation mistresses and slave women alike knew full well the brutal lessons of slavery and war and used them to construct new political roles for themselves. Determined to challenge white men's political and sexual power—power that had informed every aspect of their prewar lives—southern women sought to become formidable players in the racial and sexual politics of the postwar South.

Felton's primary identity as a plantation mistress shaped every facet of her life, yet it was her wartime experience that inspired her postwar attitudes toward rape and lynching. The trauma and devastation that white women endured during the Civil War transformed them irrevocably and set the stage for the subsequent emergence of a new and powerful southern woman. In the postwar years, Felton became politically adept at using her former status and wartime experiences to demand protection in the form of women's rights. But before leading white women into the rough and tumble world of southern racial and sexual politics, she first had to make sense of her own place in a world turned upside down.

The Making of a Plantation Mistress

Born in 1835 to a prosperous slaveholding family in De Kalb, Georgia, Rebecca Ann Latimer was Charles and Eleanor Swift Latimer's firstborn child. Growing up on Panola, a 725-acre plantation fifteen miles east of Atlanta, she had a seemingly ideal childhood. The South River ran through the estate and several public roads converged on the property where her family owned a flour mill, blacksmith shop, wood shop, tavern, and the general store in which her father also served as the local postmaster. Rebecca's childhood memories reflected the joys of growing up on a wealthy slave plantation with a doting father, a devoted mother, and an adoring black "Mammy." The eldest of four siblings, Rebecca was pampered by her father and wanted for nothing. His gifts ranged from a pony to the best education then available for southern women. While he tolerated her tomboy antics and encouraged her intellectual development and interest in politics, her mother did the day-to-day work of preparing Rebecca for her future as a plantation mistress.[2]

Devout Methodists, the Latimers attended church and revival meetings regularly. Thus, Rebecca's daily activities represented a mixture of disciplined leisure and strict moral guidance. After attending to her chores and reading her bible, she rode her pony, learned to play the guitar and piano to her father's accompaniment on the violin, and frolicked about the property with the family's pet dog. As Rebecca grew older her mother required that she assist her in managing the household and accompany her on the daily rounds. A "close observer" of both her grandmother and mother's housekeeping methods, she acquired many of the skills she would one day need to run her own household. Seventy years later, she would remember her grandmother's "industry, her management and her executive ability in caring for and carrying on her household affairs."[3] Rebecca's "Mammy" also played an important part in her training. It was under her supervision that she learned to knit, to sew, to card cotton rolls, and to appreciate the importance of table manners. "I can see in memory a little child intent on learning things Mammy could teach her . . . and trying to do what Mammy did," she recalled.[4]

Along with cooking, cleaning, sewing, and tending a garden, Rebecca also had to learn to manage house slaves. Free to discipline slaves, but at the same time demand their affections, Rebecca learned how and when to wield her power. When, as a young girl, she slapped her "Mammy," she quickly realized the limits and consequences of her authority. "I had to beg Mammy's pardon, and also have her hug me once again to her bosom in token of a better peace." Rebecca described herself as having "some temper then and later on," so it is unlikely that this was the only time that she became "impatient" with a female slave.[5] However, her freedom to command and discipline slaves was limited by her mother and later by her husband when she became the mistress of her own household.[6]

From an early age, Rebecca was integrated into a hierarchical social order that sanctioned male dominance and discouraged female autonomy. Because southern white women were legally subordinated to and economically dependent on their fathers and husbands, they had little choice but to accept paternalistic domination in exchange for male protection and a measure of discrete power within the household.[7] As an obedient and dutiful daughter, Rebecca could count on her father's care. It was he who came to her rescue when she found "a drunken man hanging on their front gate shouting the most awful things."[8] The strange man served as a reminder of the dangers that lay outside the "sheltered security" of the plantation and her father's protective and watchful eye. Rebecca and the other young women of her class were always closely guarded and never traveled without male chaperones.[9]

Charles Latimer not only protected Rebecca from the dangers that existed outside their front gate, but also ensured that she had access to a formal education of the kind considered appropriate for a young lady of her status and background. When she reached the age of five, he donated land to the community to build a school for her to attend. Three years later, when the schoolhouse burned, he sent her to a private school in

Oxford where she boarded with a minister's family. Along with "readin, writin, and cipheren," she learned social graces and practical domestic skills. She recalled being "privately instructed that small girls [such] as myself should be only seen and not heard."[10] Eventually, Rebecca's family moved to Decatur so that she could attend a girl's academy; at fifteen, she enrolled in the Methodist Female College at Madison, one of the few schools available to southern women. She took a range of courses, from philosophy to chemistry, but her interests ran toward art and music. While the college encouraged rigorous study, it also emphasized the importance "of pure morals and unblemished character." All students were required to attend prayers or religious services twice a day and forbidden from attending parties or dances, and it was during her studies in Madison that Rebecca joined the "Washingtonians," a junior temperance society, and began her lifelong commitment to abstinence from alcohol.[11]

Despite the strict moral code, female students could enjoy chaperoned visits with young men who had been previously approved by their parents. In the end, courtship, not education, determined a young woman's future in the plantation South and, as in the North, parents and educators believed that female colleges served as training grounds for a woman's future career as a wife and mother.[12] Like those of most girls her age, Rebecca's teenage thoughts dwelt on marriage and motherhood. Years later, she recalled, "it was nothing uncommon to get married as early as fourteen or fifteen and an unmarried woman of thirty was rated an 'old maid.'"[13] Spinsterhood was not in the cards for Rebecca; her father's investment in her education would soon pay off.

Graduating at the head of her class, seventeen-year-old Rebecca delivered the class valedictory address. According to one newspaper, her first public lecture, titled "Poetry—Its Practical Nature and Moral Tendency," was so moving that "strong men wept under the power of sentiments at once so strong and natural." Certainly, William Harrell Felton, the thirty-year-old widowed doctor and Methodist minister who had been invited to deliver the keynote commencement address, must have found the "freshness of her religious emotions and her genuine enthusiasm" inspiring.[14] Already at home at the podium, Rebecca proved a tough act to follow, but Dr. Felton, a noted orator, was prepared for the task. He spoke of the need for educated wives and mothers and explained, "Man requires a home where the affections are refined, the passions are schooled, cares are lulled and thought is strengthened. Mind and virtue are impaired by continual contact with the throngs of pleasure or business. Patriotism resolves itself into theory unless watched and kindled by the vestal attendant at home."[15] Rebecca was no doubt impressed by his vision of Victorian motherhood, which elevated women's status in the home, and by his argument that true manhood required the moral and virtuous influence of an educated wife and mother.

William Felton came from a family of yeomen farmers who had migrated from North Carolina to north Georgia in the early 1800s. Born in June 1823 near Lexington in Oglethorpe County, William was Captain John and Mary Felton's only child. His father, who had served in the War of 1812, moved the family to Athens in 1835, where William attended Franklin College, graduating in 1843. After earning his medical degree from the Medical College of Augusta in 1844, he returned to Athens, opened a practice, and soon married Ann Carlton, the daughter of a prominent family. In 1847, when life as a physician began to take a toll on his already fragile health, he gave up his medical practice to return to the land. He moved to Cass County, three miles outside Cartersville, where he and his father farmed the rich soil of the Etowah Valley with the help of slave labor. A year later, Dr. Felton entered the Methodist ministry. His early years in Cartersville were not without hardship. His wife, Ann, died soon after giving birth to their only child, also named Ann. To help put the sorrow of his wife's premature death behind him, he turned his attention to politics; in 1851, he campaigned as a Whig and won a seat in the Georgia legislature.[16] A well-educated planter and doctor, Dr. Felton would have no difficulty finding himself a new wife and stepmother for his daughter. Indeed, given his prominent position and credentials, it was not difficult for Dr. Felton to convince Rebecca and her family that she should become his new wife.

Less than a year after the graduation ceremonies at Madison Female College, Rebecca and Dr. Felton were married and settled on his Cartersville farm. Her transition at the age of eighteen from dutiful daughter and dedicated student to wife, stepmother, and plantation mistress apparently went smoothly, although Felton's one-story farmhouse on the Tennessee River near the Western and Atlantic railroad tracks paled in comparison with Panola, her childhood home. The Feltons owned fifty slaves, making them part of the planter elite, but they lacked many of the luxuries found among the wealthiest members of their class.[17] Neighbors were scarce, and for Rebecca the trip home to her father's plantation was over a hundred miles.

Years later, Rebecca Felton recalled missing her family but having no time for moping. She had a two-year-old stepdaughter to care for, a mother-in-law looking over her shoulder, slaves to manage, and a multitude of household chores to keep her busy.

In 1854 she gave birth to her first child, John Latimer, and in 1857 grieved over the loss of her new daughter, Mary Eleanor.[18] Two years later her second son, William Harrell Jr., was born. As she later remembered, "For eight or ten years my life was so absorbed in my children that it was cloister-like, months elapsing sometimes when my feet were never outside the front gate."[19] As a minister's wife, devoted mother, and efficient mistress, there was nothing unusual about this cloistered life; isolation was common among the wives of planters.

Sanctioned by morality and domesticity, the ideals of southern womanhood represented a combination of myth and reality that informed every aspect of Rebecca's life. Besides being expected to embrace the virtues of religious piety, maternal devotion, moral uprightness, and female dependency in exchange for male protection, women of the planter class served as the imagined repositories of southern values and the appointed guardians of racial purity. Relegated to the domestic sphere, they were excluded from the "corruptive" influence of formal politics.[20] Rebecca, however, did pay attention to political affairs. Her father was, after all, an active member of the Whig Party and her husband a Whig state legislator. As a young girl, she had listened to her father read aloud to his illiterate neighbors from the popular Whig newspaper, *Southern Recorder*. At age nine she shared his disappointment when Democrat James Polk defeated Whig party candidate Henry Clay in the 1844 presidential election.[21] Of course, even as Rebecca wept over Clay's defeat, she understood that the world of politics remained a male domain. Young girls were not expected to spend their time thinking about politics; they had to focus on domestic matters such as marriage, motherhood, and creating a moral household. Yet her interest in politics never faded. More than anything, her passion for politics would sustain her in the decades to come.

Sexual Warfare

When the southern states seceded from the Union, Rebecca Felton's life changed forever. Many years after the Civil War, she blamed Confederate officers for failing to protect southern women against the horrors of invasion. In 1919, at the end of War World I, she remembered, "In the hour of her [Georgia's] deepest humiliation the commander-in-chief of Georgia's reserves had nothing, not a man to offer to stand between her innocent women and what an invading army might inflict upon them."[22] Southern men, especially the planter elite, Felton argued, had put "the profit of slavery" before the protection of southern womanhood.[23] Felton was not alone in her sentiments. During the Civil War, Mary Chesnut, a plantation mistress in South Carolina, complained in her diary: "I think these times make all women feel their humiliation in the affairs of the world. With men it is on the field—'glory, honour, praise & power.' Women can only stay at home—& every paper reminds us that women are to be violated—ravished & all manner of humiliation. How are the daughters of Eve punished."[24] Her words, like Felton's, capture the sense of vulnerability and fear that women, white and black, felt during the Civil War, and reveal her frustration and anger over white men's failure to protect white women against wartime sexual violence. While their husbands and fathers sought "glory, honor, praise and power" on the battlefield, elite southern white women were effectively abandoned and left to fend for themselves in the face of an invading army.

Like many of the residents of Cass County, Felton disapproved when Georgia broke from the Union, but despite her initial dismay, she supported and remained loyal to the Confederacy. Many years later she explained, "There never was a more loyal woman in the South after we were forced by our political leaders to go to battle to defend our rights in ownership of African slaves, but they called it 'State's Rights,' and all I owned was invested in slaves and my people were loyal and I stood by them to the end."[25] Whatever their opinions of secession, white southern women quickly rallied to war and formed a solid bloc of moral and material support.[26] Eager to fulfill the duties required of southern womanhood and convinced that southern white men would do their part to defend home and hearth, Felton too made the sacrifices demanded by the Confederacy. "Upon nobody," explained Felton, "did the storm [war] fall more dreadful and unexpectedly than upon the women of the South." Even though her children were too young to fight and her husband was physically unfit for service, she found ways to support the war effort. She organized and became the first president of the local Ladies Aid Society. She attended the sick; made military shirts from treasured dresses, and blankets from expensive carpets; knitted socks from a dwindling supply of wool; found substitutes for coffee, tea, and sugar; and boiled the earth of her smokehouse for salt.[27] When food shortages became a problem, the Feltons began growing corn on their farm for the Confederate armies.

Throughout the war, Dr. Felton used his medical and religious training to attend the sick at a nearby military camp, which meant that he spent many nights away from the farm. His absence forced Rebecca to take on the responsibility of managing the plantation. As the Confederacy became more dependent on female labor and communities were stripped of able-bodied men, the mistresses frequently took charge of plantations and assumed more active public roles.[28] Discarding long-held beliefs about female frailty and dependence often proved difficult, but Felton (like many others) soon came to embrace the challenge. In retrospect, she believed that it was "the fortitude of women of the Confederacy" that kept southern homes and families intact.[29]

If some plantation mistresses embraced their new independence however, there were others who simply felt overwhelmed, especially when it came to managing slaves. Unprepared or unwilling to take on the responsibilities of running a plantation and managing slaves full time, some sold their slaves and abandoned their plantations. Others persevered amid bitter complaints.[30] Women's anxieties about managing slaves had to do with their ideas about women's proper roles. South Carolinian Emily Harrison confided in her diary, "I shall never get used to being left as the head of the affairs at home. I am constituted so as to crave a guide and protector. I am not an independent woman nor ever shall be." In a letter written to the Confederate Secretary of War, Amanda Walker of Georgia declared she was not "a fit and proper person" to supervise slaves. The *Macon Daily Telegraph* agreed: "Is it possible that Congress thinks . . . our women can control the slaves and oversee the farms? Do they suppose that our patriotic mothers, sisters and daughters can assume and discharge the active duties and drudgery of an overseer?"[31] It was in order to address this issue that the Confederate Congress passed the much contested "Twenty-Nigger Law," which exempted from service one white man on each plantation of twenty or more slaves. In the end, however, most plantation mistresses had little choice but to manage as best they could. They either rose to the challenge or they failed miserably.

White women's anxieties about managing slaves were partly rooted in their fear of slave insurrections. John Brown's 1859 raid on Harper's Ferry had made it difficult for slaveholding women to maintain the pretense that their "servants" were content with the system of slavery.[32] As far away as Florida, Susan Bradford sighed, "We feel that we can trust none of the dear black folk. I am afraid to say a word for fear it will prove to be just what should have been left unsaid."[33] In 1861, a widow moaned in a letter to her sister, "Can we cope with an enemy abroad & one at home—negroes are fully alive to the state of things & are much more sensible than one would suppose . . . I can imagine all sorts of noise at night and sometimes think they are right at my door."[34] Felton received a letter from her mother in which she worried, "I am the only white person on the place tonight."[35] For white women living on isolated farms and plantations without male protection, the fear of slave violence spread quickly, and even though examples were rare, it only took one case or rumor of a planned insurrection to further escalate white women's fears.[36] In the fall of 1861, for example, only five months after the bombardment of Fort Sumter, Mary Chesnut wrote in her diary, "I broke down; horror and amazement was too much for me. Poor cousin Betsey Witherspoon was murdered! She did not die peacefully in her bed, as we supposed, but was murdered by her own people, her Negroes."[37] According to Chesnut, Witherspoon "lived alone" on Society Hill Plantation, where she "indulged and spoiled" her "insolent" and "insubordinate" slaves. When slaves William and Rhody, "Betsey's old maid," were put in jail "on strong suspicions," Chesnut explained with horror how some of the men had suggested burning the Negroes at the stake. "Lynching proposed!" she wrote. "But it is all idle talk. They will be tried as the law directs, and not otherwise. John Witherspoon will not allow anything wrong or violent to be done. He has a detective there from Charleston."[38]

According to Chesnut, the murder investigation revealed that the slaves had killed Mrs. Witherspoon to avoid a threatened "thrashing" by her son, John Witherspoon. Chesnut explained how on the day before the murder John had informed his mother that while she was away, William and Rhody had given a party fifteen miles away from Society Hill and had taken her china, silver, and house linen to use. As he left the plantation, John allegedly shook his whip at William and scolded, "Tomorrow I mean to come here and give every one of you a thrashing." William and Rhody were furious that John had made such a threat. "Mars' John more than apt to do what he say he will do," William warned the other slaves, "but you all follow what I say and he'll have something else to think of beside stealing and breaking glass and china."[39] At midnight, Rhody and William, with the aid of two other slaves, entered Betsey's bedroom, where they smothered their sleeping mistress with a quilt. As the slaves began the work of cleaning up the crime scene, Betsey supposedly came to and begged for her life, but Rhody stuffed her mouth with a quilt, William held her head and hands down, and the other two slaves sat on her legs.

In the weeks and months after the murder, Chesnut recorded how the women on Mulberry, the Chesnut plantation, were driven "wild" with fear and suspicion.[40] When her sister Kate's "maid" insisted on sleeping at the foot of her mistress's bed, Kate confessed her fears: " 'For the life of me . . . I cannot make up my mind. Does she mean to take care of me, or to murder me?' " That night, Kate decided to sleep in her sister Mary's room—"The thought of those black hands strangling and smothering Mrs. Witherspoon's grey head under the counterpane haunted her."[41] Chesnut's mother-in-law became convinced that the slaves were trying to poison the family. "I warn you, don't touch that soup! It is bitter. There is something wrong about it!" she cautioned.[42] Chesnut confessed her own fears: "Hitherto I have never thought of being afraid of Negroes. I had never injured any of them. Why should they want to hurt me?" Giving in to her fears, Chesnut wrote, "I feel that the ground is cut away from under my feet," and asked, "Why should they treat me any better than they have done Cousin Betsy?"[43] Slaveholding women all over the South must have asked themselves the same question. Yet, like Chesnut, many mistresses suppressed their worst fears and hoped that their slaves would remain loyal and offer protection against invading Yankees.

Some plantation mistresses construed the nonviolence of the slaves not as a conscious moral choice, but as the reflexive loyalty of servants. In Fayetteville, North Carolina, Anne K. Kyle recalled: "But for the kindness of my servants I don't know what would have become of me. They were very faithful. One walked up and down the passage all night and the other stayed on the back porch. Still I was afraid to close my eyes."[44] As to the question of slave violence, Felton explained, "When the majority of white men were in the army and plantations were crowded with slaves large and small there were fewer disturbances than occurred before or since the Civil War."[45] Elizabeth Saxon of Alabama shared her opinion: "Able-bodied white men all gone, the women and children were under their care; their willing hands labored, and by their sweat and toil our coarse fare was provided. Not an outrage was perpetrated, no house was burned. Afar off on lonely farms women with little children slept at peace, guarded by a sable crowd, whom they perfectly trusted."[46]

Many white women believed that black women played a key role in restraining black men during the war. Chesnut explained, "I would go down on the plantation tomorrow and stay there even if there were not a white person in twenty miles. My Molly and all the rest I believe would keep me as safe as I should be in the Tower of London."[47] Felton also specifically argued that the "fidelity and general excellence" of colored women "scattered all over the Southland" had prevented slaves from turning on their masters. Southerners, she explained, "owed the security of Confederate homes" to their faithful female slaves.[48]

As the war progressed and federal troops began occupying southern territory, white women's fears shifted from their slaves to Yankee troops. Rumors that northern soldiers planned to rape their way through the South spread, and refugees and local newspapers reported "outrages against women" and other atrocities allegedly committed by Union soldiers.[49] Even though the federal military defined rape as a crime worthy of court-martial and execution, Union officers used rape and the threat of sexual violence as weapons of warfare against southern women, black and white. As early as 1862, General Benjamin Butler tacitly sanctioned the use of sexual violence to subdue and punish Confederate women in New Orleans who insulted or offended federal troops.[50] In charge of forces garrisoning the city, Butler issued the infamous *General Orders, No. 28*. "As the officers and soldiers of the United States have been subjected to repeated insults from the women (calling themselves ladies) of New Orleans" he declared, "it is ordered that hereafter when any female shall . . . insult or show contempt for any officer or solider of the United States, she shall be regarded and held liable to be treated as a woman of the town plying her avocation."[51] In this way Butler reduced southern ladies who resisted federal occupation to the status of a common prostitute, thereby also making them unworthy of protection. If rape happened, then they would be responsible for their own victimization. In defense of the order, Butler wrote to New Orleans Mayor John Monroe, "There can be, there has been, no room for misunderstanding of General Orders, No. 28. No lady will take any notice of a strange gentleman, and *a fortiori* of stranger, in such form as to attract attention. Common women do . . . I shall not, as I have not, abated a single word of that order; it was well considered. If obeyed, it will protect the true and modest woman from all possible insult. The others will take care of themselves."[52]

In a letter to the editor of the *New York Times*, Goldwin Smith, a British abolitionist, historian, and journalist, criticized Butler's order as "coarse"

and "highly reprehensible," but he also agreed with the general that southern white women were "unsexing themselves" and "provoking a dangerous collision between the citizens and the garrison." Smith not only
blamed southern women for provoking Butler, but also argued that "in
spite of all the 'tenderness' and 'grace' ascribed to them by their admir-
ers," southern women were not above "sending their female servants to a
public flogging house to be flogged naked by the hands of men."[53] Such
monsters should expect little mercy at the hands of federal troops, he
thought.

Jefferson Davis, president of the Confederacy, characterized Butler's
order as an invitation to soldiers "to insult and outrage the wives, the mothers, and the sisters of our citizens" and declared him "a felon, deserving
of capital punishment."[54] Butler's "Woman's Order" provoked criticism
throughout the Confederacy as an affront to southern womanhood and
confirmed white women's fears that northern men were brutes intent on
waging war against "defenseless" women.[55] Women saw Butler's order as a
direct assault on southern womanhood as well as an attack against southern manhood. "I cannot express to you the indignation this thing awakened," fumed New Orleanian Clara Solomon in her diary, "I hear that the
men were perfectly exasperated for you know the insult offered to us is also
to them."[56] In South Carolina, both Mary Chesnut and Emma Edward
Holmes wrote in their diaries that Butler's orders confirmed that Yankee
soldiers were "fiends" and "beasts" determined to dishonor southern women
and men.[57]

At the same time that southern women expressed their outrage at Butler's threat, they revealed that they were not completely defenseless. Before federal troops ever arrived in Louisiana, Sarah Morgan of Baton
Rouge confided in her journal that she had a "pistol and carving knife
ready." And after learning of Butler's Order No. 28, she wrote, "Come to
my bosom, O my discarded carving-knife, laid aside under the impression
that these men were gentlemen." Other women also armed themselves
against Butler's "army of fiends."[58] Julia LeGrand of New Orleans recorded
in her diary that "Mrs. Norton has a hatchet, a tomahawk, and a vial of
some kind of spirits with which she intends to blind all invaders."[59] In August 1862, Miss Emma Holmes of Charleston wrote, "Mrs. Henry M.
Hyams of New Orleans, the wife of the Lieut. Governor of the State has
rendered her name historic among Southern women, who have nobly

avenged the insults of 'Butler, the Beast.'" She explained in detail how a "Yankee officer" stopped Hyams and demanded that she bow in accordance with Butler's order. When she refused, "the vile wretch threw his arms around her and kissed her," and upon his release Hyams "drew a pistol and shot him dead in all the flush of his insolence."[60] Mrs. Hyams, the story went, was spirited away by a sympathetic Union officer who helped her reach southern lines.[61]

Women all over the South armed themselves. On her family plantation, Oakland, eight miles north of Holly Springs, Mississippi, nineteen-year-old Cordelia Lewis Scales wrote to a dear friend, "I wish you could see me now with my hair parted on the side with my black velvet zouave on & pistol by my side & riding my fine colt, Beula. I know you would take me for a Guerilla. I never ride now or walk without my pistol. Quite warlike, you see."[62] In Macon, a man explained that his mother and sister who lived in the country felt "quite secure" with the pistol and long knife that he had given them. In a letter to her husband, Julia Pope Stanley of Georgia wrote, "Oh that I had more faith. But when I hear of how our women are insulted by the Yankees, my heart almost faints within me." In the end, however, she concluded, "every woman ought to be armed with a dagger to defend herself."[63] Even President Davis made sure his wife Varina had a pistol for her protection. Although he taught her how to use it, he suggested, "You can at least, if reduced to the last extremity, force your assailants to kill you."[64] If death represented a better alternative than rape, then it is not surprising that southern white women went to extremes to protect themselves.

Whether or not Union soldiers and officers read Butler's order as a free pass to assault white women, a few officers followed his example and used the threat of sexual violence to subdue Confederate women. Union Major Thomas J. Jordan told women in Sparta, Tennessee, that if they refused to cook for his troops he would be forced to "turn his men loose upon them and he would not be responsible for anything they might do." In the town of Selina, he advised, "They had better sew up the bottoms of their petticoats" if they were unwilling to serve his troops. In Rome, Georgia, after stripping and spanking a group of young women who had emptied their chamber pots on passing soldiers, Union troops—who were aware of Butler's declaration—justified their actions accordingly: "No one but an abandoned woman would do a thing like that. Abandoned women had no rights that anyone was bound to respect."[65]

While it is difficult to know how many white women suffered a so-called fate worse than death during the war, a number of white women were raped. In North Carolina during the spring of 1865, Private James Preble "attempted to rape" both "Mrs. Rebecca Drake and Miss Louis Bedard" and "did by physical force and violence commit rape upon the person of one Miss Letitia Craft."[66] When Perry Holland, 1st Missouri, confessed to the rape of Miss Julia Anderson in Tennessee, he was sentenced to be shot, but it was later commuted.[67] Mrs. Catherine Farmer, also of Tennessee, testified that Lieutenant Harvey John, 49th Ohio, dragged her into the bushes and told her he would kill her if she did not "give it to him." He tore her dress, broke her hoops, and "put his private parts into her," for which he got ten years in prison.[68] In Georgia, Albert Lane, Company B, 100th Regiment of Ohio Volunteers, was also sentenced to ten years because he "did on or about the 11th day of July, 1864 . . . upon one Miss Louisa Dickerson, violently and feloniously did make an assault . . . then and there forcibly and against her will, feloniously did ravish and carnally know her."[69] Despite scholarly claims that the Civil War was a low-rape war, the fact that many women feared sexual assault and that hundreds, and possibly thousands, of women suffered rape cannot be ignored. Men and women not only wrote about sexual assaults and the fear of rape in their diaries and letters, but women, black and white, free and enslaved, pressed charges against alleged rapists. At least 250 Union soldiers were court-martialed for the crime of rape.

Significantly, a large number of the 250 rape cases in the Union record were either of black women raped by white men or white women raped by black men, suggesting that race played a key role not only in the cases the Union Army sought to pursue, but also in who was willing to report rape.[70] Because rape was considered a fate worse than death, and because southern culture discouraged white women from even discussing sex, it is likely that most rapes involving elite white women, which often took place on lonely farms like Felton's, went unreported. After all, in a society where a white woman's virtue represented her most valuable commodity, a sexual assault was a theft from which few could recover. Rape symbolized the loss of virtue as well as a failure of southern manhood. White southern men would have been loath to let their neighbors know that they had been unable to protect their wives and daughters from rape. Thus, elite white women had much to lose from reporting rape. The same was

not true, of course, for black women, who had everything to gain from reporting rape.

In the fall of 1863, the Western & Atlantic railroad tracks that ran by the
Felton farm brought the harsh realities of war to Rebecca's doorstep. The
trains carried wounded soldiers and supplies through Cartersville. As
early as September, battles on the outskirts of town had sent folks to seek
refuge further south. Every day the news spread that Union soldiers were
waging war against citizens, liberating and arming slaves, burning homes,
and raping women.[71] The Confederate Congress whipped up the rumors
of atrocities and intensified white women's fears when it declared, "The
conduct of the enemy has been destitute of that forbearance and magna-
nimity which civilization and Christianity have introduced . . . clothing
of women and infants is stripped from their persons . . . helpless women
have been exposed to the most cruel outrages and to that dishonor which
is infinitely worse than death."[72] Rebecca pleaded with her husband to
find safer quarters for her and the children, but not until 1864 did the Feltons, their three children, and fifteen slaves abandon their home for a
small farmhouse in a pine forest three miles outside of Macon.[73] Through
the spring and summer months, the family reestablished a household and
Dr. Felton put the slaves to work clearing land while he continued to attend wounded soldiers in nearby medical camps. No longer in the direct
line of fire, it seemed they were safe. Three months later, however, Rebecca awakened to find federal troops raiding her food supplies and invading the slaves' quarters.[74] With her husband by her side, she could
expect Yankee soldiers to treat her with some respect. Her female slaves,
however, could not count on the same courtesy.[75]

It comes as no surprise that most documented southern accounts of Yankee rape were of black women. In the spring of 1863, John N. Williams of
the 7th Tennessee Regiment wrote in his diary, "Heard from home. The
Yankees have been through there. Seem to be their object to commit rape
on every Negro woman they can find."[76] In Columbia, South Carolina, Dr.
Daniel Heywards Trezevant recounted how seven Yankees raped and murdered "Mr. Shane's old Negro woman."[77] When federal soldiers raped
black women they often did so in the presence of white women. B. E. Harrison of Leesburg, Virginia, wrote a letter to President Abraham Lincoln
complaining that federal troops had raped his "servant girl" in the presence
of his wife, and Union general William Dwight reported from Louisiana in

1863 that "Negro women were ravished in the presence of white women and children."[78]

As a demonstration of their power over black women and as a threat to white women, these public acts of sexual violence also served to mark southern defeat. Just as the rape of white women implied that southern men were unable to protect their mothers, wives, and daughters, the rape of slave women meant they could no longer protect their property. In Sperryville, Virginia, Mrs. Swindler witnessed the rape of her "Negro Servant" Polly Walker by three men of the 1st New York Light Artillery.[79] In Sandtown, Georgia, Mrs. Campbell and her mother witnessed the rape of their slave Sylvia Campbell when three men of the 2nd Kentucky Cavalry (Union) broke into their home. Sylvia testified that the sergeant held a gun to her head and raped her four times before another man dragged her into the woods. The unsympathetic senior Mrs. Campbell testified: "Yes, they dragged the nigger into the woods. She has not been able to do a lick of work since, but lies around useless. Her mistress has to wash all her own clothes." The sergeant was sentenced to two years hard labor.[80]

Because so many northerners viewed themselves as liberators of slaves, federal officials certainly did not openly condone the rape of slave women. While no federal soldiers were executed for raping black women, a few were court-martialed and convicted. In the summer of 1864, Lieutenant Andrew J. Smith, 11th Pennsylvania Calvary, was sentenced to ten years of hard labor for "committing a rape on the person of a colored woman" in Richmond, Virginia. His victim testified, "He threw me on the floor, pulled up my dress. He held my hands with one hand, held part of himself with the other hand and went into me. It hurt. He did what married people do. I am but a child."[81] In reviewing the sentence of the court-martial, General Benjamin Butler supported the guilty verdict. Summarizing the case, he explained, "A female negro child quits Slavery, and comes into the protection of the federal government, and upon first reaching the limits of the federal lines, receives the brutal treatment from an officer, himself a husband and a father, of violation of her person."[82] Unwilling to entertain pleas for mercy on Smith's behalf, Butler defended the sentence and declared the officer lucky to walk away with his life.

The summer raid on Felton's farm marked the beginning of a deluge of catastrophe for Rebecca. After federal soldiers captured Atlanta, an epidemic of measles struck the Felton farm. Five-year-old Willie Felton and six slaves died.[83] When Sherman began his "March to the Sea," destroying and burning all in his path, the Feltons were besieged with Confederate commissary officers, embittered deserters, and liberated slaves all desperate for food and anything else they could plunder. In the spring of 1865, as the surrender approached, she found herself again caught up directly in the path of war. This time, however, she faced federal troops alone, as Dr. Felton was away attending wounded soldiers. Upon hearing rumors that Union soldiers were advancing on the city, Rebecca rode on horseback into East Macon to find out if they were true. She learned at Burke's bookstore on Mulberry Street that Union troops "attended by hundreds of Negroes" were less than twenty miles away. She recalled, "The citizens expected the worst and that squad[s] of citizens were asking for protection from loot, rapine and the torch. . . . I still wonder that I had the temerity to undertake that lonely ride. It was a deserted road, much of it still in forest growth, and the poor little horse was slow."[84] The following day, a Confederate soldier informed her that Macon would be surrendered and civilians, especially women, should leave immediately. Felton refused to flee, declaring, "I can run no further. I have nowhere to go."[85] When troops finally arrived, "they took whatever we had that they wanted, and trampled down our crops," recalled Felton. She recounted how a soldier rummaged through her bedroom.[86]

Southern white women felt the threat of sexual violence most when soldiers invaded their private spaces to search for contraband or to plunder. Clara D. MacLean of North Carolina described her terror when a soldier forced his way into her home: "Before I was aware of his intention, he had locked the door. I rose and walked toward it. 'Come,' I said, 'and I will show you the trunks in the other room, as there is nothing here, you see, in the way of arms.' But he had stationed himself in front of the door, his back toward it. For a moment, nay, a long minute—centuries it seemed to me—we stood thus." Eventually she was able to maneuver out of the room and the soldier's clutches.[87] In Virginia, Judith McGuire raged, "It makes my blood boil when I remember that our private rooms, our chambers, our very inner sanctums, are thrown open to a ruthless soldiery."[88]

Southern white women had to worry about their own soldiers as well. Confederate deserters, camp followers, and southern men also took advantage of women who stood in the line of their struggles. Men, black and white, roamed the countryside and it was often difficult for elite white women, who were accustomed to only acknowledging men they knew, to avoid contact with strangers. Indeed, the experience of having to deal with strange men heightened fears. As women fled their homes and communities in quest of safer accommodations they found themselves more vulnerable.[89] Elizabeth Saxon recounted "a night of terror" during her trek from Alabama to Arkansas. Twenty-three miles outside of Memphis, she was forced to rent a room in a small cottage in the woods from "a mean-looking, ferret-faced man." After eating dinner prepared by "a small black woman, who disappeared as soon as she cooked it," Elizabeth purchased some candles from a man who sold things in a tiny shed off the portico and with her two small children retired for the evening. She had planned to ask the "negro woman" to stay in the room with her, but she was long gone. Upon returning to her room, she realized that the sliding bolt had been removed from the inside of the door, the lock was broken, and there was "no security whatever."[90] She was terrified. While her children slept, Saxon stayed awake writing letters to her friends. She soon heard a soft step outside her door. Whoever lurked outside might not have imagined that she carried a pistol in the pocket of her dress. "No man could send a bullet straighter to its mark than I," she explained. She flung the door wide open and found the man who had rented her the room standing outside her door in his stocking feet. "I thought I heard you," she said, "I am glad you are here. I want to ask you some questions. Come in." She backed into the room. When they sat down, she drew the pistol from her pocket. "This is a very lonely place," she began, "and in troublous times like these it seems a poor place to sleep in with neither lock nor bolt on the door. How am I to fast it?" He scoffed, "Nobody is going to hurt you. I only came to ask you what time you wanted to be called in the morning. What are you doing with that pistol?" Saxon threatened, "I am only holding it in my hand now and I expect to be up all night. I have much writing to do. I have carried this pistol in my pocket since I left home; it is heavy and I am tired. I have not had any use for it, and it is not likely that I shall, but if there should be any need to use it, I shall most certainly do it."[91]

In hopes of avoiding situations similar to Saxon's and seeking refuge from their fears, many women of the planter class found themselves forced to turn to federal troops for protection, and sympathetic soldiers sometimes complied. Felton was no exception. She recounted, "A trooper named Dowling, a youth from Cincinnati, was billeted in my house. . . . There were stragglers and camp followers roaming the country, and he left a loaded musket for my protection when he was not around."[92] In Camden, Arkansas, Virginia McCollum Stinson not only managed to get a Yankee guard, but also to take in a federal officer to board for extra protection. She explained, "After the guard came and the federal officer, I had no more serious trouble." When it came time for the officer to leave, she recalled, "Woman like I burst in tears and said 'Oh!! Capt. Rohadaback what will become of me and my little children, when you are gone?' He tried to comfort me and said 'I don't think my men will molest you at all.' "[93] Cornelia Peake McDonald, a refugee in Lexington, Virginia, explained that when Union troops captured the city, she was relieved to "see at least one Yankee, Maj. Quinn," who remained on her front porch to protect her and her property from "marauding parties."[94]

Yet, as the war dragged on and Sherman marched through the South destroying all in his path, Union patience wore thin, and officers were less likely to respond to white women's pleas for protection. Determined to bring the South to its knees by terrorizing and depriving civilians of the means of maintaining the Confederacy, Sherman and his men had little sympathy for white women they believed were responsible for keeping the war going by aiding and abetting Confederate soldiers. Still, elite white women believed that their gender and social position should trump all. Josephine Bryan Worth recounted that when Sherman raided Fayetteville, North Carolina, her aunt's plea for a guard was rejected: "You'll git no protection. That's played out long ago."[95] In February 1865, Charlotte St. Julien Ravenel, who lived at Pooshee Plantation in Berkeley County, South Carolina, complained in her diary when a Yankee general refused her family's request for a guard on the grounds that "his army did not straggle and that he could not leave a guard at every place he passed."[96]

Taking to heart Sherman's declaration to "make Georgia howl," Union soldiers not only deprived women of guards, but they also robbed them of food, livestock, and anything of value that they could find. What property could not be carried away was often burned. As destruction and violence escalated, women waited in terror and despair for the Yankees to arrive. Again, rape figured large. More hated than Butler, Sherman and his troops represented southern white women's worst nightmares. In fearful anticipation of Sherman's march through South Carolina, Emma Holmes wrote, "the progress has been like the commencement—all the barbarities of savage warfare followed in Sherman's wake. Fire, desolation, destruction of

all property unremovable—all provisions, cattle & negroes carried away—
the rape and consequent death or insanity of many ladies of the best families. Alas what pen can portray the sufferings inflicted by that army of
demons, white and black."[97]

Sherman was demonized during and after the war, and the South's image of him as a beast eventually became a national legend. Yet, even at
the time, there were some who were willing to concede that he was not
an absolute monster. According to one story that circulated after the war,
he had gone out of his way to offer protection to a southern woman he
had courted during his time at West Point. Reports have it that some-
where outside of Cartersville, not very far from Felton's plantation in the
Etowah valley, Sherman learned that his troops were looting the home of
Cecilia Stovall Shelman, an old sweetheart. He ordered the soldiers to
leave the house unharmed and left a letter explaining his actions: "You
once said that you would pity the man who would ever become my
enemy. My answer was that I would ever protect and shield you. That I
have done. Forgive me all else. I am but a soldier."[98] In general, however,
he was not in the business of "protecting and shielding" southern women.
When he burned Columbia, South Carolina, and the women came to
ask him for protection, he taunted them, "Where are your fathers and
husbands and sons? Why are they not here to protect you?"[99]

If Sherman was guilty of waging war against defenseless women and
children, then Confederate soldiers were guilty of failing to protect them,
which was, after all, one of the ideological rationales for the war. Confederate officers and soldiers were notorious for abandoning cities and towns
as federal troops advanced. Time and time again, as southern white men
fled for their lives, they left women to the mercy of their enemies. In May
1863, Mary Ann Loughborough, who had followed her husband's regiment from Jackson to Vicksburg, recorded how the women of the city
greeted Confederate soldiers who confessed they were "running" from
federal troops. "Why don't you stand your ground?" "Shame on you all!"
and "We are disappointed in you! Who shall we look to now for protection?" cried the women.[100] In a letter to her husband, Julia Davidson
complained, "The men of Atlanta have brought an everlasting stain on
their name. Instead of remaining to defend their homes, they have run off
and left Atlanta to be defended by an army of women and children." She
concluded, "God help us for there is no help in man."[101] In Virginia, a

group of women declared the Confederate Army incompetent and suggested the formation of a ladies regiment in the Army of the Shenan-
doah.[102] In a letter to the governor of North Carolina, a group of women
pleaded for protection and explained that "in absence of all protection
the female portion of this community may be subjected to a system of outrage that may be justly denominated the harrow of harrows more terrible
to the contemplation of the virtuous maiden and matron than death."[103]
In Jasper County, Mississippi, a group of "Ladies" petitioned the Confederate secretary of war for male protection as well as weapons to defend
themselves from "the demonic invasion."[104] Even as elite white women
clung to traditional notions of manhood in their demands for protection,
their actions challenged images of frail and defenseless womanhood.
White women's acts of public protest and violent self-defense not only
served as a political challenge to the image of the dependent and fragile
southern belle, but also called into question southern white men's ability
to protect southern womanhood, a complaint that would carry over into
the racial and sexual politics of Reconstruction and the New South.

Many years after the war, Felton blamed Confederate officers for failing to protect southern women against the horrors of invasion. Southern
white men's failure was grist for a conservative feminist reproach. Felton
later came to a more general view of the sexual vulnerability of white
women of all classes, but the discourse of horror and the danger of rape
was essentially founded in the grievances of "ladies," first articulated during the war. Southern men, especially the planter elite, Felton argued,
had put "the profit of slavery" before the protection of southern womanhood.[105] Whereas elite white women had held up their end of the bargain, to the point of "unsexing" themselves, southern manhood had failed
miserably. White women all over the South had been left unprotected,
and some had even suffered rape. Felton and other women of her class
emerged from the war battered by the responsibilities, devastated by the
death of so many men and children, dismayed by the failure of southern
manhood, and traumatized by war and the threat of sexual violence.
They compressed these sentiments into a postwar narrative in which rape
was the dominant theme. Certainly, the postbellum rape hysteria cannot
be fully understood without serious consideration of the sexual vulnerability and violation that women have experienced in all wars, and which
the Civil War in particular marked for southern women.[106]

Gone with the War

When General Robert E. Lee surrendered at Appomattox in the spring of 1865, the only way of life that Felton had known was destroyed. Everywhere widespread food shortages, extreme poverty, drought, and epidemics outlasted the war. With her slaves gone, food supplies scarce, and two surviving children to feed (her son John and her stepdaughter Ann), Felton had few options. Fortunately, not all their crops had been trampled; they would not starve. Along with corn and other vegetables, however, the summer heat brought deadly mosquitoes. In June the Feltons contracted malaria and John died. Stricken with fever and grief, her thirtieth birthday passed unnoticed. With all the children she had borne now dead, she carried only her sorrow when she finally returned to Cartersville in August 1865. Years later she remembered, "When I reached the gate I picked up the springs that had been a part of my dead child's fine baby carriage . . . desolation and destruction everywhere, bitter, grinding poverty—slaves all gone, money also. We certainly paid the price while we were in refugee conditions."[107] Assessing her wartime losses long after the Civil War and Reconstruction, Felton questioned, "Was slave ownership ever worth the sacrifice of blood and treasure that resulted from that secession ordinance?"[108]

Felton continued to be bitter about slavery all of her life. In later years, she critiqued the antebellum racial and sexual politics that she believed had brought on "four years of bloody war." She asked why the South had not compromised on the issue of slavery or taken the advice of "those who were afraid of war." It was "the profit" of slavery, she concluded, that had made southern slaveholders rush "unwisely" into secession. Lacking in "foresight" and "statesmanship," southern men foolishly gambled on slavery and ultimately lost everything—"their slaves, their real estate and personal property, lost their surplus money and lost their lives in many cases."[109] Felton argued that it was a mistake to fight for the perpetuation of domestic slavery, but also complained, "I was only a woman, and nobody asked me for an opinion."[110]

Felton, however, was no abolitionist. A product of the planter elite, she was a white supremacist who had been brought up to believe that slavery was "commanded by the Bible and ordained of God." Slavery, Felton insisted, extended benevolent paternalism to slaves who benefited from the moral influence of whites, especially white women. In exchange for subsistence, protection, and moral guidance, they were happy to serve. She conceded that slavery had its dark side and that "there were abuses, many of them." This was all common enough—pro forma for whites before and after the war, but in conceding that slavery had a dark side, she turned those commonplace views to the service of a critique of white men. The "curse of slavery," she argued, lay in the behavior of "cruel masters" and "bad white men" who violated the moral law and "made mulattoes as common as blackberries." She concluded, "When white men were willing to put their own offspring in the kitchen and corn field and allowed them to be sold into bondage as slaves and degraded them as another man's slave, the retribution of wrath was hanging over this country and the South paid penance in four years of bloody war."[111]

Her critique of southern white men who blatantly defied anti-miscegenation and marriage laws rested on the assumption that slave women willingly participated in this "sin." For Felton, as well as for many other southern white women, the increasing mulatto population served not only as a reminder of white men's infidelity, but also as a confirmation of black women's licentiousness. Only a few southern white women had been able to come to terms with and speak publicly about the sexual exploitation of slave women in the antebellum period. In fact, Sarah and Angelina Grimké were the only antebellum southern white women to address publicly the rape of slave women by white masters; they had to leave the South to do so.[112]

Thus, while Felton could see that southern white men's abuse of sexuality and power could be directly linked to slavery, she could not comprehend that black women were among their victims. When Felton condemned a "rich man" who she claimed "lived in open *alliance* with a colored woman," she made clear her ideas about black women.[113] Viewing black women as sexual competition, Felton, like many southern white women, placed the female slave in collusion with the licentious master and ignored the unequal power relations between white men and slave women.[114] "We live surrounded by prostitutes," Mary Boykin Chesnut famously complained in her pre-war dairy, "An abandoned woman is sent out of any decent house elsewhere. Who thinks any worse of a Negro or Mulatto woman for being a thing we can't name."[115] Chesnut understood the sexual double standard that allowed southern white men to engage in sex across the color line, but she, like Felton, had difficulty acknowledging that the rape of slave women made such a standard possible. More accustomed to low whispers about white men's illicit sexual behavior, quiet rumors of bloody slave insurrections, and deafening silences regarding the sexual exploitation of slave women, women of the planter elite accepted and perpetuated long-held beliefs that black women lacked virtue.

Yet Felton did not view *all* female slaves as morally depraved. In "Southern Women in the Civil War," an address she delivered to the United Daughters of the Confederacy in Augusta, Georgia, Felton gave "honorable mention" to slave women: "I shall tell you something about a class of women who lived in plantation homes," she began, "who belonged there, and who raised families and whose work in the fields and the kitchen, in the loom-house and the dwelling, that we occupied in the Southern States . . . I allude to the colored women, who were the cooks, the nurses, and the main reliance of the white women in their arduous duties." "Mammy" was a symbol of the regenerative power of slavery, white benevolence, and what Felton referred to as slave "fidelity and general excellence."[116] By envisioning female house slaves as loyal and diligent "mammies," Felton and other former slaveholders could claim slavery had its virtues.

Her understanding of slave women's behavior during the Civil War reveals how she negotiated complicated and contradictory visions of black womanhood. "There were bad men then, also bad men now," she explained, "but the colored women on the farms were glad to go to the mistress for protection when raiders came along and the roar of the enemy's cannon could be heard in the distance." And it was in memory of these "good slaves," she concluded, "It is proposed to raise a monument of either marble or bronze."[117] Only when she shifted her attention to the behavior of northern white men could she see black women as victims of sexual violence and admit that slave women needed and expected white women to protect them from white men. Still, Felton made a distinction between slave women who were "glad" to seek protection from "raiders" and the "colored women" with whom "bad" southern white men "lived in open alliance" before the war.[118]

In Felton's postwar writings she argued that white men's lapses contributed to white women's sexual vulnerability in the antebellum South. In an undated and unpublished short story entitled "A Farm House Experience," she imagined how one white woman escaped "a fate worse than death"—black rape.[119] In doing so, she took the opportunity to criticize antebellum southern white men for placing the profit of slavery before the protection of southern womanhood at the same time that she reinforced the myth of black rape. The main character, Mrs. Mary Simpson, a new wife and mother, worn down by the summer heat and nursing her infant son, leaves town to rest at her aunt and uncle's small country farm. During her visit she experiences what Felton describes as a "horror of horrors!" Mary had grown up on the small farm and was surprised to learn that her uncle had placed locks on the barn doors to keep his neighbor's slaves from plundering his farm. Her uncle explains that Squire Masters, "a stingy man" who "half" fed and clothed his "niggers," had forced his slaves to resort to stealing for food. He concludes, "A mean master makes a mean nigger" and threatens the safety of the whole community.

When Mary and the baby have retired for the evening, she notices "a big black hand" reaching out from under her bed for a glass of water. It is one of Squire Masters's unruly slaves, and there is little doubt he wants more than a drink. She clutches her newborn in her arms hoping he will cry out, but the child barely wakes. Forced to pinch the baby, who screams in agony, she musters enough courage to cross the room and exit. Upon fleeing the room, she collapses down the staircase and screams for help. Falling in and out of consciousness she is unable to "tell what she had suffered" until some hours later, long after the slave has run away.[120]

Felton's story is intended as a tribute to white women's ability to protect themselves and yet it is also a critique of southern white manhood. Not so different from her postwar critique of Confederate soldiers who failed to protect home and hearth, "A Farm House Experience" reflects what she understood as southern white men's abandonment of white women. In other words, mean masters bred black rapists. At the same time, her tale illuminates how fear of rape during the Civil War not only informed southern women's postwar anxieties, but also drove their remembrance of the past.

A New Southern Woman in the Making

The harsh realities of military defeat and unprecedented poverty made obsolete the plantation mistress. Without slave labor, elite white women found it impossible to return to their former lives. No longer could Felton and the other women of her class confine themselves to managing a household. Many had to enter the public world of paid work. Before the war, recalled Felton, "it was almost unheard of for a woman of any means at all to go out and work by day or by the hour. But necessity spoke now."[121] Because teaching was one of the few jobs considered respectable and safe enough for an elite white woman, the Feltons established a school in Cartersville, where Rebecca taught mathematics and music for two years.

Felton's involuntary entry into the waged labor force, like her wartime experience, had a profound impact on how she envisioned women's place in postwar southern society. It challenged her to rethink long-held beliefs that poor white people, especially poor white women, were lacking in honor and respectability. Prior to the war she, like most elite white southerners, accepted the idea that poor white women were morally corrupt. In the antebellum South, poor white women were seen as the polar opposite of the pure and virtuous elite white woman.[122] Indeed, whites who engaged in menial labor were often perceived as only a few steps above slaves. To lack property or a profession in the slave-holding South was to lack honor and respectability, and to be "regarded as a social parasite and a potential threat to social harmony and order."[123] Poverty was particularly shameful for white women because it violated norms of white femininity. Lower-class white women who labored alongside slaves were an absolute contradiction of the southern lady, who symbolized leisure, luxury, wealth, and refinement. Thus elite white women sought to maintain a "clear and often militant defense" of their class privilege and their distance from lower-class white women.[124] Popular images of "depraved" poor white women—in the language of social and political reformers—helped license a host of abuses against lower-class white women.

When poor white women suffered physical and sexual abuse at the hands of white men in the antebellum South, they, like slaves, often were blamed for their victimization and denied legal protection.[125] Southern legal codes had long defined *rape* as a forced and nonconsensual sexual attack; in most antebellum cases, however, it was not enough for a poor white woman to prove force and lack of consent. She also had to establish that she was a woman of previous "good fame," provide evidence that she had disclosed the assault to a third party immediately, show signs of physical injury, and provide proof of her efforts to resist.[126] Such requirements meant that poor white women, who were already perceived to be sexually voracious, were effectively excluded from the class of women who were deemed likely victims of rape. Because class was so central to a woman's veracity in a rape trial, those who were most successful in the courts were frequently young white girls under the age of consent or married white women. In both cases, the issue of consent was irrelevant; children under the age of ten were not capable of consent and it was commonly believed that no self-respecting married white women would agree to sex with a man other than her husband.[127]

The legal treatment of poor white women who brought rape charges reinforced cultural stereotypes about their presumed depravity.[128] Even a black man accused of raping a poor white woman in the antebellum South was likely to obtain a fair trial.[129] Their value as property meant that black slaves were often protected against rape charges brought by non-elite white women. Poverty combined with "deviant" behavior severely undercut a white woman's ability to demand protection in the Old South. Such attitudes, however, proved difficult to maintain in the aftermath of war as poverty swept across the southern landscape and required many elite white women to abandon the privacy of their households to work in the fields. Food shortages and the departure of former slaves meant that, at least for a while, Felton's "plight was that of nearly everyone else."[130] Experiencing firsthand the harsh realities of poverty and forced into close contact with poor white people, Felton came to believe that lower-class white women not only deserved respect, but protection as well.

After two years of teaching, the Feltons were again able to make a living from their land with the aid of black hired hands. During the turbulent politics of Reconstruction government, Felton gave birth to her third son, Howard Erwin, in 1869 and her last, Paul Aiken, in 1871. In 1873 Paul died, and her husband again decided to enter politics. In 1874, just two years after Democrats brought a violent end to Reconstruction by regaining control of the Georgia legislature, forcing the Republican governor to resign and electing a Democrat to fill the vacancy, Dr. Felton decided to run for Congress as an Independent Democrat.[131] Unhappy with the Democratic alliance between the former planter elite and new big business, he declared himself a representative of the yeomen. The Independent platform sought a free ballot and a fair count of ballots, promoted the payment of national and state debts, advocated a liberal system of internal improvement and support for public schools; and demanded the abolishment of the convict lease system. Furthermore, they condemned the political caucus, sought liberalized sectional prejudice, and declared that the national government was the supreme authority. The Independents favored a protective tariff, supported "sound money," and denounced monopolies.

More than twenty years had passed since Dr. Felton had run a political campaign, but he had an intuitive grasp of the rough and tumble politics of the postwar South and he knew that if he planned to win a seat in the U.S. House of Representatives as an Independent, he would need all the help he could get. He turned to the smartest person he knew—his wife. A keen strategist and confident speechwriter, Felton possessed all the skills necessary to run her husband's campaign. "I found myself suddenly in the thick of a campaign," recounted Felton, "I did not stop to think what a radical change this was for a young woman reared on an old-fashioned plantation. . . . It seemed perfectly natural that I should take an active part in my husband's campaign."[132] And actively participate she did— from arranging his speaking engagements to writing letters for him, to answering newspaper attacks, to helping write his speeches, to attending political meetings. Dr. Felton's choice of his wife as his campaign manager paid off. He won a seat in the 44th Congress and reclaimed it twice. During his three terms in Congress, Rebecca accompanied him to Washington and she served as his personal secretary. Many years later she recalled, "I was up and ready for a six years' struggle in and out of Washington, where I still wrote letters, wrote for the newspaper, worked for constituents before the departments, doing the work of the present clerks to congressmen."[133]

Felton's active and public involvement in her husband's political career did not go unnoticed or unchallenged in Georgia. Pre-war southern society had not generated the thin web of benevolent, philanthropic, and reform groups supported by the woman's sphere in the North and West. After the war, even without the right to vote, northern women continued to get involved in politics. Such was not the case for the old planter class. In 1876, after she attended a political rally with Dr. Felton, the editor of the *Tri-Weekly Courier* of Rome, Georgia, complained, "The disgusting spectacle of one or two white ladies in a rough and tumble political meeting was seen for the first time in the city yesterday. This may be very nice in the higher circle at Washington, but it doesn't exactly come up to the southern standard of propriety."[134] What may have seemed "perfectly natural" to Felton was considered by most white southerners as unacceptable behavior for a woman, especially one of her status. Desperate to rehabilitate the image of southern white manhood and determined to reestablish their political power in white supremacist and patriarchal terms, the majority of southern Democrats had no interest in sharing political power with women. The return of home rule, as far as they were concerned, meant a return to domesticity. "We sincerely trust that the example set by Mrs. Felton will not be followed by southern ladies," scolded the *Thomasville Times* editor, "Let the dirty work in politics be confined to men. It is bad enough for them to engage in it, but infinitely worse for women. There is a higher, nobler, purer sphere for women; let her fill it."[135] Undeterred, Felton remained involved in her husband's political career, so much so that in 1878, when Dr. Felton won his third term to the House, one newspaper declared, "Mrs. Felton and Doctor Reelected."[136] By 1880, however, such criticisms proved the least of their worries.

Determined to stamp out the Independent movement, Democrats guaranteed Felton's defeat not by pointing to his wife's political activity, but by accusing him of allying with Republicans and being weak in his support of white supremacy. Democrats circulated rumors that Dr. Felton had turned a needy Confederate soldier away, supported the Republican governor and his radical allies during Reconstruction, and campaigned for black votes. Worst of all they whispered that his daughter had married a mulatto.[137] Unable to fend off such accusations, Dr. Felton was defeated in the election of 1880 and the Independent movement was fully squashed. Back in Georgia, the Feltons soon became entrenched in state and local politics. In 1884, Dr. Felton successfully campaigned for a seat in the state House of Representatives, but while Rebecca remained deeply involved in her husband's career, in the 1880s she began pursuing political interests of her own that went well beyond keeping Dr. Felton in office.

Felton's Civil War experiences exposed her for the first time to the problem of rape, the limits of white manhood, and the hollowness of the southern gender politics of protection. During the war men of the planter class had proved incapable of holding up their end of the antebellum bargain that required female dependence and obedience in exchange for male protection. Left to their own defenses, southern women had suffered unspeakable humiliations at the hands of an occupying military force. In Felton's view, southern white men had done little to protect southern womanhood from the sexual horrors of war. The battle over slavery cost Felton all that she held dear, except her husband and stepdaughter. Her initial sense of grievance and helplessness following the Confederate defeat faded into an angry determination to never again depend solely on men. Yet, as a woman who had been born and reared in the plantation South, the promise of protection was too powerful to discard completely. In the 1890s she would try to fashion another resolution between white women and men by projecting a lurid, sensationalized vision of the "black rapist."

2

THE VIOLENT TRANSITION FROM
FREEDOM TO SEGREGATION

Ida B. Wells was a generation younger than Felton. She was born a slave during the Civil War and came of age during Reconstruction. Like Felton, Wells saw the origins of the connection between rape and lynching in the institution of slavery. And while the two might have agreed on the roots of the problem, they disagreed about the fundamental details. For Felton, the narrative of sexual violation and lynching centered on the protection of the southern lady; for Wells, it focused on the rape of slave women and the absence of punishment for white perpetrators. In her memoir, *Crusade for Justice*, Wells reasoned that the white men who had "created a race of mulattoes" by raping slave women were in fact the "same white men" who lynched, burned, and tortured black men for allegedly raping white women: "I found that in order to justify these horrible atrocities [lynchings] to the world, the Negro was being branded as a race of rapists, who were especially mad after white women." At the same time, she argued, white men continued, "without let or hindrance, check or reproof from church, state, or press" to rape black women wherever and whenever they could.[1]

During Reconstruction and the rise of Jim Crow, Wells became keenly aware of black women's sexual vulnerability and began to think in political terms about how best to protect black womanhood. Refusing to accept the racial and sexual terms of the antebellum hierarchy that defined protection as a right guaranteed only to elite white women, Wells sought to broaden notions of female protection by insisting that it was a basic right of citizenship. But before she could do so, she, like Felton, had to make sense of her own place in the new world of emancipation. Wells, however, would have to do so as a young black woman with little privilege and no status.

Defining Freedom

Wells was born in 1862 in Holly Springs, Mississippi, to slave parents James Wells and Elizabeth Warrenton.[2] James Wells came to the bustling town in 1858 when his white father, also his master, apprenticed him to a carpenter and contractor named Bolling. Sold away from her family in Virginia as a young girl, Elizabeth Warrenton came to Holly Springs after being bought to serve as Bolling's cook.[3] Denied the right to legally marry, the young couple had already set up household and Elizabeth was pregnant with Ida when Union soldiers captured the town. During the first three years of Ida's life, Holly Springs exchanged hands many times and at least twelve clashes between Union and Confederate soldiers took place in and around the town.[4] Elizabeth and James survived these tumultuous times and were there to welcome the arrival of Federal troops and the 1863 announcement of Lincoln's Emancipation Proclamation.

As James and Elizabeth sought to deal with the implications of their new freedom, white southerners with the aid of President Andrew Johnson moved quickly to reassert control over their lives and labor.[5] By the time Congress reconvened in December of 1865, all the former Confederate states, except Texas, had met the president's terms for readmission into the Union.[6] The Wellses' home state of Mississippi (where blacks outnumbered whites) set the tone of "Presidential Reconstruction" when it refused to ratify the Thirteenth Amendment, declined to repudiate state debts incurred during the war, revived its state militia and manned it with Confederate veterans, and passed its infamous Black Codes.[7] By defining the limits of black freedom, by restricting economic mobility to ensure black men and women's roles as a labor force in the South, and by seeking to maintain unequal categories of race, the Black Codes had an immediate impact on freed people's daily lives.[8] The codes outlawed interracial cohabitation and marriage and denied blacks the right to vote, to hold public office, to serve on juries, or to bear arms. Other measures of control included exclusion from many occupations, restrictions on conducting certain businesses, limitations on where blacks could own land, and apprenticeship laws that allowed indigent young blacks to be apprenticed involuntarily to whites, with former slave masters receiving preference. A black person accused of theft, "running away," drunkenness, wanton conduct or speech, neglecting job or family, handling money carelessly, or "idle and disorderly" behavior could be charged and fined for vagrancy.[9]

Within the confines of the Black Codes, Ida's parents began to carve out new lives for themselves. They legalized their marriage and James accepted Bolling's offer to stay on as a carpenter in his shop. Elizabeth, however, retired to become a full-time wife and mother and eventually gave birth to seven more children (Eugenia, James, George, Annie, Eddie, Lily, and Stanley).[10] Like many freed people, she eagerly sought education for herself and the children.[11] Thus, when the Freedman's Aid Society of the Methodist Episcopal Church established Shaw University (later renamed Rust College) in Holly Springs in 1866, Elizabeth and four-year-old Ida attended the first day of classes together and James accepted a seat on the university's first board of trustees. The curriculum ranged from elementary education to normal school training for teachers. Elizabeth attended long enough to acquire the necessary skills to read the Bible. After completing her basic elementary education, Ida officially enrolled in the university's teacher training program. The mostly white faculty offered students "a broad, thorough and practical education" that included religious and moral instruction.[12] Students were required to attend daily chapel, weekly prayer meetings, and church on Sunday. The northern white missionaries who taught at Rust College took extra care to train young black men and women in accordance with Victorian ideals of manhood and womanhood.[13]

Ida's childhood education also included powerful lessons about the racial and sexual politics of the antebellum South. Stories from her family's past taught her about the harsh realities of slavery and the particular horrors that female slaves suffered. Her mother had recounted "the hard times she had as a slave" and how one of her masters had "seared her flesh and her mind with torturous beatings."[14] It is not clear if her mother's tales of hard times included accounts regarding white men's sexual aggression against slave women. One can only speculate as to why Elizabeth's master had beaten her and eventually sold her to a Mississippi slave trader. Regardless of whether or not her own mother chose to recount stories of sexual violence under slavery, Ida knew that her paternal grandmother, Peggy, had most likely been raped by her white master and had given birth to the man's only child—her father, James Wells.

Slave women, as Ida learned, not only suffered at the hands of their male masters, but also incurred the wrath of unsympathetic mistresses. "The only thing" Wells claimed to remember about her father's stories of slavery underscores how white men's illicit sexual behavior influenced relations between female slaves and white women.[15] As a young child, Wells overheard a conversation between her father and her grandmother that gave her "insight to slavery." Her grandmother Peggy and her husband, who owned a farm in Tippah County, had come to Holly Springs to sell their cotton and corn at the market. As always, Ida sat quietly listening as her grandmother and father caught up on old news. At some point in the discussion Peggy mentioned "Miss Polly," their former mistress. According to Wells, her grandmother informed her father that "Miss Polly" wanted to see him and his children. It was not the request that surprised young Ida but her father's response: "I never want to see that old woman as long as I live. I will never forget how she had you stripped and whipped the day after the old man died, and I am never going to see her." Her father's severe tone and harsh words did not go unnoticed. "Burning to ask what he meant," Ida remained silent, because, as she explained, "children were seen and not heard in those days."[16] As a child, Wells may have failed to understand the significance of her father's words but they left a profound impression.

Word of the violent episode between Peggy and "Miss Polly" marked a new level of understanding in Ida's childhood education. It signaled the huge divide that existed between white women's perceptions and black women's realities in the South. Deeply invested in the myth of black female immorality and unable to confront or control their husbands' sexual behavior, southern white women viewed slave women with jealousy and contempt.[17] Even if a mistress overlooked her husband's late night visits to the slave quarters, it proved difficult if not almost impossible to ignore the birth of a mixed race child. A reminder of her husband's infidelity as well as her infertility, the birth of James would have been especially painful for "Miss Polly."

Harriet Jacobs summed up a white mistress's violent rage and the slave's vulnerability in her memoir: "[the white mistress] felt that her marriage vows were desecrated, her dignity insulted; but she had no compassion for the poor victim of her husband's perfidy. She pitied herself as a martyr; but she was incapable of feeling for the condition of shame and misery in which her unfortunate, helpless slave was placed."[18] Almost a century later, civil rights activist and feminist Pauli Murray, the great granddaughter of a North Carolina slave woman raped by her master's son, drew a similar conclusion: "The southern woman was never sure of her husband's fidelity or her sons' morals as long as there was a slave woman in the household. The

slave woman's presence threatened her sovereignty, insulted her womanhood and often humiliated her before her friends. She was confronted with
a rival by compulsion, whose helplessness she could not fight."[19] The racial
and gender hierarchies produced by the institution of slavery and reinforced by white men's sexual behavior created a gulf between black and
white women that in most cases proved almost impossible to bridge.

It was not long before Ida figured out the meaning of her father's words
and came to fully understand the racial and sexual dynamics of master/
slave relations and the long shadow it cast on black women's lives. But as a
young black girl growing up during the pitched battles of Reconstruction,
she learned firsthand that the brutality and violence that characterized
black/white relations in the plantation South had not vanished with Lincoln's Emancipation Proclamation. Newly freed black women were unwilling to return to the antebellum sexual and racial status quo that allowed
white men to rape and brutalize them with impunity. Indeed, for Ida B.
Wells and the millions of black women in the South, another war had just
begun. Their battle for legal protection not only made visible the previously
muted racial and sexual violence against black women, but also radically
influenced the politics of Reconstruction and the rise of Jim Crow.

James and Elizabeth Wells joined the newly founded Asbury Methodist
Church (a branch of the Methodist Episcopal Church); James then became a Mason and eventually joined the Loyal League, a Republican organization created to protect black voting rights. Eager to put the painful
and violent memories of slavery behind them, freed men and women all
over the South built churches, formed lodges, created newspapers, established political organizations, took control of their labor, and ran for political office when possible. They no longer had to meet under the cover of
darkness to worship, to organize politically, or to educate themselves and
their children. Former slaves organized "Negro Conventions" and passed
resolutions demanding the full rights of citizenship, including the franchise, access to land, fair wages, and protection against white violence.
In June 1865, black Mississippians held a mass meeting in Vicksburg at
which they condemned the exclusion of "loyal citizens" from the upcoming elections and called on Congress to refuse the state readmission until
black men were given the right to vote.[20] In Jackson, black washerwomen
organized a labor strike and called on the mayor to support their demands
for "a uniform rate" of pay for their work.[21] Indeed, from Mississippi to

Virginia black men and women articulated their desire for economic and political power and insisted on the right to control their labor, defend their families, and live without white interference.[22]

Emancipation, however, had not changed the way many southern whites viewed black men and women—as property. Former slaves felt the limits of their freedom most when they acted politically or sought to manage their own labor. Southern whites resorted to intimidation, ostracism, theft, whippings, rape, and even murder to regain control over black people.[23] In December 1865, Colonel Samuel Thomas, Assistant Commissioner of the Freedmen's Bureau, reported to Congress: "Wherever I go—the street, the shop, the house, or the steamboat—I hear the people talk in such a way as to indicate that they are yet unable to conceive of the Negro as possessing any rights at all. . . . To kill a Negro they do not deem murder; to debauch a Negro woman they do not think fornication; to take the property away from a Negro they do not consider robbery." Thus, Colonel Thomas rightfully observed of southern whites, "They may admit that the individual relations of masters and slaves have been destroyed by the war and the President's emancipation proclamation, [but] they still have an ingrained feeling that the blacks at large belong to the whites at large, and whenever opportunity serves they treat the colored people just as their profit, caprice or passion may dictate."[24] Intent on treating newly freed men and women as they had under slavery and unwilling to relinquish notions of white supremacy that held blacks as undeserving of civil and political rights, southern planters, whether compelled by "caprice" or "passion," unleashed an unprecedented wave of violence against their former slaves who were no longer valued as property worthy of protection.

In the years immediately following emancipation, white violence tended to be localized and personal, usually having to do with disputes over labor or rules of proper racial etiquette. In vivid testimony before the U.S. Senate, former slave Henry Adams of Louisiana recalled how in 1865 southern whites used threats and violence to limit black freedom, to ensure black deference, and to establish a cheap labor force. Adams explained how his former master intimidated ex-slaves into signing labor contracts by promising to "protect" them from "the bad white men" who would kill them just "for fun." Of his master's sixty former slaves, Adams was one of only two men who refused to sign a contract. Even when blacks refused to commit their labor to a single planter, they found it difficult to move from one plantation to another. According to Adams, whites used a combination of violence and the pre-war pass system to prevent former slaves from moving freely.[25] As a test of his freedom and against the wishes of his former master, Adams refused to carry a pass during a weeklong trip to Shreveport. Four white men stopped him six miles south of Keachie and asked him whom he "belonged to." When Adams declared he "belonged" to no one, three of the men beat him with a stick and threatened to kill him before letting him go at the request of the fourth man. "I seen over twelve colored men and women, beat, shot and hung between there and Shreveport," he testified. Convinced that freedom meant that "every man" would have "rights" and the power to protect himself, Adams, like many ex-slaves, challenged whites' assumed power over him and his family. When his fifteen-year-old sister suffered brutal beatings from both "the madame" and "the boss," he, along with "a large number of young colored people," decided to leave the plantation in protest. En route to Shreveport the group fell victim to a mob of forty white men who shot at them, took Adams's horse, robbed them of their "clothes, and bedclothing and money," and forced their return. According to Adams, the "crowd of white men broke up five churches" as well. Thousands, he concluded, had been killed for trying "to be free."[26]

Riots, Rape, and Radical Reconstruction

Former slaves had many reasons for wanting to escape plantations for towns and cities. Cities like Shreveport, or even smaller towns like Holly Springs, not only provided anonymity and freedom from white surveillance but also made possible better education, financial independence, and new political opportunities. Finding wage labor was not always easy, but for those with skills, like James Wells, there was usually plenty of work. Tradesmen faired much better than their rural counterparts who were often forced to live hand to mouth in search of a steady income. As a skilled carpenter Wells was able to earn enough money to provide for his family. More importantly, his economic success meant that Elizabeth and the children did not have to labor as domestics in the homes of white folks. Because Elizabeth worked at home and the children's only "job," as Ida explained, "was to go to school and learn all we could," they escaped the violence inherent in black/white labor relations.

Town and city life, however, was not without hardship or free of white violence. In the postwar period, urban riots were the most visible sign of the efforts by white southerners to stamp down black political mobilization and prevent economic independence. Ida was four years old when reports came from Memphis, only thirty miles away, that whites angered by the presence of black militiamen had attacked the city's black community, murdering, beating, and raping its inhabitants and burning homes and businesses in a three-day riot. Even though the riot did not directly affect Ida's immediate family, they must have felt the sense of menace and terror that swept through their community and the surrounding area as news spread that white rioters had killed forty-six blacks, raped at least five black women, and injured hundreds more.

The riot drew national attention and a congressional committee traveled to Memphis to investigate.[27] For the first time, black women asserted their legal claim to personal and sexual autonomy before a national audience.[28] The committee found: "It is a singular fact, that while this mob was breathing vengeance against the negroes and shooting them down like dogs, yet when they found unprotected colored women they at once 'conquered their prejudices,' and proceeded to violate them under circumstances of the most licentious brutality."[29] Black women and men bravely testified before the committee. Sixteen-year-old Lucy Smith testified that seven white men, two of them police officers, broke into her home during the riot and brutally raped her. "One of them," she explained, "choked me by the neck. . . . After the first man had connexion with me, another got hold of me and tried to violate me, but I was so bad he did not. He gave me a lick with his fist and said I was so damned near dead he would not have anything to do with me . . . I bled from what the first man had done to me. I was injured right smart."[30] Denied legal protection against rape under slavery, Smith and the four other rape victims challenged long-held beliefs that black women welcomed white men's sexual advances. In response to their testimonies, the committee's final report concluded, "The crowning acts of atrocity and diabolism committed during these terrible nights were the ravishing of five different colored women by these fiends in human shape."[31]

For black women, such a declaration confirmed their new rights as citizens and marked a radical change in national politics. These rights, which were based on ideas that had begun with abolitionist literature on the violation of slave women, gained currency during the Civil War when black women testified to sexual assaults at court-martial trials. In the postwar context, such testimony gave voice to black women's suffering and their demands for legal protection. The congressional committee's declaration defined black women as political persons worthy of federal protection against racial and sexual violence. Even though Ida Wells was too young at the time to appreciate the significance of the women's testimony, their actions paved the way for her and a new generation of black women determined to defend themselves against such violence in the future.

The Memphis riot, along with similar incidents in New Orleans, Chattanooga, Louisville, and Vicksburg, confirmed northern beliefs that the federal government had to do more to protect southern blacks and guarantee their rights as citizens.[32] Outraged by President Johnson's failure to act and inspired by black resistance and determination, the radical wing of the Republican Congress seized control of Reconstruction. In 1866, they refused to seat former Confederates elected to Congress. Making use of their congressional majority, Republicans passed two bills over Johnson's veto. The first bill strengthened and extended the life of the Freedmen's Bureau (established in March 1865), which initially helped ex-slaves and white refugees by providing food, clothing, supplies, and medical services. The Bureau eventually performed marriage ceremonies, established schools, supervised contracts between ex-slaves and their employers, managed confiscated or abandoned lands, and arbitrated legal disputes between black employees and their white employers.[33] The second bill passed by Congress, the Civil Rights Act of 1866, declared that all persons born in the United States were citizens, "without regard to race, color, or previous condition."[34] Again in opposition to Johnson's wishes, Congress wrote the Fourteenth Amendment into the Constitution, making it illegal for any state to enforce or make any laws abridging the "privileges and immunities" of citizens; to deny "equal protection of the law"; and/or to deprive citizens of life, liberty, or property without "due process of the law."[35]

While Tennessee willingly ratified the Fourteenth Amendment, the other ten ex-Confederate states refused to adopt the amendment, forcing Congress to pass the Reconstruction Act of 1867, which divided those ten states into five districts commanded by generals empowered to protect with military force the life and property of blacks.[36] In a follow-up measure, Congress empowered military officials to register voters and oversee new elections. Ex-Confederate states would now have to draft new constitutions, enfranchise black voters, and ratify the Fourteenth Amendment before being readmitted into the Union.

In the fall of 1867, James Wells, along with over sixty thousand black men and fewer than fifty thousand white men, registered to vote in Mississippi.

Soon afterwards, voters elected one hundred delegates (sixty-seven Republicans, seventeen of them African Americans) to serve at the constitutional convention. In January 1868, the delegates drafted a new state constitution, which accepted the requirement of the Fourteenth Amendment, disfranchised ex-Confederates, granted universal adult male suffrage, and allowed interracial marriages. In protest, a group of leading white men met in Jackson and wrote a white supremacist manifesto in which they resolved to defend the state against "negro domination." They accused the Republican Party of plotting "to place the white men of the Southern States under the governmental control of their late slaves" and called "upon the people of Mississippi to vindicate alike the superiority of their race over the negro and their political power, and to maintain constitutional liberty."[37] Waving the banner of white supremacy, they rallied the Democratic Party and organized to defeat the constitutional referendum by any means necessary.

Democrats threatened blacks with loss of employment, evictions from farms, and death if they voted Republican. When James Wells's employer, Bolling, threatened to fire him if he did not vote the Democratic ticket, he "bought a new set of tools, and went across the street and rented another house."[38] Most black men, however, could not afford to disobey their white employers. Indeed, the threats of violence and loss of livelihood were all too real. The Democratic campaign of terror succeeded. The new state constitution was defeated in June 1868 by almost eight thousand votes, and Democrats won the governorship and four of the five congressional posts. Failure to pass the constitution, however, made the elections invalid.

At the same time that Mississippi Democrats learned to make violent use of the political rhetoric of white supremacy, Republicans realized that they would have to organize, educate, and protect a new electorate if they hoped to reconstruct the state. The Loyal League was critical to this effort. Organized in the North during the war, the League had worked to rally support for the Union. Now it branched into the South to ensure black rights. By the fall of 1867, Leagues existed in almost every southern state. The League often operated in secrecy and held night meetings to attract black members, who feared for their safety. Not until after the 1868 elections did the League begin to gain ground in the Delta State. James Wells became a member of the Holly Springs branch. The League's efforts paid off when citizens voted in November 1869 to accept the revised constitution (now shorn of the disfranchising clauses) and elected James

Alcorn, a substantial delta planter and former slaveholder, as the new Republican Governor. Alcorn's administration took office early in 1870, and the new legislature, which included forty black men, ratified the Fourteenth and Fifteenth amendments and appointed the first black man, Hiram Rhodes Revels, to the U.S. Senate to fulfill the unexpired term of Jefferson Davis.[39]

On February 23, 1870, Congress readmitted Mississippi into the Union; over the next four years the state legislature approved public education and invested in public buildings and institutions for the poor, the mentally ill, and the physically handicapped. They eliminated racial discrimination from the state laws and in 1873 passed a civil rights bill guaranteeing blacks equal access to all places of public entertainment. While blacks outnumbered whites and voted in large numbers during Mississippi's Reconstruction years, they represented only a small percentage of elected officials. In the first Reconstruction legislature (1869) there were thirty black members, some of whom had been slaves, and by 1871 that number had risen to thirty-eight. In 1872, John R. Lynch served as the first black speaker of the state House of Representatives and in 1874 blacks held several significant positions: A. K. Davis was elected Lieutenant Governor; James Hill of Holly Springs was appointed Secretary of State; and T. W. Cardozo was elected State Superintendent of Education. In 1875, Blanche K. Bruce, a former slave, was the second black man elected to the Senate.[40] Although black Mississippians never held offices in proportion to their numbers, they did find inspiration in the few black leaders elected to public office. Indeed, the accomplishments of black men like Lynch, Davis, and Bruce left a lasting impression on Ida B. Wells and young black people coming of age in Mississippi during "Radical" Reconstruction. If a black man from Mississippi could replace Jefferson Davis in the U.S. Senate, anything seemed possible.

"Redemption" Politics and the Rise of the Rape Myth

Of course, black political participation did not go unchallenged. The Mississippi Democratic Party, with the assistance of paramilitary groups such as the Ku Klux Klan (KKK), the White Rose Society, the Native Sons of the South, and the Seventy-Six Society were determined to regain power over former slaves and to seize control of local and state governments. Thus, they waged war against black people and their Republican allies.[41] Even in the relatively peaceful town of Holly Springs, Ida and her family could not ignore the upsurge of violence that left so many freed people brutalized or dead. When reading newspaper articles to her father and his "admiring group" of friends and listening to her parents discuss postwar politics, Ida struggled to grasp the meaning of words like Ku Klux Klan. Her mother's worried pacing at night whenever James attended a political meeting and reports of the Klan's failed attempt to assassinate Nelson Gill, a founder and leader of the local Loyal League, made Ida keenly aware that the KKK "meant something fearful."[42] Indeed, by 1871, Elizabeth had reason to worry and Ida much to fear.

At first, white violence against ex-slaves had been unorganized and directed at individual blacks, but by the 1870s black communities all over the South had become targets of a systematic campaign of political terror. The KKK, an unofficial arm of the Democratic Party founded in Pulaski, Tennessee, in 1865/66, became the most visible symbol of white supremacy and southern white men's illicit effort to "redeem" the South. In the early 1870s, during the height of Mississippi Klan violence, nightriders, as they were called by southern blacks, dressed in robes that included pointed hoods and masks that covered their faces, rode through black communities at night terrifying, threatening, flogging, raping, and murdering blacks and their white allies. In the eastern counties, the Klan was notorious for killing or driving out teachers and burning black schools and churches. Terrorist groups all over the state targeted black men who voted Republican, participated in the Union League, or held political offices. Nightriders murdered politically active black men and raped their wives and daughters.[43] In 1870, organized whites killed two black men who were members of the Lauderdale County board of supervisors. In Monroe County, white supremacists disemboweled and cut the throat of Jack Dupree, president of a club of black Republicans, and Klansmen severely whipped A. P. Huggins, the black school superintendent.[44] G. Wiley Wells, district attorney for the northern district of the state and a resident of Holly Springs, argued before a congressional committee that Klan violence served to keep blacks away from the polls so that Democrats would carry the elections. He testified that in the summer of 1871, despite the passage of the state's anti-KKK law the year before, "Negroes were coming into Holly Springs imploring [him] to protect them."[45] It seemed no one was safe.

Black women and men who demanded fair pay, broke labor contracts, rented or owned land, or displayed economic success in any way risked having their homes invaded by gun-toting nightriders. In Winston County, when Nancy Edmonds left her employer's plantation in pursuit of a better job, the Klan whipped her "unmercifully" and forced her to return.[46] One white Mississippian explained that the Klan sought "to keep them [blacks] from renting land, so that the majority of the white citizens may control labor."[47] In Tippah County, organized whites drove blacks off good land, and in Alcorn County, they tried to drive away black laborers on the Gulf and Ohio Railroad. Former slaves who had achieved a modicum of economic success by challenging the exploitative systems of wage labor contracts and sharecropping were seen as threatening white political hegemony and white supremacist ideas. They became the targets of white vigilante terror.

White southerners, like most Americans, understood citizenship in terms of manhood and patriarchal rights and prerogatives. However, resistance to black citizenship, with its implied rights of political, economic, and social equality, took on a sexual connotation because of the association of equality with sexual license.[48] For example, when a congressional committee asked Joseph Beckwith of Columbus, Mississippi, why the Klan had whipped him and his wife, he explained, "They said that they understood I had talked some talk concerning some white woman that was not nice . . . they wanted to run me off, the man I lived with did, on account of my crop, and that was why they got the Ku-Klux to get after me, and that night tried to make me own it, and I told them I didn't say it."[49] Although Beckwith's economic success was probably at the root of the Klan's resentment, by linking it to the supposed insult to white womanhood Klansmen justified their violent behavior as chivalrous and honorable, while portraying Beckwith as unmanly and unworthy. Beckwith's beating reveals how the alleged protection of white womanhood from insult or injury was tied to the question of black citizenship and thus became part of the political discourse of Reconstruction.[50]

The Beckwith case signaled the postwar emergence of a strict color line that shored up white men's sexual and political power. Whereas black men and women who dared to push up against these new racial boundaries (or were merely perceived by whites as doing so) risked deadly consequences, white men were at liberty to cross racial lines, especially if doing so reinforced white dominance and Democratic power. For example, when Edward Carter of Mississippi testified that the Klan "ravished" his daughter and ran him off his land because they "wanted what [he] had," he revealed not only how nightriders denied him the traditional rights of manhood that would allow him to protect his daughter against rape, but also made clear their complete disregard for the rights of black women.[51] The men who beat Beckwith and his wife and those who raped Carter's daughter wanted to prevent blacks from having what whites had: the rights as citizens to control their labor, to successfully own land, to exercise political power, to protect their families, and to live as respectable men and women. By accusing black men of dishonoring white womanhood and at the same time raping black women, southern white men articulated, on the one hand, deep anxieties about what they understood as the consequences of forced "social equality" and, on the other hand, a strong desire to maintain sexual dominance over black women.

Democrats first expressed their concerns about the question of social equality during the 1864 presidential election when they accused Lincoln and the Republican Party of promoting interracial sex, or in their words, "miscegenation"—a new coinage.[52] In the postwar context, southern Democrats reasoned that if black men were given the full rights of citizenship they would inevitably pursue intimate relationships with white women, which for many white southerners meant the eventual degeneration of the white race. J. R. Smith, a white postmaster and clerk of the chancery court in Meridian, argued that the Democratic Party had successfully convinced whites, especially poor whites, that the Republican Party intended "to put the negro in control, to make a sort of negro supremacy, to give him the control of the affairs of the Government, to put him in office, and gradually to force him into social relations with the white people . . . to intermingle by marriage with the whites."[53] Joshua S. Morris, a white lawyer in Jackson, agreed: "Multitudes of middle and lower classes of whites . . . are induced to believe that republicanism means social equality; that, if a man is a republican, he must necessarily be in favor of white people and negroes marrying and associating on terms of perfect equality in the social circle."[54] Convinced that interracial sex would undermine racial hierarchy, nightriders policed and punished men and women, most of them black, accused of engaging in interracial sex. Three black women, Betsy Lucas, Eliza Hinton, and Lydia Anderson of Noxubee County, suffered brutal whippings by nightriders who accused them of "cohabitating" with white men. In Columbus, the Klan whipped George Irion, a black man, for allegedly "keeping a white woman."[55]

In the context of black freedom, sex across the color line signified a radical political act, especially on the part of black men and white women. Weaving together fears about black political power and anxieties about miscegenation into a single design, southern whites converted black men's desires for economic and political equality into a desire for "social equality," which they then translated into a threat against white womanhood. This scenario of race, sex, and politics created a powerful alibi for denying black people the basic rights of citizenship and for bringing whites together across class lines.[56] Bringing white men and women together across class divisions was no easy task, but the Democratic Party's success at confounding black male citizenship and interracial sex proved extremely powerful in achieving it. When nightriders accused Beckwith of speaking inappropriately about "some white woman" while they sought to gain control of his crops, they signaled a slight shift in their ideas about which white women deserved protection. It now seemed that all southern white women, regardless of class status, were worthy of protection if their alleged assailants were black. Southern whites in many ways had always been cautious regarding interactions between black men and white women, but in the postwar context these concerns began to take on new meanings and acquire a sense of urgency as whites imagined "social equality" as tantamount to forced sexual relations between black men and white women.[57]

With the confederacy's defeat, the simplest exchanges between black men and white women assumed a more menacing tone for many white southerners. Southern white men anxiously sought the reinstitution of a strict gender and racial hierarchy dependent on black deference and white female subordination. Postwar, however, they extended protection to all white women, not just southern "ladies." In the antebellum South and during the Civil War, protection devolved upon the honor of elite white women. When the nightriders portrayed Beckwith's economic success as an insult to white womanhood generally, they intentionally encompassed all white women so that whites would stand together across class lines. The sexualized language of "social equality" resonated with most southern white men and women, regardless of class, because it squared with their ideas about white supremacy and traditional gender roles. What honorable white man would not heed the call to protect white womanhood and what self-respecting white woman would not deem herself worthy of protection?

Ironically, at the same time that white supremacists began constructing political arguments about the need to protect all white women against black men, Klansmen and gangs of white men were using sexual violence to intimidate or punish black women and their families. Southern white men were not merely concerned with reconstructing and maintaining a caste defined by race, they were also determined to preserve traditional forms of racial patriarchy which allowed them complete control over black and white women's sexuality. Thus, while emancipation deprived wealthy white men of easy sexual access to and greater control over black women, black women remained vulnerable to sexual and racial violence at the hands of white men.[58] Certainly, Ida's mother feared for James Wells's safety when he attended political meetings, but she would have also worried about her own protection and that of her daughters. Nightriders threatened, flogged, and raped black women for a range of perceived transgressions—from participating in Republican Party politics, to engaging in interracial sex, to challenging white authority. After a Klansman's failed attempt to assault Miss Davis, one of the white northern teachers at Wells's school, he abducted and raped Davis's favorite black student.[59]

Mississippi was no exception. In Georgia, during the height of Klan violence, a group of nightriders brutally beat and raped Rhoda Ann Childs when they could not find her Republican husband. In testimony given to an officer of the Freedmen's Bureau, she described the horrible events: "They then seized me and took me some distance from the house, where they 'bucked' me down across a log, stripped my clothes over my head, one of the men standing astride my neck and beat me across my posterior, two men holding my legs. . . . Then a man, supposed to be an ex-confederate soldier, as he was on crutches, fell upon me and ravished me."[60] While the rape of black women by white men still represented an assertion of white men's racial and sexual power, in the postwar context it served also as both a punishment and a threat to black women's bodily rights as citizens.

Even when nightriders refrained from raping their female victims, they engaged in a pattern of ritualized sexual torture. The Klan forced most black women to take off their clothes before whipping them and threatened them with worse if they did not change their ways. In testimony given before a congressional committee, Caroline Smith of Georgia stated: "Felker then said, 'Take off this,' pointing to my dress, 'and fasten it around you.' They made me fasten it to my waist. He whipped me some and then he made me take my body off which I wore under my dress. He gave me fifty more and then said, 'Don't let's hear any big talk from you, and don't sass any white ladies.' "[61] While the Klan commonly dragged women from their homes in the middle of night, they sometimes tortured and threatened blacks, especially black women, inside their homes. A group of white men invaded the home of Cheany Ransom, a former slave, who had filed a successful complaint against Mrs. Hunt, her white employer, for refusing to pay her for services rendered. Ordered by the Freedman's Bureau in Calhoun, Georgia, to pay Cheany the twenty dollars that she owed her, Mrs. Hunt declared, "If she had to pay her that Cheany should not live here to enjoy it." That very night three white men forced their way into Cheany's bedroom and while she lay in bed they rubbed a pistol over her face and said they would blow her brains out if she did not leave town.[62]

Free to articulate their outrage at the way white men violated and insulted black womanhood, freed people pointed out the contradictions in notions of white supremacy and argued that as citizens black women deserved the same protections and rights guaranteed white women. At an Emancipation celebration in 1866, Henry McNeal Turner, a minister in the African Methodist Episcopal Church (AME), countered white supremacist concerns about "social equality" by drawing attention to the rape of black women by white men: "It was said, and Southern fanatics rode that hobby everywhere, 'That if you free the negro he will want to marry our daughters and sisters,' that was another foolish dream. What do we want with their daughters and sisters? We have as much beauty as they. . . . All we ask of the white man is to let our ladies alone, and they need not fear us."[63] More importantly, black women themselves challenged white men's assumed sexual power over them by reporting injustices to the Freedman's Bureau and seeking legal redress. No doubt the men who invaded Cheany's bedroom and threatened her with death for reporting Mrs. Hunt to the Freedman's Bureau must have feared that she might report them as well. In fact, her previous actions may have prevented them from raping her. Whenever possible, former slaves courageously challenged white violence and countered images of degraded black manhood and womanhood with declarations of citizenship and demands for state and federal protection.

The story of the 1871 riot in Meridian, Mississippi, reveals how members of one black community sought to defend their rights as citizens and to protect themselves against organized white violence. The upsurge of Klan activity in the nearby Alabama counties of Sumter and Greene had forced many black people to seek refuge across the state border in Meridian. Feeling the effects of the labor shortage produced by black refugees, Alabama nightriders crossed the state line and forced many black workers at gunpoint to return to their former employers. In protest, black Meridians marched through the town. White officials arrested Aaron Moore, William Clopton, and Warren Tyler for making "incendiary" speeches. Democrats held a public meeting in which they resolved to remove Republicans from office, called for the appointment of new officials to disarm black citizens and to break up their organizations, and invited Klansmen from Alabama back to help them.[64] At the trial of Moore, Clopton, and Tyler, shots rang out in the courtroom and mayhem broke loose. When the smoke settled, the white Republican judge and two black men lay dead. Two days of rioting followed. Searching from house to house for black leaders, confiscating weapons, and burning churches, organized mobs of white men beat, raped, murdered, and arrested black citizens and white Republicans. At least four black women were raped.[65] As in most race riots, blacks were outnumbered and outgunned. In the end, thirty African Americans were brutally murdered and the black community was terrorized. Only six white men were charged and arrested with unlawful assembly, intent to kill, and assault. The grand jury, however, refused to indict.[66]

The Meridian riot contributed to Congress's belated passage of the 1871 Ku Klux Klan Act, which made it illegal to "conspire together or go in disguise upon the public highway, or upon the premise of another for the purpose . . . of depriving any person or any class of persons of the equal protection of the laws, or of equal privileges or immunities under the laws," or hindering state authorities from affording equal protection of the laws to all citizens. The law authorized the president to use military force to prevent organized violence and to suspend the writ of habeas corpus in order to suppress "armed combinations."[67] During the height of Klan violence, President Ulysses S. Grant suspended habeas corpus in nine South Carolina counties and thousands of suspected Klansmen were arrested and hundreds convicted. Federal intervention did much to suppress Klan activity, however, it was too little and too late. By 1871 a pattern of political oppression and intimidation of black voters and their white Republican allies was well established. By 1874 Democrats had gained control in the governments of Virginia, North Carolina, Georgia, Tennessee, Alabama, and Texas. That same year Democrats also won control of the U.S. House of Representatives.

The battle over Reconstruction and the claims of black citizenship continued in Mississippi. In 1875, Democrats initiated the "First Mississippi Plan" to deter black political participation. No longer depending on Klansmen and nightriders, Democrats openly used violence and fraud to control the black vote. Mobs of whites killed black voters and rioted in the towns of Clinton and Aberdeen, and in the counties of Yazoo and Coahoma. Unmasked men attacked Republican rallies, stuffed ballot boxes, and killed black political leaders like Charles Caldwell, who served as a delegate at the 1868 Constitutional Convention and as a state senator. As a result, Democrat "Redeemers" won five of the six congressional seats and secured a four-to-one majority in the legislature in the 1876 state election. With a majority in the state legislature, the Democrats impeached and removed the black lieutenant governor before forcing the Republican governor to resign and leave the state. By 1876 Republicans remained in power in only three southern states (Florida, South Carolina, and Louisiana). As part of the bargaining that resolved the disputed presidential election in favor of Rutherford B. Hayes, Republicans promised to end Radical Reconstruction, thereby leaving most of the South in the hands of the Democratic Party. Upholding the Republican end of the bargain, in 1877 President Hayes withdrew the remaining federal troops from the South and abandoned southern black people.

The Sexual Politics of Segregation

The failure of Radical Reconstruction to secure the political well-being of blacks in the South left millions of former slaves vulnerable, lacking land, and dependent on the white planter elite. The withdrawal of federal troops meant that hopes of federal protection vanished and the possibility of black citizenship dwindled as white Democrats regained complete power in the former Confederacy. By 1877, James and Elizabeth Wells would have been among the millions disheartened by events and their future prospects. The rise of Democratic power in 1876 led to the passage of poll taxes, making it difficult for poor blacks and whites to vote. That same year the Mississippi legislature passed the infamous "Pig Law," which made the theft of a pig or property valued over ten dollars an act of grand larceny and subject to at least five years' imprisonment. Claims that black men were raping white women—which had served to justify Klan violence and the violent overthrow of Republican governments—were now being used to defend legal segregation.[68] Regardless, young black men and women who had experienced the freedom and possibilities of Radical Reconstruction remained determined to exercise their rights as citizens.

The bleak political realities that southern blacks faced were often overshadowed by the harshness and meanness of everyday life. Poverty and disease dominated the southern landscape and for most black people money was rare and hunger was common. Even when former slaves were able to acquire wealth, they, like their white neighbors, were not immune to disease and death. In 1878, when a yellow fever epidemic brought by mosquitoes swept through the Mississippi Valley, the issue of social equality hardly mattered as citizens, black and white, rich and poor, Democrats and Republicans, fought for survival against the deadly disease. The fever claimed twenty thousand lives in the region and reduced the Holly Springs' population by one-fifth. Some three hundred people, including James and Elizabeth Wells and their youngest son, lost their lives.[69] Left to care for her five younger siblings (Eugenia, the next oldest, who was paralyzed from the waist down due to a severe case of scoliosis; James, age eleven; George, age nine; Annie, age five; and Lily, age two), sixteen-year-old Ida had little time to mourn the death of her parents. Many years later, she explained, "Life became a reality to me."[70] Desperate to keep her family together, Ida opposed efforts to place her siblings in various homes in the black community. Her fiery and outspoken determination to keep her brothers and sisters together in the family home was met with suspicion. Rumors began to circulate that she had asked a white man for money, that she "wanted the house for illicit assignation," and that her siblings were actually her own children.[71] Her parents' status in the community had previously shielded Ida from the harsh stereotypes that often circulated about black women's sexuality. Never before had her virtue or respectability been publicly questioned and, she recalled, "I am quite sure that never in all my life have I suffered such a shock as I did when I heard this misconstruction that had been placed upon my determination to keep my brothers and sisters together."[72] To counter the gossip, Ida's grandmother, Peggy, came to stay and help with the children.

At this point Ida sought paid employment for the first time and eventually found a job teaching in a small country school in Marshall County, six miles outside of Holly Springs. Riding to and from work on the back of a "big mule," she spent five days each week teaching in the countryside and on the weekends she cleaned, cooked, and cared for her siblings. Between teaching and caring for her siblings, she tried to continue her studies at Rust College. Sometime between 1880 and 1881, however, a confrontation with the president of the college, in which she allegedly "questioned his authority," led to her expulsion. Years later she explained (without giving further details) that her "tempestuous, rebellious, hard headed willfulness" had been the reason why her "scholastic career was cut short."[73] Unable to continue her education, she accepted an invitation from her aunt Fannie Butler (whose husband had died during the yellow fever epidemic, leaving her with three children to care for) to move to Memphis, Tennessee. Sometime in 1882, Ida left her handicapped sister Eugenia in Holly Springs with her mother's sister Belle, found apprenticeships for her brothers, and took her two younger sisters, Annie and Lily, with her to Memphis. She soon secured a teaching position ten miles outside the city, where she earned three times more than she had in Mississippi and no longer had to commute to work on the back of a mule; she was now able to ride to work on a train.

The move to Memphis allowed her to escape some of the trauma and misery she had suffered in Holly Springs. In the two years since the deaths of her parents, she had fallen victim to vicious rumors and had been expelled from college. In such a small town there was no escape from the "base slanderous lie that had blackened [her] life." Memphis, however, offered her the possibility of a new beginning. In fact, she hoped it would be a place "to cast the dark shadows out and exorcise the spirit that haunt[ed] [her]."[74]

During the Civil War, African Americans first began migrating to Memphis from the surrounding countrysides of Tennessee, Mississippi, and Arkansas. Fugitive slaves escaped from farms and plantations to find refuge there among Union soldiers at Fort Pickering. The black population in Memphis increased from four thousand in 1860 to seventeen thousand in 1865. Despite the 1866 race riot and the yellow fever epidemic that devastated black neighborhoods, the black population of Memphis continued to grow. In 1880, blacks in Shelby County, which includes Memphis, represented 55 percent of the population and managed to elect two black men to serve in the state legislature. In "South Memphis," blacks created opportunities for themselves and built a community complete with churches, schools, businesses, benevolent societies, associations, and clubs.

When Ida arrived in the early 1880s a small but thriving black middle class already existed. Included in this community was Robert Church, the wealthiest black man in the South. Also born in Holly Springs, Church was the son of a white steamboat captain, Charles B. Church, and a slave seamstress, Emmeline. As a young boy, he worked as a cabin boy and a steward on his father's boat. During the war he settled in Memphis, where he subsequently opened a saloon after the war. Shot in the head during the 1866 race riot, he barely survived. After the 1878 epidemic, as white residents abandoned their homes and businesses, Church used his inheritance to take advantage of the low real estate prices and bought the city's first bond in an effort to help Memphis regain its charter.[75] However, most of the city's black residents could only dream of having the financial means to one day own property. Even though Ida's job as a teacher placed her in the tiny, fragile black middle class that included teachers, ministers, doctors, shopkeepers, lawyers, and housewives, she barely made enough money to make ends meet during her first years in the city.

As Wells sought to take advantage of the many opportunities that Memphis offered the black middle class, southern whites, united in the Democratic Party, chipped away at those opportunities. Southern Democrats continued the work of imposing white supremacy and reestablishing a society divided along racial lines. They believed legal segregation would prevent interracial contact and reinforce white solidarity. As early as 1866 the Tennessee legislature passed the state's first Jim Crow law requiring separate schools for white and black children. In 1870, interracial marriages were outlawed. A few years later, in response to the Civil Rights Act of 1875, which guaranteed blacks equal access to public accommodations and the right to serve as jurors, the Tennessee legislature passed a statute that made it legal for hotels, restaurants, railway companies, and places of amusement to discriminate based on race.

In 1881 the state legislature initiated what would eventually be recognized as the "separate but equal" doctrine when it passed a law requiring railroad companies to furnish separate cars for colored passengers who paid first-class rates. In actuality this meant that black people who could afford first-class tickets were to be relegated to the smoking car. Referred to as the "ladies' car," the first-class car provided passengers with cushioned seats, clean floors, a toilet, and prohibited smoking and the use of obscene language. On most railways men were not allowed in the ladies' car unless they accompanied a woman or child. The "smoking car" was exactly that—a rowdy, smoke-filled car close to the engine where passengers who could not afford first-class tickets rode. It was no place for "a lady."

For black women, the battle over the ladies' car had as much to do with challenging segregation as it had to do with defending their reputations as respectable women worthy of protection and insisting on their rights as female citizens to be treated with respect and dignity. While the number of southern blacks who could afford first-class tickets was relatively low, the fight to maintain access to the ladies' car became one of the most visible signs of black resistance to the rise of Jim Crow.[76] In 1879, a Mrs. Richard Robinson unsuccessfully sued the Memphis and Charleston Railroad when she was denied access to the first-class car. A year later, however, a federal court awarded Jane Brown three thousand dollars when she sued the company for physically removing her from a ladies' car and forcing her to ride in the smoking car, which was "crowded with passengers, mostly immigrants traveling on cheap rate." Rather than ride in the smoker's car, Brown disembarked from the train at the next stop. The lawyer for the Memphis and Charleston Railroad Company argued that Brown had been removed from the ladies' car because she was no lady. By claiming that Brown was "a notorious and public courtesan, addicted to the use of profane language and offensive conduct in public places," the defense relied on antebellum legal precedent that defined black women as unworthy of the rights and protections guaranteed to respectable and virtuous white women.[77] The company claimed that the smoking car was equal to the ladies' car and that Brown had no right to refuse it. The court, however, was not convinced and held that the Tennessee law of 1875 was in conflict with the federal regulation of interstate commerce and thus unconstitutional. Brown had paid for a first-class ticket and was entitled to first-class accommodations "equal in all respects to the best which the company offered on that train to other female passengers traveling alone as the plaintiff was."[78] The court's verdict in favor of Brown was celebrated as a victory for black womanhood.

Wells, who was only nineteen years old and had been riding the trains for less than a year, grasped the significance of white southerners' efforts to relegate black passengers, especially black women, to the smoking car. A signifier of the race, class, and gender contradictions that plagued ideas of white supremacy, the battle over the ladies' car was a fight neither side could afford to lose. Segregated transportation would be a new platform for Wells—an issue that was implicitly about womanhood and protection from harassment and insult. Thus, it was with this in mind that Wells, who was traveling in the ladies' car between Memphis and Woodstock, ignored a white conductor's request that she move to the smoking car. According to Wells's testimony, the conductor asked her twice to leave the ladies' car before trying to forcibly remove her. Wells explained: "He tried to drag me out of the seat, but the moment he caught hold of my arm I fastened my teeth in the back of his hand. . . . He went forward and got the baggage-man and another man to help him and of course they succeeded in dragging me out." Whites, women and men both, added to her humiliation by standing in their seats to get a good view and applauding as the conductor physically evicted her from the car.[79] Refusing to stand in the smoking car, Wells got off at the next stop and decided to sue the company for discrimination.

Eight months later a state judge ruled in Wells's favor on the grounds that the railroad company had violated the 1881 law that required them to furnish "colored passengers" with "separate but equal" first-class cars. Wells was awarded two hundred dollars and the railroad company appealed; in the same month, Wells was again refused admittance to the ladies' car and again she filed suit. In December 1884 the judge again found in Wells's favor and awarded her five hundred dollars in damages. The railroad filed another appeal, which reached the state supreme court in the spring of 1887. To Wells's dismay, the judges reversed the lower court's decision, making clear Tennessee's commitment to a society divided by race, class, and gender. Bitterly disappointed, Wells confided in her diary, "I had hoped such great things from the suit for my people generally. I have firmly believed all along that the law was on our side and would, when we appealed to it, give us justice. I feel shorn of that belief and utterly discouraged, and just now if it were possible would gather my race in my arms and fly far away with them."[80]

Born during the Civil War, Wells had not suffered the dehumanizing effects of slavery and thus had not been forced to defer to whites or to concede her rights as a citizen to white authority without a fight. Her parents' economic and social standing in the black community allowed her to grow up with racial pride and a strong sense of self. In her autobiography, Wells credited her mother for her religious, intellectual, and domestic educations: "A deeply religious woman, she won the prize for regular atten-

dance at Sunday school, taking the whole brood of six. . . . She ta
how to do the work of the home—each had a regular task besides ;
work, and I often compare her in training her children to that oi otner
women who had not her handicaps." With much pride, Wells concluded,
"She was not forty when she died, but she had borne eight children and
brought us up with a strict discipline that many mothers who have had educational advantages have not exceeded."[81] Her father provided for the
family financially and fulfilled his civic duty. His fierce independence
and unwillingness to submit to Bolling's political demands or Miss Polly's
wishes to see the children made lasting impressions on Wells. Taking lessons from both her parents, Wells would spend most of her adult life
struggling to balance her political ambitions with her desire to represent
the best of black womanhood. Her family's slave past, the violent politics
of Reconstruction, the tragic loss of both her parents at a young age, the
vicious rumors that circulated about her character in the aftermath of her
parents' death, and the relentless and violent rise of Jim Crow segregation
shaped the woman that she would become and informed her entry into
the racial and sexual politics of the New South.

3

SOUTHERN WHITE WOMEN AND THE
ANTI-RAPE MOVEMENT

The tumultuous consequences of the Civil War and Reconstruction brought new opportunities and burdens for both black and white southern women. The combination of military defeat, the emancipation of slaves, and Radical Reconstruction politics transformed class, gender, and race relations in the American South and gave rise to both a "New Southern Woman" and a "New Southern Negro."[1] However, southern white men, especially those responsible for "redeeming" the South, had not significantly changed their ideas about the "place" of women and black people in politics and society. During the pitched battles of Reconstruction southern Democrats had made clear their intentions of excluding black men from politics, "protecting" white women from the perceived "dangers" of black citizenship, and maintaining sexual and political power over both black and white women. Elite southern white men set out to rebuild a society segregated by race, organized by class, and restricted by sex.

Felton and Wells, like many others of both races, refused to accept the subordinate roles ascribed to them. Instead, armed with painful lessons from their past and motivated by hopes for the future, they seized upon women's postwar concern with protection of body and property and forcefully entered into the violent racial and sexual politics of the "New South." Felton and Wells would call southern white men's ideas about female protection to account, each in her own way. Patriarchy offered precious little room for women to find their political voices, but both women found that space and occupied it fully.

Postwar realities made it difficult for Felton to ignore the contradictions embedded in antebellum notions of chivalry. She complained that at its best, chivalry required that "a woman's name was protected with threat of duel"; at its worst, it "permitted a man to beat his wife." Chivalry in the form of "bows and curtsies" and "high-flown words" had done little to protect women during the war and seemed to be doing even less in the post-Reconstruction period.[2] Such antiquated notions, she argued, shored up white men's economic and political power while leaving women dependent and vulnerable to a host of abuses ranging from rape to financial ruin. "Before the war," she criticized, "a married woman of Georgia could not even own her clothes." All was the property of her husband and he was her sole support. The Civil War had taught Felton that women, regardless of race and class, could not and should not depend solely on individual men for security. It was too dangerous and unreliable in times of crisis. For Felton, the politics of Reconstruction introduced radical alternatives for acquiring and safeguarding female protection. Pointing to the 1868 constitutional convention, "a radical body controlled by scalawags and carpet-baggers," she noted that it was the first group of elected southern officials to guarantee women the right to own property. Felton contended that better laws, not individual men, could do more to protect the virtue and rights of southern womanhood than southern honor.[3] She argued that in the New South, judges and legislatures should do the work of defending southern womanhood and "legislate domestic protection."[4] Chivalry was a dead letter.

Defining *protection* as a right to which all women were entitled, she initiated a radical view of female protection that encouraged women's independence and political power. In its own way, her argument was as strong as anything women's rights advocates in the North were setting forth. She believed that postwar realities required not only modern forms of protection enshrined in the state, but also an assertive "new" southern woman to demand it. Felton used her husband's political position and the influence of the Woman's Christian Temperance Union (WCTU) to broaden her concern with protection to include black women and poor white women. Convinced that women would have to enter politics to secure legal protection, Felton began a militant campaign for southern women's rights and joined the WCTU. Acknowledging black women's sexual vulnerability and the inadequate protection for poor white women, she challenged the elite white male hierarchy that shored up white men's sexual and political power and reinforced women's second-class status. In doing so, Felton inspired southern white men's worst fears: the political empowerment of southern womanhood.

Protection for Black Female Convicts

Ironically, it was on behalf of black women that Felton, in the 1880s, initiated her own political career. After reading in the *Atlanta Constitution* that a judge had sentenced Adaline Maddox, "a little fifteen-year-old colored girl," to five years of hard labor for stealing fifty cents, she decided to inquire into the state's convict lease system. The system had had critics from its inception. Created after the Civil War to reduce state debt, it exercised repressive control over black men and women and created a vast, cheap black labor force for southern business and industry. In the early 1870s Felton had already declared the system an invention of corrupt Democrats and greedy businessmen. The leasing of convicts to private employers allowed any person or company in need of workers to lease prisoners from the state for a small fee. Convicts labored in backbreaking industries—logging, phosphate mining, farming, railroad building, sawmilling, and turpentining. The state required lessees to assume all responsibility for the care, housing, and security of the prisoners in their employ. This relieved the state of the burden of paying to house and feed inmates, and enabled the government to make a profit on those remanded to its care. The income received from convict leasing eventually came to form a significant portion of the state's total revenue. Thus, the many politicians who were also businessmen had little incentive to reform a system from which they, as well as the state, profited.[5]

Felton began her research by reading the recently murdered Georgia legislator Robert Alston's report on convict leasing. As early as 1879 Alston spoke out against the convict lease system. After investigating and writing a legislative report revealing the brutality and corruption embedded in the system, Alston set out to introduce a bill to reform the system, but before he could do so he was shot and killed in the state house by an opponent of the forthcoming bill.[6] Felton learned from Alston's report that the system was more corrupt and brutal than she had imagined—prison conditions were abominable; guards enforced discipline through beatings; food and sanitation were vile; and inmates were brutalized and subjected to unspeakable degradation. She also discovered that the camps had high mortality rates due to a combination of poor food and water, unsanitary conditions, disease, accidents, overwork, beatings at the hands of guards, and lack of medical care.[7]

In 1881, African Americans represented over 90 percent of the convict lease population and, as Felton discovered, Adaline Maddox was just one of hundreds of teenaged girls and boys who had received long terms for relatively minor offenses. According to Felton's sources, women and children as young as twelve labored in these camps. Housed together with what she perceived as "hardened criminals," young prisoners, male and female, were shackled during the day and chained together at night. At the time of her investigation, Felton found that 137 children under age sixteen and some fifty women and girls lived in convict labor camps across the state.

The treatment of young black women was, to her, the most horrifying aspect of the system. Rape was commonplace. Worse, it was interracial: white guards raped black female convicts, forcing many of them to give birth to "illegitimate babies" of mixed race. The image of Adaline Maddox chained with "hardened criminals," most of them men, and subjected to sexual abuses at the hands of white guards deeply offended Felton's moral sensibilities. "She was in degradation so vile that a woman's soul was horrified to think of it," explained Felton. "I thought the sentence so disproportionate to the offense that I could not forget it. How much kinder it would have been to have shot her before she donned the stripes."[8] For Felton, then Adaline's sentence was a fate worse than death. Outraged at the "herding of women and small criminals in the same prison pens with men, and the working of convict women under brutal overseers who were made to submit to these brutal guards, and which resulted in placing infants in these prison pens," Felton instigated a campaign against the convict lease systems, emphasizing the sexual exploitation of female convicts.

No longer willing to accept the double standard that allowed southern white men to abuse black women with impunity, Felton revealed a shift in her ideas about black women's sexuality and her understanding of who deserved protection in the postwar South. In a radical move, she wrote letters to local and state newspapers calling on the state legislature to protect its black female convicts. She argued that white men's desire for profit had again left southern womanhood vulnerable. In this case, however, the women in desperate need of protection were not white. Felton's attack on the convict lease systems exposed not only her effort to bring black women under the umbrella of protection, but also her desire to constrain white men. Her critique was not so different from the arguments that the Grimké sisters had made against the sexual exploitation of slave women. Prison guards who raped female convicts, like slaveholders who sexually exploited female slaves, not only abused their power over black women, but also, according to Felton, betrayed the fundamental principles of white supremacy and their wives by fathering mixed race children.

Four years later, still haunted by the "forsaken little colored girl," Felton convinced her husband, recently elected to the state legislature, to introduce a bill to establish a reformatory for female convicts and juvenile delinquents. "He fathered the movement in the General Assembly and together we opened up a war on convict leasing," Felton explained; sanctioning her own efforts with the presence of her husband.[9] In 1885 when Dr. Felton first introduced the bill on the floor of the legislature, he took cues from his wife and declared the Georgia convict system "unchristian and uncivilized."[10] Leases, he raged, had created a "deeper, darker, and more fearful hell for women than for the male criminal."[11] Acknowledging that efforts were made to keep white women out of such camps, Dr. Felton nonetheless insisted that no woman, white or black, should be forced to suffer this "shame and degradation." To drive home his point, he asked a clerk to read aloud from an investigative report regarding a white overseer's rape of four black women in one camp. One woman, read the clerk, was pregnant and the father was most likely the overseer. "It is a shame! Yes a shame!" he declared after the reading. "A disgrace, dishonor to Georgia. In the name of humanity and justice to womanhood in the name of virtue and all that is good, let us rescue Georgia from the foul blot today."[12] No longer able to restrain themselves, the large number of citizens—most of them women—who had crowded into the galleries in support of Dr. Felton's bill burst into applause, making clear that Rebecca was not alone in her political crusade. Rarely had southern whites, especially southern white men, used words such as "virtue," "justice," and "honor" in regards to black womanhood.

Yet the trump card was not the principle of equal treatment, but the fear of black vengeance. The convict lease system, Dr. Felton warned, was not only barbaric in its treatment of female convicts, but also a "great school of vice, of immorality and of crime" that graduated hardened and dangerous criminals who returned to society "the enemies of white people" and "determined to have revenge."[13] He refused to speculate about how black convicts might seek revenge against white people, yet he knew his audience well and could count on his fellow congressmen to imagine the worst: the rape of a white woman by a black man. In fact, by the mid-1880s, in response to political activity on the part of both newly freed slaves and white women, many southern whites perpetuated the growing belief that black men were raping white women in increasing numbers.[14] Dr. Felton's suggestion that white guards who raped black female convicts were partially responsible for the alleged rise in sexual assaults against white women by black men placed the problem of rape squarely on the shoulders of white men. Like his wife, he accused southern white men of putting profits before the protection of southern womanhood. Passage of the reformatory bill, he concluded, would serve to protect all the citizens of Georgia, black and white.

In the end, however, the bill was defeated. Opponents insisted that black female convicts were "the veriest fiends that walked the earth;" altogether deserving of sexual violence and beyond reform.[15] Felton recalled, "These women were represented as crime centers, and vilest of the vile."[16] Few southern whites openly challenged the emerging postwar notion that black men and women freed from the discipline of slavery were reverting to their "natural" primitive, brutish ways. As the dominant image of blacks shifted from inferior child to aggressive and dangerous savage, the easier it became for white southerners to justify a host of abuses including not just convict leasing and rape, but also lynching, disenfranchisement, and segregation.

Despite the bill's defeat, the Feltons persevered and in the spring of 1886 Rebecca traveled to Macon to attend the third annual state convention of the Georgia WCTU. Founded in 1874 as an interracial organization, the WCTU adopted the motto "For God, Home and Native Land" and gave impetus to a nascent women's rights movement.[17] The WCTU grew rapidly as white and black women joined local chapters throughout the Midwest and the Northeast.[18] Still recovering from the devastation of war and coming to terms with the end of Reconstruction politics, most southern women had little time or energy to participate in the political crusade against alcohol, and few were interested in organizing across regional or racial boundaries. Not until the spring of 1880 did a small group of white women in Atlanta form an all white chapter of the WCTU, the first sign of southern white women's growing interest in organized temperance work.[19] A year later, WCTU president Frances Willard gave a series of lectures in Atlanta as part of her campaign to recruit more southern women to the organization. She returned to Atlanta in 1883 to attend the first WCTU state convention and to encourage the women of Georgia to expand their work beyond temperance and fully accept the organization's "do everything" policy.[20] By the 1880s this policy included a range of issues encompassing prison reform , tougher rape laws, protective labor laws, child welfare, public health, and female suffrage.[21]

In the South, the WCTU was extremely selective about which issues to tackle, and separate chapters were organized for black and white women.[22] Still somewhat wary about the role of women in politics and unwilling to commit to female suffrage, white southern branches re- mained quite conservative compared to their northern counterparts. The combination of white supremacy and political conservatism required not only a segregated WCTU in the South, but also a national leadership open to regional difference. In order to build a southern membership and keep southern white women from seceding, the national WCTU ac- cepted a policy of "state's rights" that allowed southern white women both to pick and choose the issues they wanted to support and to espouse a discourse of white supremacy in their temperance work.

In spite of segregation, when Felton joined the WCTU, black and white temperance women in the state had worked together to win prohi- bition elections in close to twenty-four counties.[23] In 1885, Georgia's union had twenty chapters and almost seven hundred dues-paying mem- bers. With forty-five locals and a little over a thousand white members, the organization peaked in 1893. By the time Felton joined, Willard had inaugurated the WCTU's department of social purity to work for laws and public policies that would protect women's and girl's "chastity" and the Georgia chapters had joined the national campaign to raise the legal age of consent, which was set at the age of ten in most states.[24] Consent laws required that a man who had sex with a child under the age of ten be charged with rape regardless of whether or not the young girl had con- sented, thus making irrelevant her moral character, which was often de- termined by her race and/or class status.[25] Convinced that raising the age of consent would reduce the number of sexual assaults against young girls (which, the WCTU believed, led to prostitution), temperance women across the country instigated public debates to reform predatory male sex- ual behavior.[26]

Fully aware of the WCTU's success at the polls and its crusade to protect young girls from sexual assault, Felton approached the organization in the spring of 1886 to solicit its support for her campaign against convict leasing and the sexual exploitation of female convicts. Years later she explained, "Up to that time I had not joined any organization, but there had been so many dreadful publications concerning the enormities of chain gang camps . . . that I determined to join the organization, to be able to fight these evils with numbers."[27] Felton introduced a resolution calling on the organization to support Dr. Felton's defeated bill. Reading from Alston's report, Felton "gave forth the astounding fact that 25 little children under three years of age resided in camps along with their convict mothers—helpless little innocents, born into the lowest depths of human degradation."[28] The children, she bemoaned, were not just any children, but the sons and daughters of white guards who had raped black female prisoners. She recounted all that she had learned about the dreaded system and begged the temperance women of Georgia to dedicate themselves to fighting these "evils."[29] Reverend W. H. Potter, editor of the *Wesleyan Christian Advocate*, endorsed Felton's resolution and the women of the WCTU "authorized" her to write and present a memorial petition to the Georgia Legislature.[30] The petition called on the state to separate women and juvenile criminals from "the older and more hardened criminals." As women, they declared it their "privilege" to suggest reforms "pertaining to the welfare of our race." They refrained, however, from pushing too hard and explained they were willing to "leave the remedy . . . to consideration and good judgment" of the legislature. To avoid accusations of meddling in politics, moreover, they specifically requested that their petition "not be mingled with political platforms or used for political effects."[31]

Despite this effort to distance the petition from political debates, Felton's presence in the state house could, in the end, only be read as a political act. It was one thing for Felton to write angry letters to the editors of local newspapers, but another for her to organize signatures on behalf of black women and publicly demand elected officials to legislate reform.[32] Felton later recalled, "I, myself, a woman without ballot, and no weapon but an active pen, was attacked in that legislative body because I obeyed the mandate of the WCTU and presented the memorial."[33] She was referring to Representative E. G. Simmons's speech in opposition to the reformatory bill and what she perceived as a personal attack on both herself and Dr. Felton. Simmons, speaking from the floor of the legislature, accused Dr. Felton of pandering to black voters: "With the banner of prohibition in one hand, he will appeal to the whites, and with the banner of the reform prison, he will appeal to the colored race."[34] After running down the merits of the bill, he branded Rebecca Felton "the political she of Georgia." Simmons mocked Dr. Felton and accused his wife of actively participating in politics—which in some elite circles was tantamount to being labeled a "fallen woman." Indeed, as far as the Feltons were concerned, Simmons had "gone as far as the law allowed" in an attempt to "defame" Felton's character.[35]

In the antebellum South such words would have instigated a duel, but much had changed since the war and Dr. Felton was no longer the man of his youth. Nonetheless, he needed to defend his honor and his wife's good name. In his reply he resorted to the familiar rhetoric of ladyhood and conjured up his oratory power to protect her. He reprimanded Simmons as a "ruffian" and "slanderer," declared his wife "one of the noblest and purest and most intellectual women of Georgia . . . who has only the interest of Georgia at heart, her native State, and its future welfare," and vowed that as long as he had breath in his body he would do everything in his power to defend her.[36] Regardless of Dr. Felton's fiery defense of his wife and the bill, the all-white male legislature refused again to pass the measure.

Simmons's verbal assault against the Feltons and the bill's repeated defeat reveal the strength of male resistance to white women's efforts to police their sexual behavior and to participate in politics. Not until 1897, when an alignment of southern progressives was in place, did the state finally respond to social reformers by employing wardens for each prison camp and creating a Prison Commission of three elected members to manage the convict leasing system to make sure prisoners were treated humanely. Eventually, in 1900, the state constructed a prison in Milledgeville where men, women, and juveniles were separated. The legislature, however, did not abolish the convict lease system until 1908.[37] In spite of this slow progress, Felton happily took credit for leading the prison reform movement and claimed that as early as 1890 she was "secretly" informed that "negro women convicts were removed from association with males in convict camps."[38] Her campaign against the "evils" of convict leasing marked just the first of many battles she would have with the Georgia legislature over the failure of southern white men to protect southern women.

WCTU and Reforming Rape Laws in the South

The same year that Felton, backed by the WCTU, called on the state to create a female reformatory, temperance women all over the country were circulating a petition demanding that state legislatures raise the age of consent.[39] The petition opened with lurid social purity rhetoric: "The increasing and alarming frequency of assaults upon women, and the frightful indignities to which even little girls are subject, have become the shame of our boasted civilization." A review of laws, explained the WCTU, had exposed an "utter failure" to meet new public demands for "better legal protection of womanhood and girlhood." Calling on state legislatures to "enact such statutes as shall provide for the adequate punishment of crimes against women and girls" and urging that "the age at which a girl can legally consent to her own ruin be raised to at least eighteen years," the WCTU concluded that the laws on the books did more to protect "the purse" than "the person."[40] On this issue, too, Felton jumped into the campaign to lobby the Georgia legislature. Her participation in the WCTU's thirty-year campaign to change consent laws from ten to eighteen, like her campaign for prison reform, reflected a dramatic shift in her public thinking about the problem of rape and white men's sexual behavior. Her primary motivation for pushing the reform of rape laws was to prevent elite white men from engaging in sexual intercourse with black girls. She believed the sexual exploitation of black women and girls not only revealed a violent disregard for black womanhood, but also exposed a profound disrespect for white womanhood and the supremacy of the race.

The WCTU's national campaign to reform consent laws sought to guarantee legal protection for all women regardless of class, race, or "previous chaste character" and to police the sexual behavior of white men, especially men of the upper classes. All over the country reformers believed raising the legal age of consent would provide better legal protection for working-class women, whom they perceived to be particularly vulnerable to their employers.[41] As the anonymous author of "Protection of Girlhood," an article published in the journal *Philanthropist*, argued: "For the daughters of the wealthy and favored classes, shielded from exposure and protected by good home environments, there is relatively little need for legislative interposition. For the poor and dependent, for the multitudes of young and greatly exposed working girls in our large cities, the situation is very different and the need to add legal safeguards is most urgent."[42] The WCTU made no secret about the class implications of raising the legal age of consent. On the one hand, they sought to protect poor women; on the other hand, they wanted to police middle-class and elite white men whom they believed preyed on the sexual innocence of young working girls.[43] Not surprisingly, male legislatures opposed increasing the age of consent for exactly these reasons and argued that young men and boys of the upper class would become the victims of designing poor women. Some even went so far as to appeal for the protection of boys. The WCTU, in typical fashion, responded to such calls for male protection with both candor and wit: "If the legislature should think it necessary to enact a law protecting boys under eighteen . . . the advocates of this movement would doubtless give it their endorsement. . . . When old women of eighty, and married and unmarried women of middle age, *in good society and of fine social standing*, go about ruining boys of ten and twelve and sixteen, it will be time to sound the alarm for boys as we are now sounding it for girls."[44] Placing particular emphasis on *"good society and of fine social standing,"* the WCTU openly challenged the sexual double standard that ignored elite white men's sexual indiscretions while holding women to an almost impossible moral standard.[45] Like Felton's campaign against convict leasing, the crusade to raise the legal age of consent required social reformers to rethink their ideas about lower-class white and black women's sexuality at the same time they called into question white men's sexual behavior.

While the national WCTU carefully crafted their discussions in class terms and avoided discussing the racial significance of reforming rape laws, white southerners understood that race and class went hand in hand in a society where the majority of "working girls" were black women laboring in white homes. If the WCTU hoped to avoid explicitly raising the issue of race, southern white legislatures had no problem pointing out that reforming rape laws would provide protection to poor black women at the expense of elite white men.[46] Southern white men understood that raising the legal age of consent presented a challenge to their racial power as well as their sexual prerogative. In Tennessee, one legislator warned, "to raise the age of consent . . . would enable loose young women, both white and black, to wreak a fearful vengeance on unsuspecting young men. . . . Who of us that has a boy 16 years old would be willing to see him sent to the penitentiary on the accusation of a servant girl?"[47]

Southern temperance women, however, held firm and spoke publicly in favor of protecting young black girls. Texas WCTU president Helen Stoddard explained her racial commitment to raising the age of consent: "As I pass along the streets of our cities and see the mulatto children, I think the colored girl needs protection, and more than that, the Anglo-Saxon man needs the restraints of this law to help him realize the dignity and sacred heritage he possesses by being born in the dominant race of the world."[48] In Georgia when "certain legislators had openly objected to the protection [that an age-of-consent] bill would afford colored girls," the WCTU responded that the protection of black women "added" to the reasons why the bill should pass and a group of Methodist women passed a resolution that called for "the protection of the childhood and womanhood of Georgia without regard to race."[49] Felton joined the chorus of southern women who defended the reform on the grounds that it would both provide black girls the protection they so desperately needed and would serve to regulate the sexual behavior of southern white men, especially elite white men. In a speech titled "The Rights of Children," Felton asked, "What is a ten year old girl but a child—a helpless child, if left to her own devices or exposed to the wiles of lust and selfish depravity?" Responding to white men's concerns that they would be vulnerable to prosecution, Felton continued, "It was gravely hinted that the liberty to prosecute offenders was not safe legislation, for it might give trouble to so-called respectable people in defending such cases. . . . This world needs wholesome restraint, and the age of consent might safely be raised to twenty-one, rather than left at ten, if it placed a wholesome check on sensual debauchery." As the "coming mothers of the race," she declared it "preposterous" that little girls, white or black, are not "defended on all sides from impurity and violence."[50]

White men in Georgia, eager to maintain their racial and sexual status, endeavored to prevent white women from engaging in and setting the tone of public discussions regarding rape. They took particular aim at the WCTU organizers who had successfully raised their voices in public spaces. The temperance stance on rape engendered bitter reaction that was often couched as sexual insult. In the fall of 1886, the *Atlanta Constitution* hoped to shame the organization into silence when it printed an article, "Morality That Is Immoral." The article condemned the WCTU for sending telegrams across the country that declared, "The Woman's National Temperance Union has secured 200,000 signatures of women to a petition asking Congress to raise the age of legal consent to eighteen years," and urged the press to "advocate the measure." Outraged at the publication of the telegram in "all the daily papers," the *Constitution* refused to support the petition and declared it "a public indecency for a lot of women to be moving about, discussing such a matter, getting up petitions and signatures, and bringing the subject into such prominence as to make it common talk." The editor claimed that some "social evils" were unfit for public discussion and should not "be spoken of in a mixed company or mentioned in print," because such publicity "lowers the tone of public morals." More importantly, the issue "should be left entirely to the men who make our laws."[51]

Such gendered rhetoric may have silenced some women, but it held little sway over WCTU women who had given up the notion that respectable women had no place in politics. In their national newspaper, the *Union Signal*, organizers took to task the *Constitution* editor for being hypocritical in his coverage of rape and contended that temperance women were only doing the work that men had failed to do. They complained that the *Constitution* had no problem "dish[ing] up with startling headlines and needlessly disgusting particulars" three stories of rape in the same issue in which they sought to censure the WCTU: "Does not 'such publicity lower the tone of public morals' quite as much as it does for the mothers of the nation to circulate a petition asking protection for their girls till they reach an age in which they are legally responsible for their acts?" Furthermore, they questioned, "If the sins can be 'mentioned in print,' why cannot the safeguards against the sins?"

As to the issue of leaving the reforms to men, the WCTU rebutted, "We have left it entirely to the men for three hundred years, for this disgrace our civilization dates back to the common law of England. . . . We think three hundred years is long enough to wait the tardy action of 'the men who make our laws.'" The consent laws, they reminded their readers, were fixed at ten in most states and as low as seven in Delaware, which meant that the "most fearful crimes" could be committed against a little girl as young as eight "with impunity, if the demon committing it can make a jury of men believe that she 'did not resist to the extent of her physical power.'"[52] As southern men so clearly understood, and the "good" temperance women did not fail to point out, there was much more at stake in this debate than the tone of public morals.

As these heated exchanges suggest, southern men and women were far from being in agreement about the problem of rape. The one point they did agree on was "the increasing and alarming frequency of assaults upon women," but the question of who was responsible for these crimes was still up for debate. Indeed, the coverage of rape in the *Constitution* suggests that the terms of the public debate about sexual violence remained very much up for grabs as late as 1886. Some of the "needlessly disgusting particulars" of the cases of sexual assault that appeared on the second page of the September 17, 1886, edition of the *Constitution*, for example, showed white men working hard to construct a rape/lynch narrative contingent on white female dependency and antiquated notions of chivalry. But at the same time, the stories also reveal both white and black women's challenges to a racial narrative that defined rape as a crime committed solely by black men against white women.

The first story, a "special" report from Macon, appeared under the heading "ATTEMPTED RAPE: SCOTT RICHARDS UP FOR A CRIMINAL ASSAULT" and recounted a white man's attempted rape of a black woman. This account more than any other directly challenged the postwar emergence of the rape/lynch myth that excused white men's sexual crimes and ignored black women's victimization. Rarely did white newspapers report the rape or attempted rape of a black woman by a white man, but when such articles did appear they revealed black women's efforts to defend themselves and to seek justice. Richards was fined two hundred dollars or sixty days on the chain gang for assaulting and knocking down a black woman. His "brutality," described the article, "was fiendish." According to all accounts, he had knocked the "negro woman" down and when she "raised an outcry" he struck her repeatedly as he "attempted to execute his villainous designs." The woman's screams brought the police to her rescue. The *Constitution* concluded, "By the time the various courts get through with him he will probably be a wiser if not a better man."[53] Regardless of whether or not Richards's conviction would make him a "wiser or better man," his sentencing and its publication served as a warning to all white men that black women were not always easy prey. Refusing to suffer in silence, black women sought to take advantage of their rights as citizens by taking white men to court.[54]

Needless to say, white men's sexual crimes, unlike black men's, were not perceived as threats to the emerging social and political order. The *Constitution* article never identified Richards by race; the absence of an overt racial identifier reveals more than it sought to hide—that race was not considered a significant factor in rape cases when the alleged assailant was a white man. Yet race mattered. When the victim was a black woman, as in the Richards case, she usually went unnamed and was denied all markers of respectability. Never was a black victim given the title "Miss" or "Mrs.," and she was always referred to as a "woman," not "a lady." Although white assailants could be labeled "brutes" or "fiends," their crimes never provoked discussion of mob violence. An assault on a black woman by a white man was not deemed worthy of mob violence, at least not in the minds of white southerners and the white press. Between 1880 and 1930 only six white men were lynched in Georgia for assaults against women, and none of their alleged victims were black.[55] But the Richards case does suggest that some judges were willing to convict white men for crimes against black women, especially if white police officers had witnessed the crime. And, as the *Constitution* suggested, a white man could be reformed and emerge from punishment a "wiser man."

Another story in the *Constitution* better fits the narrative of rape and retribution that white southern newspapers found most compelling and that white men ultimately sought to perpetuate. A "special" report from Savannah recounted the attempted rape of "Mrs. Thomas Willis, wife of a respectable white farmer" in the town of Millen by "a negro, S. Wilkinson." Despite the newspaper's growing commitment to a rape narrative that portrayed southern white women as helpless and in need of protection by white men against alleged black rapists, the details regarding the attack on Mrs. Willis exposed the difficultly of maintaining a narrative of female dependency. Describing Mrs. Willis as the wife of a "respectable white farmer," the *Constitution* established Willis's race and status as an honorable woman worthy of protection and framed the assault as an affront to white southern manhood everywhere. On the night of the alleged assault, the newspaper reported that Mrs. Willis, "*alone* in her house . . . her husband being temporarily absent," was confronted by "a negro man" who pushed his way into her home. He "seized [her] and endeavored to do violence to her person," but Mrs. Willis fought back. Breaking free of her attacker, she grabbed a gun to defend herself. Her assailant, however, wrenched the gun from her and knocked her to the floor. Fortunately, Mrs. Willis was not "alone," as the *Constitution* insisted; a "colored girl" who was working in Mrs. Willis's kitchen heard the violent scuffle and came rushing to the aid of "her mistress." Wielding an axe handle, the colored woman beat the man over the head and the two women fought him until he retreated. Once outside the house he fired a round of shots at the front door before fleeing.[56]

Regardless of the black woman's heroic effort in protecting her employer and Mrs. Willis's violent defense of herself, the *Constitution* focused its attention on the role that white men played in tracking, capturing, and eventually punishing the alleged culprit. Shifting attention away from

Mrs. Willis, the article described how Major Ed Toy had captured S. Wilkinson after noticing "a strange negro" near the train station in Rogers who fit the description that Mrs. Willis had given of her alleged assailant. The ex-Confederate soldier arrested Wilkinson and took him back to Millen where he allegedly denied the attack on Mrs. Willis, but instead confessed to having "attempted outrage" on the eleven-year-old white daughter of Mr. Brunson a year before. Few had forgotten that "outrage" according the *Constitution*, but just in case, the article reminded: "The Brunson girl was on her way home from school, with a young brother, when attacked by the negro, who tore all her clothing off, before he was frightened away." After his alleged confession, the newspaper explained, the child was sent for and immediately recognized him. "With a cry of horror," recounted the *Constitution*, "she fell to the ground in a dead faint."[57] If Mrs. Willis refused to play the part of the frightened and fragile victim in need of male protection, the image of a terrified and helpless white child passing out at the sight of her alleged attacker would more than suffice. The *Constitution* concluded there was "no doubt about his guilt, and it is believed the indignant citizens will dispose of him summarily."[58]

The third article in that issue of the *Constitution* highlights how white women and white men differed on addressing the problem of rape. No doubt connected to the hysteria surrounding the attempted rape of Mrs. Willis in Millen, the *Constitution* reported a lynching in the same town: "LYNCHING AT MILLEN: A NEGRO BRUTE TAKEN FROM A TRAIN AND HUNG." The story brought home the point that southern white men hoped to make—lynching of black men would protect white womanhood and keep blacks in their place. In three brief sentences the article explained that Henry Barnes, a "colored man," was taken by a party of masked men from a train near Millen and riddled with bullets for allegedly "outraging a white lady" at Rogers station, on the Central railroad.[59] What exactly constituted "an outrage" on the part of a black man against a white woman in a public space ranged from speaking to a white woman to touching her while helping her to board a train. In this case the "outrage" went unstated. What is clear, however, is that a black man had in some way offended an unescorted white woman. Short on detail, the article underscored the violent extremes to which southern white men were willing to go to punish a black man who dared to offend a white woman's sensibilities.

Compared with southern white women's age of consent campaigns, these stories reveal that women and men were not only in disagreement about who was responsible for the increasing numbers of rapes, but also about how to prevent the crime. Temperance women were focused on creating legal "safeguards against the sins," while men were more interested in "safeguarding" their sexual privilege. Women were invested in the passage of laws for protection, but white men were aware that tougher rape laws were targeted at policing their sexual behavior. Moreover, they were more interested in using extralegal means to solve the problem of rape, which they linked to black men and white women's efforts to exercise political power in the public sphere. White men argued that tougher rape laws would deny them the privilege of exercising extralegal violence.[60] In the cases printed in the *Constitution* all the alleged rapists were strangers; it was implied in the age of consent campaigns that victims most likely knew their alleged assailants. In all but one of the newspaper cases the "rapist" was black and the victim white. Not surprisingly, it was only in the two cases that involved black men and white women that extralegal violence was an issue. The locations of the alleged attacks, however, follow no set script: Richards attacked the unnamed "negro woman" on a public street; Mrs. Willis was in her home "alone" when she was assaulted; the "little Brunson girl" was on her way home from school when she was allegedly attacked; and Barnes was accused of "outraging a white lady" in a train station. Rape could occur at almost any time and place as black and white women and girls went about daily activities, yet alleged rape of white women by black men on isolated farms and in rural districts were the kind of stories that white southern presses were most interested in covering.

While white southern women were stepping into the public sphere to demand legal protection against rape for black women and restraints on their male family members' sexual aggressions, southern white men were actively mobilizing the image of the black rapist for their political advantage. According to one popular theory, blacks had undergone a salutary civilizing process through enslavement, but that had been tragically ended by emancipation.[61] In his widely read 1889 study, *The Plantation Negro as Freeman*, Philip Alexander Bruce alleged a dangerous moral regression among post-emancipation African Americans. For Bruce, the most striking example of the return to black savagery was the increasing frequency of "that most frightful crime"—the rape of white women by black men. According to Bruce, "There is something strangely alluring and seductive to them in the appearance of a white woman; they are aroused and stimulated by its foreignness to their experience of sexual pleasure, and it moves them to gratify their lust at any cost and in spite of every obstacle. This proneness of the negro is so well understood that the white women of every class, from the highest to the lowest are afraid to venture any distance alone, or even wander unprotected in the immediate vicinity of their home."[62] Along with this theory, the belief grew that "bad Negroes" who had never known slavery were supplanting the "good Negroes" who had once been slaves.[63] By arguing that the assault on white women was a new feature of black activity after slavery, Bruce and others claimed that black emancipation was tantamount to an initial breach of white supremacy. Not surprisingly, the politicization and dissemination of such menacing images served both to justify the disenfranchisement of blacks and to inaugurate a particularly barbarous period of widespread lynching of black men on the most spurious evidence.

As for the Georgia WCTU's campaign to raise the age of consent, the *Constitution* ignored it, not only because it did not fit with the narrative of rape that justified lynching black men and reinforced southern white men's autonomy, but also because it challenged white men's sexual prerogatives. Not until 1918 did the Georgia legislature finally raise the age of consent from ten to fourteen.[64] In the meantime, southern temperance women continued to fight for female protection on a host of terrains. In the South, white women assumed prohibition was their best bet at securing legal protection against rape, domestic violence, and financial ruin. Subsequently, temperance work would eventually lead reluctant southern white women down the path of woman suffrage.[65]

Prohibition, Rape, and Lynching

Felton's decision to join the WCTU in 1886 had as much to do with her longtime commitment to temperance as it did with her dedication to the movement against convict leasing and her postwar challenge to the double standard that left southern women unprotected against white men's abuses. Her ideas about the "evils of drink" had changed somewhat from the days of her youth when she first joined a temperance club and took a personal vow of abstinence. As a member of the WCTU, she insisted that temperance was not merely a moral question to be decided by the individual, but a social and political problem that needed to be regulated by the state. She believed that the sale and consumption of alcohol spawned a range of societal problems that adversely impacted the lives of women and children: domestic violence, sexual conflict, financial irresponsibility, child neglect, rape, corrupt politics, and race problems.[66] Embracing the WCTU battle cry "Home Protection," she traveled all over the state "pleading" before white and black audiences for the "protection" of mothers and their children from the dangers of drink.[67] She recalled, "I expect I was the first Georgia woman to take the platform to urge voters to remember their homes and their children in prohibition contests."[68] Those who supported liquor interests or defined southern politics as a male domain denounced Felton for not knowing her place and behaving in ways unbecoming of a respectable lady. Felton, however, met their criticism head on.

At the WCTU 1894 state convention in Atlanta, Felton directly challenged assertions that temperance women were "unwomanly." With the skills of a brilliant politician, she deployed a discourse of protection to both shame southern men into action and to justify women's political activity. Southern women, she argued, had been forced into politics because southern men had failed in their duties. Felton stated that she was neither seeking political office nor intent on usurping "any power or privilege that belongs of right to men"; yet she was charged with "unwomanliness" for petitioning lawmakers to protect the virtue of women and children. Referring to her critics as "beardless boys" and "small, sapheaded editors," she called into question their manhood by playing up white womanhood. She asked rhetorically, "Is it manly to force us to the extremity? . . . Can it be womanly to endure such evils quietly? Can it be unwomanly to seek to avert them? . . . Say, oh! Men of Georgia wouldn't I be less than a woman not to cry out for safety?" Turning the tables on her critics, Felton argued that her political actions reflected southern womanhood at its best and exposed a profound failure in southern manhood. "Sneer at women's weak effort, if you will," she berated, "but the time thus wasted, would be better employed in vindicating your own patriotism and manhood."[69] Felton ridiculed southern white men for creating a world of politics that they deemed "too filthy for woman's touch" and accused them of being "too indifferent" to women's safety.[70] If male politicians ignored their duties as husbands and fathers, she reiterated, then what choice did wives and mothers have but to enter the political fray?

Like other temperance women, Felton strategically defined the work of the WCTU as a "natural" extension of motherhood and sought both to justify women's political participation and to politicize the dilemmas of women's private lives.[71] Postwar southern politics, she argued, had to take into account once private issues of "the home," such as alcoholism, domestic violence, sexual exploitation, and children's rights. Lecturing across the state, Felton made the case that a "mother's touch" could "clean up and purify" southern politics. In the face of perceived threats to the sanctity of home, she demanded accountability from southern men and sought to naturalize women's political activity. "The uprising of the women of America on temperance is a natural sequence to their mother love," she told one female audience.[72] And, in a prohibition address before the all-male Joint Committee of the House and Senate, Felton insisted, "Motherhood should be carefully protected, guarded and defended as no other interest." As to whether southern women could "lean" on their men folk, Felton was clear—"The clinging ivy and the sturdy oak is a pretty simile of domestic dependency but nevertheless the ivy is sometimes so foreshortened at the top and so closely trimmed at the sides that it must stand alone per-force"— the answer was a resounding No![73]

As Felton traveled through the South in the early 1890s campaigning for prohibition, she seemed hardly concerned with the image of the black rapist that circulated in the daily press. Yet by 1890 it had become an issue that even the WCTU could not ignore. That year Frances Willard felt it necessary to address the so-called "southern problem" of rape and lynching. The occasion was the 1890 National Woman's Christian Temperance Union's Seventeenth Annual Meeting in Atlanta. Willard declared in her opening address that the decision to convene in Georgia confirmed "that the national WCTU is for 'native land,' not for a section, and is guided by the southern cross as well as the north star."[74] Just two weeks prior to the conference, in an interview published in *The Voice*, a progressive journal, Willard had made clear her political commitment to bringing southern white women under the banner of "Home Protection." To push prohibition in the South and rally southern white women's support, Willard raised the specter of the "black rapist" despite the fact that the National WCTU opposed lynching.

Playing on southern fears, Willard exploited the rape/lynch myth to her political advantage: "The problem on their hands is immeasurable. The colored race multiplies like the locusts of Egypt. The grog-shop is its center of power. The safety of woman, of childhood, of the home, is menaced in a thousand localities at this moment, so that the men dare not go beyond the sight of their own roof-tree."[75] Tying the rape of white women by black men to drink, she explained, "An average colored man when sober is loyal to the purity of white women; but when under the influence of intoxicating liquors the tendency in all men is toward a loss of self-control."[76] Even as Willard pointed out that "half drunken white roughs" murdered black men at the polls and intimidated them so they would not vote, she contended that "great dark-faced mobs" threatened the vote for prohibition. Utilizing both the language of white supremacy and the discourse of protection, Willard declared without regard to region, "The Anglo-Saxon race will never submit to be dominated by the Negro so long as his altitude reaches no higher than the personal liberty of the saloon."[77]

Willard's words affirmed the power of the rape/lynch narrative and showed how northern white women seized upon it to ally themselves with southern white women. Even though white women and men in the North adopted the myth of the black rapist, however, they were more ambivalent about lynching and rarely defended it, at least in print. When liberal northern white women condemned lynching, they usually accepted the southern claim that African American men represented a sexual threat to white women. Jane Addams, perhaps the most powerful woman of the Progressive Era, accepted the assertion of the ubiquitous black rapist even as she argued against lynch law.[78] In an article published in the 1901 edition of the *Independent*, a progressive journal, Addams decided to "give the Southern citizens the full benefit of their position," by accepting "that they have set aside trial by jury and all processes of law because they have become convinced that this brutal method of theirs is the most efficient method in dealing with a peculiar class of crime committed by one race against another" — namely, rape.[79]

Southern white women continued to define their temperance work as a crusade to reform white men's behavior and to bring protection to women without regard to race or class. Even Felton, who by the mid-1890s linked both rape and lynching to the "drink evil," defined the problem as one ultimately created by southern white men. In 1894, in two separate speeches, Felton declared, "Race troubles and whisky go hand in hand." The whisky-jug, she contended, was at the root of 90 percent of lynchings: "What are our white citizens thinking about to install a crime-producer at their very doors, when their young daughters are not safe on the public highway?" She insisted, "A sober man, black or white, will not rashly enter into crime and villainy." Not only did whiskey provoke sexual violence, but mob violence as well. She declared, "We owe it to the colored people of Georgia to remove far from ignorance the poison which makes demons of human beings, and destroys womanhood and our young maidens on the public highway. And we owe it to our white men, young and old, to keep their minds and hearts clear, that law may rule in dealing with crime and thus keep the nation from anarchy and bloodshed."[80] While Felton highlighted sexual violence on the part of black men, she was not willing to concede that white men did not rape or that lynching was a necessary means of protection.

More concerned about the agricultural depression of the early 1890s than the so-called threat of black rape, Felton joined the southern agrarian revolt and sought protection for poor white farmwomen in the form of temperance, economic independence, and education—not lynching. Felton had not forgotten the losses she had suffered because southern white men had put the profit of slavery before the security of their wives and daughters. The Civil War had cost her more than she could ever recover. The experiences of poor white farmwomen did not seem so different from her postwar suffering. Both economically and politically dependent on their husbands and fathers, these women had little or no control over the fate of their families. In 1891, Felton proposed a program to the state agricultural society called the "Wife's Farm," in which she asked every farmer to put aside land for his wife. In return for her household labor, he would work her plot of land, which would consist of crops for home consumption and whatever she saw fit. Regardless of what choices the farmer made about his market crops, the wife's crop would be able to provide the family with security. Economic independence required education, so Felton also argued for educational opportunities for underprivileged white girls. She called on organized white women to petition local governments to improve rural schools, to pass compulsory education laws, and to create a technical college for poor white girls.

Determined that poor white women should have the protection they deserved, Felton not only pushed temperance and her "Wife's Farm" plan but also joined the Georgia Populist movement.[81] In the late 1880s an agricultural society called the Farmers' Alliance swept across the South, enrolling more than 100,000 black and white members. Convinced that the American political and economic systems were rigged to serve the interests of the rich at the expense of farmers, the Alliance demanded that the government expand the money supply by printing more notes and coining more silver. Such action would cause inflation and drive up cotton prices. It also argued for the subtreasury plan, a scheme by which farmers at harvest could borrow money against the value of crops stored in government warehouses while waiting for prices to improve. When neither the Democrats nor the Republicans would adopt these demands, the Alliance founded the People's Party—or, as it was more commonly called, the Populist Party. Felton was drawn to the movement not just because it was invested in the issues she had spent her life working on, but also because Populists seemed more open to women's political participation and goals of education and economic equality. Indeed, women attended meetings, held offices, published and wrote for the Alliance newspapers, gave numerous speeches, and were directly involved in forming the national People's Party.[82]

Populism attracted followers in all of the southern states, but it was especially strong in Georgia where it tended to flourish in regions that possessed little love for the Democratic Party. It was most successful in the old plantation country where the Feltons lived—where before the Civil War, the Whig Party had dominated. Even after the decline of the Whigs, the region only reluctantly embraced the Democratic Party and Independents like Dr. Felton were elected to the U.S. Congress. Led by Thomas Watson, who had been elected to the U.S. Congress in 1890 as a Southern Alliance Democrat, the Georgia Populist Party drew national attention.[83] Realizing that the white vote would probably split between the Populist and Democratic parties, the Populists—and Tom Watson in particular—tried to gain the support of African Americans. Although never going so far as to call for social equality, the Populists invited two black delegates to their state convention in 1892, appointed a black man to the state campaign committee in 1894, and insisted on black voting rights. They also demanded an end to the convict lease system. Democrats quickly accused the Populists of allying with former slaves and of being soft on rape of white women by black men. They also depicted Populist women as aggressive and vicious. Such claims, accompanied by violence and corruption on the part of the Democrats, helped to easily defeat the Populist candidate for governor in the 1892 election.

Within a year more hardship was on its way as the United States was shaken by the Panic of 1893. Railroads, banks, and businesses collapsed, and millions of people lost their jobs. The average price of cotton fell to less than five cents per pound, creating a promising opportunity for Populists during the Georgia elections of 1894. Dr. Felton took the opportunity to run on the Populist Party ticket for what he hoped would be a fourth term in the Georgia legislature. In support of her husband's campaign and the temperance movement, Felton wrote an editorial in the summer of 1894 in which she specifically denounced lynch law and called for the defense of black political rights. The Populist Party, she argued, was "an immense concourse of farmers—the bone and sinew of this republic," who had organized in support of prohibition, to denounce "lynch law," and to call "on our public officials to enforce our laws against crime."[84] Felton was no doubt responding to extralegal campaigns of physical and psychological intimidation led by Democrats intent on destroying the fragile alliance between black and white farmers. Arguing that Populist politics would lead to "Negro domination," Democrats had used the image of the "black rapist" to agitate against southern Populists.[85] Indeed, during the years of the Populist voting strength the number of persons lynched reached an all-time high in the South—over 200 persons were lynched in 1892 alone. The 1894 election was bitterly contested and Dr. Felton, along with Watson, was defeated despite their charge of election fraud. Once again the Democratic Party successfully wielded the racist and sexist whip of white supremacy to their political advantage. Rebecca Felton, no doubt, took note, and by 1896 the Feltons had returned to the Democratic Party.

Rebecca Felton's campaigns on behalf of black female convicts, for the reform of rape laws, and for the economic empowerment of poor white women shows clearly that southern white women did not always see the problem of rape in racial terms. In the post-Reconstruction years she and others like her sought to broaden the definition of protection to include black women and poor white women. She demanded protection that did not require dependency on fathers and husbands, and that insisted on women's ability as well as their right to participate in their own protection. It was hardly a coincidence that the popularization of the myth of the black rapist emerged at the same time that southern white women organized to rein in white men's sexual and political behavior. The allegation of black rape and the need for vigilante justice took hold of the American imagination as white women stepped up their political campaigns for temperance, better education, economic independence, and suffrage. Felton and other southern women resisted white men's attempts to keep them at home with threats of what lurked outside. White women did not lock themselves in their homes; instead, they actively tried to manipulate the rape hysteria and the language of lynching in their struggle for women's rights. The shift from defining rape as a problem between white men and black and white women to one of black men and white women revealed not only the impact of white women's organized campaigns for political and social rights, but also white men's success at turning attention away from their own sexual activities to those of black men. Felton needed now to create new and powerful weapons in her campaign for white women's rights.

4

ORGANIZING IN DEFENSE OF
BLACK WOMANHOOD

The stories of rape and lynching that began appearing almost daily in the white southern press in the mid-1880s were cause for great concern in black communities. Despite suspicions on the part of some leading African Americans that southern whites were fabricating rapes to justify lynching, most refrained from publicly expressing their doubt. Yet a few dared to speak against southern mob violence. As early as 1883, Frederick Douglass, a national figure who had made his reputation as a fugitive slave turned abolitionist and advisor to President Lincoln, was among the first to speak out against lynching. In an address delivered in Washington, D.C., at the Congregational Church to celebrate the twenty-first anniversary of emancipation in the District of Columbia, Douglass declared the rape cry a false justification for the lynching of black men. Careful not to mention the "unspeakable," he argued, "A crime almost unknown to the colored man in the time of slavery seems now, from report, the most common. I do not believe these reports. There are too many reasons for trumping up such charges."[1] Although Ida Wells wrote an editorial as early as 1886 protesting the lynching of Julia Wood in Tennessee, a year later she confided in her diary, "It seems awful to take human life but hardly more so than to take a woman's reputation & make it the jest & byword of the street; in view of these things, if he really did them, one is strongly tempted to say his killing was justifiable."[2] Certainly, it proved difficult for African Americans to make a case against lynching as long as rape served as the primary justification.

The upsurge of racial violence in the early 1890s, however, changed that. The mob violence that accompanied the Populist revolt made clear to some, black and white, that lynching had much more to do with preventing black political and economic mobility than protecting white women from rape. Southern white Populists, like Felton and Watson, who spoke out against lynching in the early 1890s had unintentionally helped to create a precarious opening for African Americans to publicly denounce southern mob violence. When mobs lynched over two hundred African American men and women throughout the South in 1892, Wells was compelled to reconsider her views about southern mob violence. She courageously launched a campaign against lynching that initiated one of the first public hearings to simultaneously address the problems of racial and sexual violence against black women and men. As the most outspoken leader in the crusade against lynching at the turn of the century, Wells introduced an anti-lynching platform that called for the end of lynching and the protection of black women against white rape. In doing so she inspired the emergence of the black women's club movement.

Indeed, just as the 1890s ushered in a new wave of white supremacist violence, it also marked the emergence of an organized black women's movement. The Woman's Christian Temperance Union (WCTU) represented the largest and only integrated women's organization in the United States; it also served as a model and training ground for black women to create their own organizations. At the same time that southern white women like Rebecca Felton found their political voice, so too did Wells and the black women who organized on her behalf. Wells knew she could not challenge the violent racial and sexual politics of the New South alone—she needed the force of numbers that only an organization like the WCTU could provide. To do this, Wells would first have to challenge the rape myth that was used to justify lynching. She would have to inspire black women to create and define a movement of their own before gaining the support of white female social reformers like Frances Willard, president of the WCTU. Acquiring white women's support was a challenge that required Wells to walk a deadly tightrope—held at one end by sexual politics and pulled by racial politics at the other. On more than one occasion, however, she would lose her footing as racial and sexual politics violently shifted between 1880 and 1915. Nonetheless, with the aid of a new generation of educated middle-class black women, she would lead the way.

Protection in Black and White

If Ida B. Wells had learned anything from her failed lawsuit against the Southwestern Railroad Company in 1887, it was that black women would have to fight tooth and nail to gain legal protection and respect in the

New South. Even as her faith in the legal system faltered, she remained vigilantly committed to challenging the violent politics of white supremacy that sought to deny African Americans and women their rights as citizens. In 1883, with a pen as her only weapon, Wells began to write in protest. Her first articles, recounting her lawsuits against the railroad company, appeared in the *Living Way*, a black journal based in Memphis and run by two Baptist ministers, R. N. Countee and William A. Bickley. Under the pseudonym Iola, she wrote editorials on issues ranging from temperance to suffrage. By 1891 she had acquired co-ownership of a black newspaper, *Free Speech*, and had developed a reputation as a hard-hitting writer. In March 1892, after her dear friend Thomas Moss along with Calvin McDowell and Henry Stewart were lynched in Memphis, Wells launched her career as a radical activist. Determined to expose the rape myth that justified white mob violence and masked sexual violence against black women, she became an outspoken anti-lynching activist.

The lynchings of Moss, McDowell, and Stewart, co-owners of the People's Cooperative Grocery, exposed Wells to the reality of southern mob violence. The People's Grocery had taken black customers from a white competitor, W. H. Barret. When friction developed between the managers of the two stores, Barret instigated several incidents of violence against the black storeowners and complained to legal authorities that the People's Grocery was a public nuisance. Members of the black community held a meeting to address the growing tension. In response, Barret filed charges of conspiracy and threatened the black owners with a white mob. When nine plainclothes deputies arrived at the grocery store, the men armed in defense of themselves fired. Thirty blacks, including Moss, McDowell, and Stewart, were arrested. Four days later, a mob dragged the three men from the jail and lynched them.[3]

In response, Wells wrote a series of editorials condemning the lynchings and calling for organized black protest. In *Free Speech*, she supported a boycott of the city streetcars, encouraged blacks to move west to Oklahoma, and advised armed self-defense.[4] Wells bemoaned, "Where are our 'leaders' when the race is being burnt, shot and hanged?"[5] Encouraging self-defense, she advised, "A Winchester rifle should have a place of honor in every black home, and it should be used for that protection which the law refuses to use."[6] Denied legal protection, she argued that whites left blacks with no alternative but armed self-defense: "I had bought a pistol the first thing after Tom Moss was lynched, because I expected some cowardly retaliation from the lynchers. I felt that one had better die fighting against injustice than to die like a dog or a rat in a trap. I had already determined to sell my life as dearly as possible if attacked. I felt if I could take one lyncher with me, this would even up the score a little bit."[7] Wells, however, took aim with her pen and not her pistol. In the months following the Memphis lynchings, she investigated and compiled data on as many reported lynchings as she could track. Her discoveries were shocking. Not only were the majority of victims not accused of rape, but young boys and girls as young as fourteen and sixteen had fallen victim to white mobs.

It was the hard facts that led Wells to challenge the claim that lynching served as punishment for rape. The rape/lynch association that had begun during Reconstruction and was now being wielded against southern Populists and African Americans who challenged white men's political power and economic dominance, had been accepted without question. Before the Memphis lynching, Wells confessed, "Like many another person who had read of lynching in the South, I had accepted the idea meant to convey—that although lynching was irregular and contrary to law and order, unreasoning anger over the terrible crime of rape led to the lynching; that perhaps the brute deserved death anyhow and the mob was justified in taking his life."[8] Wells was not alone in accepting the rape/lynch myth as truth and acceptable justification for mob violence.

The Memphis lynching, however, revealed that mob violence had little to do with black men raping white women or white men's claims of protection. Instead, it suggested that economic competition, not rape, was the cause of mob violence. In a May editorial, Wells openly challenged the narrative of rape that whites employed. "Nobody in this section of the country believes the old threadbare lie that Negro men rape white women," she warned. "If southern white men are not careful, they will over-reach themselves and public sentiment will have a reaction: a conclusion will then be reached which will be very damaging to the moral reputation of their women."[9] Wells had put into print what others had dared not say—some white women were not so pure and innocent after all.

As far as southern whites were concerned it was Wells who had "over-reached" herself. The mere suggestion that a white woman would willingly consent to sex with a black man was enough to send white men into violent hysterics. One local newspaper responded, "The fact that a black scoundrel is allowed to live and utter such loathsome and repulsive calumnies is a volume of evidence as to the wonderful patience of Southern whites. But we have had enough of it. There are some things that the Southern white man will not tolerate, and the obscene intimations of the foregoing have brought the writer to the very outermost limits of patience. We hope we have said enough."[10] It was not, however, enough for some whites. The office of *Free Speech* was attacked, the press destroyed, and Wells's partner, J. L. Fleming, barely escaped the city with his life. Traveling in Philadelphia and New York when her editorial appeared, Wells was warned that if she valued her life she would not return south.

"Exiled" in New York, Wells refused to be terrorized into silence. Invited by T. Thomas Fortune, a leading African American journalist, to join the staff of his national black newspaper the *New York Age*, she stepped up her campaign against lynching.[11] Her editorials became more aggressive and forceful. "Having lost my paper, had a price put on my life, and been made an exile from home for hinting at the truth . . . I felt that I owed it to myself and to my race to tell the whole truth now that I was where I could do so freely."[12] And speak freely she did. In the *Age* under the heading "Exiled," Wells recounted the events leading to the destruction of *Free Speech* and repeated her claim that lynching was not a punishment for rape, but a means to "keep the race terrorized and 'keep the nigger down,'" especially those who were "acquiring wealth and property."[13] The publication of over ten thousand copies of the paper made Wells a national celebrity in the black press and inspired a group of elite black women in New York to organize a dinner in her honor. The women raised over four hundred dollars to help Wells reestablish *Free Speech* in New York. Wells, however, used the funds to publish her *New York Age* article into a pamphlet, *Southern Horrors*, instead. She dedicated the pamphlet to the "Afro-American women of New York and Brooklyn, whose race love, earnest zeal and unselfish effort . . . made possible its publication."[14] The dinner celebration inspired also the founding of two black women's clubs: the Woman's Loyal Union led by Victoria Matthews, a New York journalist, and the Woman's Era Club led by community activist Josephine Ruffin in Boston.[15]

In *Southern Horrors*, Wells introduced a scenario in which black women suffered sexual violence at the hands of white men and black men fell victim to white mob violence for engaging in consensual sexual relationships with white women.[16] Here and in a second pamphlet (*A Red Record*, published in 1895), Wells challenged the idea that lynching resulted from

rape and presented statistics showing that only one-third of the black victims of lynch mobs had actually been accused of rape.[17] She argued that
the portrayal of blacks as rapists made them "moral monsters" and placed
them "beyond the pale of human sympathy."[18] Wells suggested that the
focus and attention placed on the alleged black rapist masked the rape of
black women and justified white southerners' violent efforts to deprive
African Americans of social, political, and economic rights in the New
South. Using white men's words and actions, she took to task southern
notions of chivalry and challenged the racial double standard embedded
in the rape/lynch discourse. "True chivalry," she declared "respects all womanhood" and "can hope for little respect from the civilized world, when it
confines itself entirely to the women who happen to be white."[19] Wells
echoed southern white women when she proclaimed, "Not one who reads
the record as it is written in the faces of the million mulattos in the South
will for a minute conceive that the southern white man had a very chivalrous regard for the honor due the women of his own race or respect for
the womanhood which circumstance placed in his power."[20] White men,
she argued, not only dishonored their manhood when they raped black
women, but also desecrated their marriage vows.

Wells drew no distinctions between white men who raped black women
and those who lynched black men.[21] A close examination of "the facts,"
she concluded, would reveal that white men, regardless of their claims,
were not invested in punishing rapists. By highlighting two alleged rape
cases that occurred in Nashville in the months following the Memphis
lynchings, Wells exposed the racial and sexual double standard embedded
in the stories of rape and lynching told by white southerners.

According to local newspapers, in May 1892 a mob of two hundred men
armed with Winchester rifles, shotguns, muskets, and pistols gathered outside Lem Thompson's home on South Spruce Street in Nashville. Earlier
in the day, Thompson's son, Lem G. Thompson Jr., had been arrested on
a charge of raping eight-year-old Maggie Reece. The girl claimed that
Thompson Jr. assaulted her in Meacham's Drug Store, on the corner of
Ewing Avenue and Fogg Street, where the boy worked as a clerk and she
had gone on an errand for her mother. Not long after Thompson's arrest
and subsequent release on bail, rumors spread that a mob of five hundred
men were organizing to lynch the boy.[22] This was not the first time an accusation of rape had caused "considerable excitement" among the citizens
of Nashville. Just two days before a mob had invaded the county jail and

injured several police officers in an effort to lynch Frank Weems, who had been arrested for the attempted rape of Mrs. Amelia Maverty near Chattanooga. Luckily for Weems, local authorities had already taken him to Memphis for "safe keeping.[23] Less fortunate were Henry and Eph Grizzard, who were lynched a month prior to the Reese-Thompson incident for allegedly raping Mollie and Sadie Bruce in the nearby town of Goodlettsville.[24] Confirming black and white southerners' worst fears, these stories splashed repeatedly across local newspapers captured in vivid detail the rape/lynch drama of the New South.

A close examination of the Reese-Thompson and Bruce-Grizzard cases exposes the contradictions in the stories that white southerners told themselves about rape and lynching. To start with, the eight-year-old rape victim, Maggie Reece, was African American and her alleged assailant was white. The armed men that organized at Thompson's residence late that Monday night were white and they had come to protect the young man from a rumored "mob of five hundred negroes."[25] In the Bruce-Grizzard case, two black brothers were accused of raping two white sisters. A white mob lynched them. While the Bruce-Grizzard case in many ways typified the late nineteenth-century rape/lynch scenario perpetuated by white southerners, the Reese-Thompson case revealed a counter narrative that placed black women and girls at the center. The dominant narrative, as white southerners told it, usually unfolded in rural districts where "unprotected white women" lived on isolated farms, "lustful black men" lurked around every corner, and "honorable white men" lynched "black rapists" to protect white womanhood. Yet, as Wells persuasively argued in *Southern Horrors* under the heading "The Black and White of It," such narratives merely functioned to distort the reality of racial and sexual violence in the South.

In the weeks and months that both proceeded and followed the Bruce-Grizzard and the Reese-Thompson cases, the *Nashville Banner* reported almost daily stories of rape and attempted rape against both white and black women. Headlines varied from "ATTEMPTED ASSAULT: Mrs. Newton Cowgill *Attacked* at Her Residence by an Unknown Negro," "ANOTHER OUTRAGE: A Respectable White Woman *Assaulted* by a Negro Near Chattanooga," "A TOO FAMILIAR STORY: Another Rape *Committed* by a Negro on a White Woman," and "ANOTHER OUTRAGE: *Attempted* by a Negro Boy on a Little White Girl," when the victims were white and their assailants black. But when black women were victimized the tone of the headlines changed: "A MEMPHIS SENSA-TION: He [A Prominent Society Man] Is *Accused* of Attempting an Out-rage Upon a Negro Woman," "WAS LODGED IN JAIL: A Negro *Charged* with Criminally Assaulting a Young Colored Girl," and "A SE-RIOUS CHARGE: Ben George *Accused* of Attempting to Outrage a Ne-gro Girl."[26] Stories announcing the rape or attempted rape of a white woman by a black man ignored the legal maxim "innocent until proven guilty." Guilt was a foregone conclusion as headlines declared "Another Outrage." In stark contrast, reports regarding black female victims of rape rarely accepted as true black women's charges. Most headlines merely an-nounced that a "claim" or "accusation" had been made and in many cases reporters explained, "there is not much in the charge" or "it is the unanimous opinion . . . that he is not guilty of the crime charged."[27] Rapes of white women by white men went largely unreported.

Even as white newspapers dismissed black women's rape charges as un-founded, they could not ignore African Americans' insistent demands for legal protection and urgent calls for self-defense. White southerners must have read with concern the numerous reports in local and national news-papers detailing black resistance to white violence.[28] "A SECRET OR-GANIZATION: Texas Negroes Form a Society to Protect the Race" and "RACE CONFLICT: A Negro Mob and White Citizens Fight in Vir-ginia" read the headlines on the front page of the May 14 issue of the *Nashville Banner*. The Texas organization, explained the *Banner*, was headed by a committee known as "The Bloody Three," whose responsi-bility it was to decide what punishments the organization would mete out to whites caught participating in lynchings.[29] Under the headline "HE IS OPPOSED TO BOMB-THROWING," the *Banner* published an inter-view with Frederick Douglass, who was scheduled to give a public lecture at Nashville's Spruce Baptist Church. The interview focused on whether or not Douglass had advised southern blacks to use bombs or other explo-sives in retaliation to lynching. Douglass wisely denied the charge, but conceded that he had "playfully [said] that the negro, if not let alone, will begin to study chemistry." He concluded without hesitation, "if the South continues to sow the wind, it must reap the whirlwind. That violence begets violence."[30] As for organized self-defense, the specter of armed blacks taking the law into their own hands, he warned, was certain to en-rage the white community and produce a further escalation of violence from which blacks would not recover. "It would be the signal for death and a race war if attempted," predicted Douglass.[31]

Three days later, when the Nashville *Daily American* published an article announcing that "certain colored men of Cambridge and Boston, belonging to secret societies" were preparing "dynamite bombs" and planning to come South to take "revenge unless the outrages [lynchings] are stopped," it was more than some whites could tolerate.[32] The following day, the *American* published an angry response signed "Saxon," who declared the article a hoax and rebuked Douglass and other race leaders for not doing more to prevent black men from raping white women. "Instead of advising negroes to revenge the lynching of negro criminals," he chided, "They should rather advise the race to purge itself of this particular class of criminals. . . . The negroes owe it to themselves; to their protection; to the peace of their families and homes; to their race's respect; to their claims to the rights of citizenships, to take this matter of negro rapine in white settlements and communities, into their own hands." Calling upon blacks to lynch their own when they raped white women, "Saxon" ignored sexual violence committed by white men against black women.[33] He even conveniently ignored the alleged assault on Maggie Reese, but did not hesitate to remind his readers of the alleged rape of the Bruce sisters.

The alleged rape of Mollie and Sadie Bruce took place in Goodlettsville, twelve miles north of Nashville, where the two young women lived with their "poor but respectable" mother, Mrs. Lee Bruce, the keeper of the first tollgate on the Long Hollow turnpike. Three weeks before the attack their father, Mr. Lee Bruce, an ex-Confederate, had died of pneumonia. Mrs. Bruce was with her two eldest daughters, Mollie and Sadie, aged twenty and fifteen, at the bedside of twelve-year-old Sallie Bruce, who was suffering from pneumonia, when two men allegedly broke into their home. The papers reported that around midnight two black men with revolvers forced their way into the Bruce household and "after a brave struggle" Mollie and Sadie were brutally raped. Having satisfied their "fiendish desires" and robbed the family of eight dollars, the men fled.[34] News of the crime "spread like wildfire." Couriers rode in all directions to alarm white citizens and before daylight a hundred "desperate men" armed with double-barreled shotguns and Winchester rifles had gathered at the Bruce home. The house was searched for clues and "a certificate from the Health Officer" made out in the name of Henry Grizzard was found in the kitchen where the young women were reportedly raped. This was considered sufficient evidence of guilt and a "howling mob" went in search of Grizzard. By mid-day a group of "deputized citizens" had captured Grizzard and taken him to the Bruce household for identification. After the Bruce sisters identified him as one of their assailants, he was promptly turned over to local authorities. Once in Sheriff Hill's custody, Grizzard allegedly confessed to being in the Bruce house, but denied committing any crime. Upon hearing "this confession," the angry mob insisted the sheriff hand over the prisoner. "Faced with such odds," explained the *Nashville Banner*, "the Sheriff, who was alone, turned the prisoner over" and by noon Grizzard's bullet-riddled body was hanging from a tree, only a few hundred yards from the Bruce home, with a sign pinned to his chest that read: "Death to anyone who cuts this body down before 12 o'clock to-night."[35]

The lunchtime lynching failed to satisfy the mob's taste for revenge. Later in the evening, when Detectives McGuire and Moran returned to Nashville with three men that Mrs. Bruce failed to identify, the blood-thirsty mob rushed the wagon and fired shots injuring the officers and their captives. Only after much pleading on the part of Sheriff Hill and Reverend A. H. Manely, pastor of the Cumberland Presbyterian Church, did the mob retreat. Despite Mrs. Bruce's request "that the law be allowed to take its course," the next morning, when the *Nashville Banner* published rumors that one of the men in custody, Eph Grizzard, had been seen with his brother Henry on the night of the crime "heading in the direction of Mrs. Bruce's house" and that he had suspiciously burned his clothes and shoes, the mob organized an assault on the jail.[36] During two failed attacks on the jailhouse the mob of white men chanted: "Our mothers and daughters!" "Remember our homes!" and "Think of our wives and daughters!"[37] In many ways the mob's call to action was not so different from the WCTU's home protection slogans. Invoking the image of innocent and pure white women in constant need of protection, the men endeavored to perform their manly duties as fathers, husbands, and brothers.

Sworn in their duty to uphold the law and protect their prisoners, officers defending the jail fatally wounded A. B. Guthrie and Charles Rear and arrested many more before the mob heeded Governor John Price Buchanan's plea for law and order. After negotiating the release of those who had been arrested, the mob leaders promised not to attack the jail. As the mob dispersed, a rumor began circulating that the "negroes around Goodlettsville were holding a meeting and intended to burn and pillage the town." The *Banner* reported that in the face of these rumors many remained behind "in order to protect their wives and families in case of a negro uprising."[38] The governor's influence was short lived. By lunchtime the next day the mob outside the police station had grown from one hundred to over a thousand. "Several prominent citizens" had already made speeches feeding the mob's frenzy when Dr. W. T. Davis of Goodlettsville mounted an ash box on the southeast corner of the public square.[39] The *Daily American* reported that Davis, "the leader," had the rough and tumble crowd "absolutely at his bidding," and when he recounted in vivid detail the alleged assaults on the Bruce sisters, "strong men" broke into tears. "Fellow-citizens," he entreated, "for this negro to go unpunished would be a fearful encouragement for other negroes to commit the same kind of outrage. Justice has been meted out to one negro . . . and it is a bad time to wait for the tardy justice of a Court in Davidson. Boys, will you see that justice is done now?"[40]

Despite the sheriff's best efforts to protect Eph Grizzard, an early morning visit by "several colored preachers" to Governor Buchanan to beg for state protection, and a last minute attempt to dress Grizzard in women's clothes "preparatory to spiriting him away," several armed men gained access to the jail, secured the keys from Jailer Willis, and dragged Grizzard into the street where thousands of screaming white citizens waited.[41] As Grizzard was dragged through the street he "received blow after blow from the open palms of enraged citizens" and one man "at intervals stuck a knife into his body." Within fifteen minutes, Grizzard's severely mutilated body was hanging from the Nashville & Edgefield Bridge; over fifty shots were fired into his lifeless body and a sign was pinned to his shirt that read, "Look at him till the sun goes down. Death to the man who takes him down before the sun goes down."[42]

After an inquest jury declared that Grizzard had come to death "at the hands of parties unknown," his body was taken to Goodlettsville where local men debated whether or not it should be "shown to the ladies of the town so that they might be advised of the summary vengeance that threatened such fiends."[43] No doubt "the younger and wilder heads" wanted to show off their manly revenge so that their mothers, wives, and daughters would be proud of them and reassured of their protection. Such a violent demonstration, however, also functioned as a form of terror against white women. The message of fear—stay in your place or you might get raped—was implicit; more subtle was the violent threat to white women who might be willing to consider sex across the color line. It is difficult to know exactly why some men believed such a gruesome display was necessary and others did not. Unless, as Wells suggested, the Bruce girls had engaged in consensual sexual relations with the Grizzard brothers. According to all public accounts, however, the Bruce sisters had not chosen their fate, and thus, the "older heads" who were opposed to the "revolting exhibition" carried the day and at eight o'clock Grizzard's remains were turned over to a black undertaker.

Every effort had been made to portray Mollie and Sadie Bruce as respectable young ladies worthy of protection. Both the *American* and the *Banner* described them as "the most estimable young ladies" who lived with their widowed mother in "a lonely cottage beyond the pale of police protection."[44] They were "poor, but respectable people," concluded the *Banner*.[45] While on the one hand acknowledging long-held beliefs that poor and working-class women might well be lacking in virtue, and on the other hand marking a shift in who was *now* eligible for protection, the *Banner* placed class on the back burner and served rape up in racial terms. No longer relegated to the status of immoral and unworthy, poor white female victims of rape—or more specifically poor white women raped by black men—were *now* deemed respectable and deserving of violent protection. And, in this case, financial support as well. Over two hundred dollars had already been collected in "a subscription fund" for the Bruce family and the King's Daughters were busy organizing a performance of the "The Old District Skule and Modern Blending" to be performed by the Literary Club of Madison on Friday for the "benefit of the unfortunate family." For poor white women, whose rape cases had never fared well in the legal system, extralegal violence meant that for the first time their charges might be taken seriously; or, as the young men of Goodlettsville suggested, poor white women who engaged in consensual sex with black men would now "be advised of the summary vengeance that threatened" such actions.[46]

It would take days before all was quiet in Nashville and the surrounding area. No sooner had the undertaker buried Grizzard's body, at the county's expense, then rumors spread that "a mob of Negroes" from Nashville set on revenge were planning to attack the town. "Goodlettsville Ready," declared a headline in the *Daily American*.[47] While hundreds of white folks from nearby communities were flocking into the little town, leading black citizens were desperately trying to convince white authorities that the rumors were false. W. H. Young, a prominent black attorney, politician, journalist, and magistrate, and W. A. Crosthwait, also a black attorney, met with leading white officials to reassure them that black citizens were not planning to attack the town, and to make clear that "they deplored that anything like an uprising by the negroes should have been expected by the whites, and that they deeply regretted that the race was not regarded as law abiding citizens, as their interests lay in the enforcement of the law."[48] The two men sought to ease white fears, but they took the opportunity to point out that black citizens, not whites, had acted in accordance with the law. No doubt the lynchings angered and frightened many African Americans; in fact, a few bravely expressed their outrage during the white parade that followed the wagon that carried Grizzard's body out of town. At the corner of Deaderick and Cherry streets, "a young negro expressed disapproval of the lynching" and "in a twinkle he was felled to the earth by a stalwart country man." On Summer Street, another Negro "for a similar remark was left lying on the sidewalk with blood gushing from his nose and mouth."[49] Indeed, like the lynchings, such assaults served their purposes of terrorizing African Americans and preventing them from speaking out in protest against white violence.

There was also "considerable talk" of a white mob coming from Edgefield Junction to get Sergeant Davis, who was accused of fatally wounding two members of the mob. Such a lynching, explained the *American*, would "certainly be followed by bloodshed" and therefore was unlikely.[50] Just in case, however, Davis was taken to the country for safekeeping. The odds of a white man being lynched in 1892 were about as good as they would ever be in the South.[51] Even though mobs executed an estimated seventy-one whites in that year, that number paled in comparison with the number of blacks lynched. Between 1890 and 1899, the ratio of black lynching victims to white was at least seven to one and after 1900 it increased to more than seventeen to one.[52]

For weeks following the Grizzard lynchings, whites continued to justify the mob's actions. In an editorial published in the *Nashville Banner*, Jasper L. Watts unwittingly exposed the racial dynamics of the case. The young girls, he explained, were brutalized in the presence of their "helpless" mother and dying sister by "burly, brutal men—to state it stronger— two brutal black men."[53] It was not enough that the girls had been raped, but the fact that their assailants were black only added insult to injury. Perpetuating the claim that black men had a natural tendency to rape white women, he advocated lynching as the only reasonable punishment. He asked rhetorically, "Would the men of that community have deserved the name if they had failed to act and act promptly?"[54] Ironically, he concluded, "The color of the offender has nothing whatever to do with the punishment, for a like offense a white man is lynched as speedily as a black man."[55] However, as Wells reminded her readers, "the color of the offender" as well as the color of the victim had everything to do with the punishment and the Reece-Thompson story was a case in point.

Occurring almost a month after the Grizzard lynchings, the alleged rape of Maggie Reese left little doubt that race mattered. According to the *Daily American*, Reece had entered the drug store to purchase Jamaica ginger when Lem Thompson Jr., who was working alone, allegedly assaulted her. Ms. Reece, the young girl's mother, returned to the store soon after the assault and accused the boy of raping her daughter and promised to have him legally punished. After Reece reported the alleged assault to local authorities news quickly spread and a group of black men began gathering in front of the store. Tom White, who lived next door to the shop, heard the "commotion" and came out to see what was going on. Upon entering the shop, he found Thompson crouched behind the counter crying. White retrieved a shotgun and handed Thompson a pistol and when three black men "started in the store with the avowed intention of taking the boy and hanging him," he threatened to shoot if they dared to enter the store.[56] Prepared to let the law run its course, the black men withdrew and waited for Patrolmen Hill and Womack to arrest Thompson.

Not long after authorities released Thompson on a $250 bond, reports circulated that three unidentified black men in a spring wagon had made tours of "Black Bottom, Hell's Half Acre and Varmint Town [the city's black districts] admonishing their race to prepare to avenge the outrage." Charles Gibbs, a black citizen of Nashville, was "overhauled" by whites for allegedly making "incendiary remarks" and inciting his friends to take up arms to "get even with the white people for the nigger [Grizzard] they hung off the bridge" a few weeks before.[57] Undoubtedly the black community was still reeling from the recent lynchings of the Grizzard brothers. And some, in fact many, must have wanted to see Lem Thompson suffer a similar fate for his alleged assault of Maggie Reese. Despite talk of revenge, leading citizens in the black community understood the deadly consequences of such actions and instead organized meetings to calm those who may have been taking seriously the violent calls to action.

While black citizens gathered in two of the city's largest churches to discuss a legal plan of action, white citizens were busy arming themselves. Twenty-five white men gathered at the Thompson place and Lem was escorted to an undisclosed place in "the country" for safekeeping.[58] Fearing a "negro uprising," officers Campbell and Curran instructed the night detail to be particularly vigilant and to disperse any suspicious groups of either race. "Despite the vigilance of the officers," explained the Banner, "little knots of negroes formed in all parts of the city and discussed the matter and for several hours the indications of trouble were ominous."[59] By eleven o'clock, two hundred white men had surrounded Thompson's home. In the presence of at least twelve police officers, a cannon used in practice by the cadets at Brennan's Military Academy was brought down and stationed in front of the house and loaded with six pounds of tenpenny nails. When an anonymous message warned that a mob of black men had left Black Bottom and was on its way, the women and children in the vicinity were moved to "places of safety" and "armed forces" formed into double lines across Spruce Street, ready to "repel the attack." Surely, this mob now armed for the protection of an accused rapist must have included many of the same men who had lynched Henry and Eph Grizzard just weeks before. After waiting an hour without any signs of the approaching "black mob," the "crowd" dispersed, with the exception of a dozen men who remained on guard at the Thompson residence until morning. The "black mob" never materialized, but perhaps those in the African American community who wanted vengeance had made their point—no longer were black men and women willing to sit silently by as white men raped and lynched African Americans.[60]

The next morning "the excitement continued" as hundreds of black and white citizens crowded into the city court to hear the preliminary case against Lem. Mr. Marks, a white lawyer for the defense, began by asking whether the city, or anyone else, had the right to charge a boy under fourteen years of age with rape and read from "Greenleaf on Evidence [Simon Greenleaf, A Treatise on the Law of Evidence (1892)]" under the heading of rape: "It may also be shown in evidence that the prisoner was, at the time, under the age of fourteen years, prior to which the law presumes that he was unable to commit the offense, and this presumption is by common law conclusive."[61] Mr. Marks then asked permission to introduce the boy's father to establish the fact that he was under fourteen years of age, and claimed under the section quoted that Lem could not be held under the charge. Mr. Samuel McElwee, a black lawyer who had served three terms in the Tennessee General Assembly, entered a demurrer against the proposition, and said it would require other evidence than the father's word to establish the boy's age. Judge Bell held that as his court was merely a court of inquiry he would rather wait and hear the evidence in the case, and set the trial for a later date.[62] The *Banner* concluded, "It is the unanimous opinion of those who know young Thompson that he is not guilty of the crime charged. He bears the reputation of being a manly little fellow and above committing such a deed."[63]

The rape of Maggie Reece, the rumored plot to lynch Thompson, the white mob that organized to protect him, and the legal proceedings that followed marked the shifting terrain on which black and white southerners vied for justice in cases of alleged interracial rape. Just as it had mattered that the Bruce sisters were white and the Grizzard brothers were black, it mattered that Maggie Reese was black and Lem Thompson Jr. was white. The more closely the circumstances of the crime resembled the imagined postwar scenario of black male villainy and white female helplessness, the greater the chances that a mob would succeed in lynching its victim.

As the Reese-Thompson case reveals, African Americans sought to intervene in and restructure alternative rape/lynch narratives. For some African Americans, lynching Lem would have been the appropriate justice. It is important to note, however, that in the Reese case, when blacks threatened to lynch, whites were more than eager to maintain "law and order." Regardless of white southerners' claims that lynching was reserved for heinous crimes such as rape, they were committed to employing lynching primarily as a form of racial terror and believed that such a violent show of power on the part of African Americans would prove disastrous to the construction of a social order rooted in white male supremacy.

While African Americans were prevented from lynching white men who raped black women, they were at times allowed to use extralegal means to punish black men accused of rape. Even though white authorities were likely to protect black men who raped black women, black mobs, like white mobs, were in some cases allowed to police and punish their own. Of the 284 white victims of white mobs, under 9 percent were lynched for rape; of the 148 black men lynched by black mobs, 25 percent were lynched for rape.[64] The higher percentage of black men accused of rape and lynched by black mobs had as much to do with concerns about rape as it did with the lack of legal protection offered black women. Because white authorities rarely took seriously sexual violence against black women and girls, it comes as no surprise that some African Americans felt compelled to use extralegal violence. The *Nashville Banner* reported on June 30, 1892, that George Marvel, a young black man from Murfreesboro, Tennessee, accused of raping twelve-year-old Josie Floyd, barely escaped a black mob. Rescued from "the infuriated negroes" and lodged in the city jail, Marvel, reported the local newspaper, was safe. "It is altogether improbable, that the negroes will undertake to do anything lawless, as they hardly possess sufficient nerve to attack a jail, especially such a strongly-built one as Murfreesboro has," concluded the article.[65] Two weeks later, the *Nashville Banner* reported on the front page, "RAPIST LYNCHED: A Negro Mob in Arkansas String Up One of Their Own Race." For whites, such headlines suggested that sexual attacks by African American men had become so common that even blacks were resorting to mob violence. More importantly, as Wells so painfully pointed out, such stories helped to justify the actions of white lynch mobs.

Despite what white southerners told themselves and wanted the rest of the world to believe, less then 25 percent of black victims of lynching were accused of rape and very few white men were lynched for sexual crimes.[66] According to Wells, white mobs never lynched on behalf of black women. Highlighting such cases as Reece-Thompson and Bruce-Grizzard, Wells argued that the rape/lynch narrative depended on a variety of racialized gender constructions: the chaste and dependent white woman; the sexually violent black man; the immoral and unredeemable black woman; and the honorable and civilized white man.[67] It was clear to Wells that a successful campaign against rape and lynching would require proving all of these false.

Defining a Movement

Wells's aggressive call to action in *Southern Horrors* won her both enemies and allies. Her opponents in both the black and white press criticized her for not knowing her place. Some members of the black press accused Wells of writing in a way unbecoming of a lady and called on her to practice "moderation and conservatism."[68] The white press tried to discredit her by attacking her moral character. The *Memphis Commercial* called her a "wench" and a "black harlot" in pursuit of a white husband.[69] The assault on Wells's moral character was not a new tactic. Novel, however, was the swiftness with which black women responded to the attack. Black women in Boston organized the Woman's Era Club in the defense of Wells and published an anti-lynching leaflet. After electing Josephine St. Pierre Ruffin as president, the newly formed club passed a resolution condemning the *Commercial* and expressing their "confidence in Miss Wells' purity of purpose and character."[70] Ruffin would remain one of Wells's life-long supporters.[71]

Just months before Ruffin founded the Woman's Era Club, Anna Julia Cooper helped to organize the Colored Women's League of Washington, D.C. In the same year that Wells published *Southern Horrors*, Cooper published *A Voice from the South*, a collection of essays and lectures addressing many of the problems African American women faced at the turn of the century. Born into slavery in Raleigh, North Carolina, Cooper graduated from St. Augustine Normal School in 1869. She obtained a master's degree in 1884 from Oberlin College; later, in 1925, she earned a doctorate in Latin at the Sorbonne in Paris. She spent most of her life as an educator in Washington, D.C., serving as the district's second female school principal at the "M" Street High School for Negroes. Cooper pleaded for the protection of black women in the South. Using language less explicit than Wells, Cooper dismissed white fears of black rape and suggested that black women were the real victims of sexual violence: "The social equality scare then is all humbug, conscious or unconscious, I know not which. And were it not too bitter a thought to utter here, I might add that the overtures for forced association in the past history of these races were not made by the manacled black man nor by *the silent and suffering black woman!*"[72] Careful not to offend the sensibilities of her reader and to preserve her image as a respectable woman, she refrained from using sexually explicit language. Using the coded discourse of "social equality" and tracing the problem of "forced association" back to days of slavery, Cooper went as far as she could without being deemed improper.

Espousing a politics of racial uplift, Cooper called on blacks to change their behavior. In contrast to Wells, who called on whites to do just that, Cooper believed that redeeming the image of black womanhood would guarantee protection. Cooper's appeal for the defense of black womanhood was a direct response to Alexander Crummell's article, "The Black Woman of the South: Her Neglects and Her Needs." Crummell was born free in New York in 1819. He was ordained as an Episcopal priest in 1844 and in 1873 founded and served as the pastor of St. Luke's Episcopal Church in Washington, D.C. In his 1883 article, Crummell declared that middle-class black women, "as well as their ignorant sisters in rude huts, are followed and tempted and insulted by the ruffianly element of Southern society, who think that black *men* have no rights which white men should regard, and black *women* no virtue which white men should respect!"[73] Building on Crummell's claims, Cooper urged black ministers to offer protection as well as religious and educational training to black women who "were often without a father to whom they dare apply the loving term, often without a stronger brother to espouse their cause and defend their honor with his life's blood." Even as Cooper accepted that white men were responsible for the "destruction" of black womanhood, she argued that with God's help, a bit of training, and proper protection, black womanhood could be "regenerated."[74]

Like many black social reformers of the period, Cooper muted her condemnation of white southerners and turned her critique inward. While admitting that white racism was the cause of the social, economic, and political difficulties that African Americans faced at the turn of century, Cooper argued the race could do much to shield itself.[75] Committed to an ideology of racial uplift, Cooper criticized black men for failing to defend black womanhood. Describing black men as "callous" and "nerveless," she questioned "why there should not be an organized effort for the protection and elevation" of black women.[76] Cooper knew that African Americans were being murdered under the guise of an "organized effort to protect and strengthen" white womanhood. She did not, however, mention the southern practice of lynching in her plea for protection.

Cooper turned not to southern white men for her example of chivalry and true manhood, but to the White Cross League of England. Led by the bishop of the Anglican Church, the organization was committed to building "bulwarks around their wronged sisters." According to Cooper, "English women are strengthened and protected by more than twelve centuries of Christian influences, freedom and civilization; English girls are dispirited and crushed down by no such all-leveling prejudice as that supercilious caste spirit in America which cynically assumes 'A Negro woman cannot be a lady.' "[77] As far as she was concerned, no woman was truly protected in a society that did not value "Christian influences, freedom and civilization." What was lynching, if not a contradiction of the ideals put forth by the White Cross League of England? Her call for the protection and elevation of black womanhood stressed both the advancement of British civilization and a Christian manhood that sought to honor and protect all women. Cooper called on black men to do their part to ensure the safety of black womanhood.

Southern Horrors, along with Wells's articles in *New York Age*, made her a celebrity in the black press and a visible player in the national social reform movement. Speaking before black and white audiences, she was embraced by leading figures such as Frederick Douglass; Albion Tourgee, a white lawyer, judge, writer, and civil rights activist; Josephine Ruffin; Susan B. Anthony, a leading suffragist; and Jane Addams of Chicago's Hull House, among others. As Wells's national reputation grew, she was soon recognized on the international stage as a race leader. In April 1893, she was invited to England by social reformers Catherine Impey, a British Quaker and founding editor of the *Anti-Caste*, and Isabelle Mayo, a Scottish writer. Impey and Mayo were part of a growing liberal movement in Great Britain that was challenging Britain's imperialist policy. Many of them had links to the abolitionist movement and were deeply committed to racial justice as well as women's rights. As news of southern lynchings reached Britain, Impey took up the issue in *Anti-Caste* and set out to help remedy the problem. It was with the intention of educating themselves about the evils of lynching and organizing for its end that the British women invited Wells to deliver a series of lectures.[78]

After Wells's first lecture the women founded the Society for the Recognition of the Brotherhood of Man (SRBM) to oppose racial segregation, lynchings, and "other forms of brutal injustice."[79] Despite a falling out between Impey and Mayo during her visit, Wells managed to give a series of lectures and interviews that garnered praise and support in Scotland, Birmingham, Manchester, and London.[80] When Wells returned to the states in June she was heralded by the *Indianapolis Freeman* as the "modern Joan of the race."[81] The white southern press, however, was far less enthusiastic. The *Memphis Appeal-Avalanche* continued its attack on her character and called her a "negro adventuress."[82]

Back in the states Wells focused on the 1893 Columbian Exposition in Chicago and its failure to acknowledge the progress and accomplishments of African Americans. Working with Frederick Douglass and Ferdinand Lee Barnett, a prominent black lawyer and founding editor of the Chicago *Conservator*, Wells published *The Reason Why the Colored American Is Not in the World's Columbian Exposition: The Afro-American's Contribution to Columbian Literature.*[83] It was while in Chicago working on the World's Fair pamphlet that a romance blossomed between Wells and Barnett. The courtship no doubt informed her decision to relocate to the windy city. Born in 1856 in Nashville, Tennessee, Barnett was the son of a slave who had bought his freedom and moved the family to Canada and then, in 1869, to Chicago. Ferdinand graduated from Northwestern University Law School in 1878 and established the *Chicago Conservator*. He married Mary Graham, the first black woman to graduate from the University of Michigan, in 1882. After giving birth to two boys, she died in 1888.[84]

Like Wells, Barnett was a race activist who spoke out against lynching. In the early 1880s, he published an editorial in which he protested southern mob violence: "A colored man was lynched upon the charge of an attempt at outrage. An attempt, mind you. This is a comprehensive term in the South. It embraces a wink by a colored man at a white girl a half a mile off. Such a crime is worthy of lynching, but a beastly attack upon a colored girl by a white man is only a wayward indiscretion."[85] It comes as no surprise that the two hit it off and that Barnett joined Wells's campaign against lynching. In 1893, Barnett became the founding president of the Illinois Anti-Lynching League.[86] He also hired Wells as a writer for his newspaper.

Once settled in Chicago, Wells helped organize the first black women's club in Illinois—later chartered as the Ida B. Wells Club—to protest racial injustice. Founded in September of 1893, it had more than three hundred members by February 1894.[87] The black women's club movement had taken on a life of its own in just a few short years. All over the country black women were organizing in defense of themselves.[88] Established in 1892, the Colored Women's League of Washington, D.C., had branches in the South and as far west as Kansas; the Woman's Loyal Union of New York had sister clubs in Memphis, Charleston, and Philadelphia; and in 1893 the Woman's Era Club of Boston developed branches throughout New England. Responding to disenfranchisement, the indignities of Jim Crow, the increase in lynching, the attacks on the moral and sexual character of black women, as well as the multitude of political and economic problems that faced African American communities at the turn of the century, a new generation of educated black women committed themselves to racial uplift through self-help.[89]

A few months into the New Year, Wells received an invitation from the SRBM to return to Great Britain. Back among British social reformers, Wells explained how white Christian leaders and social reformers in America refused to speak out against lynching and in some cases had even condoned mob violence. When British Reverend S. A. Steinthal, a leading antislavery Unitarian, led an effort to pass an anti-lynching resolution at the national conference of the "Unitarian, Liberal Christian, Free Christian, Presbyterian, and other Non-Subscribing Conferences" that was meeting in Manchester, two American delegates, Reverend Brooke Herford and Mrs. Ormistan Chant, a prominent Boston Unitarian and social reformer, spoke out against the resolution by challenging Wells's claim that the American pulpit had encouraged lynching with its silence. Chant helped to defeat the resolution when she declared that Wells's accusation and the proposed resolution were "unjust to their Unitarian brethren in America."[90]

Back in Boston, the Woman's Era Club again came to Wells's defense and sent a letter to the *Manchester Guardian* expressing its members' particular disappointment that Chant, who had addressed the Club at its first public meeting, had played a role in defeating the resolution.[91] Florida Ruffin Ridley, corresponding secretary of the Woman's Era Club and daughter of Josephine St. Pierre Ruffin, opened, "We do not pretend to say there are no black villains. Baseness is not confined to race. We read with horror of two different colored girls who recently have been horribly assaulted by white men in the South. We should regret any lynchings of the offenders by black men, but we shall not have occasion. Should these offenders receive any punishment at all, it will be a marvel." Ridley concluded that "we do not expect that white women shall feel as deeply as we" and dedicated her protest to the suffering and unprotected black women of the South. The letter made it clear that Wells was not alone in her crusade and that an organized group of black women supported her work and her claims.

Determined to prove her point about the lack of support from whites against lynching, Wells took aim at the most famous American reformer — Frances Willard, president of the WCTU. Making use of Willard's 1890 interview in which she had subtly excused lynching and declared, "The safety of womanhood, of childhood, of the home, is menaced in a thousand localities at this moment, so that the men dare not go beyond the sight of their own roof tree," Wells accused Willard of not only failing to speak out against lynching, but also of condoning segregation by allowing for segregated unions in the South.[92] Wells held the WCTU to high standards because it was an interracial organization and she hoped to force Willard's hand and compel the WCTU, the largest women's organization in the States, to come out publicly against the rape and lynching of African Americans.[93] Willard, however, desperate to hold on to her white southern membership and to save face among British social reformers, challenged the validity of Wells's accusations. She accused Wells of misrepresenting the WCTU and declared herself opposed to mob violence by highlighting the WCTU's 1893 anti-lynching resolution.[94] Despite Willard's attempts to discredit Wells, the British continued to support Wells's campaign and founded the London Anti-Lynching Committee.[95]

The heated exchange between Wells and Willard, which continued when Wells returned to the States and climaxed at the November national meeting of the WCTU in Cleveland, Ohio, left some black clubwomen feeling that they had to take sides. And take sides they did. Some black temperance women who had been working diligently for over a decade to create and maintain alliances with white social reformers felt it necessary to come out in support of Willard. Yet few could ignore what lay at the heart of Wells's critique — that white women were all too willing to accept the myth of black rape while ignoring the rape and murder of black women and men.

After the WCTU convention, Wells continued to travel and speak out against lynching. Her schedule did not ease up until June 27, when she married Ferdinand Lee Barnett Jr. and hyphenated her name. Wells-Barnett soon took over the editorship of the *Conservator* and settled into her new life as a wife and soon-to-be mother. She did so, however, knowing that the work that she had begun would continue. Indeed, she was back on the lecture circuit within two months of her marriage, speaking before black and white women's clubs. While marriage and motherhood slowed the pace of Wells's anti-lynching crusade, the black women's club movement rallied on her behalf.

Black Clubwomen Enter the Fray

By 1895, many black clubwomen believed that a national organization was necessary to challenge the negative images of African Americans that served to justify rape and lynching. If black women could convince white women, like Willard, that rape was not a one-sided problem, and that lynching was not a "natural and commendable outburst" but a racist act of lawlessness, then they would gain a formidable ally in their campaign for protection.[96] They believed, however, that they would first have to show themselves as worthy of protection. And who better than they could refute the racist image of the "black whore?"

In the summer of 1895, the Woman's Era Club of Boston, in response to "a foul slander hurled" at Wells and black womanhood in general, organized the "The First National Conference of Colored Women of America." In an effort to discredit Wells's anti-lynching campaign, James W. Jacks, president of the Missouri Press Association, sent a letter to Miss Florence Belgarnie, the Secretary of the London Anti-Lynching Committee, in which he declared that most black women were "prostitutes" and "natural liars and thieves" and concluded that "out of 200 in this vicinity it is doubtful if there are a dozen virtuous women of that number who are not daily thieving from the white people."[97] Belgarnie forwarded the letter to Ruffin, who in turn sent copies of the letter to the "leading men and women" of the race "for an expression of opinion."[98] Mary Church Terrell, a founding member of the Women's League of Washington and daughter of Memphis millionaire Robert Church, described the letter as "the most unjustifiable and venomous attack ever made upon the womanhood of any race by a man."[99] Black women, explained Margaret Murray Washington of the Tuskegee Women's Club and the second wife of Booker T. Washington, were "suddenly awakened by the wholesale charges of the lack of virtue and character."[100] Fannie Barrier Williams of Chicago reported that the letter was "instantly and vehemently resented. . . . [It] stirred the intelligent colored women of America as nothing ever had done."[101] Ruffin responded to Jack's letter with a national call to action on the editorial page of the club's magazine, *Woman's Era*. Under the heading "Let Us Confer Together," she challenged, "Read this document carefully and discriminatingly and decide if it be not time for us to stand before the world and declare ourselves and our principles. The time is short, but everything is ripe; and remember, earnest women

can do anything."[102] Ruffin's call to organize in defense of black womanhood marked the beginning of a national black woman's movement committed to the protection of black women.[103] Answering Ruffin's call and
marking "a new era," a hundred black women from across the country
traveled to Boston, where they made clear their determination to defend black womanhood. They founded the National Federation of Afro-
American Women, electing Margaret Murray Washington as president.

Wells-Barnett, a new bride and expectant mother, was unable to attend. Despite her absence her presence was strongly felt. Indeed, one
woman described the conference as reinforcing "the efforts of our leading women such as Ida B. Wells-Barnett."[104] A resolution passed praising
Wells-Barnett's work "against the lying charge of rape" as "noble and truth-
ful."[105] Declaring her as their "noble 'Joanna of Arc,'" they endorsed
Wells-Barnett's campaign against lynching and rape. Support for Wells-
Barnett, however, was not unanimous.

Some clubwomen believed that Wells-Barnett's "fierce denunciations
of 'southern white women'" had provoked Jack's letter and feared that her
presence at the convention would harm the movement's image and their
efforts to build alliances with white women. Prior to 1895 few black
women had spoken publicly about rape and lynching and none as forcefully as Wells-Barnett.[106] Fearing their words would be perceived as condoning rape and would alienate their few white allies, many refused to
discuss the problem outside of private circles. In an attempt to distance itself from Wells-Barnett's critique of Willard, the convention passed a resolution, although not without protest, stating their support of the WCTU.
Despite passage of the resolution, which was never published, the
Woman's Era Club published an editorial criticizing the WCTU and declared "let it be understood that the editors of this paper stand by Mrs.
Wells-Barnett squarely in her position on this matter and fully endorse
it."[107] Wells-Barnett mistakenly read this as a "unanimous endorsement of
the course [she] had pursued in [her] agitation against lynching."[108] True,
many black clubwomen supported her campaign against rape and lynching, but some were not happy with her "course" of action. Indeed, some
black clubwomen found her aggressive and confrontational style of protest
more than distasteful and even harmful to the movement.

When Josephine St. Pierre Ruffin addressed the First National Conference of Colored Women, she inaugurated a national campaign for the
protection of black womanhood. She explained that the attacks on black

womanhood were often "so humiliating" that they served "to protect the accuser by driving the helpless accused into mortified silence." Long enough had black women remained silent. Ruffin declared, "With an army of organized women standing for purity and mental worth," black women could now "deny the charge and open the eyes of the world." A national black women's club movement would "break this silence, not by noisy protestations of what we are not, but by a dignified showing of what we are and hope to become," she concluded.[109] Whereas Wells-Barnett believed that armed resistance and agitation for federal intervention would guarantee protection and foster black progress, Ruffin called on black clubwomen to serve as models of true womanhood to ensure protection. Embracing a "politics of respectability" rooted in racial uplift, the national movement avoided Wells-Barnett's confrontational tactics and opted for the more conservative style of protest exercised by Anna Julia Cooper.[110]

The National Federation of Afro-American Women, which joined with the Colored Women's League in 1896 to become the National Association of Colored Women (NACW), embraced the challenge put forward by both Wells-Barnett and Cooper and spoke out publicly against rape and lynching. The NACW became an umbrella group for black women's organizations at the state and local levels. It operated through a series of departments and a strong executive cabinet. Its official newsletter, *National Notes*, served as an instrument to unite black clubwomen and educate them in the science and techniques of reform. Integrating Wells-Barnett's and Cooper's ideas and different styles, black clubwomen were able to create a national anti-lynching debate that called for the protection of black womanhood. With every story of lynching and rape, the press presented a more horrifying and dehumanizing image of African American women. Stereotypes portraying the race as uncivilized and lustful could be read in almost every southern white newspaper. Black clubwomen believed that if they could convey a moral and respectable image of black womanhood, they would elicit sympathy and protection for all black women. To this end, they organized nationally and locally, and published articles, pamphlets, novels, and a range of essays that challenged the racist and sexist presumptions concerning rape and lynching.

By the time the NACW was founded and had elected Mary Church Terrell as its first president in 1896, Wells-Barnett had already published her second anti-lynching pamphlet, *A Red Record*, resettled in Chicago with her husband, and given birth to their first child, Charles Barnett. In the four years that had passed since Wells-Barnett's exile from Memphis and the publication of *Southern Horrors,* little had changed in regards to the racial and sexual politics of the South. The lynching and rape of African Americans remained a weekly event in southern states and the assault on the moral character of black women had only intensified. Between 1892 and 1896 close to nine hundred men and women had been lynched.

Frederick Douglass's death in 1895 at the age of seventy-seven placed Booker T. Washington, head of the Tuskegee Institute, as the leading African American voice. The same year, Washington delivered what his critics called the "Atlanta Compromise Speech" at the Cotton States and International Exposition in Atlanta. He advised black southerners to "cast down your bucket where you are" and reassured white southerners, "In all things that are purely social we can be as separate as the fingers, yet one as the hand in all things essential to mutual progress."[111] In 1896, the Supreme Court agreed with Washington and handed down its famous "separate but equal" ruling in *Plessy v. Ferguson.* By a vote of eight to one, the justices ended three decades of struggle over keeping public spaces integrated, ruling that states could force railroad companies to exclude African Americans from first-class, or "ladies," cars. Justice John Marshall Harlan, who was the only southerner on the Court and a former slaveholder, cast the lone dissenting vote. "The arbitrary separation of citizens, on the basis of race," he argued, "while they are on a public highway, is a badge of servitude wholly inconsistent with civil freedom and the equality before the law established by the Constitution."[112]

When black clubwomen decided to convene in Washington, D.C., in the summer of 1896, Wells-Barnett was eager to attend. With her four-month-old son in tow, she actively participated in the meeting and helped set the organization's agenda. For the majority of black clubwomen who attended the conference, redeeming the image of black womanhood was the first step in eradicating racial and sexual violence. They believed, like Cooper, that the negative portrayals of black women served to keep the race politically, economically, and socially degraded. "Until the present stigma is removed from the home and the women of its race," argued Fannie Barrier Williams, president of the Illinois Federation of Colored Women's Clubs, "there will never be an unchallenged vote, a respected political power, or an unquestioned claim to position of influence and importance."[113] According to Terrell, the newly elected president of the NACW, the duty of black clubwomen was "setting a high moral standard and living up to it."[114] To counter the slander circulated by the press, she explained, it was necessary for black women, who represented "the intelligence and virtue" of the race, to "avoid even the appearance of evil" in both their public and private lives.[115] In short, Terrell believed that black clubwomen should resist engaging in political protest that had the potential for instigating the kind of vicious and slanderous attacks suffered by Wells-Barnett.

Even as black clubwomen refused to blame their poorer black sisters for their own victimization, they adopted the slogan "Lifting as We Climb," implying that a change on the part of black women was necessary. Committed to a "politics of respectability" and a discourse of racial uplift, they naturally turned their criticism inward.[116] They believed that if they could "uplift" the demoralized class of poor black women, their demands for protection would no longer go unheard. Racial uplift, argued many black clubwomen, would chip away at white supremacy and guarantee blacks fair treatment and equal protection under the law. Good manners, social purity, cleanliness, and homecare would serve as weapons of protest. As Ruffin had declared in 1895, black clubwomen hoped to achieve protection and respectability "not by noisy protestation," but by a "dignified showing." Emphasizing domesticity, clubwomen sought to improve family life, health, and morality in the black community. Both Nannie Burroughs, founder and longtime president of the National Training School for Women and Girls in Washington, D.C., and Charlotte Hawkins Brown, founder of the Palmer Memorial Institute, made sure that the students at their schools learned good manners and social graces. Burroughs preached a "politics of respectability" to the working-class female students who attended the National Training School and emphasized reform of individual manners and morals as crucial to racial self-help.[117] At the turn of the century, black clubwomen directed most of their energy into building day care programs, old age homes, or community houses and programs that would both improve the living conditions of poor blacks and eradicate the image of the inferior Negro.

As president of the NACW, Terrell argued that "in spite" of slavery, temptations, sexual assaults, and the lack of "safeguards usually thrown around maidenly youth and innocence," many black women had managed to maintain dignity and respectability.[118] Pointing to statistics compiled "by men not inclined to falsify" the record, Terrell explained that immorality among black women was not as common as among white women in countries "like Austria, Italy, Germany, Sweden, and France."[119] By identifying white women of Europe as less virtuous than black women, Terrell severed the link between morality and race. Acknowledging that immorality existed among black women just as it did among women of all races, she argued that black women were victims of circumstances that made it extremely difficult for them to live virtuous and respectable lives. Furthermore, by living under an institution that denied them the rights of womanhood, many black women were innocent victims in a demoralized and corrupt society. If black women's morals were "as loose and as lax" as white southerners claimed, she contended, the South had nobody to blame but itself, slavery, and white men.[120] One black woman commented, "No amount of discussion will alter a fact, and it is a fact that a very great number of negro women are depraved. It also a fact that . . . Christian men and women of the South sold wives away from their husbands and then compelled them to live with other men . . . the negro woman's immorality shows more plainly than her white sister's because she is poor and ignorant."[121]

White female social reformers, like Rebecca Latimer Felton, saw things differently. Many were quick to lay the blame for lynching at black women's feet. In a speech titled "The Rights of Children," Felton linked the "black rapist" and the "black whore": "The great mass of these indifferent women are shameless in their prostitution and brazen in defiance of moral laws. Their children are brought up in wanton disregard of decent living—and when the question is asked why so much violence and so much lynching, I can readily understand the miserable condition under which these miserable violators of the law came into being."[122] Because the Victorian ideology of true womanhood held women as morally superior and responsible for the moral training of their men folk, southern white women blamed black women for the "black rapist."[123] Most white women, however, rarely acknowledged the rape of black women by white men and even when they did so they refused to accept any of the blame. It was much easier to point fingers, like the white woman who complained in the *Independent* that "When a man's mother, wife, and daughters are all immoral women, there is no room in his fallen nature for the aspiration of honor and virtue."[124]

Admitting immorality among black women and tracing its roots to slavery, black clubwomen sought to prove that black women were not naturally promiscuous. In "Negro Womanhood Defended," Addie Hunton, a teacher and principal active in the NACW and the Young Women's Christian Association (YWCA), explained, "There is an unwritten and an almost unmentionable history of the burdens of those soul-trying times when, to bring profit to the slave trade and to satisfy the base desires of a stronger hand, the Negro woman was subject of compulsory immorality."[125] Using language quite similar to Cooper's, Hunton blamed white southerners for black women's plight. Slavery had placed no value on the black family and had denied black women control over their bodies. Victims of rape, a crime "more bitter than death," black women had survived. In their defense Hunton attacked white morality and argued that southern virtue had "its basis on the souls and bodies of Negro women."[126] In other words, the rape of black women by white men allowed white women to maintain their status as pure and virtuous.

Like Wells-Barnett, Hunton lumped together the mobs of southern white men who tortured and murdered black men for allegedly assaulting white women with those who raped and lynched black women. Her plea for the protection of black womanhood called to task the ideology of chivalry espoused by southern whites. Since, according to southern whites, lynching sought to "keep pure and undefiled the spirit that worships at the family shrine," Hunton asked why no arms were being lifted in defense of black womanhood.[127] Burroughs also accused white men of failing in their manhood: "A man who is truly a gentleman, respects a woman, not because she is white or black, as the case may be, but because she is a woman, and he has been taught that there is a certain amount of respect due every woman."[128] Making use of Wells's argument, both Burroughs and Hunton complained that if white men were truly chivalrous they would extend respect and protection to black women. Black clubwomen made no distinctions between respect and protection — one afforded the other. They found themselves denied protection because they were not perceived as respectable. But without respectability, they could hardly demand protection.

Just as slavery had denied black women the rights of womanhood, it had also stripped black men of their ability to protect black women. This inability to protect black women during slavery, black clubwomen argued, had carried over into freedom. As late as 1912, a black woman who had worked as a cook in a white southern home published an editorial in which she described her husband's failed attempt to protect her from her white employer's sexual advances. A black woman, she explains, "has only herself to depend upon for protection. If their fathers, brothers, and husbands seek to redress their wrongs under our peculiar conditions, the guiltless negroes will be severely punished, if not killed, and the white blackleg will go free!"[129] While some women clearly recognized the dangers black men faced when and if they attempted to protect black women, others complained that black men exacerbated the problem of protection by refusing to defend black women's honor with their "life's blood."[130] Espousing a Victorian notion of manhood, Burroughs blamed black men for the lack of respect shown black women. She complained, "Our men have permitted many encroachments upon the moral life of the race by not entering manly protests against all who insist on having social equality of the wrong sort. White men offer more protection to their prostitutes than many black men offer to their best women." Burroughs argued that until black men were prepared to "defiantly stand for the protection" of black womanhood, the women of the race would continue to be viewed as lacking in virtue and the easy prey of "the hands of the most vile."[131] Convinced that the womanhood of the race depended on the manhood, black clubwomen understood that images of the black rapist and the depraved black woman were intricately linked and would have to be tackled simultaneously. The myth of the black rapist reinforced the idea of the immoral and hypersexual black woman and vice versa.

From its inception, the NACW formed anti-lynching committees at the local and national levels and publicized lynching and violence against black women. The Michigan Federation of Colored Women's Clubs followed Wells-Barnett's lead in 1898, when it petitioned President William McKinley to appropriate forty thousand dollars for the widow of a lynched South Carolina postmaster. In January 1904, former NACW president Terrell responded to Thomas Nelson Page's article, "The Lynching of Negroes — Its Causes and Its Prevention," in which he blamed the increasing number of lynchings on the rape of white women by Negroes, the justice system's delay in meting out punishment for such crimes, and the need for a punishment to match the brutality of rape.[132] In "Lynching from a Negro's Point of View," Terrell argued, like Wells, that lynching was "due to race hatred" and southern "lawlessness."[133] She insisted that the race problem could not be solved until *whites* were "educated and lifted to a higher moral plane." Taking a page from Wells's book, she declared, "It is a great mistake to suppose that rape is the real cause of lynching in the South."[134] Challenging the stereotypes of both the black whore and the black rapist, Terrell recounted the history of black women's sexual exploitation by southern white men and questioned: if lynching functioned to protect and honor womanhood, then why had mobs not organized to punish white men for violating colored women and girls? "Throughout their entire period of bondage colored women were debauched by their masters," she contended. "From the day they were liberated to the present time, prepossessing young colored girls have been considered the rightful prey of white gentlemen in the South, and they have been protected neither by public sentiment nor by law. In the South, the negro's home is not considered sacred by the superior race. White men are neither punished for invading it, nor lynched for violating colored women and girls."[135]

In 1904, at the NACW's St. Louis biennial, the organization took Wells's advice and passed a resolution calling on the federal government to take a firmer stance against lynching. At the same time, however, the NACW became closely allied with the conservative politics of Booker T. Washington, who believed that patience and a commitment to racial uplift would do more to solve the race problem than "noisy protest." His wife, Margaret Murray Washington, was editor of the organization newsletter—*National Notes*—for the first decade of the twentieth century and served as the organization's president from 1912 to 1918. In a 1906 letter to Margaret Washington praising her editing of the newsletter, Josephine Yates, president of the NACW at the time, expressed the organization's commitment to the accommodationist philosophy traditionally attributed to Washington. Yates wrote, "Our paper must be kept in a conservative tone that will show that we are not ranters, not seeking notoriety, that the matter of race elevation through intelligent and continuous work in the right direction is all we are seeking."[136] The NACW's conservative politics, however, forced radical members like Wells-Barnett to find alternative organizations through which to engage in militant protest.

Wells-Barnett had begun to be alienated from the NACW as early as 1900.[137] Her radical politics and aggressive personality made her difficult to work with and ran counter to the conservative ideology promoted by the NACW.[138] During her 1899 presidency of the NACW, Terrell made clear her dislike for Wells-Barnett when, at the request of Fannie

Williams, she prevented Wells-Barnett from participating in the second meeting of the NACW, which was held in Wells's own town of Chicago.[139] While it is difficult to know exactly why Williams and Terrell felt it necessary to exclude Wells-Barnett from the meeting, it is clear that her confrontational and at times combative style proved to be too much for a movement rooted in Victorian notions of womanhood. Uncompromising in her commitment to radical protest politics, Wells found herself constantly running up against the NACW's leadership. Her problematic relationship with Terrell (as well as other leading club women) ensured her relegation to the margins of the national black club women's movement.

Wells-Barnett sought out organizations that better suited her radical and uncompromising style of protest. In 1898, when T. Thomas Fortune revitalized the National Afro-American Council, an interracial organization founded in 1890 and committed to confronting racial discrimination and violence, Wells-Barnett was elected to serve as the organization's financial secretary. She was later appointed director of the council's Anti-Lynching Bureau. As an active member of the Afro-American Council, Wells-Barnett was able to maintain a national voice in the campaign against lynching. During her time as head of the Anti-Lynching Bureau she published *Lynch Law in Georgia* (1899) in response to the lynching of Sam Hose, and *Mob Rule in New Orleans* (1900) regarding the lynching of Robert Charles. Again Wells-Barnett would find her influence at the national level short lived as the council succumbed to the influence of Booker T. Washington in 1902.

Wells-Barnett's public disdain for Washington placed her on the more radical side of the national black protest movement. In 1904, Wells-Barnett wrote an article titled "Booker T. Washington and His Critics" that was published in *World Today*. She declared, "Mr. Washington says in substance: Give me money to educate the Negro and when he is taught how to work, he will not commit the crime for which lynching is done. Mr. Washington knows when he says this that lynching is not invoked to punish crime but color, and not even industrial education will change that."[140] While Washington believed that black economic success would overcome the legitimate class prejudices of whites and gain their respect and acceptance, Wells-Barnett argued that economic success and Puritan virtue would not save blacks from rape and lynching. Her personal experiences and investigation of racial violence had shown that turning inward to self-help and money making did not abate lynching but instead provoked it. If she had learned anything from the Memphis lynching of her friend Thomas Moss, it was that black economic success provoked white violence. "The more the Afro-American yields and cringes and begs," she argued, "the more he has to do so, the more he is insulted, outraged and lynched."[141] It was her belief that African Americans would have to force change not through conciliation, but with militant protest and, if necessary, violent resistance. Unfortunately for Wells-Barnett, Washington was the best-known race leader in the United States and exercised great influence over black organizations. He also was known for his ability to silence his black critics.[142]

Forced yet again from the national movement, Wells-Barnett put her energy into the local politics of Chicago. As editor of the *Conservator*, president of the Ida B. Wells Club, and the mother of four, she had more than enough to keep her busy. Nevertheless, the 1909 founding of the National Association for the Advancement of Colored People (NAACP), an interracial organization committed to the improvement of race relations, gave Wells-Barnett hope that her anti-lynching campaign would find a national home. It comes as no surprise that her attendance at the National Negro Conference in New York, the founding meeting of the NAACP, was not without controversy. She was one of only three African Americans asked to speak at the meeting. In her speech, "Lynching: Our National Crime," Wells-Barnett proposed a campaign for federal anti-lynching legislation and called for "a bureau for the investigation and publication of the details of every lynching."[143]

Controversy flared, however, when Wells-Barnett learned she had been excluded from the "Committee of Forty," the group that would do the work of defining the organization's programs, structure, and long-term goals. After Du Bois read the names for the committee, Wells-Barnett along with William Monroe Trotter, who was also excluded from the forty, stormed out of the meeting. According to Wells-Barnett, the two had been kept off the committee because they opposed "Mr. Washington's industrial ideas." This, however, was unlikely, considering Du Bois was also a critic of Washington. It was more likely, as Mary White Ovington, secretary of the NAACP, explained, that the all-white nominating committee (with the exception of Du Bois), opting for a "middle course," had omitted Wells-Barnett along with other "powerful personalities, who had gone their own way, fitted for courageous work, but perhaps not fitted to accept the restraints of organization."[144] Regardless of their reasons, Wells-Barnett was outraged. After much protest on the part of Wells-Barnett and several of her white allies, she was eventually put on the Committee of Forty and the next year became a member of the organization's executive committee. Yet she remained skeptical of the white leadership and wielded little if any influence in the organization.

As an executive member of the NAACP, Wells-Barnett hoped to bring the NACW into protest politics. Elizabeth Carter, president of the NACW in 1910, invited Wells-Barnett to speak about the NAACP's work at the biennial meeting in Louisville and placed her at the head of the committee on resolution. Wells-Barnett found the NACW still committed to conservative politics. When she moved that the organization's newsletter, the *National Notes*, which for more than a decade had been edited by Margaret Murray Washington and printed by the Tuskegee Institute, be placed under the organization's control and an editor elected, she was hissed off the convention floor.[145] She and others complained that no critical articles about Booker T. Washington ever appeared in the newsletter. They insisted that the post of editor was becoming important enough to require election. Even though the motion failed, the NACW did endorse the goals of the NAACP, "provided it did not interfere with the treasury or divide the working force of the National Association of Colored Women." This support demonstrated that not all members of the NACW were supporters of Washington's conservative politics. More importantly, it suggested that, like Terrell, who had finally started moving toward direct protest, some black clubwomen were beginning to realize the limitations of racial uplift.

The NAACP waited almost six years before making use of Wells-Barnett's recommendations to establish an anti-lynching bureau and canvass for federal legislation. Finally, in 1914, the NAACP set out to investigate and publish the facts about southern lynchings. It comes as no surprise that the NAACP's anti-lynching campaign was strongly influenced by the politics of respectability and racial uplift ideology espoused by black club women.[146] In fact, a close look at the NAACP's response to the rape and lynching of Marie Scott in the spring of 1914 in Wagoner County, Oklahoma, reveals how a politics of respectability shaped and at times may have hindered the NAACP's early campaign against lynching.

By 1914, thousands of African Americans had lost their lives to southern lynch mobs. So when a mob of three hundred "masked men" pulled Marie

Scott from her prison cell, tied a rope about her neck, dragged her kicking and screaming to a telephone pole, and hanged her, it did not come as a great shock to African Americans. In typical fashion the southern white press vilified Scott and justified the mob's actions. According to the white press, Marie Scott was lynched because she had killed Lemuel Pearce, a young white man, "by driving a knife into his heart."[147] While no attempts were made to explain why Pearce "with a party of other young whites" had gone to the "negro section of town" or why Scott "sprang upon Pearce and plunged a knife into his heart, killing him almost instantly," one paper suggested that the "ostensible reason" given for the lynching "was the fear that even if the negress was convicted and sentenced to death, Governor Cruce," who opposed capital punishment, "would prevent her execution."[148] Described as a "murderess" in most white newspapers, Scott's guilt was assumed and her lynching thereby justified. But the various accounts told among African Americans reveal a different and disturbing story.

Almost three weeks after the lynching, M. Scott Brown Jr., attorney for the Muskogee, Oklahoma, branch of the NAACP, wrote a letter to May Childs Nerney, secretary of the NAACP Executive Committee, about the lynching.[149] Brown's letter was extremely vague and almost cryptic. In the first half he described the "Bottoms" where Marie Scott lived and allegedly killed Pearce as the "red light district." He explained that while "reliable information" about the case was "entirely lacking," he believed that "the details and the circumstances surrounding the death of the young man, [were] so revolting, and so shocking in the very nature of the case, that [he] should hesitate to discuss them with [Miss Nerney] (or any other lady)." Brown explained that he would have no problem giving Chapin Brinsmade, the NAACP's first full-time staff lawyer, or "any other man, the gist of the rumor, which indicates the real facts in the case."[150] Accepting the idea that it was inappropriate to discuss anything sexual in nature, rape included, in mixed company, Brown's letter left much to the imagination. Unfortunately, in this case, Brown's hesitation was read as an indication that Scott's reputation was less than respectable. Indeed, those in the national office interpreted Brown's letter as evidence that Scott was a prostitute and concluded that her case was unworthy of investigation.

In a letter to Mrs. C. H. Dodge, president of the Friday Club of San Diego, Brinsmade made clear the NAACP's reasons for not taking on the case. Three weeks after the lynching, Dodge had written to Brinsmade calling for an investigation: "The time has come that something practical should be done to prevent further atrocities, and since our motto is, 'Deeds not Words' we would suggest that the matter be taken up by the Colored Women's Clubs of the country and financed by them." Brinsmade declined the offer to help finance the employment of a detective "to go into Oklahoma and get evidence to convict" Mary Scott's lynchers. He explained, "There are two considerations however, which make me feel that this is not the crime we should choose for such an investigation. In the first place, it seems that a complete investigation and the publication of the facts will not result in obtaining public sympathy for the victim of the lynching, because her character was as bad as possible and because the circumstances of her crime were revolting and shocking."[151] His letter was more than enough to convince Dodge, who closed her letter with "Yours for the Uplift." A month later, however, the NAACP received information that directly contradicted their assumptions that Scott was a depraved and immoral black woman who had viciously murdered a white man. According to Jas. Harold Coleman, Marie Scott belonged to a family of "respectable people." She was brutally raped by "two drunken white men" who had broken into her home.[152] Her brother attempted to rescue Scott and killed one of her assailants. Since he fled the scene of the crime, his sister was accused of the murder and ultimately lynched. Still, the NAACP refused to take up the case in fear that doing so might call into question the moral character of black womanhood.

Indeed it seems the NAACP misunderstood Brown's letter. It is safe to assume that what made the case so "shocking and revolting" to Brown had less to do with Scott's moral character than with the fact that she was raped. Unfortunately, Brown's unwillingness to discuss in detail with Nerney the events surrounding the lynching of Scott allowed the NAACP to assume the worst about the woman's reputation. Having embraced the anti-lynching campaign as set forth by black clubwomen, the NAACP was extremely concerned about presenting a respectable image of black womanhood. In the end, the NAACP never did send investigators into Oklahoma and said very little about the case publicly.[153] It was a tragic miscarriage of justice that was never acknowledged or punished.

It was extremely difficult to strike the right public stance against lynching. The stakes were high, sometimes deadly, for blacks who failed to find the right balance. As Wells-Barnett and the black clubwomen who supported her discovered, it would take a range of tactics and criticism to make even a little difference in the racial and sexual politics of the New South. The delicate balance between racial uplift and political protest that black women forged in the early fight against lynching made the struggle even more difficult. In the end, however, these women anticipated the rise of an interracial anti-lynching movement that would ultimately succeed in the years to come.

Rebecca Ann Latimer (left) and her younger sister Mary photographed in the early 1850s. The Civil War would make it impossible for Rebecca and the women of her slaveholding class to live up to the ideals of southern womanhood. (Courtesy of University of Georgia Press)

"THE LADIES OF NEW ORLEANS before GENERAL BUTLER'S Proclamation. After GENERAL BUTLER'S Proclamation." In 1862 General Benjamin Butler passed "General Orders, No. 28" to prevent the women of New Orleans from insulting federal soldiers, whose occupation they resisted. (John McLenan, Harper's Weekly, July 12, 1862, provided courtesy of HarpWeek., LLC)

Ida B. Wells came of age during the pitched battles of Reconstruction. The granddaughter of a slave woman and her white master, Wells was attuned to southern racial and sexual politics at an early age. (Courtesy of Sophia Smith Collection, Smith College)

During Reconstruction white vigilantes attacked African American men and women who sought to exercise their new rights as citizens. Black women were whipped, raped, and murdered by ex-Confederates eager to regain economic and political power. (Harper's Weekly, September 14, 1867, cover "Whipping a Negro Girl in North Carolina by 'Unconstructed' Johnsonians." Provided courtesy HarpWeek., LLC)

Ida B. Wells *(left)* was photographed with a lynching victim's widow, Betty Moss, and two children in 1896 after being forced into exile from the South because of her editorials protesting lynching and calling into question the crime of rape as justification for mob violence. (Courtesy of Special Collections Center, University of Chicago Library)

Photograph of Rebecca Latimer Felton taken in 1910 when she was seventy-five years old. (Courtesy of Southern Historical Collection, University of North Carolina at Chapel Hill)

Postcard of the lynching of Laura Nelson in Okemah, Oklahoma, May 25, 1911. Nelson and her son were accused of murdering a white deputy. (Courtesy of Without Sanctuary Collection, National Center for Civil and Human Rights)

White men, women, and children posing for a photograph with the corpses of Laura Nelson and her son. The image became one of many postcards of victims of lynching that whites collected as souvenirs or used as threats against African Americans. (Courtesy of Without Sanctuary Collection, National Center for Civil and Human Rights)

Rubin Stacy was accused of raping a white woman and lynched in Fort Lauderdale, Florida, on July 19, 1935, by a mob of white men and women. Southern white women and girls were most visible at lynchings of black men accused of sexually threatening or assaulting a white woman. (Courtesy of Library of Congress, Prints and Photographs Division)

"This is her first lynching."

Reginal Marsh's sketch, "Her First Lynching," appeared in *The New Yorker* in 1934. (The New Yorker Collection 1934 Reginald Marsh from cartoonbank.com)

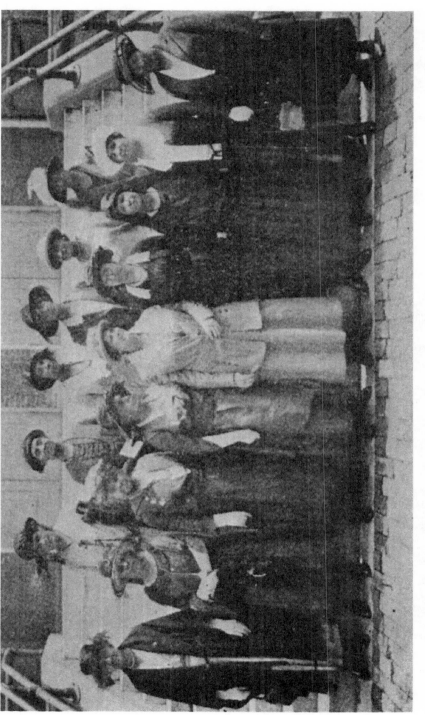

In 1922, Ida Wells-Barnett (front row, third from the left) and members of the National Association of Colored Women met with President Warren Harding to urge him to hasten final action on the Dyer Anti-Lynching Bill, the first of such laws to reach the U.S. Senate. (*The Crisis*, October 1922, p. 260)

Rebecca Latimer Felton (seated) on the steps of Congress with white female political activists in Washington, D.C., after being sworn in as the first woman to serve in the U.S. Senate on November 21, 1922, as a replacement for Thomas E. Watson, who died while in office. (Courtesy of Library of Congress, Prints and Photographs Division)

5

NEW SOUTHERN WOMEN AND THE TRIUMPH OF WHITE SUPREMACY

Whether by insisting stridently on legal protection, or by calling on white men to lynch a suspected black man, or by participating in mob violence, white women came to play powerful roles in the racial and sexual politics of the New South. Following Rebecca Felton's lead, many southern white women engaged in public debates about rape and lynching and organized their protection campaigns to accord with the dominant political fact of white supremacy. From presenting petitions on the floor of the legislature to taking center stage at lynchings, southern white women not only challenged gender restrictions and class assumptions about women's proper public place and role, but also managed to exercise political and racial authority at a time when they had no formal power. In the 1880s and afterwards they proclaimed their political concerns about rape in the press, before state legislatures, and at lynchings. They laid claim to their rights to legal and/or extralegal protection and expressed their desire to move freely without fear of sexual violence. In so doing, they transformed the "problem" of black rape into a discussion about white women's rights.

Southern white women's behavior can be better understood in light of the changes in women's status and the violent power that lynching gave them. As the South experienced rapid industrial, political, and social change, middle-class southern white women began to shed their traditional roles as wives and mothers and to move into the public world of politics. They campaigned for prison reform, temperance, and suffrage. While holding men to traditional standards of male chivalry and honor, they also began to redefine southern womanhood. Some organized for prohibition and participated in mob violence in the name of "home protection" and white supremacy. Others campaigned for suffrage, against convict leasing, for better education, and for tougher rape laws to improve the status of women. Engaging in public debate and protest about these issues, they revealed a "New Southern Woman" who clamored for a public role and sought political power.

No longer the weak and submissive female of the antebellum period who had little choice but to sit at home under the watchful eye of her male protector, the increasingly independent and spirited southern woman questioned societal constraints as she entered into a sexually and racially charged public sphere. Without regard to class or social status, she insisted on her share of privileges in the New South. One major means to this end was to use the threat of black rape to make demands of white men and thereby achieve a modicum of political power.

In the blistering heat of August 1897, Rebecca Felton addressed the annual meeting of the Georgia Agricultural Society on Tybee Island.[1] In her speech, "Woman on the Farm," she unabashedly employed the political lessons she had learned over the last twenty years campaigning for the protection of black female convicts, for prohibition laws, for raising the legal age of consent, and for Populist reform, to make the case for the empowerment and protection of poor farm women. In general, Felton, the radical social reformer, blamed farmers for keeping their wives and daughters in a perpetual state of poverty and repeated her earlier plea for coeducation.[2] But the forceful address she gave that hot summer day was also the beginning of a change in her ideas about how best to protect women from men's transgressions. It brought together the concerns of elite southern white women and poor white women regarding the issues of rape and lynching.

"Why has the crime [rape] assumed such proportions in the years following the war?" Felton asked. The answer, she argued, was not the alleged uncontrollable sexual desire of black men, but in fact southern white men's refusal to provide women with adequate protection in the form of better education, tougher rape laws, prohibition, and honest politics. Hearkening back to themes of male betrayal that had preoccupied her since the Civil War, she argued that the brutal combination of rape and lynching that framed southern politics was, in other words, the direct result of white men's abuse of political power, as well as their inability to make proper use of the church and the courts for the protection and empowerment of white womanhood.

Felton argued that the rape of poor white women by black men was a by-product of white men's corrupt politics and the ongoing economic and political subordination of white women. Using sexually suggestive language, she proclaimed, "With due respect to your politics, I say that when you take the negro into your embrace on election day to control his vote and use liquor to befuddle his understanding and make him believe he is a man and your brother, when you honey snuggle him at the polls and make him familiar with dirty tricks in politics, so long will lynchings prevail, because the cause will grow and increase with every election." In essence, white men's lawlessness and corrupt practices in the form of election fraud and the manipulation and subjugation of black men fed black criminality, and thereby increased the sexual vulnerability of white women. Simply put, black men, enraged by white men's avoidance of punishment for breaking the law and by their unjust treatment at the polls, were more inclined to commit crimes of "theft, rape, and murder." The corollary of this, Felton warned, was that if white men were not manly enough to clean up their politics and provide poor white women with economic opportunity and the legal protection they so desperately needed, then they would have to continue to lynch. "Lynch, a thousand times a week if necessary," she declared.[3] In this context, Felton believed that lynching was yet another sign of white men's failure to provide the South with democratic political practices and its women with protection and basic civil rights.

In highlighting and deploying the image of the "black rapist" in this way, Felton tapped a political vein so provocative and powerful that the editors of the two major newspapers in Georgia, the *Atlanta Journal* and the *Atlanta Constitution*, quickly published parts of her speech on the front pages of their newspapers. Not surprisingly, both editors ignored those sections in which she blamed white men for the problem of rape and declared lynching an unmanly act. Instead, they lauded her as a champion of mob violence and positioned her now as the leading spokeswoman on the question of rape and lynching: " 'Lynch,' Says Mrs. Felton," read the headline in the *Atlanta Journal*, and "Lynch 1,000 Weekly, Declares Mrs. Felton: White Women of the South Must Be Protected from the Ravening Human Beast and Lynching Is Unwritten Law Here," declared the headline in the *Atlanta Constitution*.[4] Taken out of context, Felton's "lynch a thousand times a week" declaration took on new meaning as southerners and northerners, white and black, male and female, read her speech as confirmation of their worst fears about rape and lynching.

Neither the press nor the southern public grasped that Felton's speech had, in fact, been a wholesale indictment of Democratic politics and white men's failures. Instead, white southerners were excited and inspired by the misrepresentation of her argument and embraced Felton as the voice of new southern white womanhood. Her address, now reduced to a slogan, seemed to capture what they persistently defined as the root of southern political problems: black men's uncontrollable sexual desire for white women encouraged by Northern interference. Indeed, southern white men, like the local newspaper editors, only heard what they wanted to hear. Ulla Hardiman of Atlanta wrote to Felton, "I thank you for your speech made at Tybee. It is the sentiment of a true Southern woman, and it reiterates the sentiment of every true southern man. The horrible crimes that have been committed in the South incited by the sentiment of the North and with its approbation, make it necessary for southern men to commit the deeds that they do. We certainly will hang not only a thousand a week, but ten thousand, if necessary, to protect the honor and virtue of our women." Perpetuating the myth of the black rapist and justifying lynching as a means of protecting and honoring white womanhood, he shifted blame to interfering northerners, ignorant black voters, and a handful of overly ambitious southern politicians: "You are perfectly right in stating that we are a little too free in our cordial manner toward the negro voters, filling them full of whiskey on election day, and spurning them during the balance of the year." He, however, refused to accept responsibility. Black men, he reasoned, "know our position; they ought to understand our civil and social rights—and for their own protection they should be wise in refusing to listen to the element of the Southern people who care nothing for the honor and integrity of manhood and womanhood in their politics."[5]

Southern white women, however, heard other things in Felton's speech. Eager to hold their men folk accountable, desperate for proper protection against rape, and determined to maintain independence and freedom, many women expressed their support of Felton's political efforts on behalf of poor white farm women. An anonymous woman from Virginia wrote, "We with your voice may rend the heavens in calling a halt to this political corruption. Don't let your words die, nor sleep, send up the cry of Lamentation for your sisters all over our once beautiful South Land."[6] Mrs.

Fannie H. Williams of Chicago—who had lived in Florida for ten years—after reading Felton's speech in the *New York World*, wrote, "I wish to say that I heartily endorse your views on the subject of the crime of Negroes against white women. . . . It is the duty of white men to those whom God has given them, their greatest blessing, to put a stop [underlined three times in the text] to this awful state of terror and danger in which ample evidence proves we live. Every southern (or northern either) woman should lend their voice to bring about a state of affairs in which we may breathe the breath of life without cowering in terror from the most dreadful threatening dangers."[7] For her, Felton's words were a moral and political call to action that southern white women could not afford to ignore. Female respondents agreed it was necessary to hold white men accountable and to raise their voices for proper protection against black rape, better education, and economic independence.

Of course, not all southern women rushed to support Felton. Marie Louis Myrick, editor of the *Americus-Times-Recorder*, responded to the Tybee Island address by warning the young white women of Georgia to avoid making the same "sad mistake" as Felton in assuming "the political or professional prerogatives of men."[8] Less interested in what Felton had to say about rape and lynching than in the fact that she was engaging politics through public speaking, Myrick condemned Felton for not knowing her place as a woman. Speaking from "personal experience," she advised women to avoid politics unless "impelled by necessity" and warned, "Occupy the sphere properly accorded heaven's best gift to man and just as long as you can, for a public life with its snares and cares is killing, and in the end must bring precious little comfort to a woman. Let our women beware and take care, and not like 'fools rush in where angels fear to tread.'"[9] In a response written almost a year later, Felton insisted that the meeting of the State Agricultural Society at Tybee was "non-political" and that she had "made no mention of politics" in her address.[10] But despite this disclaimer, Myrick was undoubtedly right to suggest that Felton's speech had the potential to serve as a political call to action for white women in the South.

Even in the North, Felton's speech quickly attracted attention. The *Boston Transcript*, for example, picked up Felton's speech and lamented, "We should be sorry to believe that the women of the South would now be foremost in stimulating and developing that tendency to the employment of lynch law, which has already reached a point where it casts a reproach and a blight upon the state."[11] Felton could not ignore northern criticism and what she saw as a gross misinterpretation of her words. In an open letter published in newspapers throughout the South, she reminded readers that she had called for lynching as only a "last resort" and insisted that "my rebuke was intended for the inertness of our pulpits in this crisis; my indignation was expended on the incapacity of our courts, and my contempt was freely expressed for the deficient manhood which could not protect the innocent and helpless." She also stressed again that "rape would be more common and lynching increase" so long as southern politicians continued to "debase" black voters and engage in "political trickery." Lynch law, she argued, was in the same category as crimes against the franchise, "such as registration frauds, ballot box stuffing and false counting," all of which testified to the failure of white men to act lawfully.[12]

While reiterating the basic tenets of her critique of white men in this way, however, Felton also took the opportunity to directly draw upon the powerful image of the "black rapist." Deeply offended by the *Transcript's* lament that southern white women were espousing "fiendish sentiment" and taking the lead in "stimulating and developing the tendency to the employment of lynch law," Felton accused the northern editor of being soft on rape when "committed by his pet and political favorite, the negro" against southern white women. Taking a page from her long-time political rivals, Felton now fully deployed the sexualized discourse of white supremacy. She reasoned, "It is positively unsafe to allow young white women to walk alone on the highways, or to be left at home without male protectors. The brutal lust of the half-civilized gorillas seems to be inflamed to madness—for five lynchings took place in Georgia for the crime of rape in the week preceding my address at Tybee." While she admitted that there "are bad men of the white race," she nevertheless insisted that in the South black men were responsible for 90 percent of rapes against white women. She bemoaned the fact that the editor of the *Boston Transcript* branded as fiends "the women of the South who demand protection for these country homes that courts and pulpits have failed to give them. . . . Where was the word of sympathy for the innocent and helpless victim of such villainy?" In defending her earlier words, then, Felton had begun to back away from her critique of southern manhood, and to suggest that it was, in fact, white northerners and young African Americans who were responsible for the problems of rape and lynching that plagued the southern political landscape. Deploying the now common rhetorical strategy of asking "What if your daughter or wife was raped by a black man?" Felton implied that chivalrous southern white men were justified in their violent actions.[13]

Thus, while Felton had no problem criticizing the white men of the South in her own back yard, she found it much more difficult to do so before a national audience. Felton explained, "There has been injustice to the negro in many cases, but there is no law, human or divine, that forbids the protection of our homes in their innocence and purity, even if it needs the lynchers' rope to do it." Responding to northern criticism, she made clear that when push came to shove her political allegiance lay with the white men of the South, regardless of party affiliations. The "North" should mind its own business and "let us protect our Southern households from violence and outrage without interference or malevolent criticism."[14] If this response was, in part, a product of genuine sentiment, it is also true that Felton was no fool and understood better than most how southern politics worked. The mere suggestion that her opinions reflected Northern sentiments could make her a political outcast in the South; and in the end, she clearly chose to align herself solidly with the white supremacist South.

A year after Felton's Tybee Island speech, the *Wilmington Messenger* resurrected its message in the service of the North Carolina Democratic Party's election campaign.[15] In an attempt to beat back recent political gains made by black and white Republicans and Populists, white Democrats invoked the specter of the black rapist and deployed Felton's speech as a rallying call to disenfranchise black voters. Their efforts culminated in the "Wilmington Race Riot."[16] A witness to the violent power of her words, Felton seized on the moment not as an example of the corrupt politics she had deplored and denounced in her "Women on the Farm" speech, but as an opportunity to reframe her ideas about the protection of poor white women to fit more comfortably with the powerful political discourse of white supremacy.

Alexander Manly, the black editor of the *Wilmington Record*, tried to exploit the crack between white men and women by challenging the *Messenger's* use of Felton's speech. Building on her claim that white, not black, men were ultimately responsible for rape and lynching, Manly accused poor white men of being "careless in the manner of protecting their women" from the "human fiend, be he white or black."[17] He also agreed with Felton that white men were the source of the problem, but following in the tradition of Ida B. Wells he argued that white men raped black women with impunity and held white women partially responsible for lynching. White men's resort to mob violence, he continued, was not a reaction to rape (or, as Felton had earlier claimed, a failure on the part of white men to make proper use of the courts), but a violent response to consensual sexual relationships between white women and black men. He explained, "Our experience among poor white people in the country teaches us that the women of the [white] race are not any more particular in the matter of clandestine meeting with colored men, than are the white men with colored women."[18]

In the years following Wells's exile from the South in 1892, few if any southern African Americans had dared to suggest that white women desired sexual relations with black men. Adding fuel to the fire, Manly warned, "You set yourselves down as a lot of carping hypocrites; in fact, you cry aloud for the virtue of your women, while you seek to destroy the morality of ours. Don't think ever that your women will remain pure while you are debauching ours. You sow the seed—the harvest will come in due time."[19] While Felton had already warned that lynching and election fraud compelled black men to seek revenge against white men by raping white women, Manly made a far more incendiary charge, implying that it was, in fact, the rape of black women by white men that provoked black men to retaliate against southern whites. In effect, Manly sought to flip back the script that white supremacist discourse had earlier inverted. The real problem, he insisted, lay with white men who raped black women and then lynched African Africans who challenged their racial and sexual dominance.

White newspapers, of course, immediately pounced on Manly's editorial: "White Women Slandered: Leading Negro Republican Newspaper Excuses Rapists" read the headline of the North Carolinian.[20] And in the hands of Democrats, the concoction of Manly's and Felton's words together served to whip white North Carolinians into a violent frenzy which led to a two-day massacre that left an unknown number of African Americans dead. Fortunately for Manly he had already left the city before the riot began.

The 1898 Wilmington race riot exposed the tremendous power of Felton's words and forced her once again to articulate publicly where she stood on the political question of rape and lynching. In the twelve months that had passed since she gave her "Women on the Farm" speech, she had been lauded by southern whites, especially white men, as "a true southern woman" and hailed in the southern white press as the leading female voice of the South. Making use of her new prominence, Felton now chose to exploit the Wilmington race riot to further her political advantage. When asked her opinion of Manly's editorial and the Wilmington riot, she said, "When the Negro Manly attributed the crime of rape to intimacy between negro men and white women of the South, the slanderer should be made to fear a lyncher's rope rather than occupy a place in New York newspapers." Revealing a strategic reversal in her own political thinking, she added, "It is the unwritten law in Georgia that the black fiend who destroys a white woman in her home or on the highway, and is identified with proof positive, must die without clergy, judge, or jury."[21] Just a year earlier Felton had insisted that lynching should only be used as a "last resort" and pointed to its spread primarily as evidence of white Southern men's corruption and their failure to implement appropriate measures to protect white women. Now, however (intoxicated by public attention and accolades), she put aside her critique of white southern manhood to fully endorse the idea that black men who raped white women and, indeed, black journalists who dared to question the racial purity of southern white women, "must die without clergy, judge, or jury." No longer a sign of white male failure, lynching, she now suggested, was indeed a proud and honorable part of the traditions of Georgia and the South.

In the aftermath of the Wilmington massacre, Felton would continue to build her reputation as a defender of southern mob violence. When newspapers reported a protest meeting of African Americans at the Cooper Union in New York City, at which Elizabeth Grannis, president of the National Christian League for the Promotion of Purity, denounced the North Carolina riot and, like Manly, called into question the racial purity of southern white womanhood, southerners turned to Felton to counterattack. Targeting Grannis's claim that "white women and white girls of the South are full of colored blood," Felton labeled Grannis a "vile slanderer," guilty of "telling a willful and venomous untruth."[22] Clearly, Felton suggested, Grannis was not a woman worthy of protection, and happily threw her to the wolves: "I ask you to pass her around in southern newspapers, that she may obtain little more of this notorious advertising."[23]

Felton's increasingly clear-cut and opportunistic stance on the issue of rape and lynching did not go uncriticized, even in the South. In December 1898, a month after the Wilmington massacre, Reverend J. B. Hawthorne of the First Baptist Church of Nashville, Tennessee, denounced her views on lynching. "When she exclaims 'Hang a thousand of them!'" he preached, "She represents humanity verging toward the animal and the fiend. She makes us think of a misanthrope to whose soul summer had never come and spring has forever faded. She writes like one whose reason is dethroned by anger and revenge." Newspapers across the South published Hawthorne's sermon under headlines such as "Takes Mrs. Felton to Task for Speech: Dr. Hawthorne Criticizes the Lady's Advocacy of Mob Law."[24] Notorious for her scathing letters, Felton's defensive response, in which she reframed Dr. Hawthorn's rebuke as "an attack" on southern womanhood, came as no surprise to southern readers. Reiterating the main points of her 1897 address at Tybee, Felton opened fire: "I gave warning at Tybee. I deprecated mob law. I pleaded for more religion in the churches, more promptness in the courthouse, more manhood than the incitement of evil passions in the degraded and vicious; and while Georgians thanked me, I am carried by name into a Nashville pulpit by a slick-haired, slick-tongue, Pecksniffian pulpit blatherskite to be reviled by the enemies of the southern people, because of this earnest defense of my own race and sex of the wives and daughters of southern men in their unprotected rural homes!"[25] In this way, Felton sought to salvage elements of her earlier position, but at the same time she did not back away from her justification of mob violence.

Instead, she sought to portray lynching as a natural response to the horrors of sexual violence, by recounting the rape of a black woman by a black man. "Some years ago on our farm," she explained in one of the little stories that were her rhetorical stock in trade, "a negro girl was assaulted by a negro brute. Her colored grandmother rescued her in her agony and frantic struggles. The father of that girl, himself a negro, pursued the rapist through out the field with blood hounds, and if the county officers had not reached the offender first, he would have died right there without judge or jury. That's the verdict of fatherhood regardless of color, gentlemen!" She was, thus still willing to acknowledge that black women were victims of rape, but now she did so only in order to reinforce the myth of the black rapist. "In Georgia we draw the line around our daughters," she declared, "Stop the crime and lynching will stop!" Hawthorne, she concluded, "allied himself with miscreants." In attacking her, he, like her other critics, Grannis and Manly, had joined "the malicious defamers of southern womanhood."[26]

Clearly, then, 1898 was a turning point. Felton had abandoned the idea of bringing black and white women together under the umbrella of protection as she had sought to do in her earliest forays into prison reform and temperance in the 1880s. Instead, what had begun in the aftermath of the Civil War as a campaign to protect both white and black women from white men's sexual behavior now quickly gave way to a movement committed solely to the defense of white womanhood against the perceived threat of black rape. Up until this point Felton consistently maintained that all southern women, regardless of race, class, or status, were worthy of protection and that all men, especially white men, were capable of sexual violence. In their unwillingness to raise the legal age of consent, the white men of Georgia had, after all, made perfectly clear the terms on which they would allow white women to enter the public debate about rape. Felton, however, now accepted the Democratic bargain that demanded unquestioning allegiance to the ideology of white supremacy in order to ensure support for the protection of poor white women. She may have taken one step forward by claiming protection for poor white women against rape by black men, but she took two steps backward in both her refusal to demand protection for black women and, more generally, to hold white men accountable for their sexual crimes.

In Felton's reply to Manly's editorial and the Wilmington massacre, she claimed that the number of lynchings (and thus the number of rapes) in Georgia had decreased by "fifty percent" since she delivered her "Woman on the Farm" speech. Felton's claim suggests that in some small way she still believed her address was a critique of lynching. Even so, she must have known that her "lynch a thousand a week" declaration had done more to justify mob violence than to prevent it. The reality, in fact, was that lynching in Georgia was on the rise. Between 1897 and 1898 mobs lynched a total of twenty men (eighteen black men and two white men), and the total number of lynchings more than doubled between 1889 and 1899. In 1899 alone at least twenty-five black men and one white man were lynched, making it the most deadly year in Georgia's history.[27] And, if Felton's Tybee Island speech had already set the stage for elite white women's entry into the sexual and racial drama of southern politics, then one particular lynching, in the spring of that year, provided the elite women of Georgia with a new opportunity to step into the political spotlight.

According to Georgia newspapers, on the afternoon of April 12, 1899, Sam Hose, a black man, killed his white employer Alfred Cranford, a successful farmer, abused his children, and raped his wife, Mattie. It was reported that the two men had argued in the days before the murder and that Cranford had scolded Hose for "slighting his work." The white press agreed that Hose then murdered Cranford with an axe as he sat eating dinner with his wife and four children. What shocked white readers most, however, was not Hose's deadly assault on Cranford, but the report of his alleged rape of Mattie Cranford. "The poor little woman was forced to submit to the most shameful outrage which one of her sex can suffer," reported the *Constitution*. According to E. D. Sharkey, Alfred's brother-in-law, "Sam Hose assaulted Mrs. Cranford literally within arm's reach of where the brains were oozing from her husband's head," and Alfred's father insisted that Hose had killed his son specifically in order to "outrage his wife."[28] Even worse were the rumors that circulated. In a letter written to Dr. Felton, Wells B. Whitmore went well beyond what any newspaper would have considered publishable: "He carried her helpless body to another room, and there *stripped* her person of every thread and vestige of clothing, there keeping her till time enough had elapsed to permit him to accomplish his fiendish offense twice more and again! And, as to render all still more horrible and horrifying, he was afflicted with loathsome 'S******s' [syphilis]."[29]

The alleged assault on Mattie Cranford whether dished up in vivid details in the local newspapers or whispered behind closed doors and in private letters inspired a ten-day hunt for Hose—accompanied by a predicable crescendo of calls for lynching. As Hose eluded capture, local newspapers continued to recount the details of his alleged crimes, focusing primarily on the rape and the planned lynching. The *Constitution* offered a five-hundred-dollar reward for Hose's capture and explained, "A respectable farmer was murdered, his children were dipped in his blood, and his wife was submitted to an outrage, the nature of which exhausts the powers of the law to properly punish."[30] Indeed, white newspapers were in agreement that upon his capture Hose would be lynched. While the *Atlanta Constitution* simply declared he would be "burned at the stake," the *Atlanta Journal* elaborated a scenario of female honor avenged: "If Hose is caught, he will be brought back to the scene of his crime, face to face with his victim. Mrs. Cranford will be judge and jury and by her verdict death is to be the negro's penalty. She has expressed a desire to dictate the mode of death and manner of torture. Her decision as to how the death penalty is to be paid has not been announced, but it is said that death by fire is her preference."[31] The *Journal* thus invited Mattie Cranford onto the lynching stage not merely as a helpless victim but as an active and powerful participant: judge, jury, and executioner.

In the days preceding the capture and lynching of Hose, Mattie Cranford was not the only white woman asked to participate in the public discussion of the question of how to respond to the dangers of rape. The white press in Atlanta also created space for the voices of other elite southern white women. On Sunday, April 23, the same day that Hose was finally captured and a white mob of thousands brutally tortured and burned him alive, the *Atlanta Constitution* published "a symposium" sponsored by Mrs. Loulie M. Gordon, one of the city's leading social reformers and a WCTU member, on the question "How Shall the Women and the Girls in the Country Districts be Protected?" in which nine white women expressed their views, alongside nine white men.[32]

In keeping with her status as the leading white female voice on the question of rape and protection, Felton's views were the first of the female contributors to appear, following only those of Georgia governor Allen D. Candler's and former governor William J. Northen's. In her comment, Felton reiterated her new position on the issue of lynching. The burden of responsibility, she insisted, now lay with black men, and the Sam Hose case only confirmed this in her judgment. Rape of "helpless white women" placed the black perpetrator "beyond the pale of human mercy." Any "true-hearted husband or father" would happily lynch Hose with no more concern than if he were shooting down a mad dog; indeed, she insisted the dog was "more worthy of sympathy." Only the fear of mob violence, "with no torture too severe and no punishment too swift," she argued, would prevent black men from raping white women. Hose, she concluded, "may as well get ready to die."

Not all the participants in the symposium agreed with Felton on the question of lynching, however. Several women argued, as Felton herself once had, that mob violence was part of the problem. Thus, L. A. Romare, wife of Paul Romare, the president of the Atlanta National Bank and a WCTU member, worried, "The cry of 'vengeance' echoes from city to forest—from mountain to seaboard—slow torture, death, destruction are the watchwords of the hour, and are the incentives that have urged men through brake and forest, lake and swamp, heedless of self or self-preservation, if only the guilty wretched is caught at last. But what will this hot fury avail? Nothing but the stirring of a deeper strife, and the gratification of a passionate revenge."[33] Mary E. Bryan, a journalist and popular fiction writer, challenged Felton's claim that fear would deter would-be rapists: "Fear is not a salutary or lasting prevention of evil. To inflict torture and cruel death as a penalty for brutish crimes is to imitate the negro in barbarism and to develop the instinct of savagery that underlies all our civilization." Referencing Edgar Allen Poe's "The Demon of the Perverse," she concluded that the punishment of lynching would do more to excite and provoke the "evil soul" than to subdue it.[34] Annie E. Johnson, president of Georgia Federation of Clubs, also argued against mob violence: "Let the laws be strong and vigorously, but justly, enforced, and fear will go far to prevent crime."[35] Loulie Gordon, the organizer of the symposium, similarly avoided calling for lynching as a remedy and instead suggested the creation of a legislative fund to finance "an up-to-date, well equipped sufficient military force" to police and safeguard rural communities. Bryan and Sallie Chase Patillo, president of the Atlanta Woman's Club, also suggested stronger police enforcement, militia protection, and vigilante committees.[36] Bryan even recommended "colonization" of African Americans "either in Africa or in some portion of this country set apart for him as the Indian Territory is reserved for the Indians."

Regardless of how they came down on the question of lynching, however, what did unite the female participants in the symposium was their belief that women themselves had a role to play in their own protection. Several brazenly declared that women were the best defenders against rape and should take up arms to protect themselves. Mrs. W. Y. Atkinson, a leading social reformer and the wife of former governor William Y. Atkinson, suggested, "Let women who live in the rural districts learn to use firearms and be ready in any emergency to defend themselves and their homes either in the presence or in the absence of fathers or husbands. The fact that they can shoot will be circulated throughout their neighborhood and will be a check on 'brutes with crime in their blood.'"[37] Mrs. John C. Reed, wife of an Atlanta attorney and Klansman, also recommended that women be trained in the use of firearms: "They must become expert with the pistol, which they must buckle to their side, and the state should pay to every woman who lays her assailant dead at her feet a large reward, and for the assailant, death sure quick and terrible should be the unfailing penalty."[38]

Two male participants in the symposium, former Governor William Northen and Georgia Inspector General William Obear, also advocated arming women. Northen explained, "What I shall say may seem radical and revolutionary, but the time has come for heroic action, and we dare not hesitate at any demands that promise security." After suggesting that homes "be made miniature arsenals" and women "be allowed to carry weapons upon their person, concealed, if so desired," he declared, "An occasional Negro lying dead in the back yard shot by a brave woman in defense of her honor, will do more to stop this awful crime than all the lynchings that may occur in a year."[39] Unlike the women who called for armed self-defense, Northen placed limitations on when women should be allowed to participate in their own defense and maintained that the male "master of the house," when present, was fully capable of protecting the purity of white womanhood. Inspector Obear's response was not very different from the ex-governor's when he proposed, "Women may *assist* in their own protection by becoming familiar with the use of fire arms and having them at hand when the *occasion* demands."[40]

None of the male participants in the symposium suggested lynching as a remedy. In fact, during his two terms as governor beginning in 1890, Northen had spoken out regularly against mob violence. Under his leadership the state legislature in 1893 passed a law that sought to punish mob members, and required sheriffs to organize posses if necessary to protect the accused. Northen had also on several occasions deployed the state militia to thwart planned lynchings.[41] Just a month before the Hose affair, then governor Allen Candler had, in a similar vein, issued a statement denouncing the lynchings of five black men in Palmetto accused of arson as "inexcusable," and offered a reward for the apprehension of the lynchers.[42] As all the men who participated in the symposium were Democratic politicians, legal officials, or military officers sworn to uphold the law, they may have been more inclined to support legal remedies. More importantly, they saw mob violence as a threat to civic order and, of course, to their own legal and political authority. For these reasons, they called for a range of preventive measures that included strong legislation, organized militias, patrol of rural areas, and speedy trials.

While many of the women participants supported such measures, they were, however, for the most part united in their belief that white men had failed in their manly duties. "The state of affairs existing in this country must be lamentable when women are called upon to discuss how they can

protect themselves against brutes, and in many instances men of the country must be induced by the offer of large rewards to arrest their assailants,"
declared Atkinson. "Who makes the state?" Romare asked sarcastically. "It
is not the hard working unselfish mother. . . . Only one-half of creation has
the right to legislate or decide, no matter how grave the question or far-
reaching its result." In statements such as this it is possible to detect the be-
ginnings of an argument for white women's suffrage. If male voters had
failed to implement measures to address "the state of affairs existing" in the
South, then perhaps it was time for white women to arm themselves not
only with guns, but also with the ballot. Certainly, in general, the call for
white women to participate in their own protection had opened up a space
in which the racial and sexual politics of the New South could be used to
legitimize and support a new and politically powerful female voice.

This was the voice of the New Southern Woman which Felton had, in
many ways, prefigured. She deployed the political discourse of protection to push for social reform and to demand rights not just for herself,
but for lower-class white women as well. The details varied—some
southern women argued for armed self-defense, some for a reallocation
of the state's resources, and some like Romare and Felton specifically criticized men's use of the franchise. Like Felton, they were often oblivious
to the requirements of consistency, but on one point they held fast: white
women needed more power. As a group, they were both cause and consequence of a climate of greater public approbation for women's political
presence. Whereas in 1886, the editor of the *Atlanta Constitution* refused
to print a WCTU petition calling on the legislature to raise the legal age
of consent, by 1899 he was actively soliciting white women's opinions
about rape. And, as long as they were willing to define the problem primarily in terms of the need to protect white women from black rapists,
the *Constitution* happily published their views and suggestions.

Even as the space to publicly articulate their views widened, of course,
the issue of lynching remained a controversial one. Indeed, in the aftermath of Sam Hose's death, the savagery of his lynching brought out some
responses stronger in their abhorrence of the act than those published
earlier. Under the heading "A Woman's Protest," the *Constitution* printed
a letter written by Eliza E. Mell, the State Historian for the Alabama division of the Daughters of the American Revolution and wife of Patrick
Hues Mell, who described herself, to the dismay of some, as "a southern

woman, a native Georgian, a Daughter of the Confederacy."[43] Her declaration is worth quoting at length:

> Permit me, as a club woman, to express my utter horror and detestation of the awful crime committed by those parties who mutilated, tortured and burned alive Sam Hose. . . . I blush with shame for my native state. The negro should have been given the severest punishment of the law, but nothing short of the barbarity of a savage could justify such treatment as was given him. While reading the account my soul so burned within me to think that such deeds should be said to be necessary for the honor of southern women, that I write under the influence of strong emotion to urge the Georgia federation, which stands for what is best and noblest in the women of the grand ole state, to make a public protest, as solemn and strong as it can be made, against such terrible deeds. I believe that men will continue to commit these crimes in our name until we rise up in indignant protest. Woman's influence can do more than law or religion to change public opinion and put an end to such brutal violence.[44]

Implicit in Mell's argument that white women possessed the power to end lynching was the unstated belief that they also perpetuated mob violence. Challenging the idea that lynching was "necessary for the honor of southern women," she articulated an anti-lynching argument that would not gain currency among southern white women until 1930, when Jessie Daniel Ames founded the Association of Southern Women for the Prevention of Lynching (ASWPL).[45] While Annie Johnson, President of the Georgia Federation of Clubs, had herself argued against lynching in Gordon's symposium, the Federation chose to ignore Mell's plea that they use their influence to make a "public" and "powerful protest" against lynching. The fact was that in 1899 Mell's "Protest" placed her among a tiny minority of southern white women. Indeed, if public debates over the issue of protection had increasingly opened up new space for political participation by elite white women, then for many other white women all over the South the practice and rituals of lynching itself had created an arena in which they were newly able to claim and occupy positions of public authority and power.

Ladies Who Lynch

In parallel with the efforts of elite figures such as Rebecca Felton, from the 1880s ordinary white women aggressively crafted their own politics of protection: reporting rape, identifying alleged assailants, inciting crowds, directing mobs, providing fuel for and lighting execution pyres, shooting into corpses, and scavenging for souvenirs afterwards. In so doing, they expressed their commitment to white supremacy and made clear their violent determination to acquire and maintain the gendered privileges of whiteness in the New South. Despite the masculine ideology of lynching that pictured white men as manly protectors, white women's participation in mob violence countered the image of passive and weak southern womanhood that lynching ideology sought to convey. To suggest that white women were unable to participate "directly in the torture" and that their efforts really only reinforced the intentions of white men is to ignore the question of how and why white women involved themselves in lynchings in the New South.[46] Nor can their activities simply be divided into the categories of directors of white male "action" or marginal and "ambivalent" participants.[47] The sense of power that came with mob violence allowed a woman to play several roles on the stage of lynching. Whether she performed the part of the "Fair Maiden violated and avenged," or a "Lady Macbeth" who prodded and provoked the deadly act, the female participant was not simply an object of chivalry, but a powerful new woman invested in both white supremacy and women's rights.[48]

At the time, white women's participation in mob violence was widely recognized. It both bolstered justifications of lynching and informed anti-lynching arguments. For southern white newspapers it dramatized racial solidarity, provided a semblance of law and order, and legitimized the mob's brutal actions. Highlighting white women's presence, white southern newspapers unintentionally revealed the limits of a vision of social order that sought to keep white women and African Americans in their respective places, passive and dependent. In the black press, the reportage of white women's participation reinforced arguments that southern mob violence was a barbaric and uncivilized crime that degraded humanity. In particular, white women's ritualized role in identifying the mob's victim and dictating the kinds of torture to be inflicted on him gave anti-lynching activists ammunition against mob violence and also provided them with a target for reform. Often depicted in the black press as the most vicious participants at lynchings and as key instigators, white women were seen as central to the effort to end lynching. After all, if anti-lynching advocates could reach the women who triggered and encouraged mob violence and who were perceived as more likely to be swayed than men, they would surely have a chance of achieving their goals. Together, then, the white southern press and black newspapers exposed to public view a new southern woman who was playing a central role in the politics of southern horrors.

In the summer of 1887, the *Atlanta Constitution* reported that Mrs. Sarah Bush, a "respectable lady" in Dekalb County, was allegedly raped by Reuben Hudson, who was described as "almost black," about five feet ten inches tall, one hundred and eighty pounds, and "repulsive in the extreme." According to the *Constitution*, Sarah Bush had given her husband "a most accurate description of the negro," making possible his capture the following day in the nearby town of Covington. When the posse "of half a hundred of Dekalb's most sturdy and law-abiding farmers" brought Hudson back to Redan, they were greeted by a crowd of white men shouting, "Kill him! Hang him! Shoot him!" The *Constitution* explained, "EVERY MAN OF THEM HAD A MOTHER, WIFE OR SISTER" and they were determined to "see that the outrage heaped upon a defenseless lady was revenged." As the mob was preparing to lynch Hudson on the spot, a gray-bearded man cried out, "Boys, this won't do. You don't know whether that is the right negro or not." The mob's authority, he reasoned, depended upon proper identification: "Let's send for Mrs. Bush, and let her see him and say whether he is the man or not." The mob, as the story reported, realized there was "justice in the course suggested" and sent a Mr. Floyd to fetch Sarah Bush.

In less than twenty minutes Floyd returned with the twenty-seven-year-old Sarah Bush, who was described as "quite frail"—only five feet tall, eighty-seven pounds, and "very pale." The mob fell silent as Hudson was pushed forward for Sarah Bush to identify. After she had looked "carefully at the Negro," Floyd asked, "Is that the man, Mrs. Bush?" Without hesitation she declared, "Yes, that is him." Not fully satisfied with her answer, Floyd pressed, "Are you quite sure that you are not mistaken? Remember, the man's life hangs on your answer." Underscoring Sarah Bush's lethal power, Floyd, like the "old gentleman" who had insisted on her identification, sought to bring a semblance of legality to the mob's actions. In the end, however, Mrs. Bush held the power of life and death over the accused. "Yes, are you certain?" added her husband. To this, Sarah Bush responded indignantly, "Am I certain? Do you think I could have passed through such an ordeal and ever forget that man?" With her index finger pointed directly at Hudson, she testified, "Every feature is indelibly photographed upon my mind that this is the man. That is him, before God!" Having sworn before God and in the presence of the mob that Hudson had raped her, Sarah Bush both legitimized the lynching and staked her claim as a white woman worthy of protection. "Then that's enough!" confirmed Mr. Bush as he darted toward Hudson and the mob roared, "Burn him!" Again Floyd asked the men to restrain themselves and deferred to Sarah Bush, "What shall we do with him?" She directed with confidence, "He choked me, choke him." When one man challenged, "No, let us burn him!" Sarah Bush held firm, "No, don't burn him. Hang him!" And as she instructed, Reuben Hudson was then hanged from a nearby tree. According to the *Constitution*, hundreds of "ladies" and children gazed at Hudson's dead body swinging back and forth in the hot summer breeze, and "one old lady" declared, "That's where he ought to have been long ago."[49]

The article concluded with a detailed description of the appealing Sarah Bush: "She has a pretty face. Her eyes are blue and her hair almost jet black. She is quite intelligent and is a general favorite in her neighborhood. She is the mother of a daughter of eight years old." At first glance it seems odd that the article would praise the rape victim's looks and character. Yet the rape/lynch narrative that sought to project an innocent, fragile, and respectable image of white southern womanhood had to be replenished when white women alleged rape by black men. It was even more necessary when the white female victim participated in the lynching of her accused assailant. In spite of the powerful leading role that Sarah Bush played at the lynching, it was her looks and vulnerability, her status as a mother and good neighbor — in other words, her weakness — that was ultimately used to justify the mob's deadly deeds.

Sarah Bush did not tie the rope around Hudson's neck, but she did play an active role in directing the mob's actions by providing an initial description of Hudson, identifying him before the mob, and insisting that he be hanged. Southerners, male and female, black and white, who read the newspaper accounts never doubted the power that Sarah Bush wielded over Hudson. Less obvious, however, was the authority she exercised over the men who lynched him. They were all too eager to do her bidding. By the late 1880s southerners, white and black, began to realize that the practice of lynching invested white women, regardless of class and status, with enormous social and political power. Whether they merely identified their assailant in the presence of the mob or fired bullets into his hanging body, white women seized the opportunity to express a new, powerful image of southern womanhood. They articulated their concerns about sexual violence, claimed their right to protection, and exercised their racial and gender power. By the time of the Wilmington racial massacre and the subsequent Sam Hose lynching, this power was a given, and women's attendance at and avid participation in mob violence were expected.

Southern white women participated in lynchings that were provoked by a variety of crimes—from murder to petty theft, from arson to cussing, from poisoning wells to jostling a white man or woman in the street, from resisting arrest to impudence—but they were most visible at lynchings of black men accused of sexually threatening or assaulting white women and girls. More than any other alleged crime the accusation of rape or attempted rape brought white women and men together at southern lynchings. Not only an expression of racial solidarity, support for and participation in mob violence also brought white women together across class lines on the issue of sexual violence and protection.

According to popular theory, lynchings were supposed to spare the female victim the humiliation of having to appear in court to testify before her alleged assailant, an all male jury, and an audience of courthouse rowdies. In 1893 the Savannah *Morning News* published a letter, "Woman's Plea for Lynching," in which a white woman maintained, "Far rather would any delicate woman see her ravisher go free, than to have to testify against him and bring him to a legal punishment. Yea, far rather would she deliberately end her own life and lay down its burden of shame and disgrace. Let every other crime be dealt with by law—but do you see now why lynchings are the only way to deal with this?"[50] A week after the Sam Hose lynching, a correspondent for the *Atlanta Constitution* similarly argued, "The very thought of a delicate woman being forced to go into the publicity of a court and there detail her awful wrongs in the presence of the brute who had inflicted upon her a fate worse than death, is well calculated to dethrone the reason of her male relatives and friends."[51]

Lynching, of course, saved a woman from having to submit to questions about her sexual past. It assured a white woman who may have lied that she would never have to answer to contradictory evidence, and it guaranteed a guilty verdict. No doubt for some women, especially poor white women whose rape cases sometimes were thrown out of the legal system, their presence and participation at lynchings presented an opportunity to see "justice meted out" on their own terms.

A white woman not only had the power to initiate mob action by charging rape; once the process had been set in motion and a suspect captured, she also had the power to end his life by identifying him as the perpetrator. Conclusive evidence was not a requirement. In 1893, for example, a Mrs. White of Shelby County, Tennessee, sentenced to death Richard Neal, a black man whom she claimed had raped her: "I think he is the man. I am almost certain of it. If he isn't the man he is exactly like him."[52] The mob lynched him anyway. Uncertain identification hardly registered: after all, if he was not the same black man, then he was "exactly like him"—close enough—and that was sufficient. Similarly, when a widow allegedly raped by Paul Jones outside of Macon, Georgia, in 1919 could identify him only by the "blood marks" that she claimed she made on his clothing, it was more than enough to compel a mob of over a thousand white men and women to shoot, drag, and burn his body.[53]

Of course, there were cases in which the mob exerted powerful influence. For example, the mob that burned Lloyd Clay alive in Vicksburg, Mississippi, in the summer of 1919 insisted that his alleged rape victim, Miss Hattie Hudson, first identify him. This single "working girl," however, had on two separate occasions failed to pick Clay out of a police lineup. Despite her initial doubt when brought before the mob, she eventually told the mob what they wanted to hear: "that he was the guilty one."[54] One female member of the mob explained that Hudson's identification "was proof to the minds of most people of the identity of the brute," and reasoned, "Could our fathers, husbands and brothers take a chance on this man's life?" The *Chicago Defender* suggested the coercion that was at work: "Fearing bodily harm might be done her should she fail to accede to the demands of the mad mob, with a response hardly audible she said, 'I think he is the man.'" The *Defender* reported that after the lynching the young woman exclaimed, "It is terrible. I am sorry but they forced me to say he was the man"; the *Vicksburg Evening Post*, on the other hand, quoted her as saying, "It is terrible, but I'm not sorry. For the sake of other girls and women I'm glad."[55]

Regardless of whether Hattie Hudson was, in fact, ambivalent about her role, other women in the mob were sure in their determination to see Clay lynched. When his naked body, saturated in oil, was suspended from the end of a rope and set afire, "women were seen to shoot revolvers" into his dangling body. When Ida M. Keefe, a prominent white woman, requested that the city cut down the tree in her front yard where Clay had been lynched, both white men and women defended the lynching and declared the tree a monument to southern white manhood. "Madam," said one man, "the tree is a monument to the spirit of manhood of this community who will not tolerate crimes against their women folks. What was done here last night was done for you and for every woman and girl in Warren County." Emily P. Shaw of Vicksburg agreed that the tree was "a monument to our young manhood and we women and girls should stand behind men in a thing like this." She also defended women's participation in the lynching: "The day has passed when a woman, 'to be a lady,' must stay behind closed doors. There are times when she should come forth and she is none the less a lady for doing so."[56]

If identifying their supposed assailant before the mob was participation enough for some women, others chose to go further. As already seen from the case of Sarah Bush, some women gave specific instructions about the tortures they wanted the mob to use. Others gave the mob a choice. In 1897, Kittie Henderson of North Carolina offered: "You may hang him or burn."[57] In the case of Mattie Cranford, the wife of the murdered man and the alleged rape victim of Sam Hose, instructions to the mob were delivered second hand by her mother. When the mob brought Hose to the home of Cranford's parents for her to identify, it was her mother who met the mob at the front gate and confronted Hose. Mrs. McLeroy explained that her daughter was in no state to identify Hose—"she is almost crazy anyway, and it would drive her mad"—but she conveyed Mattie's request for "a slow burning."[58] The mob, of course, complied.

Far from cowering at the thought of facing their alleged assailants, other women participated directly in their torture, execution, and mutilation. In 1880, for example, Mary Marmon accused Page Wallace, a black man, of rape in Loudon County, Virginia, and identified him before the mob. After he was hanged from a tree, she fired the first bullet into his swinging body.[59] There were also women who chose to stand at the head of a mob in pursuit of an alleged assailant. In the spring of 1900, Miss Annie McIvaine of Belair, Maryland, "swore vengeance" and led the party that lynched Lewis Harris, the black man whom she claimed had attempted to assault her.[60] "With her disheveled hair flying loosely in the driving rain, and with a pistol clutched in her right hand," McIvaine directed the mob of two hundred white men who had dragged the man from his cell to a nearby tree, where he supposedly confessed his crime and "forgave" the mob. The local newspaper blared in headlines that "His Victim Heads the Mob" and excitedly described her: "With her arms crossed [she] stood on the curb in the rain, and watched with relentless eyes the struggles of the wretched negro as the men hauled him up to the limb of the tree." The *Morning Herald* reported, "She brandished a pistol in the air and swore vengeance on the negro the very moment she could catch sight of him."[61] The paper was, however, sure to note that McIvaine had left the scene before the lynching took place. This was because by around 1900, white southern newspapers were committed to protecting members of a mob from criminal prosecution. In general this meant they became less likely to highlight the female victim's participation. Such an erasure had as much to do with protecting participants from the law as with preserving the image of dependent southern womanhood.

Yet, despite the newfound reluctance of the southern white press to highlight women's public participation, women continued to speak out about their actions. The morning after Harris was hanged and his body was riddled with bullets, for example, the *American* interviewed McIvaine and reported she seemed "overjoyed that her assailant had been lynched, which she thought too good for him." In recounting the alleged assault, she highlighted her ability to fend for herself, thereby also challenging the idea that as a single white woman she needed manly protection. "His attack upon me was of the most brutal character," she explained, "and I had to fight as hard as I possibly could to keep him from getting the better of me. My throat is sore now, and bears the marks of his fingers where he tried to choke me, but outside of this, and a little nervousness, I feel alright." He had not raped her. Declaring that she "hoped this lesson would be a warning to the negroes in the future," she also wanted people to know she could take care of herself. Although McIvaine's status as a white, single, working woman living on the outskirts of town made her particularly vulnerable to the threat of rape, she explained her determination to live in "her little home near the town, the scene of the assault, preferring to remain there than to go with any of her friends or relatives." She would continue to live alone without male protection because she had proven that she was more than capable of defending herself. And, if she needed white men to administer "justice," she would not let it come at the expense of her independence.

Alleged victims of sexual assault were not the only women to participate in mob violence. Mobs were broad-based, but the widely reported presence of women in them has been generally taken to mean that women were simply bystanders. The evidence suggests otherwise. Female relatives of the injured party often joined male kin in torturing and killing victims. At the 1918 lynching of Jim McIlherron in Estill Springs, Tennessee, two thousand men, women, and children took part. During the single-file procession in which members of the mob were allowed "to look upon" the victim if they promised not to "do violence or spit in his face," a female relative nevertheless "[kicked] him in the ribs and [spat] in his face." Restrained in the interest of decorum, she became "hysterical and [cried] for a pistol" and begged to be the one to kill the man.[62] In 1934, a female relative of Lola Cannidy, who was allegedly raped and murdered by Claude Neal in Marianna, Florida, took advantage of the opportunity presented to her by the mob. When Neal's mutilated corpse was brought to her front door she drove a butcher knife into the dead man's heart. Lola's sister was reported to have shouted that no possible punishment could fit the crime.[63]

As late as 1922 headlines declared, "Woman Lights Torch for Mob Who Burns Colored Man" and "Woman Applies Torch at Southern Lynching.[64] In 1917, Ell Persons, who supposedly confessed to the murder of a young girl, Antoinette Raphal, in Memphis, Tennessee, was burned alive with approval of the victim's mother. Once Parsons's "body was soaked in oil and afterward suspended in midair from the limb of a nearby tree," the mother declared that "she wished Persons to suffer the tortures he dealt to his victim." A torch was then applied his body.[65]

Thousands of white women with no direct relationship to the victims also participated in southern lynchings as a display of racial and gender solidarity, to exercise violent power over African Americans, and to express their desire to move freely without threat of sexual violence. In this sense, mob violence served as a perverse demonstration of the New Woman's desire for authority and autonomy. In the *New York World*'s 1899 report of the lynching of Richard Coleman, who allegedly assaulted and murdered Mrs. Lashbrook, the wife of his white employer in Maysville, Kentucky, women joined the men in dragging and beating Coleman as they led him to the execution pyre. Several women later testified, "They now feel as if they could walk the loneliest country road at midnight without being molested by a white or black man."[66] Interestingly, then, they saw Coleman's death as a warning to all men, regardless of race.

Such a statement again signaled women's desires to be able to move freely through the towns, cities, and countryside of the New South. In 1903, the mob that lynched John Dennis in Greenville, Mississippi, for the alleged rape of a Miss Bishop expressed both the usual concerns of men and women about protecting the sacred home and the desire to travel and move about without fear. The mob of over a hundred white men who "strung up the negro" was cheered on by the "ladies" who viewed the lynching from "the gallery." The ladies were especially pleased when "the negroes were called on to take warning and to see that Southern homes, honor, and virtue must be protected, and that women can walk the streets of Greenville at any time of night."[67]

Some white women were able to use the chaos surrounding lynching as a way to shape male conduct in public and redefine southern manhood. On May 9, 1930, an unidentified woman in "a red dress" led the mob that lynched George Hughes in Sherman, Texas, for allegedly assaulting a white woman. After she had found the local men unwilling to go into the court-room and kidnap Hughes, she lectured them for their "yellowness." Finally, she persuaded a group of teenage boys to enter the courthouse to do their "manly duty." The boys marched around the courthouse, calling for volunteers who had "enough red blood to do something about a nigger who had raped a white woman."[68] Meanwhile, women threw rocks at the militiamen who protected the accused. Eventually men and women together set fire to the courthouse to force Hughes and his protectors out. Hughes, left in a second floor cell, died of smoke inhalation. His dead body was, however, pulled from the burning building to be mutilated and burnt. A pair of "girls" joined two men who tied the corpse to a Ford and dragged it through the African American neighborhood as a warning. Needless to say, not all of the white women in Sherman participated or approved of the lynching; in fact, by 1930 southern white women were speaking out against lynching in large numbers. In a letter to her son, a prominent white woman condemned the mob's actions and expressed her dismay at the reaction of others of her sex: "Saturday afternoon I went down town and the streets were full of country women, apparently gloating over the outcome. One woman in a group of a dozen declared she wished they had burned every 'nigger' in Sherman . . . declared she wished she had been allowed to fire the torch that burned him. It is certainly discouraging."[69]

Even after southern white newspapers began to actively avoid identifying women in mobs, evidence of their involvement still leaked out, espe-

cially when they suffered injuries, were arrested, or were captured in pho-
tos.[70] It was difficult for the southern white press to cover up women's
presence and participation in mobs when they were accidentally injured.
In Knoxville, Tennessee, for example, the newspaper reported that the police and militia who intervened to prevent the lynching of Frank Martin
had wounded two women in the mob, but the press avoided identifying
them by name.[71] In 1918, Rachael Levi was killed and Margaret George
was seriously injured at an attempted lynching in Winston-Salem, North
Carolina. The *Atlanta Independent* described them respectively as "a
young woman bystander" and "a girl spectator."[72] In 1920, the *Atlanta
Constitution* similarly reported that a Mrs. E. T. Cross, an "innocent bystander," was wounded when soldiers and police fired "point blank" into
a lynch mob.[73] Six years later, in Georgetown, Delaware, the daughter of
the county recorder of deeds was gassed by troops dispersing a mob. The
Memphis *Commercial Appeal,* in reporting the incident, tried to down-
play the woman's presence: she had just happened to walk past the courthouse when the gassing began, the story went.[74]

While southern white newspapers increasingly sought to soft-pedal, ignore, and deny white women's participation at lynchings in this way, the
black press, along with northern newspapers and anti-lynching activists,
continued to expose female brutality in southern mobs. By the early twentieth century, opponents of lynching saw that it was necessary not only to
highlight white women's involvement, but also to show that they instigated
and perpetuated mob violence. The white South, the black press argued,
had become so barbarous through lynching that the men were turning the
women into savages. In this regard, black editors followed the lead of Ida B.
Wells and Frederick Douglass, who had highlighted the role of white
women in southern lynching in the early 1890s. Referring to the lynching
of Edward Coy on February 18, 1892, in Texarkana, Arkansas, for example,
Douglass appealed to the public to "think of an American woman in this
year of grace 1892 mingling with a howling mob and with her own hand applying the torch to the fagots around the body of a negro condemned to
death."[75] Two years later, in 1894, R. C. O. Benjamin, an attorney and secretary of the Colored Lawyers National Bar Association, also sought to illus-
trate the depths to which southern white women had sunk by describing
the lynching of Coy: "The torch was about to be applied when a shout went
up, 'Let his victim apply the torch! Let Mrs. Jewell set the fire!' . . . Mrs. Jewell was pale but determined. With a male relative on either side of her she

advanced to where the Negro was chained down. A lighted match was handed her and after applying it to two places on the wretch's body where the kerosene had been poured she stepped away."[76]

Flanked by male relatives, "the pale but determined" Jewell bravely confronted her alleged black assailant. Not only did she identify him as the "rascal" who assaulted her, but also applied a "lighted match" to his kerosene-soaked body. It was Coy, not Jewell, who "quaked" in the presence of the mob. After declaring his innocence, Coy pleaded with Jewell for his life. He understood his fate was literally in her hands. Even with all the markers of dependency—pale white skin, male protectors by her side, a chained black body, and a match lighted for her—Jewell's words and actions showed her to be anything but fragile. The determined look on her face, her bold exchange with Coy, and her willingness to apply the torch to "two places" on his body before walking away branded her as a savage in the black press. Benjamin also recounted the 1892 lynching of Lee Walker: "Two or three white women, accompanied by their escorts, pushed to the front to obtain an unobstructed view, and looked on with astonishing coolness and nonchalance" as Walker was burnt alive.[77] Benjamin's descriptions both complicated and reinforced the patriarchal narrative that imagined white women as weak and in constant need of male protection.

Indeed, it was precisely to show how savage white southerners were that the black press regularly placed emphasis on the barbaric nature of the women's participation in this way.[78] One headline read, "Girls Laugh as Victims Die in Fire."[79] Women in the mobs, another newspaper declared, "were no less eager for the blood of the negroes than the men."[80] In 1929, the *Chicago Defender* reported that women's cheers goaded the mob to the most gruesome acts of torture when they lynched Charley Sheppard in Mississippi for the alleged crime of murdering a white man. The screams of the women in the mob provoked one man, who "leaped atop the pile of wood, straddled [Sheppard's] body and cut his ears off with a pocket knife."[81] More like crazed fans than innocently curious bystanders, the black press repeatedly argued, southern white women encouraged their men folk to indulge in the most brutal tortures. "Think of hundreds of the best citizens," described Francis Grimké, a black descendant of the abolitionist Grimké sisters, "struggling with each other for tickets to witness such a spectacle; think of delicate and refined southern women standing on their porches and waving their handkerchiefs in approval of the burning to death of a human being; think of five thousand people going out on the Holy Sabbath day to witness such a scene, in the same spirit as they would go out to witness the races, having but one thought, but one fear, that they might be too late to see the execution."[82]

Intent on portraying a benighted and backward South, the black press described lynchings as festive events at which both white men and women relished their power. It was often said that leaders "jested and joked with hundreds of men, women, and children, who had gathered to view the gruesome spectacle."[83] Clearly lynchings provided excitement and entertainment in the everyday lives of many white southerners. Children were excused from school, shops and businesses closed, and women abandoned their household chores and shops to view or participate in the southern spectacle.[84] In 1922, the *Chicago Defender* described "a jolly crowd" of men and women at the lynching of Charlie Atkins, a fifteen-year-old boy accused of murder. The Georgia mob of two thousand men and women that burned Atkins alive and riddled his body with over two hundred bullets were described as "merrymakers" who "chatted and laughed with gusto nonchalance" as the boy screamed for mercy.[85] The mob that lynched John Henry Williams in 1921 reportedly danced around the fire that consumed his body. "The fire was lit and a hundred men and women, old and young, grandmothers, among them, joined hands and danced around while the Negro burned. A big dance was held in a barn nearby that evening in celebration of the burning, many people coming by automobile from nearby cities to the gala event," reported the *Washington Eagle*.[86] In 1927, the *Arkansas Gazette* reported the speech that one man made to the mob after they had lynched John Carter in Little Rock: "You women take your babies home and put 'em under the covers. Then come back and everybody can stick around and have a good time."[87] The mob of men and women that lynched George Hughes in 1930 was reported to have sung "Happy Days Are Here Again" as they followed the automobile that dragged his dead body through the black community.[88]

After the turn of the twentieth century, the black press, northern newspapers, and anti-lynching activists portrayed the emergence of a powerful new woman who countered the image of the genteel southern lady. An article in the *Chicago Defender* describing the 1919 lynching of Lloyd Clay in Vicksburg, Mississippi, for the alleged crime of attempted rape noted "the dainty hands of young girls" in the mob "who were seen with guns pointed at the victim, eager for a chance to be a party in furthering [the] gruesome method of cannibalism."[89] Both women and children took part in preparing Clay for the pyre. With Clay's head pinned beneath a man's heel, little children smeared kerosene on his naked body. The *Chicago Defender* published this description: "A woman, taking advantage of the opportunity, saturated his hair with gasoline."[90]

Still maintaining their femininity, these violent participants with their "dainty hands" brought a new dimension to the masculine sport of mob violence. In 1920, one newspaper reported the role played by white women in the lynching of Phillip Gaithers in Effingham County, Georgia. After the mob of men and women had mutilated and saturated Gaithers's body with gasoline, they riddled his burning body with bullets. Four young women "pushed their way through the outer rim of the circle and emptied rifles into the negro."[91] Described as having to "push" their way to the front of the mob, these young women, who had obviously been relegated to the outer edges, made sure their presence was felt. Their actions not only violated older norms of white femininity, but also showed that they possessed the confidence and physical strength to participate in mob violence.[92]

Regardless of their role in mob violence, white women continued to be measured against the ideal of southern womanhood. Whether depicted as the passive ideal or as its aggressive counter image, these women were often portrayed simultaneously as feminine and powerful actors on the stage of lynching. The description in the St. Louis *Argus* of a woman who participated in the 1925 lynching of L. Q. Ivey, a black man accused of raping a white woman, is a case in point: "She seemed to be rather young, yet it is hard to tell about women of her type; strong and healthy, apparently a woman of the country. She walked with a firm even stride. She was beautiful in a way."[93] This woman was a model of the new southern lady. Powerful, yet feminine, she was hardly affected by the brutal tortures performed at southern lynchings.

Adhering to the idea that women were the moral standard-bearers of the race, the *Louisville News*, an African American newspaper, sounded a common theme when it used the issue of lynching to ridicule southern white womanhood: "Next to the disemboweling of a colored woman by a mob some years ago in Mississippi nothing more revolting and discouraging or shocking to the sensibilities of the patriotic Negroes has occurred than the news that a Negro youth was lynched in Arkansas by a mob of 500 persons: 'Many of Whom Were Women.' It staggers the imagination to picture women engaging in the brutal, barbaric pastime of lynching."[94] By highlighting both the lynching of a black woman and white women's participation in mob violence, the editor sought to dispel the dominant myth that white men lynched to protect women. As late as 1930 the Baltimore *Afro-American* continued to emphasize white women's presence at lynchings. Recounting the lynching of Oliver Moore in Tarboro, North Carolina, the newspaper challenged the cherished image of the southern lady with a headline that declared, "WOMEN, CHILDREN TURN LYNCHING INTO PICNIC: White Southern Womanhood Steps Down to Revel at Scene."[95] Undoubtedly, black newspapers were finally succeeding in mocking white southern womanhood. They had cracked the myth of white female frailty by underscoring women's participation in lynchings.

At the same time, however, white women's participation as actors and audience at lynchings had opened up a wider space for them in public and commercial life. If they could lynch, they could do anything. They had faced their worst fears. They had survived the Civil War and the violent politics of Reconstruction and Populism—coming out on the other side strong and confident in their ability to engage the racial and sexual politics of the New South. From demanding legal protection to participating in mob violence, the new southern woman exercised all the privileges of white supremacy to demand women's rights. In this regard, Felton and the women of her generation had set the stage for the next generation of southern white women—a younger cohort that embraced a female modernity in terms not so different from Felton.[96]

In May 1920, Dorothy Hockaday (editor) and Ruth Thomas (reporter), two young women who published an eight-page morning daily in Maysville, Kentucky, witnessed and reported the lynching of Grant Smith. When the two women received a telegram from the Associated Press reporting Smith's capture, they did what many white male reporters of the period would have done—they set out for the scene of the lynching. Afterwards, the women returned to their office, printed their story in the morning daily, and called the major city papers to report the news. Although they behaved no differently than male reporters of the period, newspapers all over the country printed articles regarding the women's coverage of the lynching.[97] Headlines declared: "Girl Editors Who 'Scooped' World on Negro Lynching Tell of Race After Mob" and "Two Girls See Lynching and Print Scoop: Watch Hanging as City Reporters Search for Mob."[98] According to the Louisville *Courier-Journal*, it "probably was the first time a woman reporter 'handled' a Negro lynching." But while the *Courier-Journal* highlighted the women's coverage of the lynching as "a laudable feat," the Cleveland *Advocate*, a black news-paper, criticized the female reporters' coverage and presented them as par-ticipants. The editor declared, "The evidence of the 'brute passion' in even the 'fair sex' is unmistakable, when one reads of the fiendish delight with which two young women raced to the scene of the southern orgy, and of the minute examination they made of the tortured man." The editor opined that "by all traditions" the two women should not have acted as they did. He mocked the image of the genteel southern woman by claiming they should "have been thrown into hysterics, have started powdering their noses—then fainted."[99]

Thomas and Hockaday, like so many other white women who attended southern lynchings, embodied a powerful and independent new southern woman. In an interview with the *Advocate*, the women recounted how, with a male chaperone close at hand, they viewed the lynching from be-hind a clump of bushes where they hid in fear of detection. Once the mob had lynched Smith, the two women, "recovering from their mo-mentary nervousness," came out to inspect the dead man's body. Describ-ing Smith as the "blackest Negro you ever saw," the women twirled his "still twitching" body around and "made notes regarding the intricate man-ner in which the Negro had been strung up."[100] The women's descrip-tion, in contrast to stories written by men of the period, utilized several feminine tropes. By emphasizing their "fear" and need for a male "chap-erone," the women were able to maintain a semblance of femininity. The *Courier-Journal* printed their photographs on the front page of the paper and highlighted their beauty.

Thomas and Hockaday exercised their right to move freely in the pub-lic world of politics and citizen action, yet they were not so different from their predecessors in their embrace of white supremacy. For at least an-other decade they would share the stage with Felton and the social re-formers of the Progressive Era who had made possible southern white women's entry into southern politics. Despite the patriarchal and sexist rhetoric of the black rape of white women and of the lynching mob, white women found their participation in racial violence empowering and essential to the privileges of their womanhood. Their engagement with mob violence can be interpreted as a refusal to live in fear and as an exercise of their power over African Americans. Indeed, white women's involvement in lynching enabled them to redefine their own feminin-ity as robust, lively, and politically active. The various roles played by women—whether actively involved or passively reading about those who were physically present—revealed their desires to obtain and maintain social and political power.

When Felton made her 1897 "Women on the Farm" speech, she predicted not only more lynchings, but also white women's violent participation. She never doubted white women's capacity for brutality. In fact, she counted on it as proof of white men's failure and as a sign of white women's newfound political power and ability to defend themselves in the New South. Following Felton's lead, many white southern women, elite and poor, took the highly ritualized male act of lynching and turned it to their own purpose. They sought revenge, shook off constraints, criticized white manhood, and indulged in brutality. Lynching facilitated a kind of gender solidarity across class lines on the issue of rape and provoked women to enter into politics through a smoke screen of protecting their bodies from assault. In this manner, the barbaric acts of rape and lynching became a path to southern white women's political activism.

6

THE LYNCHING OF BLACK AND WHITE WOMEN

In 1886, almost a decade before initiating her anti-lynching crusade, Ida B. Wells published an article protesting the lynching of Eliza Woods in Jackson, Tennessee, for the alleged poisoning of Mrs. J. P. Wooten: "The only evidence being that the stomach of the dead woman contained arsenic and a box of 'Rough on Rats' was found in this woman's house, who was a cook for the white woman." She could hardly control her outrage after reading that "a mob of 1000 or more men" had dragged Woods from a jail cell and hanged her "from a limb just in front of the courthouse door."[1] She pleaded, "O my God! Can such things be and no justice for it?"[2] Southern whites saw Woods as "a black female devil, who . . . killed an esteemed Christian lady."[3] Woods's bullet-riddled naked body hanging in the Jackson city courthouse yard left little doubt in Wells's mind that neither justice nor chivalry had been present.

From the inception of her crusade, Wells claimed that white hysteria about the rape of white women by black men effectively masked violence against women, black and white. "To justify their own barbarism," she argued, southern white men "assume a chivalry which they do not possess."[4] Lynching, she explained, was not about protecting southern womanhood, but had everything to do with shoring up white men's social and political power. Desperate to control white women's sexual behavior and maintain sexual control over black women, southern white men, reasoned Wells, had created a scapegoat in the figure of the black rapist.

Wells pointed out profound contradictions that lay at the heart of white southerners' justification of lynching: victims of lynching were seldom black men accused of rape, nor were they always men. Women, black and white, were executed by southern mobs. At least one hundred fifty women were lynched and thousands more assaulted by white mobs in the American South between 1880 and 1965, the majority occurring before 1930. Even though women represented a small minority of lynch victims, their stories highlight the violence of white male supremacy and women's desperate challenges to that supremacy.

When Wells herself was threatened with lynching, she brought into focus what the "black rapist" myth had masked: southern white men's violence against women. In her 1895 pamphlet, *A Red Record*, Wells insisted that the lynching of black women was proof that southern mob violence had little if anything to do with protecting women against rape. She reported the lynchings of Mahala Jackson and Louisia Carter in Quincy, Mississippi, and analyzed the combined claims of chivalry and civilization to make her case. According to Wells, the two women were accused of poisoning a well and hanged by a white mob after a coroner's jury had found them innocent. Even a legal acquittal did little to "protect the women from the demands of the Christian white people of that section of the country. In any other land and with any other people, the fact that these two accused persons were women would have pleaded in their favor for protection and fair play, but that had no weight with the Mississippi Christians."[5] Describing the 1893 lynching of Emma Fair for arson, she challenged, "If the Nineteenth Century has shown any advancement upon any lines of human action it is pre-eminently shown in its reverence, respect and protection of its womanhood. But the people of Alabama failed to have any regard for womanhood whatever."[6] Using the very language that white southerners deployed in their justifications for lynching black men, Wells turned the defense of southern chivalry on its head. The accusation of rape, she concluded, could not explain why black women were "put to death with unspeakable savagery."[7] Yet, Wells understood better than most how southern whites transformed black women who challenged white supremacy into "human beasts" unworthy of protection.

Strange Fruit

Between 1880 and 1930 lynch mobs murdered at least 130 black women. Many more were tortured, mutilated, tarred and feathered, shot, burned, stabbed, dragged, whipped, or raped by angry mobs all over the South. The lynching of black women exposes the multiple meanings behind mob violence as well as the ways in which individual women challenged or threatened the emergence of a new southern caste system. Most white southern newspapers that reported the lynchings of black women made every effort to demonize black womanhood and to justify the mob's brutality. To most black southerners, the lynching of black women graphically illustrated the point that black women were afforded no respect, neither political nor personal. Wells, however, noted that black female victims of lynching tended to be women who challenged white supremacy. Those who could afford to, fled the South, but those left behind had few options. Some fought back violently and others sought legal recourse, but neither action guaranteed protection against white violence. Their resistance came at a deadly cost as whites relied more and more on violence as a means of social, political, and economic control.

Between 1890 and 1920 most black women were perceived not as "loving darkies" or protective nursemaids but as dangerous and conniving wenches. The fond memories of "mammy" that southern whites conjured up were one response to the "New Negro Woman" who refused to play the part of the obliging, subservient, self-effacing, loyal servant. Whites idealized their old black mammies of yesterday on the one hand, while demonizing the new independent black woman on the other hand. They retained antebellum notions of the black woman as sexually depraved. The image of the black Jezebel captured the imagination of southern whites and served to justify the ill treatment of black women in general and the race as a whole.

Southern whites began portraying free black women as savage criminal beasts during Reconstruction. As early as 1865 white newspapers were chronicling crime and ignorance among freed people, highlighting any violence and depravity detected among African American women as well as men.[8] Black women, like black men, became targets of white hysteria about black criminality. Indeed, like black men, black female victims of lynching were typically accused of one of two types of crimes: murder or assault against a white person, or arson or theft of white property. When it came to overt aggression, the rules governing racial conduct were clearly drawn and understood: a black person accused of killing a white person, sexually assaulting a white woman, or destroying white-owned property faced a strong chance of being lynched in some communities.[9]

Negative images of black womanhood functioned to justify white mob violence as early as the 1870s, yet the vilification of black female victims of lynching in the white press suggests that when it came to lynching black women, some southern whites needed to be convinced by sensational and manipulative journalism. In the winter of 1878, when a mob lynched Maria Smith and her husband Floyd Smith in Hernando, Mississippi, the *Weekly Clarion* expressed no sympathy for the couple, who had been accused of murdering a six-year-old white girl. "A Righteous Verdict Promptly Executed" read the headline over the article reporting that the child's mother had paid the couple to murder her daughter. The report described the alleged events in detail: "The colored people built a pen in their yard and placed the child in it to starve. Instead of dying in a few days as they intended it should, the little one escaped from its prison, and too weak to walk; crawled about the yard and actually devoured the excrescence [sic] left about the place by the brutal negroes. As the poor child seemed disinclined to die a natural death, the fiends then killed it." Accused of committing "one of the most horrible crimes on record," explained the editor, the couple was taken from local authorities by a group of forty men and hanged from a nearby tree. Making no distinction based on sex, the article described both Maria and Floyd as "fiends" and "negro brutes" to justify the mob's actions.[10]

Even though black women could not rape white women, their lynchings were often portrayed as a means of protecting white womanhood. Indeed, as early as the 1880s reports show how powerfully the terms of rape set the "crime" when white women were the victims. When the Charleston News and Courier reported the lynching of Julia Brandt, a fifteen-year-old black girl, her eighteen-year-old brother Vance Brandt, and sixteen-year-old Joe Barnes for allegedly murdering their white employer, Mrs. Ada Kennedy, a twenty-year-old white woman in Claredon, South Carolina, none of the stories regarding the murder suggested that Kennedy was raped. However, the white press was able to mobilize and manipulate the same images and rhetoric used to justify the lynching of black men accused of raping white women. Under such headings as "Lynching in Clarendon: Three Black Fiends Receive a Well Merited Punishment" the News and Courier applauded the mob's actions.[11] Even the New York Times printed the story under a sensational headline that justified the lynching: "A Terrible Crime Avenged: Three Negroes, One a Woman, Lynched for Murdering a White Woman."[12]

Presuming the ever-present black urge to rape, the white press portrayed white women as innocent, white men as avenging protectors, and black men and women as violent beasts. Kennedy was "intelligent and refined and highly respected by all who knew her," while Julia Brandt was portrayed as a "brute" and a "fiend." It was the particularly gruesome details of Kennedy's death that "enraged and infuriated" the three hundred citizens who participated in the lynchings. Clarendon County white people believed that not only had they robbed and murdered a pregnant white woman, but that they had shown little or no remorse for their actions. According to the local newspaper, Julia and Vance denied their part in the murder, even after Joe "confessed" and investigators allegedly found their clothes stained with blood and bits of brain. Ensuring there would be no sympathy for Julia, the local newspaper reported that it was she who inflicted the horrible lethal blow, decapitating the victim. Accounts of the lynching reported that Vance had cried "Lord have mercy," and Joe had begged to be allowed to pray. Julia, however, refused to pray or ask forgiveness. Demonized and stripped of all signs of femininity, she was portrayed as being just as dangerous if not more so than her male counterparts. In contrast, the "white citizens" who participated in the lynching were portrayed as law-abiding white men committed to protecting white womanhood. The News and Courier reported that "after satisfactory examination" and "due deliberation" a vote was taken as to whether the alleged assailants "should be jailed and await the court or be lynched." Only twenty-three voted for due process. It is unclear whether or not the blacks in attendance were allowed to vote, but according to one report, they "begged the whites to permit them to take the prisoners and burn them alive."[13] This eyewitness description of the lynching promoted the image of barbaric and savage blacks versus a calm, avenging white civilization.[14]

It is worth noting that the lynching of a black woman for a crime less than murder was not commonly accepted or approved by the majority of white southerners in the early 1880s.[15] Without a dead white body to point to, it proved a bit more of a challenge to justify lynching a black woman. Nevertheless, only four months separated the lynching of Julia Brandt from the lynching of Eliza (Ann) Cowan (alias Judith Metts) in the nearby county of Laurens, South Carolina. Cowan, a thirty-five-year-old wife and mother, was murdered for setting fire to the barn of her employer, J. S. Blalock. After Blalock swore a warrant against Cowan, Constable Samuel Gary arrested her and was on his way to the guardhouse when a party of masked men on horseback overtook him. The men dragged Cowan about two hundred yards and hanged her from "a convenient tree." Before her execution she allegedly "confessed that she had set fire to the building of Mr. Blalock for some imaginary offense that he had given her."[16] According to the account published in the New York Times, the lynching took place not far from the spot where two black men were lynched two months earlier for rape. Although the lynching of the "two fiends," explained the *Times*, "was approved by the community," the hanging of Cowan was met with general condemnation.[17] The *Newberry Herald* declared, "The hanging of any person, especially a woman, for an offense of that kind, without law, is a very grave offense and an outrage upon civilization and law. For *one* crime lynching is excusable, if not justifiable; but the hanging of this woman was neither excusable nor justifiable."[18] As Ann Cowan had neither raped nor murdered a white woman, "there was no need to give the terrible warning that vengeance is sure which becomes necessary when women are the subjects of villainous assault."[19]

Almost every newspaper that covered the story expressed outrage, even as they continued to justify lynching black men. The Reverend A. G. Legette, "one of the most prominent ministers in the county," wrote an open letter denouncing the murder and demanding that every effort be made "to bring the parties to justice." Calling white civilization into question, Reverend Legette declared that "the County of Laurens, State of South Carolina, has been disgraced by a deed sufficient to characterize the jungles of Africa, and which ought to bring the brush of shame to the bronze cheek of a Fiji heathen of two centuries ago."[20] The *New York Herald* mocked with headlines declaring "Manly Sport of Lynching" and "Why Not Lynch Babies."[21] And the *News and Courier* declared, "The lynching in Laurens was murder, and it must be taken for granted that no effort will be spared to secure the arrest of the lynchers. A reward for their detection would probably have a good effect. Public sentiment will justify, or at least extenuate, Lynch Law in isolated atrocious cases, but will not submit to mob law for S.C."[22]

The lynching of Harriet Finch, accused of murder in North Carolina in 1885, was another case that did not receive the white community's unanimous approval. The four alleged perpetrators were charged with the triple ax murder of Edward and Sally Finch and their black teenage houseboy, Ephraim Ellington, in July 1885. In September, while awaiting trial in the Pittsboro jail of Chatham County, Harriet Finch, a thirty-year-old wife and mother of two small children, her husband Jerry Finch, John D. Pattishal, and Lee Tyson were taken from their jail cells by a "disguised mob" of approximately one hundred white men and hanged.[23] Of the four victims, only Harriet Finch had her wrist and ankles tied together — "an act of courtesy, on account of her sex," explained the *News and Observer*.[24] "Four Negroes Lynched: Suspected of Murder, but Their Guilt

Not Clearly Established," read the *New York Times* headline on September 30, 1885. A special report from Raleigh declared that a number of white men believed the Negroes were innocent and that leading citizens in the county were condemning the act and demanding "a judicial investigation that will disclose the lynchers and secure their prompt punishment." The editor of the *Chatham Record*, Henry London, who had written an anti-lynching editorial earlier that year, condemned the lynchings as well: "All good citizens regret it now, and we doubt not that most of the misguided men who participated in the lynching will themselves soon regret it. Not only was the hanging of the three men a great outrage, but the lynching of a woman was especially horrible, and we doubt not that her piercing screams and piteous appeals for mercy, as they reverberated on the midnight air, will often be recalled with a shudder of remorse by those who so cruelly put her to death."[25]

While responses varied, it appears that white southerners in the 1880s were less inclined to publicly support the lynching of a black woman who had not committed a deadly assault against a white person, or if there was substantial doubt as to guilt. Whatever factors prevented whites from lynching black women in greater numbers in the 1880s had little influence on the mobs that lynched forty-two black women in the following decade. In 1892 mobs executed an estimated one hundred fifty-five blacks, seven of whom were African American women, the largest number of lynchings in the history of both the South and the nation in one year. Lynching climaxed in this decade as white elites consolidated their power by pulling poorer whites away from Populist allies who included black tenants living the same difficult rural lives.[26] There is no question that black protest and resistance contributed to the upsurge of southern mob violence against African Americans. As more and more black men and women asserted their demands for political, economic, and social justice in the South, the image of blacks in the white mind grew from that of an inferior child to a menacing and dangerous animal. In this context, all African Americans, including women and children, were perceived as potential threats and targets for mob violence.

The defeminizing mythology of monstrous black womanhood had taken hold of the southern imagination by the end of the nineteenth century. In 1891, under the headline "Feast of Human Flesh: The Body of a Child Sold for Meat by an Inhuman Mother," the Louisville *Courier-Journal* ran a story about a black woman who supposedly killed her child, sold her flesh and "called it tender veal." The article went so far as to claim that "one Negro [said] he would be willing to tie a rope around the woman's neck, put the rope over a limb of a tree, pull her just off the ground and carry light wood knots to burn her to death."[27] If blacks were willing to lynch their own women, reasoned this report, one could hardly blame whites for arming themselves against "black fiends" in the shape of women.

As white newspapers intensified their campaign to demonize black women, the "black beast" or "black fiend" took on many additional shapes. She became the "wench" who pushed white women off the sidewalk, the "Mammy" who murdered the white child in her care, the cook who poisoned a white family, the lazy domestic who stole, or even worse, set fire to her employer's property.[28] Portrayed at best as ill-tempered and quarrelsome, at worst as destructive and spiteful, black women were often described as promiscuous, disorderly, and violent women who refused to stay in their place.

Of the forty-two black women lynched in the 1890s, seventeen were linked to the murder of a white person, five to attempted murder, and seven to arson. Nine women were lynched for unknown reasons; the remaining victims were accused of a range of crimes, from stealing a Bible to train wrecking. Even though the majority of victims were accused of violent crimes—often motivated by self-defense—a few women were killed for violating racial codes. A mob of twenty white men murdered Charlotte Morris and her white husband in their home in Jefferson, Louisiana, in 1896 for living as an interracial couple.[29] The mob invaded their bedroom, shot them, chopped their bodies to pieces with axes, and set fire to their home. Others were lynched for trivial violations such as having knowledge of a theft or singing too loudly. A mob in Rome, Tennessee, shot Ballie Crutchfield in the head and threw her lifeless body into Round Lick Creek because her brother took one hundred twenty dollars from a lost wallet he found.[30] Hannah Kearse of Colleton, South Carolina, her son, and her daughter-in-law were beaten to death by a mob in 1895 because they were accused of stealing a Bible and some pulpit furniture from a church.[31]

While the crimes that black women were accused of ranged from theft to murder, at least twelve women were lynched after being accused of poisoning white folks. Poison held a special place in the arsenal of black resistance and in the white imagination, and like witchcraft, was linked to women. Historian Eugene Genovese argues, "From the moment they embarked for the New World, [black women] resorted to poison against the whites, and they continued to practice the art throughout the eighteenth century."[32] Slaveholders were especially apprehensive about poison, although they rarely acknowledged it as a feature of their everyday lives. In 1751, South Carolinians passed a law that prescribed punishment for any black who instructed another "in the knowledge of any poisonous root, plant, herb, or poison whatever, he or she, so offending shall upon conviction thereof suffer death as a felon."[33] In Charleston, a slave woman accused of poisoning a white infant was burned alive with the slave man who had allegedly supplied the poison.[34]

The fear of poisoning by black women did not disappear with the end of slavery. Almost every white middle-class household had a black cook. As cooks, servants, or nursemaids, the relationship between black women and white families was an intimate one. White women depended on black women for domestic services, but feared and resented that dependence. Wells noted this pattern, lamenting in 1894, "No other news goes out to the world save that which stamps us a race of cut-throats, robbers, and lustful wild beasts. So great is Southern hate and prejudice, they legally hung poor little thirteen-year-old Mildrey Brown at Columbia, S.C., Oct. 7th [1892], on circumstantial evidence that she poisoned a white infant. If her guilt had been proven unmistakably, had she been white, Mildrey Brown would never have been hung."[35] Seven months prior to the legal execution of Mildrey Brown, a fifteen-year-old black girl named Ella was lynched in Rayville, Louisiana, for allegedly poisoning the white family for which she worked. "A Horrible Crime Attempted, and Swift Retribution Is Meted Out to the Criminal," declared the *Richland Beacon News*. Ella, the newspaper explained, had poisoned eight white people to obtain revenge on one black man. According to local reports, the young girl "confessed" that she had "become offended" at a colored man, who was also a domestic for the Hemler family, intended to kill him, and "did not much care who else suffered."[36]

Whether black women were falsely or justly accused of poisoning their white employers, white hysteria about black criminality made those accused of poisoning extremely vulnerable to mob violence. In 1903, when Jennie Steers was accused of poisoning a young white girl in Shreveport, Louisiana, she denied the charges. Describing Steers as "one of the most diabolical murderesses that this country has ever known," the local news-

papers transformed Steers, once described as "always so polite and obliging," into a monster and justified the actions of the mob that lynched her.
Steers was accused of putting strychnine in a glass of "malt invigorator" (a
drink used in the prohibition wards as a substitute for beer) that killed
sixteen-year-old Lizzie Dolan, the daughter of her white employers. The
white folks in Shreveport believed that Steers had attempted to kill the
girl on two previous occasions. In the first attempt, Steers supposedly gave
"the little girl some strychnine lemonade, but the evidence of the drug
was so pronounced in it that the young girl refused it." On another occasion it was reported that Steers had tried to lure Lizzie into a rowboat, but
fearing the water, the girl would not board. Jealousy and revenge, claimed
one newspaper, prompted Steers to poison Lizzie. According to "reports
on the street," Steers killed Lizzie because she was engaged to a white
man who had been "intimate with the negress."[37] In an attempt to draw
attention away from the white man implicated in the love triangle, rumors soon circulated that Steers had also played a role in the robbery and
murder of Mrs. Frank Mathews several months earlier.[38]

Clearly, white news accounts were intent on warping Steers's life history to fit conventional portraits of black criminals preying on innocent
white women. "The poisoning was harrowing in the extreme and was
accomplished by strychnine in lemonade by the modern Lucretia Borgia," explained the *Shreveport Times*.[39] Another newspaper reported that
Steers's character was so bad that even the Negroes disliked her. "One
time," explained the reporter, "she became involved in a fight while working in the field and it was a difficult matter to pull her away from the
negress with whom she was fighting." And when she was not fighting or
plotting to kill someone, according to all accounts, she spent her time
outside of a church gambling with men. Steers was portrayed as a woman
ruled by sexual passion and violent tendencies who deserved the mob's
punishment.

Labor disputes between blacks and whites were among the most common reasons for mob violence in the New South.[40] In at least thirty cases
between 1880 and 1930, black women were lynched after violent disputes
with their white employers. Evidence suggests that seven black women retaliated against their employers after having been fired.[41] Their vengeance
ranged from arson to murder. In the summer of 1891, after W. P. Davis
of Crosby, Alabama, discharged Ella Williams, his home burned to the
ground. Davis and his family narrowly escaped and none of the property

was saved. Williams was arrested and allegedly confessed that she had doused the house with kerosene oil and with the help of her husband and another couple, had set fire to the property. A mob of local whites was so outraged it took the four accused, tied them up, and threw them into the Chattahoochee River.[42] In 1902, in Greenwood, South Carolina, Emma and Oliver Wideman allegedly killed their white employer after he had ordered them off his place. When the two were arrested, Emma accused her husband of the murder, while Oliver claimed that it was Emma who had killed William K. Jay.[43] Seven hours after the inquest, on their way to the jailhouse, a "crowd of infuriated friends and neighbors" overtook local officials. Failing to get a confession from either, the mob tied them both to a tree and "literally shot them to pieces."[44]

Often the result of long simmering disputes between employee and employer, violent resistance on the part of black women was not easily ignored. Thirty-five-year-old Rosa Richardson (Rose Carson) was lynched in Elloree, South Carolina, for allegedly beating to death Essie Bell, the twelve-year-old daughter of her white employers. According to most newspaper accounts, "recent trouble with the child's family" had compelled Richardson to murder the girl to "get revenge" or "get vengeance."[45] Both the Columbia *State* and the Charleston *News and Courier* reported there was "no reason assigned for the deed except that the woman was a bad character and had refused to work for Mr. Bell on whose place she lived. On several occasions, it is alleged that she grew dissatisfied and sullen." As to what had caused Richardson's discontent and inspired her violent desire for revenge, none of the newspapers dared to speculate. Instead, local white newspapers vilified her as a woman of "bad character" who had committed "one of the most brutal crimes ever perpetrated." The community, reported local papers, was "composed of steady law abiding citizens, who have always held themselves against mob violence." The article went on: "The actions of the posse it appears, has appeased the horror of the crime. The united sentiment of both races seems to be in favor of the course taken in this case."[46]

Often the employment dispute was about debt, credit, or wages. On Thanksgiving in 1914, Jane Sullivan and her husband Fred were lynched in Byhalia, Mississippi, for allegedly burning the barn of their white employer, J. B. Williams. Newspapers reported that the couple "confessed" to burning the barn in "retaliation for the action of the planter in forcing [them] to surrender a mule which [they] had purchased but had not paid for." The couple's four-year-old daughter Agnes witnessed the lynching.[47] When it came to blacks, destruction of white property courted a lynching. When black women and men violently fought with their employers and mobs decided to take action, little if any regard was given to age, gender, or status. Indeed, the mob that lynched the Sullivans hoped it would serve as a violent lesson to all blacks, young and old, male and female, who dared to challenge white authority. Agnes, along with the thousands of black children who lost their mothers and fathers to lynch mobs, was expected to learn from her parents' mistakes. The hanging bodies of black women—grandmothers, mothers, wives, sisters, and daughters—were deadly reminders to the black community that no one, not even a mother, was safe from the lynch mob.

Not surprisingly, motherhood affected patterns of black women's resistance in the post-emancipation South. Freed from the constraints of slavery, which had allowed black women little if any rights to their children, black women now exercised their parental rights vigorously. From searching for and reuniting with children who had been sold away during slavery, to controlling their own labor, to seeking education for their children and protecting them from abusive employers, many black women asserted their rights as mothers and sought to protect their children from white violence.[48] When black people exercised their familial, marital, and parental prerogatives, they often challenged the black/white power relations embedded in daily work routines.[49] The newly defined familial obligations that came with freedom helped to establish more than just new work arrangements; by the late nineteenth century, they also provided the means by which many African American men and women articulated their resistance to white authority and violence.

In 1904, Marie Thompson of Shepherdsville County, Kentucky, was accused of murdering John Irvin, her landlord. She was lynched because she refused to "cringe" before his insults and dared to protect her child. On the day that Thompson allegedly murdered Irvin, she had been working in her vegetable garden. Irvin approached her son and demanded the return of a pair of pliers that he had lent the family. The child claimed that he had previously returned the pliers. Irvin then accused the young boy of stealing the pliers, verbally abused him, and kicked him in the back several times. Few southerners of that era, black or white, would have been surprised that Irvin had used physical violence to reprimand the child. White farmers, unable or unwilling to renounce the free-handed discipline of the antebellum plantation, whipped, shot, and killed thousands of blacks who argued with them over crop settlements, wages, and labor contracts, or simply refused to display sufficient deference.[50] African Americans resisted employers' abuse in several ways: they reported abusive employers to local officials; many packed up their belongings and moved away; and others retaliated by fighting violence with violence. But African Americans who turned against their white employers risked massive retribution.

After Irvin had verbally and physically abused her child, Thompson confronted him, and the two argued. Irvin demanded that Thompson "get off his place." Thompson claimed that she turned to leave, but intentionally walked slowly. Evidently her simple act of resistance intensified Irvin's anger. According to Thompson, he attacked her from behind with a knife. The two struggled and Thompson, a woman weighing 255 pounds, got the better of Irvin and cut his throat. Understanding the deadly consequence of her deed, Thompson sold her horse and furniture to neighbors and was preparing to flee the county when she was arrested.[51] The same day that the Courier-Journal published the story regarding Irvin's death, an armed band of some dozen white men surrounded the jail and made their first attempt to lynch Thompson. While the mob was trying to break into the jail, a group of armed African American men arrived to protect Thompson. The two groups exchanged gunfire, and eventually the white mob retreated. The black men dispersed when deputies assured them that local authorities would protect Thompson.

Two hours later, fifty white men returned to the jail. They dragged Thompson from her cell with a rope tied around her neck. After begging for mercy, she began fighting the mob. The men overpowered Thompson, then placed a rope around her neck and threw it over the branch of a tree. Thompson continued to fight. With her feet several inches off the ground, she grabbed one of the men by the collar, jerked a knife from his hands, and cut the rope that was choking her. When her feet hit the ground, she tried to run. The mob fired over a hundred shots at Thompson, and when she finally fell, they cheered. Marie Thompson did not die until the next evening in the Shepherdsville jail. On her deathbed, Thompson confided in her doctor, "I didn't want to kill him [Irvin], but wanted to pay him back for what he had done to me and my boy."[52] Marie Thompson's defense of herself and her son offers a clear view of how black family members in the postbellum South were prepared to protect their own from the physical violence integral to whites' assumed power over them.

Black female victims of extralegal violence were most often poor and economically vulnerable. They were sharecroppers, domestics, widows, mothers, sisters, and dependent daughters. In some cases, women were single heads of households and supported themselves and their families with various kinds of labor, such as nursing white infants, taking in washing and sewing, and serving as cooks and domestics for white families. As in Marie Thompson's case, her status as a young black single mother in the sharecropping South meant she was extremely poor.[53] Certainly, Thompson was outraged when Irvin evicted her from his property. In a matter of seconds she had lost her home, her annual income, and her dignity. Angry and desperate, Thompson, like so many other poor black women who had suffered the abuses of their employers, struck back.

While the overwhelming majority of black women lynched were poor, a few of higher economic and social status also lost their lives to lynch mobs because they were members of economically successful households. Dora Baker, along with several members of her family, died when a mob burned her house in 1898 because her father was appointed postmaster of Lake City, South Carolina.[54] The daughters of Ben Pettigrew were hanged from an oak tree and set on fire in 1911 because the family owned a successful cotton farm in Savannah, Tennessee.[55] In the sharecropping South, the economic prosperity of a black family challenged white racism. And because success was dependent on the labor of all members of the household, it was not uncommon for mobs to attack entire families to erase the possibility of any black security.

Because most black female victims of lynching were poor, it comes as no surprise that some had participated in illicit commerce to support themselves and their families. Some ran brothels and "blind tigers," where patrons engaged in illegal activities such as gambling and drinking. Black women in the criminal underworld became victims of mob violence not because whites were particularly concerned about their moral behavior, but because they challenged and resisted the authority of white police officers. In some of these cases black women were reacting to the excessive and often brutal physical force that officers tended to use against African Americans; in other cases they were simply making every effort to resist arrest. At least eleven lynched black women were accused of assaulting or murdering an officer of the law.[56] In 1911, Laura Nelson of Okemah, Oklahoma, shot and killed a deputy sheriff who tried to enter her home to search for stolen goods. A mob of white men hanged the woman and her fourteen-year-old son from a bridge.[57] In response to a letter from the NAACP, the governor of Oklahoma explained that while there "was no justification for this lynching," one could not ignore that "an officer in the discharge of his sworn duty was wantonly shot to death by this woman and her son."[58]

When the local police chief of Monticello, Georgia, came to the home of Daniel and Matilda Barber to arrest them on a bootlegging charge in 1915, Matilda was shot and killed by the officer when members of the family allegedly resisted arrest. The Barber children then severely beat the officer who had shot Matilda. After police subdued and arrested the Barbers, some two hundred enraged whites stormed the jail and dragged the four prisoners to a tree in the very center of the black district. With only one rope the mob hanged the entire family (Dan Barber, his two daughters Eula and Ella, and his son Jessie) one by one and riddled their bodies with bullets. The lynching of the Barber family, reported the *Eatonton Messenger*, "will cause others to be a little more considerate of the lives of others; and especially officers of the law going about the discharge of their duty."[59] The majority of newspapers, North and South, however, denounced the lynchings as particularly vicious and the governor ordered an investigation and offered a five-hundred-dollar reward for the arrest and capture of the first five members of the mob. The *New York Evening Post* declared, "From vengeance on supposed enemies of society it has come to the hanging of women. Further than this it can not go, unless it takes to stringing up negro school children."[60]

African American women were also lynched for defending themselves against white men's sexual assaults. Belle Hathaway of Hamilton, Georgia, and Alma and Maggie House of Shubuta, Mississippi, were lynched along with the black men who sought to protect them because they dared to defend themselves against white men's sexual assault.[61] In 1914, Marie Scott was hanged from a telephone cable by a mob of three hundred masked men in Wagoner, Okalahoma, for killing Lemuel Pearce, a white man who had broken into her home and raped her.[62] In 1923, Ada Robertson of Beaver Slide, Georgia, was charged with shooting Emery Manor, a white man who allegedly "invaded her home" and attempted to assault her. She narrowly escaped the masked white mob that came to lynch her. The local sheriff had moved Robertson to Atlanta for safekeeping several hours earlier when he had received a warning from another prisoner in the jail that a mob was coming for Robertson. The prisoner's wife had written him a letter explaining: "The white folks are talking about lynching that woman they put in there today. If they come in there don't you say one word, because they might kill you. They are coming after her tonight. Please keep quiet for my sake and your sake. Lovingly, Hattie."[63]

A number of employers seduced or raped black female employees who, in return, killed them. The mob that lynched sixteen-year-old Alma and twenty-year-old Maggie House days before Christmas in 1918 did not let the fact that the young girls were pregnant prevent them from placing ropes around their necks, throwing them kicking and screaming over a bridge, and riddling their bodies with bullets. The *Jackson Daily News* reported that the young women along with two black men, fifteen-year-old Andrew Clark and twenty-year-old Major Clark, had plotted and killed their white employer, Dr. E. L. Johnston, a wealthy retired dentist, because of "his trouble with the elder House woman."[64] What those "troubles" were, local newspapers refused to reveal. The NAACP, however, after initiating an investigation of the lynchings, claimed that Dr. Johnston had "seduced" both the young girls; upon learning that Maggie was planning to marry Major Clark, Johnston continued to threaten and harass her, resulting in a violent confrontation between himself and Clark. While the NAACP stopped short of concluding that Clark had murdered Dr. Johnston, the editors of the *Daily Herald* declared:

> Negro women have absolutely no protection from white monsters in the South and when they are violated and degraded by white men the only remedy is that which was used by Major Clark and resulted in his lynching by a mob. The manner of the killing by ambush cannot be excused but if he killed this man for violating and outraging a respectable woman of his race he should have done so openly and in manly fashion and then defend his life to the last ditch and his act would merit the highest praise and he would deserve to be regarded as a martyr to the cause of Negro womanhood.[65]

In reality, however, it proved extremely difficult for black men to protect black women from white men's sexual advances.

Although black men were urged to do more to defend and protect black women against sexual assault, there was little if anything that African

Americans could do to prevent white mobs from raping black female victims before lynching them. In at least two cases, newspapers reported that members of the mob raped their female victims before executing them. Laura Nelson, who was lynched with her son for killing a police officer, was raped before the mob tied a rope around her neck and threw her off a bridge.[66] In December 1915, Cordelia Stevenson's naked body was found hanging from a tree on the outskirts of Columbus, Mississippi. "Woman Raped and Lynched By Mob of Southern White Men" read the headline of the *Chicago Defender*.[67] Even though reports of only these two cases reveal that black women were raped before they were executed, there is fugitive evidence that this may have been more common. A 1938 study of lynching found that "Negro women who attract the attention of lynchers are, regardless of age, invariably mob-raped before being executed."[68]

Even when black women were not raped, they, like black men, were tortured and mutilated. The torture that mobs inflicted on their victims served as reminders that whites were free to exercise complete control over black bodies. The mob that lynched Luther Holbert and his wife in Doddsville, Mississippi, in 1904, mutilated the couple before burning them at the stake. Accused of killing James Eastman, their white employer, the Holberts were tracked through the swamps of Mississippi for three days before being captured. According to the eyewitness account made by the reporter for the *Vicksburg Evening Post*, over a thousand whites attended the lynching. Tied to a tree while the "funeral pyres were being prepared," their fingers and ears were cut off and a large corkscrew was bored into the flesh of their hands, arms, legs, and bodies.[69]

In one of the most brutal lynchings recorded, Mary Turner had her unborn child cut from her womb because she had declared that she would do everything in her power to make sure that the people who had lynched her husband were punished: "Mary Turner, pregnant Black woman, is hanged to a tree, doused with gasoline and motor oil and burned. As she dangled from the rope, a man stepped forward with a pocket knife and ripped open her abdomen in a crude Cesarean operation. Out tumbled the prematurely born child. . . . Two feeble cries it gave—and received for the answer the heel of a stalwart man, as life was ground out of the tiny form."[70] There is evidence that at least seven black women were visibly pregnant when they were lynched. If such brutal lynchings were calculated to make an impression on the black community and underscore its vulnerability, whites succeeded. Nevertheless, many black women continued to resist and refute white power, and were willing to challenge that power despite the grave risks of mob violence and lynching.

Southern White Womanhood Violently Betrayed

The escalation of lynchings functioned as a means of policing the boundaries of race and gender, but it further served to mask white men's violence against white women in the New South. Without question the focus on black men's alleged crimes diverted attention from the crimes of white men and deepened the silence about white men's abuse of women of their own race. In contrast to the newspapers' lurid descriptions of alleged crimes committed by black men against white women, white papers rarely mentioned white men's crimes against women, black or white. As the African American social reformer Nannie H. Burroughs pointed out: "To publish such crimes perpetrated by them upon their own women would deprive their women of that protection of which the Anglo-Saxon delights to boast and which he wants his women to feel secure. . . . Let the thousands of white women whose mouths are shut by pride speak out."[71] If white women were inclined to remain silent about white men's violence, then the bodies of white female victims of lynching spoke volumes.

Moreover, if the violent politics of white supremacy functioned in a small way to bring ordinary white women under the umbrella of extralegal protection, it did little for the white women who refused to live up to the gender and racial expectations that white supremacy demanded. While the threat of black rape may have functioned as a means of keeping southern white women in their place, the spectacle of lynching reminded white women of the dangers lying outside.[72] Indeed, the lynching of black men sometimes incorporated threats aimed at white women who crossed racial boundaries. The mob that lynched Jesse Washington, a black man in Waco, Texas, placed parts of Washington's charred body on the stoop of a "disrespectable" white woman's home as a warning.[73]

Mob violence against white women brought into relief how far some white communities were willing to go to rein in "disorderly" white women's behavior. Anxieties over racial contamination and a threatened revision of class and gender roles surfaced repeatedly in cases of mob violence against white women. Even though the number of white women lynched in the turn-of-the-century South is small in comparison with other groups of victims, these lynching cases, along with the hundreds of cases of mob violence against white women, call attention to southern white men's response to white women who threatened the social order by refusing to play by the rules of race, class, and gender in the New South.

"Disorderly" white females alarmed male intellectuals and politicians in the late nineteenth century.[74] Echoing the narrative of black men who remade themselves as freedmen and were suddenly afflicted with the "disease" of sexual passion, turn-of-the-century white women who asserted new sexual and political identities were reviled both as race traitors and as diseased bodies. Presumed to be capable of spreading racial and political infection in their midst, they seemed to threaten the southern caste system. From the white southern male viewpoint, the advent of the New Southern Woman and her desire for independence and political power proved the need for greater surveillance of white women, especially in a sexual context. Similarly, the emergence of an independent new class of poor white working women, and the middle-class belief that lower-class white women were immoral, fed southern whites' anxieties and made some poor white women vulnerable to mob violence.

The figure of the poor white woman as morally corrupt and as a threat to the social and racial order had deep roots in the antebellum South.[75] Representations of poor women as less worthy of legal protection from physical and sexual violence at the hands of white men had met little resistance before the war.[76] Just as the Civil War and Reconstruction had a tremendous impact on the lives of black women, those events also brought new meaning to the status of ordinary white women in the South.[77] During the pitched battles of Reconstruction, southern white men began surveying more intensely poor white women's sexuality and strictures against interracial sexuality tightened.[78] Prior to Emancipation, relationships between black men and poor white women were often tolerated, but after 1865, interracial relationships between black men and white women threatened the emergence of a segregated system.[79] The postwar policing of interracial sex between black men and white women meant that some poor white women were forced under the umbrella of protection. For instance, in the spring of 1903, over thirty unmasked white men broke into the home of a Mrs. Stephens, a white woman who ran a boardinghouse, and whipped with barbed wire and apple switches her daughters, thirteen-year-old Rebecca and sixteen-year-old Ida, and Joe Shively, a fifty-year-old Negro. The newspaper report explained the motive for the whipping as "local objection to a colored boarder living with a white family."[80] The protection southern white men extended to ordinary white women meant that all white women, regardless of class, would have to live up to the standards of southern womanhood — or suffer the consequences.

This heightened intolerance of racial mixing was marked by an epidemic of violence against white women which lasted throughout the post–Civil War era and well into the early decades of the twentieth century. Unfortunately for lower-class white women, the imposition of protection to preclude interracial sex was never separated from the politics of morality, concerns about poor women's sexuality, and the security of the larger segregated social order. In fact, the new demands for the protection of ordinary white women combined with fears of black rape meant that poor white women who transgressed racial and gender boundaries became targets of mob violence. Under the pretext of protection, lower-class white women who challenged white male supremacy risked being pulled from their beds, stripped naked, flogged, and sometimes even lynched.

There is a long history of community-sanctioned abuse against women who in some way or another have offended their communities' moral sensibilities, going back to the seventeenth century. In the persecution of women as witches, as well as in the dunking of scolds, gagging of women who gossiped or slandered their neighbors, carting of whores, and riding of adulterous women, colonial Americans often publicly and violently punished women who violated established race and gender conventions.[81] In the late nineteenth century, the heyday of southern mob violence, vigilantes, Klansmen, White Caps, regulators, and other nightriders resorting to extralegal violence did not hesitate to chastise white women who did not live up to their roles as paragons of virtue and racial purity. Any white woman who ventured outside the bounds of sexual propriety in the South did so at her own risk and was likely to find herself answering to nightriders. In many southern communities, white women who fell victim to mob violence were brutally whipped, tarred and feathered, and/or violently warned to leave town. Such action against those who behaved in sexually deviant ways was part of a more general process in which dangerous sexualities were identified and disciplined.

The shift from an agrarian to an industrial and urban economy, along with increasing activism among industrial workers and the Populist movement, exacerbated class distinctions and intensified racial tensions. As economic realities prevailed over ideas that relegated women to the domestic sphere, gender roles altered significantly.[82] Although families remained important economic units, their character changed as poverty forced women into wage work. Poor white women began leaving rural communities for cities and towns where they found jobs in factories.[83] Those who were unable to find work in mills and factories had little choice but to labor as domestics or as service workers. Employment that brought poor white women into the public sphere only reinforced the views of whites who perceived them as lacking in morality.

Certainly economic losses, political and social disruptions, and the evolution of a more industrial and urban South imposed new burdens and presented new opportunities to white women. Middle- and upper-class white women seem to have benefited most from the social, political, and economic changes of the New South. They found employment as office workers, clerks in stores, and teachers, and got involved in social reform efforts that encompassed a wide range of activities—temperance, child labor reform, day nurseries, foreign and domestic missions, penal reform, education reform, health care and public health, industrial relations, race relations, and woman's suffrage.

During this period, elite white women took an interest in reforming the behavior of lower-class white women. The moralistic tone of the WCTU was indicative of this shift. It may be no coincidence that mob violence against white women increased just as Progressive Era social reformers sought to establish an apparatus for the social control and moral reform of lower-class white women who defied middle-class standards of sexual propriety.

Progressive Era social reformers were particularly anxious about the growing class of white women who sold sex for a living.[84] By the late nineteenth century, female reformers all over the country were inventing new ways of policing poor white women's sexuality.[85] The emergence of homes for wayward girls and the increasing incarceration of immigrant and poor white women were direct responses to a new generation of "unruly women."[86] In North Carolina several women's organizations petitioned the general assembly to create "a central reformatory where [prostitutes] will be forcibly detained from breaking the moral law and have also an opportunity of reforming under moral conditions." They argued that the failure to create such an institution would allow prostitutes to "spread moral and physical decay among men and girls."[87] Just as social reformers stepped up their efforts to impose middle-class standards of propriety on poor and working-class women in their communities, many southerners came to believe that a "good whipping" or a tarring and feathering could more effectively reform these women's sexual behavior and turn them into ideal working-class daughters, wives, and mothers; that is, sober, thrifty, chaste, and humble Christian women. Social reformers soon learned, however, that many poor white women were not interested in changing their behavior or embracing middle-class standards of sexual propriety or respectability.[88]

Paradoxically, the social reformers' campaigns contributed to an overall intensification in the control of and violence against white women in the South. Mob violence against southern white women accused of sexual deviance was part of white supremacist campaigns to clarify the relationship between depraved blacks and morally superior whites, and to force ordinary white women to accept their status as embodiments of racial purity. In 1885, for example, fifty masked horsemen, described by some as "regulators" and by other as "Ku Kluxers," rode into Dalton, Georgia, and visited five houses suspected of being brothels. After wrecking the homes, they severely whipped the men and women they found. Before leaving town the mob went to the home of Mayor Samuel F. Maddox and delivered a "Notice to Citizens of DALTON," which explained that their objective was to protect "the good people" by ridding the town of thieves, prostitutes, and miscegenationists.[89]

Four years later in Calhoun, Georgia, when a group of self-proclaimed citizens attacked a group of white women accused of prostitution, they also claimed to be protecting the community. The editor of the *Calhoun Times* justified the mob's actions by explaining that the town had been plagued by a "set of lewd women who were leading the youth of this place far from the path of virtue and morality and scattering disease throughout the land."[90] After the grand jury had tried, unsuccessfully, to gather evidence against the women, the group of citizens threatened the women and warned them to leave town. When they stayed put, nightriders forced most of the women to flee by whipping them.[91]

Georgia mobs were not unique; communities all over the South took it upon themselves to police white women's sexual behavior. As one Virginian explained, mob violence in the mountains in the 1890s "started out with the purpose of cleaning up the country and making people behave themselves and do things like they should do. . . . If they found too many different men going to a woman's house after night they would lay for them and whip the woman, and the man too if they weren't afraid that he might be a little too formidable for them."[92] According to historian William

Holmes, from 1887 through 1900 no fewer than 239 episodes of "white-capping" occurred throughout the nation, mainly in the South, and white women accused of sexual immorality and racial transgression were among their victims.[93] White Caps were bands of white men who periodically came forward to police social relations in the southern up-country, in the Midwest, and in frontier communities. Named for the hoods they wore on their night-riding raids, these bands of "up-standing" white community residents terrorized those who deviated from their collective sense of right and wrong. Whether the victim of their masked flogging was an adulter-ous wife, a hard-drinking father, a rapacious businessman, or an ambitious black sharecropper, the object of the White Caps' visit was the same—to enforce the private and public conduct the world of white proprietors like themselves depended on. Mob attacks against white women who were perceived as sexually loose were part of a wider though piecemeal pro-gram to remake lower-class white women into self-disciplined "southern ladies" worthy of protection.

Between 1880 and 1930, whites who took the law into their own hands killed at least twenty-six white women.[94] Over half of the white women executed by southern mobs were lynched between 1880 and 1900.[95] Un-like the hundreds of women who were flogged or tarred and feathered for racial and sexual transgressions, the majority of white women executed by southern mobs were accused of violent crimes. Of those twenty-six known incidents, at least eleven involved women who were accused of murder and one of making violent threats. Of the remaining fourteen, five were executed for unknown reasons, five for moral or sexual transgression, one for strike activity, one for stealing cattle, one for arson, and one for being mistaken as black. Not so different from black female victims of lynching, white women who committed violent crimes were portrayed as unwom-anly and unworthy of female protection. Unlike black women, however, white women were also attacked for moral transgressions such as prostitu-tion and adultery.

White women who committed adultery were not considered to be un-happy wives, but rather as threats to the natural gender hierarchy—their subversion of male authority exposed husbands' failures and wreaked havoc in their communities. "A handful of men forced Mrs. T. J. West and William Dever to pay with their lives the penalty for their sins," began the story in the Louisville *Courier-Journal* on December 30, 1895. West, a forty-year-old mother, was burned to death in her home and Dever was shot as he tried to escape the flames. The couple was allegedly living "in open adultery," and had been warned to leave the county after Dever had killed Mrs. West's husband, Thomas, in self-defense. Prior to the killing of Thomas West, both families had "stood well in the community and were regarded as worthy people," reported the local newspaper. Thomas West was described as a fifty-year-old farmer in "fairly good circumstance." A man of "domestic habits," West seldom left the farm where he lived with his wife and seven children. A fifty-year-old widower, Dever had moved to Marion County from Knoxville, Tennessee, the previous year with his sixteen-year-old daughter, Alma. "Aside from occasional indulgence in liquor," Dever was "looked upon as rather a steady man."

Soon after Dever was found innocent of murder and moved in with Mrs. West, threats were made against the couple and demands that they leave town were issued.[96] On December 28, a mob of white men went to the West house and commanded the couple to come out. When Dever's daughter Alma answered the door, one of the men pulled her from the house and told her "to run for her life if she did not want to be killed." When the couple refused to come out, one member of the mob set fire to the house. As the flames began to consume the small log structure, Dever, a pistol in his hand, dashed out the front door. Shots were fired at him and he fell dead behind a stack of hay. Mrs. West, however, was too afraid to venture over the threshold. She crawled into the family fireplace, where neighbors later found her burnt body.

"Woman Burned to Death. Her Paramour Shot Down as He Fled. HER INFIDELITY THE CAUSE," read the Courier-Journal headlines.[97] According to those who justified the mob's actions, Mrs. West, a mother of seven children, had betrayed her husband and abandoned her family for another man. Her infidelity had not only violated community notions of right and wrong, but had also cost Thomas West his life. It seems, however, that not all members of the community believed Mrs. West's punishment just. Indeed, Mrs. West had been a respected and upstanding member of her community until her husband accused her of adultery. Other than her affair with West, the only other fault that the local newspaper could find with Mrs. West was that "she was far from good looking." A group of "indignant citizens," unconvinced by the mobs' justification, assembled at the courthouse and adopted a resolution in which they "express[ed] their horror of the crime and their determination to use every effort to discover and bring to justice the brutal perpetrators."[98] Even the governor of Kentucky condemned the lynching and declared, "I regard it as the most outrageous and barbarous crime that was ever committed in Kentucky. I shall spare not labor, money nor force to bring its perpetrators to that punishment which they so richly deserve."[99] Apparently Mrs. West's status in the community, as well as the national news coverage, provoked "the good people" of Marion County to speak out publicly against the lynching. Unfortunately for Mrs. West, the white citizens of Marion County who still believed that women who committed adultery threatened white male authority and thus were dangerous to the social order got to her first.

The shooting of Rachel Thomas by a mob of southern white men, also reflected the precarious position in southern society of white women who committed adultery. In the winter of 1901, Wesley Powell and Rachel Thomas were indicted for living in adultery in Oconee County, South Carolina. A mob of white men intent on running them out of town decided to pull the couple's house down, plank by plank. After the mob had torn most of the roof off and knocked the chimney to the ground, the couple emerged from the house, and Rachel Thomas was shot and killed.[100] The fact that Thomas was a fifty-year-old mother of five children did not prevent the mob from taking action against her. Indeed, it seems that her status as a mother who had failed in her domestic responsibilities may have provoked the mob's actions. The outbreaks of white violence against white women who committed adultery were blamed on the actions of white women who had betrayed their husbands and abandoned their duties as wives and mothers. The white men of Marion County, Kentucky, who lynched Mrs. West justified their actions and echoed the rhetoric of purity, domestic protection, and the exclusive right of white men to regulate white women's sexuality, when they declared "HER INFIDELITY THE CAUSE."[101]

Unlike West and Thompson, the majority of white female victims of lynching were usually women on the fringes of southern society who were perceived as menaces in their communities. When Jane Wade and her lover J. R. Dorsey were accused of killing Mary Davis and C. C. Jones in Chattooga County, Georgia, a mob of forty masked citizens took Wade and Dorsey from the jailhouse and hanged them from the limb of a nearby oak tree. According to local newspapers, Jane Wade was a forty-six-year-old woman "of bad character" who was undeserving of protection. By pointing out her failure to adhere to proper gender roles, the local newspaper justified the mob's actions. Undoubtedly, the journalist hoped that his readers would understand that Wade was no "lady." Involved with a man at least twenty years her senior, she was portrayed as a wanton woman who hung around the local bar drinking. While the *Atlanta Constitution* reported that Jane "wept bitterly" when the mob dragged her from the jail cell, the *Walker County Messenger* claimed, "Dorsey was pleading for his life, but Jane was made of sterner stuff and told him that if they were going to hang them, let them hang and be — to them."[102] It is worth noting that there were no attempts in this report to highlight Wade's vulnerability or to suggest that she had any feminine qualities that might have generated sympathy for her. Had the newspaper account stressed female frailty, it would have been difficult to justify the mob's actions, because gender identity based on a white woman's helplessness conferred the right to demand honor and protection.

While white female victims of mob violence varied in age and marital status, most of them were poor and socially isolated. In some cases, the absence of male protectors willing to take responsibility for their misconduct made them targets of mob violence, and in other cases the very presence of men made women vulnerable to lynch mobs. "Four Alleged Bad Characters Brought to Earth" read the headline describing the lynching of Molly Smith and her lover, Abitahl Colston, in Trigg County, Kentucky, in the summer of 1895. The mob pursuing Colston after he had allegedly murdered two white men found him with Molly Smith. The bodies of both were riddled with bullets. Smith was described as Colston's "mistress" and as an "undesirable citizen," and her execution went unchallenged. There was little mourning among "the better class of people," explained the newspaper.[103] Molly Smith, like so many poor white women who associated with criminals or were themselves perceived as criminals, could not assume that her status as a white woman would guarantee protection.

Whether as perpetrators of violence or as female accomplices to male violence, white female victims of lynching were described as "disreputable" or women of "bad character." Because women were considered responsible for male morality, such accusations functioned not only to vilify female victims of mob violence but also served to blame the women for their own victimization. "Caused by a Woman," read the headline describing the lynching of West Dixon and his wife in Gallatin, Tennessee. According to local accounts, it was at a public picnic that "a fuss arose about Mrs. Dixon," who was described as "a woman of bad character." While it is not clear as to what the argument was about, it is clear that William Davidson, a sixty-year-old man, had played a part in the dispute, because when he later passed the Dixons' wagon he was shot and killed. As soon as Davidson fell dead, Dixon and his wife "broke to a run," and a crowd of "fifteen of Davidson's friends" started in pursuit, shooting at them at every opportunity.[104] Eventually both were shot and killed by the mob. Even though it was reported that Mr. Dixon had been the one to shoot and kill William Davidson, the local newspaper blamed the tragedy on Mrs. Dixon. Her "bad character" exerted the evil influence that instigated her husband's actions and provoked the mob's attack. To absolve the lynchers, people insisted that their victims were far from fragile. Indeed, mobs saw themselves as protecting their communities from the immoral influences of women they thought of as violently aggressive and sexually corrupt. In another time and place, lower-class white women's behavior would have offered a familiar and mild challenge to public morality; but in the turn-of-the-century South, it posed serious implications for the white supremacist social order.

The wave of racist and misogynist violence that surged through the South between 1880 and 1930 reveals a riven society in which black and white women endeavored to define themselves and their roles. As objects of racial and gender anxieties, they fought for public space. The lynching of women required a convergence of beliefs on the part of whites that some females posed a serious threat to the social order; lynching thus symbolized white men's violent attempts to maintain sexual and racial power over women—black and white. But it was also evidence of black and white women's resistance to white men's authority and to a new southern caste system. Such southern horrors reveal a tragic defense of an anachronistic and unjust social dynamic that left black and white women who dared to challenge white male supremacy without protection. Although white supremacy claimed to privilege all white women on the basis of race, such privileges were contingent upon white women's acquiescence to patriarchal and class rules. Thus, it is not surprising that ordinary white women's inclusion in the category of those deserving protection at the turn of the century did not come without cost, especially for those white women who transgressed racial and gender boundaries.

As tales of warning, the lynching of women functioned to regulate the racial, class, and sexual boundaries of the New South and served to remind women who had come of age in the postbellum era of the dangers that lay beyond those boundaries. Many of the cases of female lynchings reveal black and white women's resistance to white supremacy and their struggle for economic, political, and social justice. Whether as mothers defending their children or disgruntled workers demanding respect and fair pay, female victims of mob violence were often portrayed in the press as women not only unworthy of protection, but deserving of corporal punishment and, in extreme cases, death. For both black and poor white women who had long been denied the protection offered elite white women, the new racial and sexual politics of the postbellum South left them extremely vulnerable to mob violence. Nevertheless, even in the face of deadly violence many southern women refused to accept their subordinate status.

7

EQUAL RIGHTS FOR SOUTHERN WOMEN

R ebecca Latimer Felton entered the twentieth century determined to hold on to her newly found political power and confident in her ability to shape the racial and sexual politics of the New South. Unable to disentangle the complicated intersection of race and sex that lynching presented, she and other southern white women had chosen to mobilize the threat of the so-called black rapist to their political advantage; however, it was increasingly apparent that there were limits to the usefulness of this approach. By 1908, no longer content with indirect political influence, Felton had again shifted the focus of her political activity, moving away from her support for the lynching of black men and instead calling for woman suffrage (and in some cases for the lynching of white men).

Tapping into the two major political issues of the day—"the negro problem" and "the woman question"—Felton had come to espouse a political discourse of white female supremacy in her campaign for women's rights. While W. E. B. Du Bois believed the challenge of the twentieth century was "the problem of the color line—the relation of the darker to the lighter races of men," Felton believed the "woman question"—the relation of white women to white men—was the most pressing problem that faced the New South.[1] Similar to many southern white women and especially the southern white suffragists in the National American Woman Suffrage Association (NAWSA), Felton reasoned that the solution to the "negro problem" and the answer to the "woman question" were one and the same, the protection and political empowerment of white women. At all stages of her career, Felton sought protection for women without dependence on men and criticized the male establishment for their relentless commitment to the political and domestic subordination of southern white women. She also continually exhorted southern white men to embrace the "New Southern Woman" as an equal partner in both the home and the world of politics.

Invited in 1899 by publisher Hoke Smith to write a regular column in the statewide semiweekly edition of the *Atlanta Journal*, Felton further bolstered her status as a leading political voice in Georgia and presented herself as a fierce advocate for white women's rights, especially those of poor white women. Smith initially asked her to write a column advising wives on how to "brighten" their homes. Felton, who was then sixty-four years of age, jumped at the opportunity to have her opinions published and circulated across Georgia and neighboring states, but her focus was not on how to bring cheer into their rural homes. Instead, she was concerned with educating husbands and wives about how to live as equals on the "farms," lecturing young men and women about their moral behavior, and chastising the Georgia legislature for failing to pass tougher laws for the protection of southern white women and girls. Espousing her views on everything from politics, religion, prohibition, education, and suffrage to dancing, theatre, domestic violence, and lynching, Felton articulated a radical vision of political and domestic equality between the sexes. No topic was off limits as far as she was concerned and her "plain talk" and hard-hitting editorials won her the devotion and admiration of rural white Georgians.

Over the course of three decades (1900–1930) Felton publicly grappled with the sexual and racial politics of the New South in the *Journal* and gradually shifted her strategy for acquiring women's rights in the South. Although the issues surrounding rape and lynching remained crucial components of her political campaign for female protection and equal rights, she eventually gave up praising southern white men for lynching black men, and instead came to speak again of mob violence as an inadequate means of empowering white womanhood. At the same time, she never wavered in her belief, first elaborated in the immediate aftermath of the Civil War, that white men could not be trusted to protect white women's domestic and political interests. Indeed, she remained convinced white men had done more harm than good for the cause of protecting white women against sexual and domestic violence.

For this reason, while always a white supremacist, Felton did not always accede to the positions of the southern Democratic Party, especially when it came to the question of woman suffrage. In general, she deplored the "states' rights" argument and the glorification of the "Lost Cause," which she felt were used to deny white women their rights as citizens.[2] Even so, Felton, like many progressive southern white women, would first have to witness the limits as well as the deadly and disruptive consequences of the racial and sexual politics of white supremacy (to which she had contributed) before fully embracing a more inclusive campaign for women's rights.

"The Negro Problem"

In 1901, Felton published an essay entitled "Education Is Not a Success, and Unfits the Negro for Anything," in which she strategically tied the subordination of blacks to the empowerment of white women.[3] Stopping short of calling for female suffrage, Felton nevertheless subtly laid claim to all the privileges and rights of white manhood by insisting on the disenfranchisement of black men. First and foremost she claimed that white supremacy depended on racial purity and the elevated status of white womanhood. As the appointed gatekeepers of racial purity, white women, she believed, required not only protection against black rape but also access to political power in the New South. She contended that suffrage had done little to "elevate" the minds or morals of black citizens and praised "a movement" that was "quietly" working to deny black men the franchise.[4]

Black education, like suffrage, would not solve the "negro problem" or make the black man into the white man's social equal. If anything, Felton argued, education only exacerbated southern race problems: "No white woman is safe on the public highway or unprotected in her own home after thirty years of common school education for the blacks." Education, she reasoned, arouses "desires and passions that make him obnoxious" and eager to "get even" with whites—by raping white women. She reminded her readers of the "one political principle in Dixie" embedded in every "self-respecting white man and woman in the South" and "known in every political platform. . . . This is a white man's country, and white men aim to keep it so!" But, she also insisted, "the status of women in every civilized country on the globe sets the pace for its social relations and privileges."[5] Thus, even as she conceded to the patriarchal rhetoric of white supremacy that deemed it "a white man's country," she demanded that white women be guaranteed the same powerful privileges of whiteness as their male counterparts. Indeed, for Felton, the future of the South and the white race as a whole depended on the empowerment of white womanhood.[6]

Committed to the political and social subordination of African American men, Felton continued to describe lynching as an appropriate punishment for the "black rapist" and a necessary protection of white womanhood well into the first decade of the twentieth century. In 1905, for example, she wrote, "If he [a black rapist] was torn to pieces limb by limb and burnt with slow fire, or hung by the thumbs until the buzzards swarmed around him, he would still be saved some of the revolting torture already inflicted upon a harmless victim."[7] Felton's ideas about rape and lynching represented the norm among southern whites at this time rather than the exception.[8]

The 1899 burning of Sam Hose in Georgia had, in fact, initiated a new phase of lynching in which mass mobs routinely tortured and mutilated black bodies in the name of protecting southern white womanhood.[9] In 1902 a mob of four thousand whites lynched Walter Allen in Rome, Georgia, for allegedly attempting to rape a "prominent" young white girl. After the mob hanged him from a downtown telegraph pole they fired thousands of bullets into his swinging corpse. They tied a lighted kerosene lantern to his foot and pinned a sign to his chest that warned: "Thus they die, who mistreat our women."[10]

Despite the efforts of anti-lynching activists like Ida B. Wells, at the turn of the twentieth century it was not just southerners who accepted the standard justification for mob violence. Following the 1904 lynching of Will Cato and Paul Reed by a mob of over five hundred whites in Statesboro, Georgia, New York journalist and progressive muckraker Ray Stannard Baker published an article on lynching that reflected the prevailing attitude of most white Americans. The mob that burned Cato and Reed alive believed the men had murdered a white family, Henry Hodges, his wife, and three children. After traveling to Georgia to investigate the lynching, Baker described Statesboro as "a healthy, temperate, progressive, American town—a country city, self-respecting, ambitious, with a good future before it—the splendid future of the New South." Lynching, he insisted, was simply a response to the "worthless negro . . . he prowls the roads by day and by night; he steals; he makes it unsafe for women to travel alone."[11]

Yet, even as Felton, like so many other whites, remained supportive of the lynching of black men accused of raping white women, she also began to express growing concern about southern white men's manipulation and appropriation of the threat of rape and punishment by lynching for their own personal and political gain. By playing on the image of the "black rapist" in an irresponsible way, she complained, they exacerbated racial tensions and thereby also increased white women's sexual vulnerability. In 1905, for example, Felton's readers asked her opinion of Thomas Dixon's sensationalistic play *The Clansman*. Adapted from his novel of the same name, the play was set in South Carolina after the Civil War and glorified the role of the Ku Klux Klan in overturning Reconstruction and protecting white women from newly freed and lusting slaves. Felton expressed deep concerns and frustration over Dixon's reckless exploitation of sexual and racial fear.[12] Convinced a rape scene in which four former slaves sexually assault two white women would have violent consequences for both blacks and whites, she accused Dixon of sacrificing the legitimate goal of ensuring white women's safety for his own personal fame and fortune. This white man, she wrote, "will feed a terrible flame into a consuming conflagration" for economic gain—a "flame," she believed, that came dangerously close to engulfing white women. In particular, Felton believed the rape scene in the play would instigate unnecessary white violence against black men and thus inevitably provoke black men to retaliate by raping white women. She asked, "Shall this spectacular show travel throughout the south land, to engender to promote violence and invite the incendiary torch and the midnight assassin to revenge about every home?"[13]

Determined not to be misunderstood, Felton prefaced her criticism of Dixon by noting, "Everybody that reads the *Journal* understands my loyalty to southern men and women. . . . I have stood in my little place and defended southern men who felt obliged to take the law into their own hands, when white girls and women were ravished by the bestial lust and fiendish violence." But while she had publicly "defended" white men who lynched, Felton insisted Dixon was asking far too much if he expected her to attend the theatre to have her mind "inflamed" and her soul "enraged" by "sham rape violence." Moreover, she lamented, Georgia could not bear the "kind" of violence the play was sure to incite. She pleaded, "In the name of all that is good, true, honest and God-serving, put out the flame, lower the curtain and let us work out our own salvation without this firebrand in front and rear of us making angry men ready to war on society."[14]

Felton was not alone in her criticism of Dixon and *The Clansman*. Many white southerners found the play inflammatory and took particular issue with the rape scene as well as the portrayal of the Ku Klux Klan. In Columbia, South Carolina, whites hissed and booed throughout the performance and local authorities feared a riot.[15] Felton's neighbor, James B. Heyward, wrote a letter to the *Constitution* in which he cheered the Columbia hecklers and condemned the play as a host of "horrible fabrications" designed to support "the monstrous perversion of fact that Ku-Kluxism was born of rape of white women by negroes."[16] Dixon had misrepresented not only the Klan, but also the postwar relationship between blacks and whites. Heyward insisted, "The old slave never dreamed of an assault and the old slave owner was never agitated by fear of it." Intent on representing slavery as a benevolent institution, dispelling the myth of black rape, and redeeming the Klan as a respectable political organization, Heyward explained "Ku-Kluxism" as a response to the Union League, "a secret society organized to undermine the affection and veneration which the freedman continued to have for their old owners who had raised them and always been kind to them." In other words, the Klan had redeemed the South not from black rape, but from political and economic domination at the hands of carpetbaggers, scalawags, and disloyal Negroes. Thus, Heyward sought to redeem southern manhood, black and white, when he concluded, "Let it be remembered forever and forever such a condition never, no never, existed."[17]

Dixon, for his part, challenged both Felton's suggestion that the production would incite violence and Heyward's claim that *The Clansman* was based on racial fabrications and sexual fantasies. As to the issue of whether the performances would provoke white men to lynch, he defended, "We have thus passed thirty southern towns without a lynching and in one of them, on the night of the performance, a negro was caught and put in jail for an attempted assault on a beautiful white girl." Dixon's mention of this "attempted assault," of course, might well have been seen by Felton as evidence that her fear that black men, in protest against the play, might seek revenge by raping white women was well founded. Ignoring the suggestion that blacks might take violent offense to the play, however, Dixon instead focused on the assumption that white men would "rush home from a theater in their Sunday clothes, grab a gun and kill a negro just because he is negro. I confess this is a new terror in the land."[18] Having spent the last sixteen years living in New York, Dixon had difficulty comprehending this "new terror" and failed to grasp the reality of southern mob violence. Most white and black southerners understood, however, that the mere suggestion of rape was enough to instigate a lynching in many communities.

Dixon went so far as to say that the failure of Reconstruction had now spread to the North and complained that in New York over the last twelve months, "I have seen big buck negroes parading up and down Broadway with white girls hanging on their arms." Not just any white girls, he explained, but girls of "radiant beauty . . . perfect blonds, with golden hair and soft childlike blue eyes."[19] *The Clansman*, contended Dixon, was not about a past in which he imagined that sex between an "ignorant" black man and an "innocent" white woman was always rape, but rather a future in which educated black men, who after years of political, economic, and social opportunity, would compete with white men for white women's affections. Dixon defended his play, then, as both a validation of white southerners' anxieties about the "evils" of social equality and a necessary warning against miscegenation. *The Clansman*, he argued, was "a prophecy" about "the paradox of an educated negro" and his eventual demand for "absolute equality."

While some southern whites remained worried about the play's potential for violence and its distortion of the Klan, others were now outraged by Dixon's discussion of the possibility of consensual sex between black men and white women. In a Sunday sermon, Dr. Len G. Broughton, pastor of the Baptist Tabernacle in Atlanta and longtime acquaintance of Dixon, accused him of "slandering" the white people of the South for the sake of "selfish greed." He declared the show a disgrace to southern manhood and womanhood and berated, "To claim that it is necessary today for him to go gyrating about over the south, stirring up such passions of hell, to keep the races apart and thus prevent, what he imagines, an impending amalgamation of the whites and blacks into one race of mixed bloods, is a slander of the white people of the south." The four thousand plus people attending the service cheered and applauded when Broughton challenged Dixon's assumption that southerners needed "a traveling troupe of masked men and women . . . to keep our men chivalrous, our women pure, and our children free from the blood of blacks."[20] He called on southerners to "resent" the play and northerners to boycott it. Dixon, he concluded, was part of a growing set of white men, "yelling and yelping 'Nigger! Nigger!' like a hound dog upon the track of a rabbit." As far as he was concerned, Dixon's behavior was not only un-Christian and un-American, but also unsound and unsafe.[21]

Many southerners, however, refused to heed Dr. Broughton's call to "resent" the play or Felton's plea to avoid the theatre altogether. And, as predicted, sold-out performances of *The Clansman* did indeed exacerbate racial tensions in Georgia. Atlanta at this time was already buckling under the intense pressure of white supremacy. The city's black population had grown from just nine thousand in 1880 to thirty-five thousand by 1900, while the white population exploded from thirty-seven thousand in 1890 to over a hundred thousand by 1910.[22] Such rapid growth, combined with increased job competition among blacks and poor whites, and the rise of a visible black elite made up of businessmen, academics, journalists, and church leaders, heightened white anxieties about black political, economic, and social mobility.[23] White concerns about controlling and policing interracial mixing in an urban context also took on new urgency as working-class blacks and whites defied the rules of segregation by frequenting saloons, restaurants, and dance halls on Atlanta's Decatur Street in the Five Points district.[24] When *The Clansman* premiered in Atlanta in the fall of 1905 before a racially segregated but mixed audience, then, the stage was already set for violence to ensue. As whites chanted "Lynch him" after the attempted rape scene, blacks sitting in the balcony of the theatre hissed and threw bottles down on the white spectators. One black man was dragged from the theatre and arrested after coming to blows with a white man.

This scuffle between black and white theatregoers in Atlanta only served as a prelude, however, to the explosive intensification of racial tensions that took place during the 1906 gubernatorial race between Hoke Smith, the former publisher of the *Atlanta Journal* and Secretary of the Interior in Grover Cleveland's second cabinet, and Clark Howell, owner of the *Atlanta Constitution*. During the campaign, Smith insisted on the further disenfranchisement of black men, while Howell argued that his scheme to disenfranchise black men would also deny suffrage to illiterate white men and claimed that the Democratic white primary and the poll tax were sufficient for limiting the black vote. In fact, both men were ardent white supremacists, and they both used the press to heighten anxieties about the political and economic empowerment of black men and to tap into white southerners' sexual and racial fears. Smith's former paper, the *Atlanta Journal*, insisted that Howell was a supporter of both political and social equality between the races, which translated into forced miscegenation and black political domination.[25] The campaign stoked racial friction and malaise.[26]

In the lead-up to the election, newspapers across the state added further fuel to the fire with reports of alleged assaults on white women by black men and predictions of "negro domination" and a "negro crime wave." In late August, for example, the *Atlanta Georgian* published a three-part editorial on "The Reign of Terror for Southern Women," in which editor John Temple Graves argued that lynching was no longer a sufficient means for preventing rape. He instead argued for "some new and mysterious mode of punishment—the passing over a slender bridge into a dark chamber where in utter darkness and in utter mystery the assailant of woman's virtue would meet a fate which his friends would never know and which he himself would never come back to make them understand."[27] Both the *Journal* and the *Constitution* blamed the black saloons on Decatur Street, where black men allegedly guzzled cheap whiskey and gazed upon images of scantily clad white women, as a major part of the problem, and warned that if white men failed to act, assaults on white women would continue to increase and "Negro domination" would surely follow. Howell, in turn, in order to discredit his opponent, pointed to the fact that Smith, as Secretary of the Interior, had appointed blacks to office.

Remarkably, even as the campaign played into Felton's often voiced concerns about the rape of white women, the issue of prohibition, and the problem of black suffrage, she remained unusually silent during the campaign. Days before the election, however, her husband, Dr. William Felton, published an open letter in the *Constitution* condemning the governor's race as a "blood and thunder campaign." He declared that those in favor of "negro disfranchisement are HANDLING DYNAMITE WITH VERY CARELESS HANDS" and questioned "Why couldn't our political candidates for office let 'well enough alone?'" Using language not so different from his wife's rebuke of *The Clansman*, Dr. Felton warned, "As I see the situation there has been enough race antipathy and race difficulties flung upon the citizens of Georgia to account for the present continuous acts of violence, rape and arson. . . . Do these agitators comprehend the dangers that are being forced on every rural home and every business industry in our country . . . I look for more violence . . . and I can see no motive for this madness and folly but an insane desire for political office."[28]

Both of the Feltons' fears—Rebecca's that *The Clansman* would promote violence and Dr. Felton's that "a red hot campaign for personal purposes" would encourage more violence—were soon realized. The

sold-out performances of *The Clansman* across the state, the white supremacy campaign that eventually put Smith in the governor's mansion,
and the sensationalized stories of alleged rape and black crime that circulated in the daily press together turned Atlanta into a tinderbox.

On September 22 white citizens, goaded by a relentless stream of newspaper headlines reporting that black men were assaulting one white woman
after another, attacked black residents and businesses.[29] Sparks began to
fly in the hours before the riot when newspapers reported rumors of four
attempted assaults on white women by black men. The first alleged assault occurred at 2:00 P.M. when Mrs. Lizzie Cash Chaffin "discovered a
negro lurking under the bush" while feeding her hogs. When he refused
her request that he "leave the place" Chaffin retrieved her husband's gun
and fired shots at the "gingercake colored negro," who took cover in the
nearby swamp. The second attempt was reported to have occurred around
7:30 P.M. when Mrs. Frank Arnold was allegedly "seized and knocked down"
by a black man who appeared at her back door. Thirty minutes later, Miss
Alma Allen was allegedly "grabbed" and "thrown down" by a black man in
her backyard. Finally, it was reported that Mrs. Mattie Holcombe, "an old
lady," was given a "terrible fright" when she discovered a black man looking
through her blinds.[30]

By 10:00 P.M. the reported run-ins between black men and white
women had drawn thousands of angry whites to Five Points. "Kill the Negroes!" screamed members of the mob. Despite pleas from Mayor James
G. Woodward to let the law run its course, the mob grew close to fifteen
thousand by midnight, took over the central business district, and assaulted blacks wherever they could be found. Black men and women
were pulled off trolleys, grabbed out of black-owned barbershops and
restaurants, and severely beaten, in some cases to death. In response to
the mob violence, the state militia was called out and black residents in
nearby suburbs began arming themselves. Early Sunday morning torren-
tial rain forced the mob to retreat. But despite the presence of the militia,
the white mob reemerged on Sunday afternoon. With dozens of blacks
dead and hundreds more brutalized, citizens of "Dark Town" and
"Brownsville" organized in self-defense and successfully defended their
communities from white mobs. On Monday evening, police officers entered Brownsville, a middle-class black neighborhood, to arrest six black
men for possession of weapons and ammunition. A shoot-out between
black citizens and police officers subsequently left one white officer and a

black grocer dead. The next morning, three companies of the state militia were sent into Brownsville to disarm blacks and over two hundred African American men were arrested. With blacks disarmed and many arrested, city officials were finally able to call successfully for an end to the violence.[31]

The Atlanta race riot forced many southern white progressives to speak out publicly against white mob violence for the first time. White female social reformers blamed southern politicians, newspaper editors, and saloon proprietors, not black men, for the riot. Like Felton, many southern white women had begun to lose patience with men who refused to move beyond lynching as a method of female protection. Just weeks before the riot, leading Georgia social reformers and suffragists Vara A. Marjette and Mary Latimer McLendon had dismissed the hysteria about black rape and pointed instead to white men as the real threat to white womanhood.[32] In an article titled "The White Man to Blame," Marjette, a lawyer, social worker, writer, and superintendent of "Work among Negroes" for the Georgia Woman's Christian Temperance Union, rejected extralegal violence as a form of protection and called on southern white women to participate in their own defense. She accused politicians and newspapers of exploiting the myth of black rape to justify racial violence and disenfranchisement. Unwilling to let white women off the hook, she further complained, "Again the cry of rape is started by some hysterical women when there has never been a shadow of such, only in a frenzied imagination."[33] She called on white women to stop fixating on the imagined threat of black rape and to work instead on reforming white men's sexual behavior.

Mary Latimer McLendon, president of the Georgia Women's Suffrage Association and a WCTU leader, was Rebecca Felton's younger sister. Born five years after Rebecca, she graduated from Southern Masonic Female College in Covington and moved to Atlanta after she married Nicholas A. McLendon in 1860.[34] McLendon joined Marjette in blaming southern white men for leaving white women vulnerable to sexual and domestic violence. She reasoned that not until white men were willing to control their own behavior by passing prohibition laws and raising the legal age of consent would white women be truly safe. White men, she argued, were so intent on violently policing black men's sexual behavior that they ignored "the consuming outrage of the drunkard in the home." If women were enfranchised, she insisted, they would declare "with power:

'Keep the deadly poison out of the reach of my husband, father, son or brother, and from the negro brutes whose passions are inflamed by it when they commit their dastardly outrages.'" Full protection, in other words, required female suffrage.[35]

The Georgia WCTU too pointed not to black rape as the cause of the Atlanta race riot, but to the consumption of alcohol—the all-purpose temperance villain—by both black and white men as the instigating factor. From its inception the WCTU had linked rape to alcohol and argued that prohibition would both reduce sexual crimes and prevent mob violence. At the organization's state convention in Macon, just days after the riot, WCTU leaders sent a telegram to the mayor of Atlanta thanking him for closing the public schools and the saloons during the riots and informing him that the WCTU convention had voted that he keep the saloons closed permanently.[36] They asked the *Constitution* to publish a letter written by Felton calling for the "suppression of the liquor saloon everywhere in the state." Felton explained that her plea for prohibition was "in remembrance of the race riot" and reminded her readers of "the six fiendish attempts at *assault on white women in the* [streets] of our capital city during a week, four of them in a single day!" The police, she argued, were incapable of "handling the mob or of suppressing the rape fiend." The root of the problem in both cases, she declared, was liquor— "the germ that breeds ruin and disaster."[37]

In the aftermath of the riot, many city officials accepted the argument that liquor had contributed to the so-called black crime wave, as well as to white mob violence. In an effort to police the consumption of alcohol by black citizens and to prevent interracial mixing, the city council outlawed interracial bars, restricted the sale of cheap whiskey, barred chairs from saloons, and permanently suspended the license of forty bars patronized by blacks.[38] Some temperance advocates complained that the riot was the result of a "drunken mob of low down white men and boys" and insisted the state should also police white men's alcohol consumption.[39] Taking advantage of the post-riot atmosphere, the WCTU, joined by the Anti-Saloon League, worked frantically to get a prohibition referendum on the ballot; in the spring of 1907 most counties in Georgia voted themselves dry, and in 1908 the legislature implemented mandatory statewide prohibition.

Maintaining law and order, reasoned many leading whites, would require not only prohibition laws and enforced segregation, but also further disenfranchisement of black men.[40] In keeping with Governor Smith's campaign promises, the legislature introduced a literacy test as another measure of limiting the black franchise. As the Democratic Party tightened its stranglehold on southern politics and successfully disenfranchised blacks, however, southern white women became increasingly aware that the violent politics of white supremacy had, in fact, done little to ensure white women's rights. Prohibition, despite Felton's hopes, did not solve the problems of domestic and sexual violence that plagued southern homes. The Georgia legislature still refused to raise the legal age of consent above ten years of age or to consider female suffrage. Denied legal protection and formal political power, many elite white women, following the lead of figures such as Marjette and McLendon, turned now to suffrage as the only possible solution.

"The Woman Question"

Just as white women had made use of the "black rapist" in their campaigns for temperance, they did not hesitate to do so in their fight for the ballot. If southern white men could successfully use the threat of black rape to disenfranchise African Americans, then white women believed they might be able to use the same image to gain suffrage for themselves. For the sake of political expediency, southern white women deployed the Democratic tactics of white supremacy in the early campaigns for suffrage.

The suffrage movement came late to the South and even later to Georgia. In 1890, Helen Augusta Howard of Columbus, Georgia, founded a branch of the National American Woman Suffrage Association that she called the Georgia Woman Suffrage Association (GWSA). By 1893 she had members in five counties. In 1894, Mary Latimer McLendon established a chapter of the GWSA in Atlanta called the Equal Suffrage League. The movement began to grow more quickly after 1895 when the NAWSA held its annual meeting in Atlanta—Susan B. Anthony and ninety-three delegates from twenty-eight states attended. McLendon was elected president of the state organization for the first time in 1896 and served for three years, before being elected again in 1906 and serving until her death in 1921. It was under her leadership that the GWSA held its first state convention in Atlanta in 1899 and came to support a federal constitutional amendment to enfranchise women. McLendon argued that women would use the vote to pass a comprehensive reform program that would abolish child labor, raise the legal age of consent, institute compulsory school attendance, and hire female guards for the state's female prisoners.

It was not until after the Atlanta race riot, the enactment of prohibition in Georgia, and the successful disenfranchisement of black men that Rebecca Felton turned her attention to the question of woman suffrage. It is not exactly clear why she did not come out in support of suffrage before 1908. However, with black male suffrage severely limited, it seemed Felton was finally ready to join her sister as an active suffragist. Determined in her belief that the supremacy of the race required absolute equality between the sexes, she challenged traditional gender roles that denied white women the full rights and privileges of citizenship and maintained that no race could rise above the status of its women. As a New Southern Woman, Felton insisted on her right to participate in her own protection and eventually came to argue that suffrage was a woman's best defense against white male tyranny. Although a latecomer, Felton did help to lead and redefine what has been called the "second stage of the suffrage movement" in Georgia.[41]

The first stage of the southern suffrage moment had its ideological roots in the 1890 Constitutional Convention of Mississippi, where serious consideration was given to woman's suffrage as a means of countering black suffrage and securing white political power. Mississippi legislatures reviewed a plan that called for the enfranchisement of women who owned, or whose husbands owned, three hundred dollars worth of real estate. Granting voting rights to wealthy women, argued supporters of the plan, would solve the problem of black suffrage without trampling the constitution.[42] In the end, the "Mississippi Plan" rejected female suffrage and instead adopted the "understanding clause," which used literacy tests and a poll tax to disfranchise blacks. Despite the convention's rejection of woman suffrage, white women had gained a powerful argument in their battle for the ballot: the solution to the "negro problem" was woman suffrage. Consequently, leading suffragists across the South called for the disenfranchisement of black men while making the case for their own right to the ballot as "a measure to insure white supremacy."[43] Raising the specter of black male political power to argue for the enfranchisement of white women, leading Mississippi suffragist Belle Kearney, for example, declared, "The enfranchisement of women would insure immediate and durable white supremacy, honestly attained. . . . The South is slow to grasp the great fact that the enfranchisement of women would settle the race question in politics."[44]

By the time Felton immersed herself in the suffrage movement, the tide had turned and the argument that woman suffrage would solve the "negro problem" had lost political currency. In fact, by 1910 anti-suffragists were arguing that female suffrage would undermine white male political supremacy.[45] Felton dismissed such claims as desperate attempts to deny women their rights as citizens and charged southern white men with standing in the way of progress.[46] The real reason white men opposed female suffrage was not that it posed a threat to white supremacy, she argued, but rather that it challenged the political and domestic "subjection" of white women. "The truth of the whole business," she explained, "lies in their determination to hold the whip hand over the wives and mothers of the South!" She predicted: "Woman suffrage will come to the South — despite the drastic and frantic opposition of nine-tenths of the Southern Democrats in Congress at this time. They seem to be the lineal and legal heirs to all the political debris of secession."[47] Implicit in Felton's demand for suffrage was the idea that one of the privileges of whiteness was access to the franchise and all the rights of citizenship without regard to sex.

Needless to say, the issue of race did not disappear from woman suffrage campaigns. While white southern suffragists were no longer able to draw on the idea that woman suffrage would solve the "negro problem," they did not hesitate to point to the fact that black men had been granted suffrage while they remained disenfranchised. Their campaigns now focused on white female supremacy and establishing all the rights and privileges necessary to maintain it. Appointed chairman of the committee on legislation for the GWSA, Felton appeared before the state congress on a number of occasions. In 1914, when the Georgia legislature first conducted hearings on woman's suffrage, both McLendon and Felton were among those who addressed the house committee and argued that white women had as much right to vote as black men. McLendon reasoned, "The negro men, our former slaves, have been given the right to vote and why should not we southern women have the same right?" Felton similarly asked, "Why should our women not have the right to vote? Why can't they help you make the laws the same as they help you run your homes and your churches? I do not want to see a negro man walk to the polls and vote on who shall handle my tax money while I myself can not vote at all. Is this fair?"[48] The House committee answered with a 5 to 2 vote against woman suffrage.

In 1915, Felton not only returned to the state congress but also published a pamphlet entitled *The Subjection of Women and the Enfranchisement of Women* in which she continued to argue that the ballot was an inherent right of white women. She challenged southern manhood to embrace the ideals of the "New Man," who in other sections of the country had granted women the franchise. She declared, "Fifty years from now this country will hold up hands in holy horror . . . that any man or set of men in America should assume to themselves the authority to deny to free-born white women of America the ballot, which is the badge and synonym of freedom!"[49] According to Felton, the New Man, unlike his "hard-drinking, fox-hunting, high playing" forefather, who treated his wife more like a slave than an equal partner, understands that "his mate must be his comrade" and that his own status depends on the political elevation of women. "Marriage between a master and a slave was obliged to be debasing to both," she explained. "Marriage in its true meaning rests upon absolute equality between the sexes as to rights and privileges — legal, political, and social." The New Man, she argued, must therefore embrace woman suffrage and accept the notion that the "women's movement is a great movement of the sexes toward each other, with common ideals as to government, as well as common ideals in domestic life."[50] All in all, then, Felton made clear that the New Southern Woman was not only interested in changing women's political, economic, and social status, but also in redefining southern manhood. Times had changed, explained Felton, and southern white men were lagging behind.

Remarkably, as she became more involved in the campaign for woman's suffrage, Felton quieted her call for the lynching of black men and instead focused increasingly on white men's violence against their wives and daughters. White men denied women the franchise, not black men, after all, and more white women had suffered under tyrannical and oppressive husbands and fathers than at the hands of black men. She asked her readers to consider the "breadth and depth of human misery" that occurs daily because too many men have accepted the "the brute idea that women were only made for man's use, and abuse."[51] It was this degradation and abuse of women by their husbands and fathers that fueled Felton's fight for suffrage.

In a 1914 article titled "Making Slaves of Their Wives," Felton recounted how a judge had granted a woman a divorce because "her brute of a husband" had hired her out to a farmer to hoe but kept the wages for himself. "Does it not make you indignant to see the indignities that brute husbands can thus put on their wives?" she asked her readers. She bemoaned the stories "regarding the brutality of various men to their wedded wives" that appeared in newspapers on a daily basis. "It fatigues one's patience to see how some men make a business of boasting themselves as their wives' owners and masters and the evils that grows because there are enough male fools in the world to carry their beliefs into practice." Felton concluded, "If a reason is asked for, as to why women clamor for the ballot to give themselves and their children protection, you can now see why they do it."[52]

In other articles with titles such as "Spanking the Wife," "Wife Killers Crazed by Drink," "Chopping His Wife — With an Ax," and "The Murder of Wives Getting Intolerable," Felton now consistently pointed to southern white men as the primary threat to white womanhood and demanded not just female suffrage, but punishment for white men's men crimes against women. In fact, she even went so far as to call for the lynching of some white men.[53] Under the heading "Out to be Lynched," Felton expressed her outrage over the murder of an eighteen-year-old white girl by her father. The murder of his daughter, explained Felton, "was not half so infamous as the slander he put on her good name and character in death." As to the question of what punishment should be meted out to a parent who takes his child's life and then slanders her as a "vile woman," Felton answered, "I'd lynch him. He deserves hanging for shooting the hapless girl. He deserves hanging twice for the slander he intended to blast her memory with, and he simply disgraces civilization by living an hour longer than his fellow citizens can reach him with a short rope and a ready limb. Such a monster is unfit to live."[54] Felton's plea against white men's violence echoed some of the rhetoric in her earlier calls to lynch black men for rape of white women. In response to the 1915 lynching of Leo Frank, a Jewish man accused of the rape and murder of Mary Phagan, a thirteen-year-old employee in the Atlanta pencil factory that he managed, Felton wrote, "As the Indians used to say, when they had made up their minds, 'Put this in your pipe and smoke it,' so I will say as long as rape violence prevails in Georgia then lynching is going to continue. There is nothing more certain so long as there is enough red blood and manhood in the Caucasian race to stand for the protection of their women. Smoke that brethren! It is true."[55]

While Felton was thus willing to defend the lynching of Leo Frank, it is important to note that her last public statement in support of the lynching of black men had actually come several years prior to this, in 1913.[56] Around the same time, she had also said, "It was better to allow a thousand murderers to escape than to lynch one innocent person."[57] By 1920, it is clear that her views on lynching had changed even further. In January of that year, when a journalist, Sam W. Small, published an anti-lynching editorial titled "Federal Impotence as to Lynching," Felton responded with a letter to the editor of the *Constitution* in which she closely "echoed" his condemnation of mob violence in Georgia. She opened by declaring that "the hope of the country lies in the honesty of our judiciary and the integrity of our juries."[58] And yet, she complained, all-white male juries in Georgia were refusing to punish white men guilty of raping black women and of participating in lynching. She then presented two cases to make a plea against mob violence and for the legal punishment of white men's crimes.

In the first case, "a white man, or a man born with a white skin, for there is a distinction and a difference, entered the house of a negro woman, surrounded by her children, and committed such acts of violence as to be indicted by a grand jury of white men, and convicted, on the evidence furnished at the trial, by a jury of white men, and that jury, with usual mob spirit inside of them, placed a sentence of a year in the chaingang. The indictment was for rape." Shocked at such a light sentence for the crime of rape, Felton reminded her readers that a similar crime committed by a black man on a white woman would have resulted in a lynching. Felton had no doubt that if a new trial were granted another white jury would simply issue the same verdict and sentence.

The second episode she recounted also related a case of white men's sexual violence against black women. "Two negro girls," she explained, "pursued by two drunken white rapists, also married men, escaped to a cabin inhabited by an aged negro man, over 70, and in his endeavor to shield these colored girls he shot one of the drunken rapists in the leg, or arm, perhaps. Before daylight dawned the old negro was lynched and his body shot to giblets." None of the lynchers was arrested and prosecuted. "Those lynchers were known to be white men," she bemoaned, "They [the lynchers] had but one idea, namely, to shelter the white rapists."[59]

In 1897 Felton had argued that the courts had failed to protect white women against black rape, thus making lynching a necessary evil. Now she argued that the courts were failing to properly punish white men who either raped black women or lynched black men. "More than twenty years have come and gone since that speech at Tybee," she lamented. "Painful it is to me that I now say to you, in all truth and soberness, that our courts will not deal out justice, that our judges pussyfoot around these lynching atrocities, that our country officials cannot be depended on to arrest criminals and stand by the truth and the facts of the case."[60]

Amazingly, Felton had articulated a critique of lynching that in many ways resembled the arguments that Wells and Alexander Manly had made in the 1890s. Highlighting the rape of black women and the unjust lynching of black men, Felton argued that white men were not interested in protecting women but only in maintaining their own power and privilege. Taking Manly's 1898 advice to "begin at the fountainhead if she wishes to purify the stream," Felton picked up where she had stopped short in 1897 and reasoned, "The created are not greater than their creator—the fruit is no better than its tree. The stream cannot rise higher than it source." She now publicly bemoaned the fact that the white men who had participated in the twenty-one lynchings in Georgia during 1919 would sadly escape punishment for their crimes.

Felton's astonishing turnaround did not go unnoticed. She received at least three letters from black men thanking her "for her frank and stirring appeal for justice for the Negro."[61] African American photographer C. M. Battey of the Tuskegee Institute of Alabama wrote that he had read with "sincere and deep feeling" her article and "thank[ed] God for her courage of conviction." Her letter to the editor, he explained, had revealed to him the solution to lynching: "Oh if we can but persuade more of the true and divine type of womanhood, as you, to speak more boldly, more sternly, soon will this sickening comedy be washed from our stage."[62] Lynward F. Coles, state historian and director of research work at the American Legion, wrote from Philadelphia, congratulating Felton "upon her womanly stand that [she] had taken in defense of the race." He explained that words were inadequate to express his gratitude, bid her "God speed," and warned her to "beware" of the mob. He cautioned, "For you know that those bloodthirsty hoodlums will burn colored women at the stake as quickly as they will colored men and, too, they lynched Leo Frank, not far from Atlanta, a white man, and once a mob of Georgians becomes delirious with the thirst of human blood, the fact that you are a white woman will mean little or nothing to them."[63]

Why did Felton finally come out so strongly against the rape of black women and the lynching of black men by white men in 1920? No doubt the race riots of 1919, the increase in Klan violence, and the upsurge of lynchings in Georgia gave Felton pause. In 1917 the Georgia WCTU and the Georgia Federation of Women's Clubs officially came out against lynching, and in the *Georgia Bulletin* of January 1920 the WCTU specifically challenged the white women of Georgia to ask themselves: "What can I do to put a stop to these horrors?"[64] It is not clear whether or not Felton's letter to the *Constitution* was in part a response to the WCTU's call to action. In any case, it is clear that by then, she had already come to the conclusion that claiming the protection of white men as a political ploy was a bankrupt strategy, and that women now needed to protect themselves with the vote.

By 1920, moreover, Felton no longer believed that black men were the primary threat to white womanhood. Instead, she now re-embraced the view she had held in the 1880s and early 1890s, that white men represented the great danger to southern women, both black and white. With the vote now within their grasp (no thanks to the Georgia legislature, which was first in line to oppose the ratification of the Nineteenth Amendment to the U.S. Constitution), prohibition in place, and the age of consent laws raised (in 1918), the wedge of white supremacy that Felton had so skillfully maneuvered to gain entry to the world of southern politics was no longer a necessary or even useful tool for maintaining and acquiring women's rights. Empowered with the franchise, Felton resurrected her old criticisms of southern white manhood and called on the protection of all southern women and the legal punishment of all southern men for violence against women, without regard to race or status.

Felton's last public call for lynching came in 1925. Responding to a report she had read in the *Journal* about the horrific murder of a white woman by her husband, Felton could not resist suggesting extreme measures. The victim, Felton emphasized, had a ten-month-old baby in her arms when her husband cut her throat. Surely, she concluded, "if there was ever an allowable case of lynching a criminal on the spot this is one."[65] If Felton could not quite give up the idea that lynching might in some cases still be justified, it is nonetheless deeply revealing of the general shift in her thinking that it was here again an abusive white man whom she identified as an appropriate target. Moreover, in stark contrast to her earlier calls for the lynching of black men, which she knew would be answered, the likelihood of a white man in the South actually being lynched for violence against a woman was so small that Felton surely understood this protest to be a merely rhetorical exercise.

As Felton returned to a more inclusive politics of women's rights, she also shifted back toward a more independent-minded politics that refused to embrace without question the southern Democratic Party. In 1921 she was called to Florida to confer with Republican president Warren G. Harding and also met with Vice President Calvin Coolidge in Atlanta, where she denounced the treatment of black workers in Georgia.[66] Of course, Felton's refusal to declare her allegiance to the Democratic Party did not come without cost. For the first time in decades she was openly criticized in the southern white press: "Those editors who are concerning themselves about whether the Old Lady Felton is a Watson Democrat or a Harding Republican are giving too much attention to a very unimportant personage," wrote the editor of the *Dalton Citizen*. In an all-out personal attack, the editor concluded, "The Old Lady Felton never contributes anything but advice, and a poor, disloyal brand at that. She kicks at paying taxes of any kind. She encourages the spirit of hate, and abuses without restraint her superiors. Her acts as a rule are both uncharitable and unchristian. Her example and influence are not for the best. Ask those who live near her and know her best." The *Cordele Dispatch* mocked, "We had as soon depend on the witches of Salem for political advice as that which daily emanates from the sanctum of the Old Lady Felton. . . . We do not care what people call it, it is a kind of politics unworthy of loyal Georgians."[67] Yet, despite these attacks in the local press and her advancing age, at the beginning of the 1920s Felton nonetheless remained the leading female voice in Georgia politics.

A Dream Come True?

In the winter of 1922, Rebecca Latimer Felton, now eighty-seven years old, boarded a train in Cartersville, Georgia, bound for Washington, D.C., where she hoped to become the first woman to sit in the U.S. Senate. In three days the 67th Congress would be called into session, and Felton still did not know if she would be among the class of junior senators who were to be sworn in. She was recovering from a terrible cold, yet she refused to allow her son Howard to accompany her on the long trip. That Friday morning, she looked particularly fragile as the train moved northward. Her hair was "snowy white," her back bent from age, and her wrinkled face was still pale from her recent illness, but her spirits were high. She had made the journey to the nation's capitol many times before. Her late husband had, after all, served as an Independent Democrat congressman in the 44th, 45th, and 46th Congresses, and throughout his time in the House of Representatives, Felton had worked as his secretary and speechwriter. Thus she was no stranger to Washington politics; she understood better than most how Congress worked and knew that her chances of being seated were slim. Only one senator needed to object and her hopes of being sworn in would be dashed.[68]

Six weeks earlier, Georgia's Democratic governor, Thomas W. Hardwick, had asked Felton to fill the Senate vacancy created by "the sudden and unexpected" death of the eminent and notorious Thomas Edward Watson. Watson's political career had begun in 1882, when Georgians elected him to the state house of representatives as a liberal Democrat. It was as a Populist in the 1890s, however, that Watson became a powerful force in Georgia politics. As a supporter of the Farmers' Alliance platform in 1890 he was elected to the U.S. House of Representatives as an Alliance Democrat. In 1892, when lynching reached a national high, he ran for Congress on the Populist ticket. An interracial alliance of agricultural interests, the Populist Party advocated public ownership of the railroads, steamship lines, and telephone and telegraph systems. It also supported the free and unlimited coinage of silver, the abolition of national banks, a system of graduated income tax, and the direct election of U.S. senators. During his 1892 campaign, Watson condemned lynching and argued that poor whites and blacks had common interests. He was defeated (as he would be again in 1894) by a white supremacist Democrat who accused him of supporting "negro domination." After his second defeat, he returned to work as a lawyer in Thompson, Georgia, and served as editor of the *People's Party Paper*. He was nominated for vice president by the Populist National Convention in 1896 and for president by the People's Party in 1904. Despite his defeats he continued to wield political influence in Georgia through his publications *Watson's Magazine* and *The Jeffersonian*. By 1906, however, he was no longer the radical progressive who had led the southern Populist revolt. Like most Democrats, he had instead become an active proponent of the disenfranchisement and lynching of

African Americans. He was a key figure in helping to instigate the 1906 Atlanta race riot and, in 1915, he encouraged and supported the lynching of Leo Frank.[69] In 1920, as a strong opponent of the League of Nations and the Treaty of Versailles, both of which Democratic president Woodrow Wilson supported, Watson campaigned and won a seat in the U.S. Senate as a Democrat.[70]

On September 17 of that year, Senator Watson suffered a serve asthma attack, and a week later, despite his doctor's orders to remain in bed, he participated in the closing of the second session of the 67th Congress. Three days later, the sixty-six-year-old senator suffered a second asthmatic attack, which proved fatal.[71] Felton was saddened by the death of her old friend and longtime political ally. She had supported the campaigns of both Senator Watson and Governor Hardwick; and given her prominence it hardly came as a surprise that her name appeared among those suggested to fill Watson's seat. In the end, of course, the governor's decision to appoint Felton as an interim replacement had as much to do with his own political ambitions as it did with honoring a key player in Georgia politics.[72] Hardwick himself planned to run for the vacant Senate seat in the coming November elections. He knew that the interim appointee had to be someone who would not pose a political threat to his candidacy, and who would pose less of a threat than a woman? Moreover, having opposed the ratification of the Constitution's equal suffrage amendment, he needed to make amends with the women of Georgia, who were now enfranchised despite his efforts. Against this background, Felton, whose political career by now spanned six decades, was the obvious choice.[73]

Needless to say, Felton was thrilled by the prospect of going down in history as the first female U.S. senator.[74] Hardwick's decision to nominate her was not without controversy, of course. Not only was she a woman, she was also remembered by African Americans as an ardent white supremacist, and civil rights activists who had not forgotten her call for the lynching of black men argued that Felton would bring shame to the office.[75] Southern whites, however, widely revered her as the "Grand Old Lady of Georgia," and white women reformers, in particular, rallied behind her nomination, pointing to her achievements as a suffragist and an advocate of prohibition. Yet, even with this support, it soon became apparent that Felton might not be seated.[76] Congress was not expected to convene again until after elections which were set to be held in November. This meant that Felton would be unable to take the oath of office before the citizens of Georgia elected a new senator.

In response to this situation, Felton's supporters, led by Helen Dortch Longstreet, widow of General James Longstreet (second in command to Robert E. Lee), petitioned President Harding to call a special session of the 67th Congress so that Felton could be sworn in and officially seated.[77] President Harding, however, refused the request on the grounds that a special session would prove too costly for the swearing in of a single senator whose appointment would expire in a matter of weeks.[78] As the days passed, therefore, it seemed increasingly unlikely that Felton would have her day in the Senate. The November elections came and went while she lay in an Atlanta hospital bed recovering from a bad cold.

In the end, Walter Franklin George, an ex-justice of the state supreme court, defeated Hardwick and six other candidates in the Senate race. Felton had written in support Hardwick's campaign, but she had wisely refrained from criticizing George, who had few political enemies in 1922.[79] He received the official Democratic nomination and campaigned for the Senate seat as an avid "Dry"—a temperance supporter—and an open opponent of the League of Nations, U.S. loans to foreign countries, and the Dyer Anti-Lynching Bill. Indeed, in accepting the Democratic nomination George specifically promised to work against the Dyer Bill (which had recently passed in the U.S. House of Representatives), charging that it was an affront to states' rights. The bill, he argued, "proceeds directly upon the assumption that the States or the people have lost the capacity to govern themselves."[80]

Despite Governor Hardwick's defeat and the election of a new senator, Felton continued to hope that she might be sworn in, and on November 8 she wrote the Republican president from her hospital bed. She had been personally acquainted with almost every president since Ulysses S. Grant, and President Harding was no exception. Shortly after his 1920 election, Harding had invited Felton to an advisory conference in Florida to get her opinion on America's international policies, and Felton hoped that this personal acquaintance might convince him to reconsider his decision about a special session.

The very next day newspapers reported, to Felton's delight, that President Harding had indeed issued a proclamation calling Congress into "extra session" at noon on Monday, November 20. Of course, he had not even received her letter yet, but the election results had convinced him that an extra session might be useful. The Republican majority in both houses would be greatly reduced when the next Congress took office in March 1923, and President Harding believed that he had a much better chance of getting a controversial ship subsidy bill through the incumbent Congress than through the incoming one. Out of the hospital for only three days, Felton packed her bags. But would the newly elected senator, Walter George, refrain from presenting his credentials and allow her to be sworn in? When initially asked if he would hold off presenting himself in the Senate until after Felton had claimed her seat, he explained that according to the Seventeenth Amendment her term as an appointed senator had ended the day he was elected and that there was therefore nothing he could do to help.

On November 14, however, Felton received a late-night call from George. He had reconsidered and would allow her to present her credentials, although he could not assure her that they would be accepted. In fact, he warned, she might be barred from the Senate floor. Was she willing to risk such public embarrassment? With her bags packed, Felton had already made her decision—now Congress would have to decide.

The train ride to Washington provided Felton with plenty of time to "ponder the significance" of her appointment. Thinking "back over the years and decades," she could hardly believe that someone like herself "reared in the sheltered security of an antebellum plantation," might become the first woman to sit in the U.S. Senate.[81] Her thoughts that cold winter morning took her back to the days when a southern woman of her class and race "was viewed only as an ornament and a household mistress." As she explained, "I thought back through the years and decades and remembered the first time a woman had lifted her voice in public at our little country church in my girlhood. What a stir that had caused! Who in that day would have had the hardihood to predict that the time would come when Georgia women would hold public office?"[82]

Felton hoped, then, that her lifelong campaign for women's rights would be rewarded on the Senate floor. A quarter of a century had passed since the "lynch a thousand a week" Tybee Island Speech had catapulted her into the national political spotlight and inaugurated her career as the leading female southern politician. Much had changed since the 1890s and yet much remained the same. The Eighteenth Amendment, outlawing the sale and consumption of alcohol, had been ratified. The Ku Klux

Klan had risen again and was terrorizing blacks, women, Jews, Catholics, and Republicans.[83] Race riots continued to plague urban centers and lynching remained a part of the southern political landscape. Women had won the franchise with the ratification of the Nineteenth Amendment, and the Georgia legislature had finally raised the legal age of consent. Felton had changed as well, but she had not wavered in her commitment to women's rights. As early as the 1880s, her campaign for female protection, beginning with black female convicts, placed her directly at the center of southern racial and sexual politics. Her capitulation to the politics of white supremacy in the late 1890s allowed for the emergence of a politics of white female supremacy that eventually gave way to a more inclusive feminist stance by the 1920s. Never afraid to step into the political fray, by 1922, Felton's ideas about rape and lynching had come full circle. One questioned remained: Would she be sworn in as the first female senator of the United States?

8

THE GENDER AND RACIAL POLITICS
OF THE ANTI-LYNCHING MOVEMENT

In hopes of changing history, Ida B. Wells-Barnett, like Rebecca Latimer Felton, also boarded a train bound for Washington, D.C., in 1922. Wells-Barnett, however, did not make the journey alone. She traveled with a delegation of black clubwomen who had recently attended the 13th Biennial Session of the National Association of Colored Women (NACW) in Richmond, Virginia. Dressed in their Sunday best, with extravagant hats on their heads and prim white gloves on their hands, the fifteen NACW delegates had an appointment with President Warren Harding to urge him to hasten final action on the Dyer Bill, the first anti-lynching law to reach the U.S. Senate.[1] Thirty years had passed since Wells-Barnett had single-handedly initiated the anti-lynching movement and first called on the federal government for protection for African Americans against southern lynch mobs. For Wells-Barnett, the bill's passage would mean that her lifelong anti-lynching plea would at last be answered. What were the chances that both Wells-Barnett, who had made a career campaigning against lynching and championing black women's rights, and Felton, who had worked tirelessly on behalf of southern white women and advocated lynching for their protection, would both have their life's work validated by the 67th Congress of the United States?

In 1922, as Wells-Barnett looked back over her life it must have been difficult for her to fully appreciate the slow but steady impact of her radical protest politics on the larger movement to protect black women from sexual violence and black men from lynching. The "New Negro" of the early twentieth century, like Wells-Barnett, refused to tolerate white supremacist politics that relegated blacks to second-class status. And the "New Negro Woman" now also embraced a more politically radical image of black womanhood that recognized the limits of racial uplift and acknowledged the power of political action in the form of direct protest. But although Wells-Barnett had led the way, few were willing or able to credit her for helping to redefine uplift as agitation. Nevertheless, unwilling to sit on the sidelines, and still determined to have something "to show for all those years of toil and labor," Wells-Barnett continued to challenge the racial and sexual politics that served to justify lynching while ignoring the rape of black women.

The New Negro Woman's Political Power

In 1902, Mary Church Terrell published "What Role Is the Educated Negro Woman to Play in the Uplifting of Her Race?" In an eloquent conclusion, Terrell summed up, "Seeking no favors because of their color nor charity because of their needs they knock at the door of Justice and ask for an equal chance."[2] Black clubwomen, however, would have to redefine their politics of uplift into a discourse of militant protest, force their way through the "door of Justice," and demand protection against white violence if they wanted "an equal chance" in twentieth century America. Roughly two decades later, World War I and the ratification of the Nineteenth Amendment helped foster the emergence of the New Negro Woman, who was indeed more willing to embrace militant agitation.[3]

In 1919, black clubwomen sparked a new phase of the anti-lynching campaign that called for direct action and demanded white women's active involvement. And as they continued to fight for social justice and reform, and embraced female suffrage as a crucial weapon in the battle against lynching and the sexual exploitation of black women, their politics became decidedly more radical.[4] Increasingly now, black clubwomen participated in and helped to lead the NAACP's campaign for federal anti-lynching legislation. They raised thousands of dollars for the cause, gave public lectures about the evils of lynching and the realities of rape, initiated and joined protest marches, lobbied senators, and testified before Congress. Working with the NAACP, the NACW engaged in speaking and petitioning campaigns against lynching and investigated instances of mob violence that kept the issue constantly before the American public.

In all these ways, black clubwomen were following in the footsteps of Wells-Barnett, who had paved the way for the New Negro Woman in her most radical incarnation. Although on the margins of the national movements, Wells-Barnett continued to set the pace for a new generation of activists, leading a variety of organizations and political protests locally in

Chicago. Linking disenfranchisement to rape and lynching of African Americans, she insisted that woman suffrage was vital to the goals of re-shaping local and national politics and ensuring protection. Since Reconstruction, African Americans had understood the power of the ballot and embraced black male suffrage as a means of acquiring and maintaining their rights as citizens. But Wells-Barnett, like many black women, was not willing to accept the idea that the dirty world of male politics was no place for a woman. Dedicated to ensuring equal rights and justice through direct political action, she embraced woman suffrage as essential to the survival of black communities. She understood all too well that white anti-suffragists feared the power that the ballot would extend to both white and black women. Ultimately, however, Wells-Barnett defined suffrage not simply as a woman's issue but as part of the larger campaign for racial and human justice. In this regard she formed part of a tradition of black women stretching back to the 1880s, but the new generation who came on the scene after 1910 now pushed for the right to vote more pointedly. And Wells, ever in the vanguard, sought to further sharpen the edge. The 1908 race riot in Springfield, Illinois, and the 1909 lynching in Cairo, Illinois, of William James, a black man accused of raping and murdering a white woman, reinforced not only her belief that blacks needed federal protection, but also her commitment to the ballot as black people's most powerful weapon in the battle against racial and sexual violence.

The events leading up to the Springfield riot began on August 14, 1908, when Nellie Hallam, a twenty-one-year-old white woman, alleged that George Richardson, a black man, had raped her. Although Richardson pled his innocence, he was arrested and placed in a jail cell with Joe James, a black vagrant from Birmingham, Alabama, accused of the attempted rape of a white woman and the murder of a white man. When rumors spread that a mob was en route to the jailhouse, local authorities moved the two men to Bloomington for safekeeping. The mob was furious to learn that the men had been taken to safer quarters. Prodded by Kate Howard, a white rooming-house owner, who called on the mob to live up to their duty to protect white womanhood, the men destroyed the restaurant and car of the white man whose vehicle had been used to transfer the prisoners to Bloomington.[5] Still not satisfied, the mob, which had swelled to twelve thousand, began attacking any black person they could find. They beat black porters at the railroad depot and pulled blacks off the streetcars. After setting fire to the black business district and residential area, the bloodthirsty mob then lynched two innocent black men, Scott Burton, a barber, and William Donegan, a shoe cobbler, in the public square. Hundreds of blacks were injured and four whites were dead by the time the Illinois State Militia finally arrived and restored ordered.

Horrified that a riot had occurred in Abraham Lincoln's hometown, Wells-Barnett in her Sunday school class (which consisted of young black men ranging from eighteen to thirty years of age) expressed her dismay that Chicago blacks had not taken to the streets to protest the actions of the mob. When one of her students asked, "What can we do about it?" she invited the class to her home to discuss a plan of action. The meeting led to the formation of the Negro Fellowship League (NFL), an organization that Wells-Barnett would preside over as president for the next decade. The League initially began as a debating society committed to finding solutions to problems facing young black men in the city. For two years the group met in Wells-Barnett's living room to discuss a range of self-help strategies rooted in direct action. In 1910, with a huge financial gift from Victor F. Lawson, owner of the *Chicago Daily News*, the NFL opened a settlement house on State Street in the heart of the Chicago's vice district. She explained, "I thought it was our duty to try to see that some sort of lighthouse was established on State Street."[6]

At the national level, the Springfield riot inspired the founding of the National Association for the Advancement of Colored People (NAACP). Wells-Barnett was a founding member, but the interracial organization's politics proved too conservative for her. Indeed, NAACP leaders made it quite clear that they had no interest in Wells-Barnett's radical protest tactics and made every effort to limit her participation in the organization. Disappointed, but not discouraged, Wells-Barnett put her energy into the NFL and continued her work against lynching and mob violence at the local level.

One thing that the Springfield riot had made very clear, Wells-Barnett emphasized, was that lynching was no longer just a southern problem. Northern whites were not immune to mob violence and northern white women were not above falsely crying rape—as in the case of Hallam, who two weeks after the riot signed an official statement clearing Richardson of the rape charges. She confessed that it had, in fact, been a white man (whom she refused to name) who was responsible for the assault. Wells-Barnett had long argued that black men were being lynched on trumped-up rape charges, but what had been defined as a particularly southern issue was clearly now a national problem that required federal intervention. If the Springfield riot was not enough to convince black and white skeptics that the problem of lynching would continue to spread if state and federal officials refused to offer protection to black men and women, perhaps another Illinois lynching would.

In 1909, just a year after the Springfield riot, a white mob in Cairo, Illinois, lynched William James, a black coal driver who had allegedly raped and murdered Anna Pelley, a white shop girl. The mob of over ten thousand whites followed the southern script. They first placed a rope around James's neck and forced a confession. Then the victim's sister, with the help of other women, pulled the rope to hang him, and the mob riddled his body with hundreds of bullets, dragged the mutilated corpse to the scene of the alleged crime, burned the body, and placed his severed head on a fence post. In response to James's confession, in which he implicated another black man, an "elderly gray-hair[ed] woman" pleaded with the mob not to let the other "black demon escape."[7] But when James's alleged accomplice could not be found, the mob decided instead to lynch Henry Salzner, a white man who allegedly murdered his wife and who had shared a jail cell with James. This time it was Salzner's sister-in-law who took charge of the mob's deadly actions. Again the mob dragged their victim from his jail cell, hanged him from a nearby tree, and riddled his body with bullets. No doubt because it was a white body, the mob refrained from mutilating his corpse to the same degree that they had James's.

When a committee of blacks in Chicago, which included Wells-Barnett's husband, called on her to go to Cairo to investigate the lynchings, she initially refused on the grounds that she "had already been accused by some of our men of jumping in ahead of them without giving them a chance."[8] In the end, however, she did go and interviewed twenty-five black citizens about the lynchings. Making use of her investigative report, a legal brief written by her husband, and the state's 1905 Anti-Lynching Bill that mandated "the governor to remove from office forthwith the sheriff of any county in which a man, black or white, has been taken by force from jail or the custody of that sheriff and lynched," Wells-Barnett help convince Governor Deneen to remove Sheriff Frank E. Davis from office for failing to make an effort to prevent the lynchings.[9] It no doubt helped that one of the victims in this case was a white man.

Regardless of the governor's motivations, Wells-Barnett came away from the Cairo event convinced more than ever that achieving greater political power was the only way that blacks would be able to guarantee their own protection against white violence. In a 1910 essay entitled "How Enfranchisement Stops Lynching," Wells-Barnett highlighted the Cairo lynching and the successful removal of Sheriff Davis as a model for ending mob violence. Blacks in Chicago, she explained, had used political pressure and the vote to ensure not only the passage of anti-lynching legislation in 1904, but also its enforcement in 1909. "They elected one of their number to the State Legislature in 1904," she recounted, "who secured the passage of a bill which provided for the suppression of mob violence."[10] The obvious corollary of this was that without the vote, blacks would remain powerless against mob violence: "With no sacredness of the ballot there can be no sacredness of human life itself. For if the strong can take the weak man's ballot, when it suits his purpose to do so, he will take his life also."[11]

Convinced that racial solidarity and political action were essential to the future, Wells-Barnett continued to encourage members of the NFL to engage in various forms of activism. In 1911, the League protested Thomas Dixon's play, *The Sins of the Father*, for its racist content and became actively involved in helping to free blacks falsely convicted of crimes. The League also became involved in the fight for woman suffrage at the state and national levels, participated in Republican Party work in Chicago, hosted candidates' forums, and encouraged voter participation. Made up mostly of a younger generation of activists, many of them male, the members of the NFL embraced Wells-Barnett's radical protest tactics without hesitation.

In January 1913, Wells-Barnett founded the Alpha Suffrage Club (ASC), the state's first black women's suffrage organization, to work for the passage of the Presidential and Municipal Suffrage Bill, which would provide women in Illinois with limited suffrage. In March, Wells-Barnett made news at the national suffrage parade in Washington, D.C., where she confronted the racial politics of the national women's movement. When southern suffragists threatened to boycott the parade if black women were allowed to march with their state delegations, northern suffragists, to Wells-Barnett's great disappointment, acceded to their demands. She, however, refused to march unless she was able to do so under the Illinois banner.[12] And despite a tentative compromise struck with some white delegates from

Illinois who agreed to march with the black women if they stayed to the back, Wells-Barnett instead proceeded to integrate the parade by stepping in from the sidewalk and joining the all-white Illinois delegation at the front of the procession.

Back in Chicago local black newspapers lauded her as a champion of racial justice. The *Chicago Defender* declared, "The race has no greater leader among the feminine sex than Mrs. Ida B. Wells-Barnett."[13] Still on a high from her success in Washington, Wells-Barnett mobilized the ASC and the NFL behind the fight for woman suffrage and against the passage of three discriminatory bills proposed in the Illinois legislature that included laws segregating public transportation and prohibiting interracial marriages. She organized several hundred black women to travel to the state capital to lobby against the bills. In April, when the Jim Crow transportation bill was defeated in the legislature, the *Defender* credited Wells-Barnett as one of the fourteen persons responsible: "The name of Mrs. Barnett stands alone, because that constant and fearless champion of equal rights was on the firing line all the time. Her eloquent pleas in private conferences with the legislators and in open session were eloquent and forcible. Ida B. Wells-Barnett has again endeared herself to the world."[14]

In June the state suffrage bill was signed into law and Wells-Barnett began preparing the ASC for Chicago's February 1914 primaries. The club set out to educate black women about their voting rights and organized a door-to-door campaign to get black women involved in politics. To avoid criticism, the ASC made the case that they were not interested in taking political offices from men, but were instead committed to putting "a colored man in the city council."[15] Meanwhile, Wells-Barnett had been appointed the first adult probation officer in the Domestic Relations Department of the Chicago Municipal Court, and she now used her salary and position to keep the NFL afloat financially. She also joined William Monroe Trotter's National Equal Rights League (NERL). When President Woodrow Wilson permitted racial segregation in federal offices for the first time in the country's history, Wells-Barnett and Trotter both met with him to protest.

In 1915, the League, led by Wells-Barnett, protested the showing of D. W. Griffith's *Birth of a Nation*, the film based on Thomas Dixon's *The Clansman*. Calling it "a menace to the dignity and peace of the city," they lobbied without success for the passage of a state law "to prohibit acts tending to incite ill-feeling or prejudice or to ridicule or disparage others on account of race."[16] Wells-Barnett recognized the danger the film posed to race relations not just in the South, but wherever it was shown. At best it reinforced racist and sexist stereotypes of black men and women, and at worst it had the clear potential to incite urban race riots. If indeed the film did provoke white violence, Wells-Barnett warned, blacks would not go down without a fight. In the end, although showings of *Birth of a Nation* did not immediately lead to riots in the Midwest, it was only a matter of time before the racial tensions it helped encourage exploded.

On July 2, 1917, four months after the United States entered World War I, a race riot erupted in East St. Louis after a shoot-out in a middle-class neighborhood between a group of white men intent on terrorizing the black community and blacks defending themselves. Events escalated when plainclothes officers drove into the neighborhood and were shot and killed by black citizens who believed they were whites returning to do more damage. The next day, in response to the murder of the two white detectives, a white mob marched through the city attacking blacks wherever they could be found. Black men, women, and children were again pulled off streetcars and beaten unmercifully. The white mob set fire to homes and shot those trying to escape. While there were no reported rapes, white violence against black women nevertheless carried sexual overtones, with mob members stripping black women of their clothing. After two days of rioting, two hundred homes had been burned down, five thousand blacks had fled the city, and at least forty black people were dead, with many more brutalized.

As news of the riot spread, Wells-Barnett began organizing. On July 3, she called a meeting of the NFL, which agreed to send her to East St. Louis to investigate. In a pamphlet titled *The East St. Louis Massacre: The Greatest Outrage of the Century*, Wells-Barnett recounted what she had learned during her trip. Using the victims' own words, together with reports from the white press, she exposed the brutality of the mob and the negligence and complicity of the local police and state militia. Not surprisingly, she opened her pamphlet with the words and experiences of black women and highlighted white women's brutality. Wells-Barnett was pleased when Congress, responding to outrage and protest across the country, launched an investigation. In a letter to the *Broad Ax* she praised Congress for acting, but called on people to engage in further action. Prayers, protests, and passing resolutions were not enough. She explained, "We all know that unless these parades are followed up by hard work in the trenches, and all the firing of guns by every conceivable active physical movement possible, the war will not be won."[17] She insisted that blacks raise money to attend the congressional hearings en masse to ensure justice on the part of black victims and to prevent such riots from occurring in the future.

In general, World War I served to intensify the racist climate and sparked another deadly new wave of mob violence in America. In 1919 there were twenty-five race riots across the country, including one in Wells-Barnett's hometown of Chicago. White lynch mobs nationwide killed thirty-six blacks in 1917, sixty in 1918, and seventy-six in 1919.[18] Wells-Barnett's predictions were coming to pass. In the midst of this epidemic of atrocities, the lynching of Mary Turner elicited an especially strong response from the NAACP and black clubwomen who had hoped the wartime rhetoric of democracy and justice would bring an end to mob violence. Turner was one of a total of eleven African Americans lynched in Brooks and Lowndes Counties, Georgia, between May 17 and May 22, 1918, for the alleged murder of Hampton Smith, a white farmer. Her husband, Hayes Turner, was implicated in the murder and was one of the first to be lynched. But Mary, who was eight months pregnant, complained that the lynching was unjust and called for the punishment of those responsible. As described in Chapter 6, for this, she and her unborn child were brutally murdered by a mob of over five hundred white men and women.[19]

News of the gruesome lynching spread quickly through African American communities and provoked outrage and protests across the country. Meta Vaux Warrick Fuller, one of the most prominent sculptors of the Harlem Renaissance, protested the lynching with her sculpture *Mary Turner (A Silent Protest).*[20] The painted plaster sculpture depicts a woman, clutching her pregnant belly, looking down into the faces of the mob. African American playwright Angelina Weld Grimké, great-niece of the abolitionists Sarah and Angelina Grimké, also wrote a short story about Turner's lynching called "The Creaking" (and published her first anti-lynching play *Rachel* in 1916).

Meanwhile, black clubwomen's groups responded to the general upsurge in racial violence by amplifying their calls for both political and legal action. The Northeastern Federation of Colored Women passed a resolution supporting anti-lynching legislation at their July 1918 meeting and sent a letter to President Wilson protesting the lynching of African

American men and women and attacking the idea of white women as rape victims by highlighting racial and sexual violence against black women. They insisted Wilson should instead read "the story of assaults white men have made on colored women's honor by looking at the many hued faces of the race."[21] In 1919, the Federation of Colored Women Clubs of New Jersey and the Empire State Federation of Women's Clubs passed similar resolutions. The black Baptist Women's Convention demanded congressional passage of anti-lynching legislation and asked Baptist churches to dedicate the Sunday before Thanksgiving to fasting and prayer for an end to mob violence.[22]

In May 1919, the NAACP sponsored a "National Conference on Lynching" that drew over twenty-five hundred men and women to Carnegie Hall to hear speeches by black and white leaders. The meeting resolved to support federal anti-lynching legislation, to organize state committees to create favorable public opinion, and to carry on fundraising and advertising campaigns. In response, Mary Talbert, the president of the NACW, who had worked with Congressman L. D. Dyer, sponsor of the Dyer Anti-Lynching Bill, pledged black clubwomen's organized support. Regional black women's clubs, like the Northeastern Federation of Women's Clubs, also developed anti-lynching departments that published pamphlets to increase the awareness of lynching as a national problem.[23] Wells-Barnett was not present at the NAACP conference, yet black clubwomen and the NAACP had clearly adopted many of the protest tactics that she had long insisted were necessary, and legislative action to confront the problem of lynching at a national level now seemed to be a real possibility as well.

The Dyer Anti-Lynching Bill

Republican congressman Leonidas Dyer of Missouri first introduced the Dyer Anti-Lynching Bill in 1918.[24] It held that "if any State or county fails, neglects or refuses to secure and maintain protection to the life of any person within its jurisdiction against a mob or riotous assemblage, such State or county shall by reason of such failure, neglect, or refusal be deemed to have denied to such person equal protection of the laws." It also declared that "any State or municipal officer" who refused to make all "reasonable efforts" to prevent a lynching or to pursue a person who participated in mob violence "shall be guilty of a felony and upon conviction shall be punished by imprisonment not exceeding five years or by a fine not exceeding $5,000 or both." Further, the proposed law provided

that any county in which a mob murdered a person would have to pay
$10,000 to family members of the victim.[25]

The bill drew little support until 1919, when race riots broke out in
twenty-six cities, including Washington, D.C., and Chicago, and white
mobs lynched at least seventy-six African Americans (twelve of them U.S.
soldiers).[26] The "Red Summer," as it was described by civil rights activist
and writer James Weldon Johnson, marked not only an escalation in
racial violence, but also a rise in black resistance and political mobilization.[27] In addition to the activities of black women's clubs and other
groups all over the county, new publications such as Wells-Barnett's "The
Race Conflict in Arkansas" and the NAACP's *Thirty Years of Lynching,
1889–1918* helped keep black public attention focused.[28] And at the 1920
Republican National Convention in Chicago, pressure from African American voters helped ensure that the anti-lynching bill was officially adopted
as part of the party platform.[29]

Two years later, anti-lynching advocates insisted that the Republican
Party make good on its commitment. With midterm elections less than a
year away and nearly all the members of the House and one-third of the
Senate facing election contests, the Republican-dominated House of Representatives passed the Dyer Bill by a vote of 230 to 119 in January 1922.[30]
Republicans had, of course, pushed the bill through the House to secure
black votes in the upcoming election, but as the *New York Times* suggested, they were in fact simply "passing the buck."[31] The real battle would
now come in the Senate.

With three decades of anti-lynching activism under her belt, Wells-
Barnett understood how Congress worked and the lengths to which southern Democrats would go to ensure that the bill failed in the Senate. As
early as 1894, she had testified before Congress in favor of a bill proposed
by Senator Henry W. Blair of New Hampshire that merely called for an
investigation of sexual and racial violence in the American South.[32] To
her disappointment, the Blair Bill never made it out of the House of Representatives. Four years later, when a white mob murdered postmaster
Frazier B. Baker and his daughter Dorah in Lake City, South Carolina,
Wells-Barnett again called on Congress to act. Leading a delegation that
met with President William McKinley, she had argued that Baker's status
as a "federal officer" gave Congress the "authority" to punish the white men
and women who had murdered him. After spending five unsuccessful
weeks in Washington lobbying congressmen to support a bill that would

pay $1,000 to Baker's widow and surviving children, she returned to Chicago hoping to raise money to support further efforts, but was unable to generate the necessary funds.[33]

Still, much had changed since the 1890s, when Wells-Barnett had first brought the problem of lynching into the national and international spotlight. By 1922, African Americans had raised thousands of dollars to fight the problem, and for the first time since Reconstruction a significant number of Republicans seemed genuinely committed to federal intervention for the protection of African American citizens.[34] Wells-Barnett was no longer the leading anti-lynching voice in the country, and indeed the once female-dominated campaign against southern mob violence now seemed to be giving way to the predominantly male-led NAACP.[35] But in July 1922 when the Senate Judiciary Committee voted 8 to 6 in favor of the Dyer Bill she undoubtedly celebrated.[36] Never before had anti-lynching activists come so close to getting the federal government to pass a law to protect African Americans from mob violence. The seeds she had planted all those years ago, it now seemed, might actually bear fruit. Inspired by this hope and eager to be at the dedication of Frederick Douglass's home, Wells-Barnett made plans to attend the August biennial meeting of the NACW in Virginia. A huge portion of the meeting was to be dedicated to discussing the Dyer Anti-Lynching Bill, and she planned to be part of the conversation.

Even though Wells-Barnett's late nineteenth-century campaign against southern sexual and racial violence had inspired the founding of the NACW in 1896, a decade had now passed since she had last attended one of the organization's meetings. She had not forgotten how during the NACW's fourth biennial meeting in St. Louis delegates had "hissed" her from the floor for initiating a controversial resolution regarding its publication, the *National Notes*. Wells-Barnett's motion had called for the election of the paper's editor, a move clearly intended to oust Margaret Murray Washington (wife of Booker T. Washington) from the position. Wells-Barnett had made no secret of her contempt for Booker T. Washington's conservative politics, and many perceived the resolution as a personal attack. Recounting the episode in her autobiography, Wells-Barnett complained that African American activists had allowed pettiness and personal politics to get in the way of their larger political goals.[37] Yet in 1922, her anger and hurt feelings seemed small matters with the passage of the Dyer Bill hanging in the balance. If she wanted something "to show for all those years of toil and labor," then she would clearly have to reenter the anti-lynching campaign at the national level.

At the opening of the NACW's weeklong meeting, James Weldon Johnson, secretary of the NAACP's New York branch, gave a lecture titled "The Anti-Lynching Fight of the National Association for the Advancement of Colored People," and Walter White, NAACP assistant secretary, delivered a speech titled "Practical Anti-Lynching Activities for Club Women.[38] Both men, Wells-Barnett noted, "paid high tribute to the colored women of America and appealed to them to shoulder unshrinkingly the great responsibilities which they must face."[39] Sitting in the audience, however, she surely must have cringed when Addie Hunton, a Virginia NAACP field organizer and clubwoman, introduced Johnson by crediting Virginia newspaper editor John Mitchell Jr. with starting the anti-lynching movement and praising the NAACP for continuing the fight. The next evening, Nannie Burroughs, head of the NACW Anti-Lynching Department, reintroduced Walter White, who gave another speech regarding the Dyer Bill.[40] After White's speech, former NACW president Mary B. Talbert addressed the meeting regarding the newly formed Anti-Lynching Crusaders. The organization of black clubwomen, she explained, would work to publicize the horrors of lynching in order to garner support for the Dyer Bill and raise "a million dollars" to help fund the NAACP's anti-lynching efforts.[41] Before closing the meeting, Burroughs "announced that there would be a day set apart for prayer concerning the passage of [the Dyer Bill], and urged the co-operation of every colored woman in the country."[42]

Wells-Barnett proposed an alternative to prayer. Why not make a trip to Washington and "let the Senators see that our women, who had the vote, were going to use those votes against the men who did not work and vote for the bill?" she asked.[43] Despite her call for a mass delegation, NACW leaders agreed to send only fourteen delegates—from states with key senators. Two days after the NACW meeting adjourned the clubwomen arrived in Washington to meet with President Harding and several Republican congressmen. After they presented Harding with statistics regarding eighty-three female victims of lynching between 1887 and 1922, he reiterated his commitment to the Dyer Anti-Lynching Bill and promised to encourage final congressional action as soon as consideration of the tariff and bonus measures were completed.[44] The president, however, expressed doubt as to whether passage of the bill would be possible before the 67th Congress adjourned in September. Next, the delegation called on the Republican Senate leader, Senator Lodge of Massachusetts, and the chairman of the Judiciary Committee, Senator Shortridge of California, both of whom pledged "prompt action."[45] But as President Harding predicted, the second session of the 67th Congress adjourned a month later without having considered the bill.

Congressmen had hardly packed their bags when anti-lynching activists began demanding that the president call a special session of Congress. Trotter's National Equal Rights League sent a telegram to President Harding requesting such a special session, and hundreds of anti-lynching advocates signed petitions pleading with the president "to save the great progress of twelve month's labor and wipe lynching from the Banners of the Republic."[46] With the November election just weeks away, Harding feared a discussion of the controversial Dyer Bill in a special session might prove costly for Republican candidates up for reelection. In the end, however, it was the election results that forced Harding to call members of the 67th Congress back to Washington. Troubled by the large number of Republicans who had lost their seats, and eager to have the incumbent Congress act on his ship subsidy measure, the president announced to the delight of both anti-lynching and women's rights activists that Congress would be called into extra session on November 20, 1922.

Back in Chicago, Wells-Barnett, like Rebecca Latimer Felton in Georgia, read in her local newspaper that the 67th Congress was being called back into session. A landmark year for Wells-Barnett, 1922 marked her sixtieth birthday and the thirtieth anniversary of the publication of *Southern Horrors*. The movement that she had initiated had grown from a one-woman campaign to a national effort, but despite her excitement about the Dyer Bill, she was skeptical of the Anti-Lynching Crusaders and refused to join their group. She complained that the Crusaders' agenda was too conservative and ultimately unworthy of the talents of black clubwomen. And she argued that instead of praying and raising money for the NAACP to put to unknown uses, the NACW should work for the legal defense of the race by raising money to pay lawyers. She lectured the Crusaders, "If you had started a crusade to get every voting woman out to the polls this month and next to work and vote against those congressmen and senators who are up for election who are known to be against [the bill]—then indeed you would have been doing something."[47]

Yet, even though Wells-Barnett declared the Anti-Lynching Crusaders "a direct insult to the intelligence of Negro womanhood of the land," the group, in fact, reflected a radical shift in black clubwomen's work. Taking a page from Wells-Barnett's playbook, the Crusaders sought to stop lynching by educating white Americans about the reality of southern mob violence and by raising a million dollars for the NAACP's anti-lynching fund, "to be used to pass and enforce the Dyer Anti-lynching Bill and to put down mob violence."[48] They also brought the full force of their political power to the anti-lynching movement by lobbying their congressmen, using their personal political contacts, casting their ballots for like-minded candidates, and mustering other women to political action. They organized black clubwomen at the state and local levels and asked them to hold meetings, petition public officials, persuade ministers to deliver anti-lynching sermons, sell anti-lynching buttons, and hold "sacrifice weeks" in which women were urged to contribute a dollar to the campaign.

The Crusaders were also determined to win white women to the cause. As early as 1913 the black Baptist Women's Convention had published an essay entitled "White Women and Colored Women Too Far Apart in Practical Sympathy" which called on white women to participate in anti-lynching activities and the protection of black womanhood. When Wells-Barnett had insisted in the 1890s that the rape of black women and the lynching of black men were intricately linked, black clubwomen hesitated to speak out publicly about sexual violence. No longer, however, were they willing to adhere to the etiquette that required middle-class women to refrain from speaking of such things in public. "This whole race problem will be quickly and easily solved," declared the black Baptist women, "when white women teach their children . . . to respect colored women more. . . . The race problem will never be solved until white and colored women work together for mutual respect and protection."[49] Interracial cooperation during the war years further reinforced black clubwomen's belief that white support was necessary. In July 1920, when the Women's Missionary Council Committee on Race Relations sent two white delegates as observers to the biannual conference of the NACW in Tuskegee, Alabama, the black women present prepared a statement for the white women to take back to their club to "call to the attention of white women certain conditions which affect[ed] colored women in their relations with white people."[50] Further, the statement informed white women of the "unjust and humiliating practice of which the colored women in the South have been the victims" and sought to enlist their aid in the campaign against lynching.[51]

In the fall of 1920, Charlotte Hawkins Brown, the founder of the Palmer Memorial Institute, a founding member of the National Council of Negro Women and president of the North Carolina State Federation of Negro Women's Clubs, spoke as follows to the white women who attended the Woman's Inter-Racial Conference in Memphis: "There is nothing fast looking about me. And yet I can tell you that more than a hundred times, in twenty years I have had to speak up and say, 'Mister, You have missed your woman.' I want to ask, my friends, that while you want to see the criminal who sets upon you punished won't you help us, friends, to bring justice to the criminal in your race who is just as much a criminal when he tramps on the womanhood of my race."[52] Brown also told the women how because of her color she had been expelled from a Pullman car on the train ride from North Carolina to Memphis to attend the conference. Dismayed and upset by her treatment, Brown suggested that white women could influence the actions of their men. Most importantly, she insisted that only with the support and help of white women would African Americans gain protection from violence at the hands of white men. "Just why I don't know but we all feel that you can control your men. We feel that so far as lynching is concerned that, if the white woman would take hold of the situation, that lynching would be stopped. . . . I want to say to you, when you read in the paper where a colored man has insulted a white woman, just multiply that by one thousand and you have some idea of the number of colored women insulted by white men."[53] In response to Brown's speech, the Memphis Woman's Inter-Racial Conference acknowledged white women's "responsibility for the protection of the Negro women and girls in our homes and on the streets," and urged that officers of the law do all in their power to prevent lynchings.[54] Subsequently, the white North Carolina Federation of Women's Clubs passed an anti-lynching resolution, and the National Council of Women, the Federated Council of Churches in America, the women of the Macabees, and the International Sunshine Society all endorsed the Anti-Lynching Crusaders.[55] White women were beginning to accept responsibility, and support was clearly spreading.

By this time, almost two decades had passed since Ida B. Wells had first deemed white support a necessary part of any campaign against lynching and rape. And despite Wells's earlier failure to convince the NACW to take a more confrontational approach, in the postwar years the tactics and arguments she advocated were increasingly the ones adopted by black clubwomen. As part of their effort to win support for the Dyer Bill, club-women also raised thousands of dollars for an aggressive publicity campaign that encouraged prominent whites to speak out against mob law.[56] The Anti-Lynching Crusaders represented the culmination of three decades of black women's efforts to end lynching and the sexual exploitation of black women in the United States. They stridently challenged the racist and sexist contradictions embedded in the stories that southern whites told about rape and lynching, and they presented a powerful counter-narrative in which they identified the white rapist, the black rape victim, the complicit white woman, and the politically disenfranchised black man as the real cast of characters on the stage of lynching.

In 1922, Margaret Murray Washington recognized white women's growing participation in the anti-lynching movement and declared: "The Georgia State Federation of White Women's Clubs in their last convention came out strongly in favor of law and order against mob violence and lynching. When the Women's State Federation of other Southern States take a stand against this evil, the men in authority in these states will see that lynching is put down and not until then will it be done. *It is women's work now as always.*"[57] The twentieth-century anti-lynching crusade had finally prompted black women, and now white women too, to fully embrace Wells-Barnett's radical tactics against rape and lynching.

An Extra Session

When the 67th Congress reconvened in November 1922 it was confronted with a range of issues, including whether or not to seat Rebecca Latimer Felton as the first female senator and whether or not to pass the Dyer Anti-Lynching Bill. On November 20, the first day of the extra session, Felton appeared on the floor of the Senate chambers, making it difficult for the all- male Senate to ignore the issue. Wearing a black bonnet, a fur coat, and white gloves, she was cheered by the throngs of white women crowded in the gallery and greeted with congratulations from senators she knew as she made her way to Tom Watson's empty seat. No other acknowledgment of Felton's presence was made, and the Senate adjourned early to honor the memory of Senator Watson.

The next day the session began with the presentation of credentials of all the new senators except Felton. After all the new junior senators were sworn in, William Harris, the senior senator from Georgia, gave the details of Felton's appointment and asked that she too be allowed to present her credentials. He explained that she would only serve for a day and that Justice Walter Franklin George would be sworn in the next day if no one objected. After a long pause allowing for any objections, it seemed that Felton would, indeed, be sworn in. "The Senator from Georgia will present the credentials of appointment," declared Senator Cummins of Iowa. "Mr. President," Senator Tomas Walsh, a Democrat from Montana, interrupted. Was he objecting? Recognized by Senator Cummins, Walsh proceeded to deliver a slow and deliberate speech on the constitutionality of Felton being seated. Finally he concluded, "I have said this much because I did not like to have it appear, if the lady is sworn in—as I have no doubt she is entitled to be sworn in—that the Senate had so far departed from its duty in the premises as to extend so grave a right to her as a favor, or as a mere matter of courtesy, or being moved by a spirit of gallantry, but rather that the Senate, being fully advised about it, decided that she was entitled to take the oath."[58] As Walsh took his seat, Cummins announced, to Felton's great relief, "The Secretary will read the certificate of the Junior Senator from Georgia." Felton walked to the rostrum where Cummins swore her in as the first female senator in the history of the United States.

Not quite ready to relinquish her seat, Felton appeared in the Senate chambers again the next day. After calling the session to order, Cummins recognized "the Junior Senator from Georgia." After thanking Governor Hardwick for appointing her, Justice George for allowing her to "have her day," and Senator Harris for assisting her, Felton concluded with a prediction: "Let me say, Mr. President, that when the women of the country come in and sit with you, though there may be but very few in the next few years, I pledge that you will get ability, you will get integrity of purpose, you will get exalted patriotism, and you will get unstinted usefulness."[59] Then, after the applause had ended, Felton terminated her brief senatorial career and George was sworn in. The new junior senator, who had based his campaign for the Senate on opposing the passage of the Dyer Anti-Lynching Bill, took his seat just in time to participate in the fight against the bill.

Despite President Harding's failure to mention the bill in his message to Congress on November 21, pressure from anti-lynching activists made it difficult for the Senate to ignore the issue. With money raised by the Anti-Lynching Crusaders, the NAACP placed full-page ads in daily newspapers across the country declaring, "THE SHAME OF AMERICA: Do you know that the *United States* is the *Only Land on Earth* where human beings are *BURNED AT THE STAKE?*"[60] The Anti-Lynching Crusaders themselves released press announcements highlighting white women's endorsements of the Crusade and their support for the Dyer Anti-Lynching Bill.[61] They reminded senators that rape was not the cause of lynching and pointed out that at least eighty-three women, some of them white, had been lynched between 1889 and 1921.

On November 27, when Republican senator Shortridge moved that the Senate consider the bill, however, southern Democrats were ready. They began by declaring that the motion was debatable, and from there they engaged in a range of stalling tactics that marked the beginning of a filibuster. A week into the filibuster, white women began speaking out. Ten women who were members of the Democratic Party cast aside party loyalty and protested against the action carried on by southern Democrats. They urged all women, regardless of party affiliation, to demand that the Dyer Bill be enacted.[62] Soon after, a group of white women from North Carolina's Commission on Inter-racial Co-operation also came out in support of the bill, declaring, "We resent the assertion that criminality can be controlled by lawless outbreaks and woman's honor protected by savage acts of revenge." White women in Georgia, Alabama, South Carolina, Virginia, Tennessee, and Texas made similar statements.[63] Despite the efforts of so many women, black and white, northern and southern, in the end, the filibuster was successful in stopping the Dyer Anti-Lynching bill. At the end of the extra session Senator Harrison criticized his fellow lawmakers: "Instead of debating the matter we were called into session to discuss, we did just four things. First we seated Mrs. Felton, the first woman to hold a seat in the Senate. Then we received the resignation of Senator Newberry. . . . Then we defeated the Liberian loan, and next we witnessed the death of the Anti-Lynching bill — and I want to say that these last two propositions were not offered in good faith."[64]

The fact that the 67th Congress had honored Felton, one of the most outspoken proponents of lynching in the 1890s, and at the same time delivered a deathblow to the Dyer Anti-Lynching Bill must have left a bitter taste in Wells-Barnett's mouth. Despite the brutal defeat of the bill, the anti-lynching battle would, of course, continue, but it would do so without Wells-Barnett. She would spend her remaining days on the margins of the national movement while fighting for justice and equality at the local level.

The Anti-Lynching Crusaders disbanded shortly after the bill's defeat. Although they had not accomplished their overall goal, they could take pride in having successfully brought black and white women together in the political fight against lynching. Indeed, other groups of women inspired by the Crusaders were able to bring about the enachment of anti-lynching legislation at the state level. The governor of Pennsylvania signed an anti-lynching bill into law in the spring of 1923. The southern wing of the Women's Missionary Council of the Methodist Episcopal Church passed a resolution demanding that the authorities of certain states make good on their claim to the right of local government by abolishing lynching. White women's groups in Alabama, Florida, Georgia, Texas, and Virginia again issued statements rejecting lynching carried out in the name of their protection.[65] Women of the Louisiana Commission on Interracial Cooperation issued a strong statement denouncing the argument that lynching was founded on chivalry and based on honoring womanhood.[66] Throughout the 1920s black and white women recognized their common interests and continued to work for the passage of a federal anti-lynching bill.[67]

In 1930, Jessie Daniel Ames, a white southern suffragist, founded the Association of Southern Women for the Prevention of Lynching (ASWPL) in Felton's home state of Georgia.[68] Worried by the rise in the number of lynchings in the early months of 1930, and convinced that lynching did not function to protect white women, Ames insisted it was southern white women's responsibility to combat mob violence. She was drawn to the lynching cause in 1922 after hearing Nannie Burroughs deliver a speech in Texas where she declared that lynching would not end until white women were ready to stop it.[69] The ASWPL adopted strategies originally defined by Ida B. Wells: publicly attacking the idea that lynching was punishment for rape; engaging in onsite investigations of lynching; and collecting and reporting lynching statistics. They also developed their own tactics, such as asking sheriffs to sign pledges stating their intent to assist in the eradication of lynching and publicly praising local officials who acted to prevent mob violence. They convinced over 40,000 southern white women to sign the ASWPL's anti-lynching pledge, which declared, "Public opinion has accepted too easily the claim of lynchers and mobsters that they were acting solely in defense of womanhood. In the light of facts, we dare no longer permit this claim to pass unchallenged. . . . We solemnly pledge ourselves to create a new public opinion in the South, which will not condone, for any reason whatever, acts of mobs or lynchers."[70] In many ways, the ASWPL represented an answer to the earliest calls, made by the Grimké sisters, for southern white women to take up the cause of racial justice as a women's rights issue.

One can only imagine what Felton would have thought of the ASWPL. She died on January 24, 1930, just months before the organization was founded. In the years after her day in the Senate she continued to weigh in on state and national politics. From 1922 until her death, Felton still wrote her column in the Atlanta Journal, in which she spoke out against the Ku Klux Klan and expressed her opinion on a range of issues, from air travel to the flapper. During a trip to Atlanta to attend a board meeting of the Georgia Training School for Girls, Felton suffered an attack of bronchitis, which developed into pneumonia. After eight days in the hospital, she passed away at the age of ninety-four. The following day the Senate recessed "out of respect" for the first woman to serve as a U.S. senator. Senator George eulogized her: "She had well defined and firmly fixed opinions upon social, moral, and political questions and was always ready to defend them. She possessed a remarkable insight in the character of public men of her time, with many of whom she was personally well acquainted. All and all she must be grouped among the great women of her time."[71]

No doubt Wells-Barnett, who died on March 25, 1931, soon after the founding of the ASWPL, was pleased to learn that southern white women had taken up her plea to organize against lynching. Not until June 2005, almost seventy-five years after her death, however, was Wells-Barnett's anti-lynching crusade finally recognized on the floor of the U.S. Senate. Led by Democratic senator Mary Landrieu of Louisiana, the 109th Congress passed a resolution apologizing for the Senate's failure to pass anti-lynching legislation. The resolution noted that nearly two hundred anti-lynching bills had been introduced in Congress during the first half of the twentieth century, and all had been defeated. Now, however, it resolved:

That the Senate —
(1) apologizes to the victims of lynching for the failure of the
Senate to enact anti-lynching legislation;

(2) expresses the deepest sympathies and most solemn regrets of the Senate to the descendants of victims of lynching, the ancestors of whom were deprived of life, human dignity, and the constitutional protections accorded all citizens of the United States; and

(3) remembers the history of lynching, to ensure that these tragedies will be neither forgotten nor repeated.

In the chambers of the Senate, Senator Landrieu recounted the 1892 Memphis lynching that sparked Wells-Barnett's anti-lynching crusade, and stated, "Without the work of this extraordinarily brave journalist, this story could never really have been told in the way it's being told now, today, and talked about here on the Senate floor. To her, we owe a great deal of gratitude."[72]

APPENDIX:
LIST OF FEMALE VICTIMS
OF LYNCHING

Date	Name	State	Alleged Crime
1837/04/?	*Maria del Rosario (w)	Los Angeles, California	Murder
1851/?/?	*Juanita (w)	Downieville,	?
1868/09/?	Cummins' Daughter	Pulaski Co., Kentucky	?
1870/09/?	Mrs. John Simes	Henry Co., Kentucky	Republican
1872/11/?	Mrs. Hawkins	Fayette Co., Kentucky	Republican
1872/11/?	?- Hawkins	Fayette Co. Kentucky	Republican
1876/05/?	Mrs. Ben French	Warsaw, Kentucky	Murder
1878/11/04	Maria Smith	Hernando, Mississippi	Murder
1880/12/11	Julia Brandt	Charleston, South Carolina	Murder
1881/04/09	Ann Cowan	Newberry, South Carolina	Arson
1884/01/18	Mrs. Cuddihee (w)	Denver, Colorado	Murder
1884/10/20	Jane Wade (w)	Chattooga, Georgia	Murder
1885/05/15	Elizabeth Taylor (w)	Clay Co., Nebraska	Arson
1885/09/29	Harriet Finch	Chatham Co., North Carolina	Murder
1886/07/25	Mary Hollenbeck	Tattnall, Georgia	Murder
1886/08/18	Eliza Wood	Madison, Tennessee	Murder
1887/04/28	Gracy Blanton	W. Carroll, Louisiana	Robbery
1889/04/18	Puss Kirk	Sumner, Tennessee	Arson
1889/01/19	Mrs. Smithson (w)	Timptonville, Tennessee	Murder/robbery
1889/02/20	Mrs. John Puckett (w)	Lyon Creek, Oklahoma	?
1889/07/22	Ellen Watson (w)	Sweetwater, Wyoming	Accused of cattle stealing
1891/04/15	Roxie Elliott	Bib County, Alabama	?
1891/05/09	Mrs. Lee	Lowndes, Mississippi	Son accused of murder
1891/08/06	Eliza Lowe	Henry County, Alabama	Arson
1891/08/06	Ella Williams	Henry County, Alabama	Arson
1981/08/06	Belle Williams	Henry Co., Alabama	Arson
1891/09/28	Lousie Stevenson	Hollandale, Mississippi	Murder

(continued)

Date	Name	State	Alleged Crime
1891//09/27	Grant White	Hollandale, Mississippi	Murder
1892/01/18	Mrs. Baker (w)	Arkansas	Murder
1892/02/03	Mrs. Martin	Chester, Tennessee	Mother of arsonist
1892/02/10	Jessie Dillingham	Smokeyville, Texas	Train wrecking
1892/02/10	Mrs. Brisco	England, Arkansas	Race prejudice
1892/03/13	Ella -	Rayville, Louisiana	Attempted murder
1892/10/07	Midrey Brown	Columbia, South Carolina	Poisoning
1892/11/02	Daughter of J. Hasting	Calahoula, Louisiana	Father accused of murder
1892/12/21	Cora -	Guthrie, Oklahoma	?
1893/03/19	Jessie Jones	Jellico, Tennessee	Murder
1893/07/18	Meredith Lewis	Roseland, Louisiana	Murder
1893/07/28	Ada Hiers	Waterboro, South Carolina	Murder
1893/09/14	Emma Fair	Pickens, Alabama	Arson
1893/09/14	Lousia Carter	Jackson, Mississippi	Well poisoning
1893/09/14	Mahala Jackson	Jackson, Mississippi	Well poisoning
1893/11/ ?	Evans' Daughter	Bardstown, Kentucky	Revenge
1893/11/ ?	Evans' Mother	Bardstown, Kentucky	Revenge
1893/11/ ?	Mrs. Phil Evans	Bardstown, Kentucky	Revenge
1893/11/04	Mary Motlow	Moore, Tennessee	Arson
1894/03/06	?	Pulaski Co., Arkansas	?
1894/07/24	?	Simpson Co., Mississippi	Race prejudice
1894/12/05	Mrs. Teddy Arthur (w)	Lincoln Co., West Virginia	?
1895/03/18	Harriet Talley	Petersburg, Tennessee	Arson
1895/03/18	Mrs. W. E. Holton (w)	Keyapaha Co., Nebraska	Murder
1895/04/21	Alice Greene	Greenville, Alabama	Murder
1895/04/21	Martha Greene	Greenville, Alabama	Murder
1895/04/21	Mary Dean	Greenville, Alabama	Murder
1895/05/25	Mrs. John Crocker (w)	Wharton, Texas	Murder
1895/07/01	Molly Smith (w)	Trigg Co., Kentucky	Murder
1895/07/20	Hannah E. Phillips	Sanpete Co., Texas	?
1895/07/20	Mrs. Abe Phillips	Sanpete Co., Texas	?
1895/07/20	Mrs. West Dixie (w)	Nashville, Tennessee	Murder
1895/07/23	?	Brenham, Texas	?
1895/08/02	Mrs. James Mason	Daingerfield, Texas	?
1895/08/28	?	Simpson, Mississippi	Miscegenation
1895/10/11	Catharine Matthews	Baton Rouge, Louisiana	Poisoning
1895/10/14	*Floatina Suitta (w)	Catula, Texas	Murder
1895/12/02	Hannah Kearse	Colleton, South Carolina	Knowledge of theft
1895/12/29	Mrs. T. J. West (w)	Lebanon, Kentucky	Adultery
1896/01/12	Charlotte Morris	Jefferson, Louisiana	Miscegenation
1896/08/01	Isadora Moreley	Selma, Alabama	Murder
1896/12/06	Jessie Winner (w)	Lexington, Missouri	Murder
1897/02/09	?	Carrolton, Mississippi	Robbery/arson

Date	Name	State	Alleged Crime
1897/03/02	? (w)	Morganton, North Carolina	?
1897/03/03	Mrs. William Whaley (w)	Sevier Co., Tennessee	?
1897/03/05	Otea Smith	Juliette, Florida	Murder
1897/03/12	Mrs. Joe Perry	Vance, North Carolina	?
1897/05/12	Amanda Franks	Jefferson, Alabama	Murder
1897/05/12	Molly Smith	Jefferson, Alabama	Murder
1897/10/02	Peb Falls (w)	Cowan Depot, Virginia	Disreputable character
1898/01/26	Mary Pearson (w)	Adams Co., Mississippi	Murder
1898/02/22	Dorah Baker	Lake City, South Carolina	Race prejudice
1898/08/09	Rilla Weaver	Monroe Co., Arkansas	Murder
1898/11/09	Rosa Etheridge	Phoenix, South Carolina	Murder
1898/11/13	Eliza Goode	Greenwood, South Carolina	Murder
1900/03/02	Mrs. Jim Cross	Lowndes, Alabama	?
1900/03/02	? -Cross	Lowndes, Alabama	?
1900/03/12	Cassie Boan (w)	Chesterfield, South Carolina	?
1900/07/07	Lizzie Pool	Hickory Plains, Arkansas	Race prejudice
1900/07/25	Anna Mabry	New Orleans, Louisiana	?
1901/03/16	Ballie Crutchfield	Smith, Tennessee	Theft
1901/04/06	May Hearn (w)	Oseola, Arkansas	Murder
1901/08/01	Betsy McCray	Carrolton, Mississippi	Implicated in murder
1901/08/01	Ida McCray	Carrolton, Mississippi	Implicated in murder
1901/10/04	?	Marshall, Tennessee	Assault
1901/10/08	Mrs. Ben Perkins (w)	Shelbyville, Kentucky	Jailer's wife
1901/11/24	Mrs. Rachel Powell (w)	Salem, South Carolina	Adultery
1902/02/15	Bell Duly	Fulton, Kentucky	Murder
1902/12/27	Mrs. Oliver Wideman	Greenwood, South Carolina	Murder
1903/06/08	?	Smith Co., Mississippi	Murder
1903/07/26	Jennie Steers	Shreveport, Louisiana	Poisoning
1903/10/28	Jennie McCall	Hamilton, Florida	Mistaken identity
1904/02/07	Mrs. L. Holbert	Doddsville, Mississippi	Murder
1904/06/14	Marie Thompson	Lebanon Junction, Kentucky	Murder
1904/08/30	?- Bates	Union, Arkansas	?
1906/11/08	Meta Hicks	Mitchell, Georgia	Husband accused of murder
1907/03/18	?	Stamps, Arkansas	Murderous assault
1907/03/18	?	Stamps, Arkansas	Murderous assault
1907/05/21	?-Padgett	Tattnall, Georgia	Race hatred
1907/05/21	Mrs. Padgett	Tattnall, Georgia	Race hatred
1908/10/03	Daughter of Walker	Fulton, Kentucky	Race hatred

(continued)

Date	Name	State	Alleged Crime
1908/10/03	Mrs. D. Walker	Fulton, Kentucky	Race hatred
1908/10/04	Mrs David Wallace (w)	Hickory Grove, Kentucky	Making threats
1909/02/09	Robby Buskin	Houston, Mississippi	Murder
1910/04/05	Laura Mitchell	Lonoke, Arkansas	Murder
1910/08/25	Laura Porter	Monroe, Louisiana	Disreputable house
1910/09/02	Hattie Bowman	Jackson Co., Florida	Complicit in murder
1911/05/25	Laura Nelson	Okemah, Oklahoma	Murder
1911/12/?	?-Pettigrew	Savannah, Tennessee	Race hatred
1911/12/?	?- Pettigrew	Savannah, Tennessee	Race hatred
1912/01/22	Belle Hathaway	Hamilton, Georgia	Murder
1912/02/13	Mary Jackson	Marshall, Texas	Complicit in murder
1912/06/24	Annie Barksdale	Dooly, Georgia	Murder
1912/06/25	Ann Bostwick	Pinehurst, Georgia	Murder
1912/08/05	Lew Burns	Corpus Christi, Texas	Attempted murder
1913/08/25	Virgie Swason	Greenville, Georgia	Murder
1914/03/31	Marie Scott	Wagoner Co., Oklahoma	Murder
1914/06/17	Mrs. Paralee Collins	West Plains, Missouri	?
1914/06/28	Jennie Collins	Shaw, Mississippi	Complicit in murder
1914/07/12	Rosa Richardson	Elloree, South Carolina	Murder
1914/11/25	Jane Sullivan	Byhalia, Mississippi	Arson
1915/01/14	Ella Barber	Monticello, Georgia	Assault
1915/01/14	Eula Barber	Monticello, Georgia	Assault
1915/03/13	Mrs. Joe Perry	Henderson, North Carolina	?
1915/05/?	?- Briley	Pescott, Arkansas	?
1915/12/08	Cordelia Stevenson	Lowndes, Mississippi	Son committed arson
1916/08/19	Mary Dennis	Newberry, Florida	Accessory to murder
1916/08/19	Stella Young	Newberry, Florida	Accessory to murder
1916/10/04	Mary Conley	Calhoun Co., Georgia	Complicit in murder
1917/03/01	Emma Hooper	Hammond, Louisiana	Murder
1918/05/18	Mary Turner	Lowndes, Georgia	Unwise remark
1918/06/04	Bessie Cabaniss	Huntsville, Texas	Threatening white man
1918/06/04	Sarah Cabaniss	Huntsville, Texas	Threatening white man
1918/06/04	Tenola Cabaniss	Huntsville, Texas	Threatening white man
1918/12/20	Alma House	Shubuta, Mississippi	Murder

Date	Name	State	Alleged Crime
1918/12/20	Maggie House	Shubuta, Mississippi	Murder
1919/05/05	?	Holmes, Mississippi	Race prejudice
1920/11/18	Minnie Ivory	Douglas, Georgia	Complicit in murder
1921/04/09	Rachel Moore	Rankin, Mississippi	Race prejudice
1922/02/11	W. L. Barker	Waco, Texas	?
1922/06/25	Mercy Hall	Oklahoma City, Oklahoma	Strike activity
1923/01/05	Lesty Gordon	Levy, Florida	Race prejudice
1923/09/29	?	Pickens, Mississippi	In search for brother
1923/09/31	?	Holmes, Mississippi	Race prejudice
1924/06/23	Penny Westmoreland	Spalding, Georgia	?
1924/09/11	Mrs. Sarah Williams	Shreveport, Louisiana	Son accused of murder
1925/10/11	Florence Curley (w)	Shreveport, Louisiana	Mistaken identity
1926/04/25	Lily Cobb	Birmingham, Alabama	?
1926/05/25	Mrs. Bryant	Duplin, North Carolina	Economically successful
1926/10/08	Bertha Lowman	Aiken, South Carolina	Murder
1926/11/11	Sally Brown	Houston, Texas	?
1928/05/04	Mrs. Kate Browning (w)	Shepherdsville, Kentucky	?
1928/12/25	?	Eros, Louisiana	Dispute w/ whites
1928/12/25	?	Eros, Louisiana	Dispute w/ whites
1929/09/14	Ella May Wiggins (w)	Gaston, North Carolina	Strike activity
1930/02/12	Laura Wood	Salisbury, North Carolina	?
1930/07/04	Viola Dial	Mississippi	Race prejudice
1931/05/?	Mrs. Wise	Frankfort, Virginia	Resisting Klan
1930/07/06	Mrs. James Eyer	Emelle, Alabama	Refused to stop car
1946/07/26	Mrs. Dorsey	Monroe, Georgia	?
1946/07/26	Mrs. Malcolm	Monroe, Georgia	?
1965/03/25	Viola Gregg Luizzo		Civil rights activist

* Further research may reveal that victim was Mexican.
(w) Victim was white.

NOTES

Introduction

1. David Walker, *Appeal . . . to the Coloured Citizens of the World*, ed. Charles M. Wiltse (1829; New York: Hill and Wang, 1965); and Peter P. Hinks, *To Awaken My Afflicted Brethren: David Walker and the Problem of Antebellum Slave Resistance* (University Park: Pennsylvania State University Press, 1997).

2. Jean Fagan Yellin and John Van Horne, eds., *The Abolitionist Sisterhood: Women's Political Culture in Antebellum America* (Ithaca: Cornell University Press, 1994); Julie Ray Jeffrey, *The Great Silent Army of Abolitionism: Ordinary Women in the Antislavery Movement* (Chapel Hill: University of North Carolina Press, 1998); and Erica Armstrong Dunbar, *A Fragile Freedom: African American Women and Emancipation in the Antebellum City* (New Haven: Yale University Press, 2008).

3. Frederick Douglass, *Narrative of the Life of Frederick Douglass, an American Slave, Written by Himself*, ed. Gerald Fulerson, John W. Blassingame, John R. Mckivigan, and Peter P. Hinks (1845; New Haven: Yale University Press, 2001); *My Bondage and My Freedom*, ed. William L. Andrews (1855; Urbana: University of Illinois Press, 1987); and Harriet Beecher Stowe, *Uncle Tom's Cabin* (1852; Ware, England: Wordworth Editions, 1999).

4. Angelina Grimke, "Appeal to the Christian Women of the South" (1836), in *American Political Thought: Four Hundred Years of Ideas and Ideologies*, ed. Sue Davis (Englewood Cliffs, N.J.: Prentice Hall, 1995), 228–234.

5. Sarah Grimké, "Letters on the Equality of the Sexes" (1838), in *Sarah Grimké: Letters on the Equality of the Sexes and Other Essays*, ed. Elizabeth Ann Bartlett (New Haven: Yale University Press, 1988), 59.

6. Gerda Lerner, *The Grimke Sisters from South Carolina: Pioneers for Women's Rights and Abolition*, rev. ed. (Chapel Hill: University of North Carolina Press, 2004); and Katharine Du Pre Lumpkin, *The Emancipation of Angelina Grimke* (Chapel Hill: University of North Carolina Press, 1993).

7. "Pastoral Letter of the Massachusetts Congregationalist Clergy" (1837), reprinted in *Up from the Pedestal: Selected Writings in the History of American*

Feminism, ed. Aileen Kraditor (Chicago: Quadrangle Books, 1968), 51; and Bartlett, *Sarah Grimke*, 38.

8. Nell Painter, *Sojourner Truth: A Life, a Symbol* (New York: W. W. Norton, 1996).

9. Nell Painter, "Representing Truth: Sojourner Truth's Knowing and Becoming Known," *Journal of American History* 81, no. 2 (September 1994): 461–492.

10. Harriet A. Jacobs, *Incidents in the Life of a Slave Girl* (repr.; Cambridge, Mass.: Harvard University Press, 1987). Also see Sharon Davie, " 'Reader, My Story Ends with Freedom': Harriet Jacobs's *Incidents in the Life of a Slave Girl*," in *Famous Last Words: Changes in Gender and Narrative Closure*, ed. Alison Booth (Charlottesville: University of Virginia Press, 1993); Winifred Morgan, "Gender-Related Differences in the Slave Narratives of Harriet Jacobs and Frederick Douglass," *American Studies* 35 (Fall 1994): 73–94; Jean Fagen Yellin, "Through Her Brother's Eyes: *Incidents* and 'A True Tale,' " in *Harriet Jacobs and "Incidents in the Life of a Slave Girl*," ed. Deborah M. Garfield and Rafia Zafar (New York: Cambridge University Press, 1996); Nell Irvin Painter, "Of *Lily*, 'Linda Brent,' and Freud: A Non-Exceptionalist Approach to Race, Class, and Gender in the Slave South," *Georgia Historical Quarterly* 76, no. 2 (Summer 1992): 241–260; Maggie Sale, "Critiques from Within: Antebellum Projects of Resistance," *American Literature* 64 (December 1992): 695–717; Harryette R. Mullen, "Gender and the Subjugated Body: Readings of Race, Subjectivity, and Difference in the Construction of Slave Narratives" (Ph.D. diss., University of California, Santa Cruz, 1990); and Claudia Tate, "Allegories of Black Female Desire; or, Rereading Nineteenth-Century Sentimental Narratives of Black Female Authority," in *Changing Our Own Words: Essays on Criticism, Theory, and Writing by Black Women*, ed. Cheryl A. Wall (New Brunswick, N.J.: Rutgers University Press, 1989).

11. Jacobs, *Incidents in the Life of a Slave Girl*, 18.

12. Ibid., 27–28.

13. Jacquelyn Dowd Hall, " 'The Mind That Burns in the Body': Women, Rape and Racial Violence," in *Powers of Desires: The Politics of Sexuality*, ed. Ann Snitow, Christine Stansell, and Sharon Thompson (Monthly Review Press, 1988), 328–349; and Jacquelyn Dowd Hall, *Revolt against Chivalry: Jessie Daniel Ames and the Campaign against Lynching* (New York: Columbia University Press, revised 1993); Hazel Carby, "On the Threshold of Woman's Era": Lynching, Empire, and Sexuality in Black Feminist Theory," in *"Race," Writing, and Difference*, ed. Henry Louis Gates Jr. (Chicago: University of Chicago Press, 1986), 301–316; Darlene Clark Hine, "Rape and the Inner Lives of Black Women in the Middle West: Preliminary Thoughts on the Culture of Dissemblance," *Signs* 14 (Summer 1989): 912–920; Catherine Clinton, "Bloody Ter-

rain: Freedwomen, Sexuality, and Violence during Reconstruction," *Georgia Historical Quarterly* 76 (Summer 1992): 313–332; Martha Hodes, "The Sexualization of Reconstruction Politics: White Women and Black Men in the South after the Civil War," in *American Sexual Politics: Sex, Gender, and Race since the Civil War*, ed. John C. Fout and Maura Shaw Tantillo (Chicago: University of Chicago Press, 1993), 59–74; Nancy MacLean, *Behind the Mask of Chivalry: The Making of the Second Ku Klux Klan* (New York: Oxford University Press, 1994); Elsa Barkley Brown, "Negotiating and Transforming the Public Sphere: African American Political Life in the Transition from Slavery to Freedom," *Public Culture* 7 (Fall 1994): 107–146; Elsa Barkley Brown, "To Catch the Vision of Freedom: Reconstructing Black Women's Political History, 1865–1880," in *African American Women and the Vote, 1837–1965*, ed. Ann D. Gordon (Amherst: University of Massachusetts Press, 1997), 66–99; Gail Bederman, *Manliness and Civilization: A Cultural History of Gender and Race in the United States, 1880–1917* (Chicago: University of Chicago Press, 1996); Tera Hunter, *To 'Joy My Freedom: Southern Black Women's Lives and Labors after the Civil War* (Cambridge, Mass.: Harvard University Press, 1997); Grace Hale, *Making Whiteness: The Culture of Segregation in the South* (New York: Pantheon Books, 1998); Diane Miller Sommerville, *Rape and Race in the Nineteenth-Century South* (Chapel Hill: University of North Carolina Press, 2004); Susanne Lebsock, *A Murder in Virginia: Southern Justice on Trial* (New York: W. W. Norton, 2004); Thavolia Glymph, *Out of the House of Bondage: The Transformation of the Plantation Household* (Cambridge: Cambridge University Press, 2008); and Hannah Rosen, *Terror in the Heart of Freedom: Citizenship, Sexual Violence, and the Meaning of Race in the Postemancipation South* (Chapel Hill: University of North Carolina, 2009).

14. Nell Irvin Painter, *Standing at Armageddon: The United States, 1877–1919* (New York: W. W. Norton, 1987); W. Fitzhugh Brundage, *Lynching in the New South: Georgia and Virginia, 1880–1930* (Chicago: University of Illinois Press, 1993); and W. Fitzhugh Brundage, ed., *Under Sentence of Death: Lynching in the South* (Chapel Hill: University of North Carolina Press, 1997); Glenda Elizabeth Gilmore, *Gender and Jim Crow: Women and the Politics of White Supremacy in North Carolina, 1896–1920* (Chapel Hill: University of North Carolina Press, 1996); Glenda Elizabeth Gilmore, "Murder, Memory, and the Flights of the Incubus," in *Democracy Betrayed: The Wilmington Race Riot of 1898 and Its Legacy*, ed. David S. Cecelski and Timothy B. Tyson (Chapel Hill: University of North Carolina Press, 1998), 73–93; Laura Edwards, *Gendered Strife and Confusion: The Political Culture of Reconstruction* (Chicago: University of Illinois Press, 1997); Martha Hodes, *White Women, Black Men: Illicit Sex in Nineteenth-Century South* (New Haven: Yale University

Press, 1998); Ann S. Holder, "Making the Body Politic: Narratives of Race, Sexuality and Citizenship in the United States, 1864–1909," (Ph.D. diss., Boston College, 1999); Jane Dailey, *Before Jim Crow: The Politics of Post-Emancipation Virginia* (Chapel Hill: University of North Carolina Press, 2000); Stephen Kantrowitz, *Ben Tillman and the Reconstruction of White Supremacy* (Chapel Hill: University of North Carolina Press, 2000); Steven Hahn, *A Nation under Our Feet: Black Political Struggles in the Rural South from Slavery to the Great Migration* (Cambridge, Mass.: Harvard University Press, 2003); and Rosen, *Terror in the Heart of Freedom.*

1. The Horrors of War

1. Rebecca Latimer Felton, *Country Life in Georgia in the Days of My Youth* (repr.; New York: Arno Press, 1980), 87.

2. Ibid.; Rebecca Latimer Felton, *The Romantic Story of Georgia's Women* (Atlanta: Atlanta Georgian and Sunday American, 1930). Also see John E. Talmadge, *Rebecca Latimer Felton: Nine Stormy Decades* (Athens: University of Georgia Press, 1960), and LeeAnn Whites, "Rebecca Latimer Felton and the Problem of 'Protection' in the New South," in *Visible Women: New Essays on American Activism,* ed. Nancy A. Hewitt and Susan Lebsock (Chicago: University of Illinois Press, 1993), 41–61.

3. Felton, *Country Life in Georgia,* 29.

4. Ibid., 98.

5. Ibid., 99.

6. On white women's violence against slave women, see Elizabeth Fox-Genovese, *Within the Plantation Household: Black and White Women of the Old South* (Chapel Hill: University of North Carolina Press, 1988), 112 and 132; Jacqueline Jones, *Labor of Love, Labor of Sorrow: Black Women, Work, and the Family from Slavery to the Present* (repr.; New York: Vintage, 1995), 26–27; Stephanie M. H. Camp, *Closer to Freedom: Enslaved Women and Everyday Resistance in the Plantation South* (Chapel Hill: University of North Carolina Press, 2004), 132; Winthrop D. Jordan, *Tumult and Silence at Second Creek: An Inquiry into a Civil War Slave Conspiracy* (Baton Rouge: Louisiana State University Press, 1993), 201–202; Drew Gilpin Faust, *Mothers of Invention: Women of the Slaveholding South in the American Civil War* (Chapel Hill: University of North Carolina Press, 1996), 63; and Thavolia Glymph, *Out of the House of Bondage: The Transformation of the Plantation Household* (Cambridge: Cambridge University Press, 2008).

7. Ann Firor Scott, *The Southern Lady: From Pedestal to Politics, 1830–1930* (Chicago: University of Chicago Press, 1970); Catherine Clinton, *The Plantation Mistress: Woman's World in the Old South* (New York: Pantheon Books,

1982); Fox-Genovese, *Within the Plantation Household*; Brenda E. Stevenson, *Life in Black and White: Family and Community in the Slave South* (New York: Oxford University Press, 1992); Jean E. Friedman, *The Enclosed Garden: Women and Community in the Evangelical South, 1830–1900* (Chapel Hill: University of North Carolina Press, 1985); Steven Stowe, *Intimacy and Power in the Old South: Ritual in the Lives of the Planters* (Baltimore: Johns Hopkins University Press, 1987); Stephanie McCurry, *Masters of Small World: Yeoman Households, Gender Relations, and the Political Culture of the Antebellum South Low Country* (London: Oxford University Press, 1997); Leslie A. Schwalm, *A Hard Fight for We: Women's Transition from Slavery to Freedom in South Carolina* (Urbana: University of Illinois Press, 1997); and Marli F. Weiner, *Mistresses and Slaves: Plantation Women in South Carolina, 1830–80* (Urbana: University of Illinois Press, 1998).

8. Talmadge, *Rebecca Latimer Felton*, 4.

9. For discussions about protection and rape of white women in the plantation South, see Bertram Wyatt-Brown, *Honor and Violence in the Old South* (New York: Oxford University Press, 1986); Diane Miller Sommerville, *Rape and Race in the Nineteenth-Century South* (Chapel Hill: University of North Carolina Press, 2003); Sharon Block, *Rape and Sexual Power in Early America* (Chapel Hill: University of North Carolina Press, 2006); Kristen Fischer, *Suspect Relations: Sex, Race, and Resistance in Colonial North Carolina* (Ithaca: Cornell University Press, 2001); Martha Hodes, *White Women, Black Men: Illicit Sex in the Nineteenth-Century South* (New Haven: Yale University Press, 1999); Victoria E. Bynum, *Unruly Women: The Politics of Social and Sexual Control in the Old South* (Chapel Hill: University of North Carolina Press, 1992); Peter W. Bardaglio, *Reconstructing the Household: Families, Sex, and the Law in the Nineteenth-Century South* (Chapel Hill: University of North Carolina Press, 1988); and Diane Miller Sommerville, *Rape and Race in the Nineteenth-Century South* (Chapel Hill: University of North Carolina Press, 2004).

10. Felton, *Country Life in Georgia*, 58, 66.

11. Talmadge, *Rebecca Latimer Felton*, 7–8.

12. Christie Anne Farnham, *The Education of the Southern Belle: Higher Education and Student Socialization in the Antebellum South* (New York: New York University Press, 1994); George C. Rable, *Civil Wars: Women and the Crisis of Southern Nationalism* (Urbana: University of Illinois Press, 1989), 19–22; Jane Turner Censer, *North Carolina Planters and Their Children, 1800–1860* (Baton Rouge: Louisiana State University Press, 1984); and Fox-Genovese, *Within the Plantation Household*, 45–47, 110–111, 257–259.

13. Felton, *Country Life in Georgia*, 62–63.

14. *Augusta Chronicle and Sentinel*, August 11, 1852.

15. William H. Felton, "An Address Delivered at the Annual Commencement of the Madison Female College," in Talmadge, *Rebecca Latimer Felton*, 11–12.

16. See George L. Jones, "William H. Felton and the Independent Democratic Movement in Georgia, 1870–1890" (Ph.D. diss., University of Georgia, 1971); William P. Roberts, "The Public Career of Dr. William Harrell Felton" (Ph.D. diss., University of North Carolina, 1953); and Talmadge, *Rebecca Latimer Felton*, 12–14.

17. Talmadge, *Rebecca Latimer Felton*, 15.

18. Beginning at the age of nineteen until she was thirty-six, she bore five children: John Latimer (1854–1865); Mary Eleanor (1856–1857); William Harrell Jr. (1859–1864); Howard Erwin (1869–1926); and Paul Aiken (1871–1873).

19. *Atlanta Georgian*, November 8, 1922, quoted in Talmadge, *Rebecca Latimer Felton*, 15.

20. Scott, *The Southern Lady*; Fox-Genovese, *Within the Plantation Household*; Joel Williamson, *The Crucible of Race: Black-White Relations in the American South since Emancipation* (New York: University of Oxford Press, 1984); Clinton, *The Plantation Mistress*; Julia Cherry Spruill, *Women's Life and Work in the Southern Colonies* (Chapel Hill: University of North Carolina Press, 1938); Nell Painter, "An Educated White Woman in the Eras of Slavery, War and Reconstruction," introduction to *The Secret Eye: The Journal of Ella Gertrude Clanton Thomas, 1848–1889*, ed. Virginia Ingraham Burr (Chapel Hill: University of North Carolina Press, 1990); Suzanne Lebsock, *Free Women of Petersburg: Status and Culture in a Southern Town, 1784–1860* (New York: W. W. Norton, 1984); and Kathleen M. Brown, *Good Wives, Nasty Wenches, and Anxious Patriarchs: Gender, Race, and Power in Colonial Virginia* (Chapel Hill: University of North Carolina Press, 1996).

21. Rebecca Latimer Felton, *My Memoirs of Georgia Politics* (Atlanta: Index Publishing Co., 1911), 18–19.

22. Felton, *Country Life in Georgia*, 91.

23. Ibid., 92–94.

24. C. Vann Woodward and Elisabeth Muhlenfeld, eds., *The Private Mary Chesnut: The Unpublished Civil War Diaries* (Oxford: Oxford University Press, 1984), 145.

25. Felton, *Country Life in Georgia*, 86.

26. Drew Gilpin Faust, *Mothers of Invention: Women of the Slaveholding South in the American Civil War* (New York: Vintage Books, 1997); Rable, *Civil Wars*; Catherine Clinton and Nina Silber, eds., *Divided Houses: Gender and the Civil War* (Oxford: Oxford University Press, 1992); Nancy D. Bercaw, *Gendered Freedom: Race, Rights, and the Politics of Household in the Delta, 1861–1875* (Gainesville: University Press of Florida, 2003); Lee Ann Whites, *The Civil War as a Crisis in Gender: Augusta, Georgia, 1860–1890* (Athens: University of Geor-

gia Press, 1995); and Edward D. C. Campbell Jr. and Kym S. Rice, eds., *A Woman's War: Southern Women, Civil War, and the Confederate Legacy* (Charlottesville: University of Virginia Press, 1996).

27. Felton, *Country Life in Georgia*, 88–89, 101–102.

28. Drew Gilpin Faust, "Altars of Sacrifice: Confederate Women and the Narratives of War," in *Divided Houses*, 171–199.

29. Felton, *Country Life in Georgia*, 105.

30. Faust, *Mothers of Invention*, 55–62.

31. "Emily Harris Diary, November 7, 1863," "Letter from Amanda Walker to the Confederate Secretary of War," and *Macon Daily Telegraph*, September 1, 1862, quoted in Faust, *Women of Invention*, 121–122, 57, 55.

32. Faust, "Altars of Sacrifice," 182–183.

33. Susan Eppes, *Through Some Eventful Years* (Gainesville: University Press of Florida, 1968), 119.

34. Catherine Clinton, *Tara Revisited: Women, War, and the Plantation Legend* (New York: Abbeville Press, 1995), 118.

35. Talmadge, *Rebecca Latimer Felton*, 18.

36. Steven Hahn, *A Nation under Our Feet: Black Political Struggles in the Rural South from Slavery to the Great Migration* (Cambridge, Mass.: Harvard University Press, 2003); Donald E. Reynolds, *Texas Terror: The Slave Insurrection Panic of 1860 and the Secession of the Lower South* (Baton Rouge: Louisiana State University Press, 2007); and John Hope Franklin and Loren Schweninger, *Runaway Slaves: Rebels on the Plantation* (New York: Oxford University Press, 2000).

37. Mary Boykin Chesnut, *A Diary from Dixie* (repr.; Cambridge, Mass.: Harvard University Press, 1980), 139.

38. Ibid., 140.

39. Ibid., 144–146.

40. Ibid., 140–176.

41. Ibid., 140.

42. Ibid., 151.

43. Ibid., 140.

44. United Daughters of the Confederacy, *War Days in Fayetteville, North Carolina: Reminiscences of 1861 to 1865* (Fayetteville, N.C.: Judge Printing, 1910), 44.

45. Felton, *Country Life in Georgia*, 98.

46. Elizabeth Lyle Saxon, *A Southern Woman's War Time Reminiscences* (Memphis: Pilcher, 1905), 33.

47. Ibid., 147.

48. Felton, *Country Life in Georgia*, 98–99.

49. Lee Kennett, *Marching through Georgia: The Story of Soldiers and Civilians during Sherman's Campaign* (New York: HarperCollins, 1995), 84.

50. Crystal N. Feimster, "General Benjamin Butler and the Threat of Sexual Violence during the American Civil War," *Daedalus* (Spring 2009): 126–134.

51. Benjamin F. Butler, *Autobiography and Personal Reminiscences of Major-General Benjamin F. Butler: Butler's Book* (Boston: Thayer, 1892), 418; Faust, *Mothers of Invention*, 207–214; Mary Ryan, *Women in Public: Between Banners and Ballots, 1825–1880* (Baltimore: Johns Hopkins University Press, 1990), 130–171; George Rable, "'Missing in Action': Women of the Confederacy," 134–146; and Hans L. Trefousse, *Ben Butler: The South Called Him Beast!* (New York: Twayne, 1957), 107–121.

52. Benjamin F. Butler, "Letter to John T. Monroe, May 16, 1862," in *The War of Rebellion: A Compilation of the Official Records of the Union and Confederate Armies*, ed. BVT. Lieut. Col. Robert N. Scott, ser.1, vol. 53 (Washington: Government Printing Office, 1880–1901), 1208.

53. Goldwin Smith, "The Alleged Federal Atrocities," *New York Times*, August 10, 1864.

54. Jefferson Davis, "A Proclamation," in *The War of the Rebellion*, ser. 2, vol. 5, 795–797.

55. Sarah Morgan, *Civil War Diary of Sarah Morgan*, ed. Charles East (Athens: University of Georgia Press, 1991), 76–77; Emma Holmes, *The Diary of Miss Emma Holmes, 1861–1966*, ed. John F. Marzalek (Baton Rouge: Louisiana State University Press, 1979), 165, 191; C. Vann Woodward, ed., *Mary Chesnut's Civil War* (New Haven: Yale University Press, 1981), 343; Clara Solomon, *The Civil War Diary of Clara Solomon: Growing Up in New Orleans, 1861–1862*, ed. Elliott Ashkenazi (Baton Rouge: Louisiana State University Press, 1995), 367–370; Ella Gertrude Clanton Thomas, *The Secret Eye: The Journal of Ella Gertrude Clanton Thomas, 1848–1889*, ed. Virginia Ingraham Burr (Chapel Hill: University of North Carolina Press, 1990); and Kate Stone, *Brokenburn: The Journal of Kate Stone, 1861–1868*, ed. John Q. Anderson (Baton Rouge: Louisiana State University Press, 1955), 111.

56. Ashkenazi, *The Civil War Diary of Clara Solomon*, 367–370.

57. Mary Chesnut, *Mary Chesnut's Civil War Diary*, ed. C. Vann Woodward (New Haven: Yale University Press, 1981), 343; and John F. Marszalek, *The Diary of Miss Emma Holmes, 1861–1866* (Baton Rouge: Louisiana State University Press, 1979), 165.

58. Sarah Morgan, "The Enemy Comes to Baton Rouge, May 17, 1862," in *Heroines of Dixie: Confederate Women Tell Their Story of War*, ed. Katharine M. Jones (New York: Bobbs-Merrill, 1955), 132–133.

59. Juila LeGrand, "New Orleans Is Full of Rumors, December 20, 1862," in *Heroines of Dixie*, 193–195.

60. Holmes, *The Diary of Miss Emma Holmes*, 191.

61. Robert Rosen, *The Jewish Confederates* (Columbia: University of South Carolina Press, 2000).

62. Cordelia Lewis, "I Never Walk or Ride without My Pistol, October 29, 1862," in *Heroines of Dixie*, 179–182.

63. "Julia Pope Stanley," quoted in Kennett, *Marching through Georgia*, 146.

64. Varina Howell Davis, *Jefferson Davis, Ex-President of the Confederate States of America: A Memoir by His Wife*, vol. 2 (New York: Belford, 1890), 577.

65. Reid Mitchell, *The Vacant Chair: The Northern Soldier Leaves Home* (New York: Oxford University Press, 1993), 102–103.

66. Robert I. Alotta, *Civil War Justice: Union Army Executions under Lincoln* (Shippensburg, Pa.: White Mane, 1989), 165.

67. Thomas P. Lowry, *Sexual Misbehavior in the Civil War: A Compendium* (Bloomington, Ind.: Xlibris Corporation, 2006), 154.

68. Ibid., 155.

69. Ibid., 148.

70. Ibid., 177.

71. See Kennett, *Marching through Georgia*.

72. Clinton, *Tara Revisited*, 111.

73. Felton, *Country Life in Georgia*, 88–89.

74. Talmadge, *Rebecca Latimer Felton*, 22.

75. Glymph, *Out of the House of Bondage*; Ervin Jordan, "Sleeping with the Enemy: Sex, Black Women, and the Civil War," *Western Journal of Black Studies* 18 (1994): 55–63.

76. "John N. Williams," quoted in Thomas P. Lowry, *The Story the Soldiers Wouldn't Tell: Sex in the Civil War* (Mechanicsburg, Pa.: Stackpole Books, 1994), 84.

77. "Dr. Daniel Heywards Trezevant," quoted in Clinton, *Tara Revisited*, 129–130.

78. "B. E. Harrison," quoted in Mitchell, *The Vacant Chair*, 107. General William Dwight, "Report, April 27, 1863," in *The War of Rebellion: A Compilation of the Official Records of the Union and Confederate Armies*, ed. BVT. Lieut. Col. Robert N. Scott, ser. 1, vol. 15 (Washington, D.C.: Government Printing Office, 1880–1901), 373.

79. Lowry, *Sexual Misbehaviors*, 123.

80. Ibid., 147.

81. Ibid., 122.

82. "Punishment of a Military Criminal," *New York Times*, August 2, 1864.

83. Talmadge, *Rebecca Latimer Felton*, 22.

84. Felton, *Country Life in Georgia*, 90–91.

85. Talmadge, *Rebecca Latimer Felton*, 24.

86. Felton, *The Romantic Story of Georgia Women*, 22.

87. "Clara D. MacLean," quoted in Clinton, *Tara Revisited*, 30.

88. Judith McGuire, *Diary of a Southern Refugee: By a Lady of Virginia* (repr.; Lincoln: University of Nebraska Press, 1995), 21–22, quoted in Rable, *Civil Wars*, 158.

89. Joan E. Cashin, "Chapter Two," in *A Woman's War: Southern Women, Civil War, and the Confederate Legacy*, ed. Suzanne Lebsock (Charlottesville: University of Virginia Press, 1997).

90. Saxon, *A Southern Woman's War Time Reminiscences*, 54–55.

91. Ibid., 55–57.

92. Felton, *The Romantic Story of Georgia's Women*, 22.

93. Virginia McCollum Stinson, "Yankee in Camden, Arkansas," in *Heroines of Dixie*, 283.

94. Cornelia Peake McDonald, "Hunter Burns the V. M. I," in *Heroines of Dixie*, 306.

95. "Josephine Bryan Worth," in *War Days in Fayetteville*, 50.

96. Charlotte St. Julien Ravenel, "The Enemy Comes to Our Plantation," in *Heroines of Dixie*, 372.

97. Holmes, *The Diary of Miss Emma Holmes, 1861–1866*, 384, 388.

98. Clinton, *Tara Revisited*, 110.

99. Mitchell, *The Vacant Chair*, 89.

100. Mary Ann Loughborough, "In the Cave at Vicksburg," in *Heroines of Dixie*, 225–226.

101. "Julia Davidson to John M. Davidson, July 19, 21, 26, 1864," quoted in Rable, *Civil Wars*, 171.

102. Jean V. Berlin, "Did Confederate Women Lose the War? Deprivation, Destruction, and Despair on the Home Front," in *The Collapse of the Confederacy*, ed. Mark Grimsley and Brooks D. Simpson (Lincoln: University of Nebraska Press, 2001), 179.

103. Faust, *Mothers of Invention*, 56.

104. Ibid., 59.

105. Felton, *Country Life in Georgia*, 92–94.

106. Susan Brownmiller, *Against Our Will: Men, Women, and Rape* (New York: Bantam Books, 1979).

107. Felton, *Country Life in Georgia*, 89.

108. Ibid., 84.

109. Ibid., 77, 79, 84, 92.

110. Felton, *The Romantic Story of Georgia's Women*, 18; Felton, *Country Life in Georgia*, 101.

111. Felton, *Country Life in Georgia*, 77–94.

112. Gerda Lerner, *The Feminist Thought of Sarah Grimké* (London: Oxford University Press, 1998); Gerda Lerner, *The Grimké Sisters from South Carolina: Pioneers for Women's Rights and Abolition* (London: Oxford University Press,

1998); and Ellen H. Todras, *Angelina Grimké: Voice of Abolition* (North Haven, Conn.: Linnet Books, 1999).

113. Felton, *Country Life in Georgia*, 79–93.

114. Painter, "Of Lily, 'Linda Brent,' and Freud: A Non-Exceptionalist Approach to Race, Class, and Gender in the Slave South," *Georgia Historical Quarterly* 76, 2 (Summer 1992): 241–260; Minroe Gwin, "Green-Eyed Monsters of the Slavocracy: Jealous Mistress in Two Slave Narratives," in *Black Women Conjuring: Fiction, and Literary Tradition*, ed. Marjorie Pryse and Hortense J. Spillers (Bloomington: Indiana University Press, 1986), 39–52; Glymph, *Out of the House of Bondage*; and Block, *Rape and Sexual Power in Early America*.

115. Mary Boykin Chesnut, *The Private Mary Chesnut: The Unpublished Civil War Diaries*, ed. C. Vann Woodward and Elisabeth Muhlenfeld (New York: Oxford University Press, 1984), 30–33.

116. Felton, *Country Life in Georgia*, 96–99.

117. Ibid., 100.

118. Ibid., 93.

119. Rebecca Latimer Felton, "A Farm House Experience," in Rebecca Latimer Felton Papers, 1851–1930, University of Georgia Hargrett Rare Books and Manuscript Library.

120. Felton, "A Farm House Experience."

121. Felton, *The Romantic Story of Georgia's Women*, 23.

122. McCurry, *Masters of Small Worlds*.

123. Bynum, *Unruly Women*, 6.

124. Fox-Genovese, *Within the Plantation Household*, 96–97, and McCurry, *Masters of Small Worlds*, 127.

125. See Sommerville, *Rape and Race in the Nineteenth-Century South*, and Block, *Rape and Sexual Power in Early America*.

126. Bynum, *Unruly Women*, and Bardaglio, *Reconstructing the Household*.

127. Bardaglio, *Reconstructing the Household*; Laura Edwards, *Gendered Strife and Confusion; The Political Culture of Reconstruction* (Urbana: University of Illinois Press, 1997); and Diane Miller Sommerville, "The Rape Myth Reconsidered," *Journal of Southern History* 61 (August 1995): 481–518.

128. Terri L. Snyder, "Sexual Consent and Sexual Coercion in Seventeenth-Century Virginia," in *Sex without Consent*, ed. Merril D. Smith (New York: New York University Press, 2001), 49; and Jack Marietta and G. S. Rowe, "Rape, Law, Courts and Custom in Pennsylvania, 1682–1800," in *Sex without Consent*, 90–93.

129. Peter W. Bardaglio, "Rape and the Law in the Old South: Calculated to Excite Indignation in Every Heart," *Journal of Southern History* 60, 4 (November 1994): 751.

130. Felton, *The Romantic Story of Georgia's Women*, 25.
131. Hahn, *A Nation under Our Feet*; Mark V. Wetherington, *Plain Folk's Fight: The Civil War and Reconstruction in Piney Woods Georgia* (Chapel Hill: University of North Carolina, 2006); C. Mildred Thompson, *Reconstruction in Georgia: Economic, Social, Political, 1865–1872* (Whitefish, MT: Kessinger, 2007); Edmund L. Drago, *Black Politicians and Reconstruction in Georgia: A Splendid Failure* (Athens: University of Georgia Press, 1992); Paul A. Cimbala, *Under the Guardianship of the Nation: The Freedmen's Bureau and the Reconstruction of Georgia, 1865–1870* (Athens: University of Georgia Press, 2003); and Edwin C. Woolley, *The Reconstruction of Georgia* (Whitefish, MT: Kessinger, 2007).
132. Felton, *The Romantic Story of Georgia's Women*, 25.
133. Felton, *Country Life in Georgia*, 120.
134. *Tri-Weekly Courier*, October 12, 1876.
135. *Thomasville Times*, n.d., Scrapbook No. 16, 1879–1883, in Felton Papers.
136. Quoted in Whites, "Rebecca Latimer Felton and Protection," 47.
137. See Josephine Bone Floyd, "Rebecca Latimer Felton, Political Independent," *Georgia Historical Quarterly* 30 (1946): 14–34.

2. The Violent Transition from Freedom to Segregation

1. Ida B. Wells, *Crusade for Justice: The Autobiography of Ida B. Wells* (Chicago: University of Chicago Press, 1970), 71.
2. For accounts of the life of Ida B. Wells, see ibid.; Linda O. McMurry, *To Keep the Waters Troubled: The Life of Ida B. Wells* (New York: Oxford University Press, 1998); Patricia A. Schechter, *Ida B. Wells-Barnett and American Reform, 1880–1930* (Chapel Hill: University of North Carolina Press, 2001); James West Davidson, *"They Say": Ida B. Wells and the Reconstruction of Race* (New York: Oxford University Press, 2007); Paula J. Giddings, *Ida: A Sword among Lions: Ida B. Wells and the Campaign against Lynching* (New York: HarperCollins, 2008); and Mia Bay, *To Tell the Truth Freely: The Life of Ida B. Wells* (New York: Hill and Wang, 2009).
3. Wells, *Crusade for Justice*, 8; Giddings, *Ida*, 15–39; McMurry, *To Keep the Waters Troubled*, 3–17; Schechter, *Ida B. Wells-Barnett*, 11–13; and Davidson, *"They Say,"* 12–49.
4. William Baskerville Hamilton, "The History of Holly Springs, Mississippi" (master's thesis, University of Mississippi, 1931).
5. Steven Hahn, *A Nation under Our Feet: Black Political Struggles in the Rural South from Slavery to the Great Migration* (Cambridge, Mass.: Harvard University Press, 2003); and David Warren Bowen, *Andrew Johnson and the Negro* (Knoxville: University of Tennessee Press, 1989).

6. Eric Foner, *Reconstruction: America's Unfinished Revolution, 1863–1877* (New York: Harper and Row, 1988); Dan T. Carter, *When the War Was Over: The Failure of Self-Reconstruction in the South, 1865–1867* (Baton Rouge: Louisiana University Press, 1985); and James M. McPherson, *Ordeal by Fire: The Civil War and Reconstruction* (New York: Alfred A. Knopf, 1982).

7. John C. Willis, *Forgotten Time: The Yazoo-Mississippi Delta after the Civil War* (Charlottesville: University of Virginia Press, 2000); Cecil L. Sumners, *The Governors of Mississippi* (New York: Pelican, 1998); and Vernon Lane Wharton, *The Negro in Mississippi, 1865–1890* (repr.; Westport, Conn.: Greenwood Press, 1984).

8. Ann S. Holder, "Making the Body Politic: Narratives of Race, Sexuality and Citizenship in the United States, 1864–1909" (Ph.D. diss., Boston College, 1999), 125–138.

9. Theodore B. Wilson, *Black Codes of the South* (repr.; Baton Rouge: University of Alabama Press, 2000); Paul Finkelman, "Black Codes," in *Encyclopedia of African-American Culture and History*, ed. Jack Salzman, David Lionel Smith, and Cornel West (New York: Macmillan Library Reference USA, 1996), 346–349; Edward L. Ayers, *Vengeance and Justice: Crime and Punishment in the 19th-Century American South* (New York: Oxford University Press, 1984); and Mary Frances Berry, *The Pig Farmer's Daughter and Other Tales of American Justice: Episodes of Racism and Sexism in the Courts from 1865 to the Present* (New York: Vintage Books, 2000).

10. Wells, *Crusade for Justice*, 8–9; McMurry, *To Keep the Waters Troubled*, 15; Schechter, *Ida B. Wells-Barnett*, 11–12; and Giddings, *Ida*, 22–23.

11. Heather Andrea Williams, *Self-Taught: African American Education in Slavery and Freedom* (Chapel Hill: University of North Carolina Press, 2005); James D. Anderson, *The Education of Blacks in the South, 1860–1935* (Chapel Hill: University of North Carolina Press, 1988); Ronald E. Butchart, *Northern Schools, Southern Blacks and Reconstruction: Freedmen's Education, 1862–1875* (Westport, Conn.: Greenwood Press, 1980); and Jacqueline Jones, *Soldiers of Light and Love: Northern Teachers and Georgia Blacks, 1865–1873* (Chapel Hill: University of North Carolina Press, 1980).

12. "History of Rust College," quoted in McMurry, *To Keep the Waters Troubled*, 13.

13. Barbara Welter, "The Cult of True Womanhood: 1820–1860," *American Quarterly* 18 (Summer 1966), 151–174; Welter, *Dimity Convictions: The American Woman in the 19th Century* (Athens: Ohio State University Press, 1976); Nancy Cott, *The Bonds of Womanhood: "Woman's Sphere" in New England, 1780–1835* (New Haven: Yale University Press, 1977); Cott, "Passionlessness: An Interpretation of Victorian Sexuality Ideology, 1790–1850," in *A Heritage of Her Own*, ed. Nancy Cott and Elizabeth H. Pleck (New York: Simon and Schuster, 1979); Linda K. Kerber, "Separate Spheres, Female Worlds, Woman's Place: The Rhetoric of Women's History," in *No More Separate Spheres! A Next Wave*

American Studies Reader, ed. Cathy N. Davidson and Jessamyn Hatcher (Durham, N.C.: Duke University Press, 2002), 29–65; and Bertram Wyatt-Brown, *Southern Honor: Ethics and Behavior in the Old South* (New York: Oxford University Press, 1982).

14. Wells, *Crusade for Justice,* 9.

15. Deborah Gray White, *Ar'n't I a Woman? Female Slaves in the Plantation South* (New York: W. W. Norton, 1985); Marli F. Weiner, *Mistresses and Slaves: Plantation Women in South Carolina, 1830–1880* (Urbana: University of Illinois Press, 1997); Brenda E. Stevenson, *Life in Black and White: Family and Community in the Slave South* (New York: Oxford University Press, 1996); Jennifer L. Morgan, *Laboring Women: Reproduction and Gender in New World Slavery* (Philadelphia: University of Pennsylvania Press, 2004); Thavolia Glymph, *Out of the House of Bondage* (Cambridge: Cambridge University Press, 2008); Kidada E. Williams, "In the Space of Violence: African Americans and the Dynamics of Racial Supremacy after Slavery" (Ph.D. diss, University of Michigan, 2005); and Elizabeth Fox-Genovese, *Within the Plantation Household: Black and White Women of the Old South* (Chapel Hill: University of North Carolina University Press, 1988).

16. Wells, *Crusade for Justice,* 10.

17. Nell Painter, "Of Lily, "Linda Brent," and Freud: A Non-Exceptionalist Approach to Race, Class, and Gender in the Slave South," *Georgia Historical Quarterly* 76, 2 (Summer 1992): 241–260.

18. Harriet Jacobs, *Incidents in the Life of a Slave Girl* (repr.; Cambridge, Mass.: Harvard University Press, 1987), 33.

19. Pauli Murray, *Proud Shoes: The Story of an American Family* (repr. Boston: Beacon Press, 1999), 37.

20. Wharton, *The Negro in Mississippi,* 140.

21. Tera Hunter, *To 'Joy My Freedom: Southern Black Women's Lives and Labors after the Civil War* (Cambridge, Mass.: Harvard University Press, 1997), 75–76.

22. Leslie A. Schwalm, *A Hard Fight for We: Women's Transition from Slavery to Freedom in South Carolina* (Urbana: University of Illinois Press, 1997); and Julie Saville, *The Work of Reconstruction: From Slave to Wage Laborer in South Carolina, 1860–1870* (New York: Cambridge University Press, 1994).

23. George Rable, *But There Was No Peace: The Role of Violence in the Politics of Reconstruction* (Athens: University of Georgia Press, 1984); and Dorothy Sterling, ed., *The Trouble They Seen: The Story of Reconstruction in the Words of African Americans* (New York: Da Capo Press, 1994).

24. Col. Samuel Thomas, Assistant Commissioner, Bureau of Refugees, Freedmen and Abandoned Lands, 39th Cong., 1st Sess., Senate Exec., 2 December 1865.

25. William Cohen, *At Freedom's Edge: Black Mobility and the Southern White Quest for Racial Control, 1861–1915* (Baton Rouge: Louisiana State University Press, 1991); Sally E. Hadden, *Slave Patrols: Law and Violence in Virginia and*

the Carolinas (Cambridge, Mass.: Harvard University Press, 2001); and James L. Roark, *Masters without Slaves: Southern Planters in the Civil War and Reconstruction* (New York: W. W. Norton, 1977).

26. Henry Adams, "'Testimony,' *Senate Report 693, 46th Congress, 2nd Session (1880),*" reprinted in Sterling, *The Trouble They Seen*. See also Steven Hahn, "The Education of Henry Adams," in *A Nation under Our Feet*, 317–363.

27. Hannah Rosen, "'Not That Sort of Women': Race, Gender, and Sexual Violence during the Memphis Riot of 1866," in *Sex, Love, Race: Crossing Boundaries in North American History*, ed. Martha Hodes (New York: New York University Press, 1999), 267–293; Rosen, *Terror in the Heart of Freedom: Citizenship, Sexual Violence, and the Meaning of Race in the Postemancipation South* (Chapel Hill: University of North Carolina, 2008); Kenneth W. Goings, *"Unhidden" Transcripts: Memphis and African American Agency, 1862–1920* (Thousand Oaks, Calif.: Sage, 1995); Kevin R. Hardwick, "'Your Old Father Abe Lincoln Is Dead and Damned': Black Soldiers and the Memphis Race Riot of 1866," *Journal of Social History* 27 (1993): 109–128; Altina L. Waller, "Community, Class and Race in the Memphis Riot of 1866," *Journal of Social History* 18 (1984): 223–246; and James Gilbert Ryan, "The Memphis Riots of 1866: Terror in a Black Community during Reconstruction," *Journal of Negro History* 62, 3 (1977): 243–257.

28. Rosen, "'Not That Sort of Women'" and Rosen, *Terror in the Heart of Freedom*.

29. *Memphis Riots and Massacres*, 39th Cong., 1st sess., 1865–66, H. Rept. 101, 13.

30. Testimony of Lucy Smith, *Memphis Riots and Massacres*, 39th Cong., 1st sess., 1865–66, H. Rept. 101, 197.

31. *Memphis Riots and Massacres*, 39th Cong., 1st sess., 1865–66, H. Rept. 101, 5.

32. James Hollandsworth, *An Absolute Massacre: The New Orleans Race Riot of July 30, 1866* (Baton Rouge: Louisiana State University Press, 2001).

33. Paul A. Cimbala, *Under the Guardianship of the Nation: The Freedmen's Bureau and the Reconstruction of Georgia, 1865–1870* (Athens: University of Georgia Press, 1997); and Barry A. Crouch, *The Freedmen's Bureau and Black Texans* (Austin: University of Texas Press, 1992).

34. Civil Rights Act of 1866.

35. Fourteenth Amendment to the U.S. Constitution.

36. James E. Sefton, *The United States Army and Reconstruction, 1865–1877* (Baton Rouge: Louisiana State University Press, 1967).

37. Wharton, *The Negro in Mississippi*, 151.

38. Wells, *Crusade for Justice*, 8–9.

39. Julius Eric Thompson, *Hiram R. Revels, 1827–1901: A Biography* (New York: Arno Press, 1982).

40. Willard B. Gatewood, *Aristocrats of Color: The Black Elite, 1880–1920* (Bloomington: Indiana University Press, 1990); Howard N. Rabinowitz, "Three Reconstruction Leaders: Blanche K. Bruce, Robert Brown Eliott, and Holland

Thompson," in *Black Leaders of the Nineteenth Century*, ed. Leon Litwack and August Meier (Urbana: University of Illinois Press, 1988), 191–217; and Samuel Shapiro, "A Black Senator from Mississippi: Blanche K. Bruce (1841–1898)," *Review of Politics* 44 (January 1982): 83–109.

41. Allen W. Trelease, *White Terror: The Ku Klux Klan Conspiracy and Southern Reconstruction* (Baton Rouge: Louisiana State University Press, 1971); Hahn, *A Nation under Our Feet*, 217–265; Scott Reynolds Nelson, *Iron Confederacies: Southern Railways, Klan Violence and Reconstruction* (Chapel Hill: University of North Carolina Press, 1999); George Rable, *But There Was No Peace*; and Joel Williamson, *A Rage for Order: Black-White Relations in the American South since Emancipation* (New York: Oxford University Press, 1986).

42. Well, *Crusade for Justice*, 9–10.

43. Hannah Rosen, "Sexual Violence as Political Fantasy" (paper presented at 65th Annual Meeting of the Southern Historical Association, November 3–6, 1999, in author's possession).

44. Trelease, *White Terror*, 275.

45. *Testimony Taken by the Joint Select Committee to Inquire into the Condition of Affairs in the Late Insurrectionary States* (Mississippi), vol. 12, 1149–1150.

46. *Testimony*, Mississippi, vol. 12, 1155.

47. Foner, *Reconstruction*, 429.

48. Rosen, *Terror in the Heart of Freedom*; Martha Hodes, *White Women, Black Men: Illicit Sex in the Nineteenth-Century South* (New Haven: Yale University Press, 1999), 144; and Hodes, "The Sexualization of Reconstruction Politics: White Women and Black Men in the South after the Civil War," *Journal of the History of Sexuality* 3 (January 1993): 402–417.

49. *Testimony*, Mississippi, vol. 12, 888–890.

50. Martha Hodes, "Wartime Dialogues on Illicit Sex: White Women and Black Men," in *Divided Houses: Gender and the Civil War*, ed. Catherine Clinton and Nina Silber (New York: Oxford University Press, 1992); Hodes, ed., *Sex, Love, Race: Crossing Boundaries in North American History* (New York: New York University Press, 1999); and Holder, "Making the Body Politic," 154–168.

51. *Testimony*, Mississippi, vol. 12, 1085.

52. Peggy Pascoe, *What Comes Naturally: Miscegenation Law and the Making of Race in America* (London: Oxford University Press, 2009); Pascoe, "Race, Gender, and the Privileges of Property: On the Significance of Miscegenation Law in United States History," in *New Viewpoints in Women's History: Working Papers from the Schlesinger Library Fiftieth Anniversary Conference, March 4–5, 1994*, ed. Susan Ware (Cambridge, Mass.: Arthur and Elizabeth Schlesinger Library on the History of Women in America, 1994), 99–122; James Hugo Johnson, *Race Relations in Virginia and Miscegenation in the South, 1776–1860* (Amherst: University of Massachusetts Press, 1970); Joel Williamson, *New People: Miscegena-*

tion and Mulattoes in the United States (Baton Rouge: Louisiana State University Press, 1995); and Hannah Rosen, "The Rhetoric of Miscegenation and the Reconstruction of Race: Debating Marriage, Sex, and Citizenship in Postemancipation Arkansas," in *Gender and Slave Emancipation in the Atlantic World*, ed. Diana Paton and Pamela Scully (Duke University Press, 2005), 289–309.

53. *Testimony*, Mississippi, vol. 11, 76.

54. Ibid., 310.

55. Ibid., 672.

56. Holder, "Making the Body Politic."

57. Rosen, *Terror in the Heart of Freedom*; Hodes, "Sexualization of Reconstruction Politics."

58. Rosen, *Terror in the Heart of Freedom*; Rosen, " 'Not That Sort of Women' "; Glymph, *Out of the House of Bondage*; Hunter, *To 'Joy My Freedom*; Laura Edwards, "Sexual Violence, Gender, Reconstruction, and the Extension of Patriarchy in Granville County, North Carolina," *North Carolina Historical Review* 68 (July 1991): 237–260; Laura Edwards, *Gendered Strife and Confusion: The Political Culture of Reconstruction* (Urbana: University of Illinois Press, 1997); Catherine Clinton, "Bloody Terrain: Freedom, Sexuality, and Violence during Reconstruction," *Georgia Historical Quarterly* 76, 2 (Summer 1992): 313–333; Jacquelyn Down Hall, " 'The Mind That Burns in Each Body': Women, Rape, and Racial Violence," in *Powers of Desire: The Politics of Sexuality*, ed. Amy Snitow, Christine Stansell, and Sharon Thompson (New York: Monthly Review, 1983), 328–349; Jacqueline Jones, *Labor of Love, Labor of Sorrow: Black Women, Work, and the Family from Slavery to the Present* (New York: Basic Books, 1985); and Elsa Barkley Brown, " 'To Catch the Vision of Freedom': Reconstructing Southern Black Women's Political History, 1865–1880," in *African American Women and the Vote, 1837–1965*, ed. Ann Gordon, Bettye Collier-Thomas, John H. Bracey, Arlene Voski Avakian, and Joyce Avrech Berkman (Amherst: University of Massachusetts Press, 1997), 66–99.

59. Giddings, *Ida*, 24.

60. Rhoda Ann Childs, "Affadavit of the Wife of a Discharged Georgia Black Soldier," 25 September 1866, in *Freedom: A Documentary History of Emancipation, 1861–1867*, ser. 2, vol. 2, *Black Military Experience*, ed. Ira Berlin et al. (Cambridge: Cambridge University Press, 1982), 807–808; Tera W. Hunter, *To 'Joy My Freedom*, 32–35; Catherine Clinton, "Reconstructing Freedwomen," in *Divided Houses*, 316; Rosen, "Sexual Violence as Political Fantasy," 8–9; and Holder, "Making the Body Politic," 114.

61. Sterling, *The Trouble They Seen*, 392.

62. "Statement of Matilda Frix to the Freedmen's Bureau on August 27, 1867," in *Standing upon the Mouth of a Volcano: New South Georgia*, ed. Mills Lane (Georgia: Beehive Press, 1993), 101–102.

63. Henry McNeal Turner, "Colored American, January 13, 1866," in *Moral Evil and Redemption Suffering: A History of Theodicy in African-American Religious Thought*, ed. Anthony B. Pinn (Gainesville: University Press of Florida, 2002), 102–110.

64. Trelease, *White Terror*, 290–293.

65. Rosen, *Terror in the Heart of Freedom*, 209–210.

66. Ibid.

67. United States *Statutes at Large*, XVII, 13–15; and Trelease, *White Terror*, 388.

68. Holder, "Making the Body Politic," 163.

69. Khaled J. Bloom, *The Mississippi Valley's Great Yellow Fever Epidemic of 1878* (Baton Rouge: Louisiana State University Press, 1993); Edward Blum, "The Crucible of Disease: Trauma, Memory, and National Reconciliation during the Yellow Fever Epidemic of 1878," *Journal of Southern History* 69 (November 11, 2003): 791–820; and Margaret Humphreys, *Yellow Fever and the South* (New Brunswick, N.J.: Rutgers University Press, 1992).

70. Wells, *Crusade for Justice*, 10.

71. McMurry, *To Keep the Waters Troubled*, 16; and Schechter, *Ida B. Wells-Barnett*, 16.

72. Wells, *Crusade for Justice*, 17.

73. Ida B. Wells, *The Memphis Diary of Ida B. Wells: An Intimate Portrait of the Activist as a Young Woman*, ed. Miriam Decosta-Willis (Boston: Beacon Press, 1995), 77–79.

74. Ibid, 24.

75. Beverly Washington Jones, *Quest for Equality: The Life and Writings of Mary Eliza Church Terrell, 1863–1954* (New York: Carlson, 1990).

76. Kenneth W. Mack, "Law, Society, Identity and the Making of the Jim Crow South: Travel and Segregation on Tennessee Railroads, 1875–1905," *Law and Social Inquiry* 24, 4 (Spring 1999): 377–409; R. David McCall, " 'Every Thing in Its Place:' Gender and Space on America's Railroads, 1830–1899" (master's thesis, Virginia Polytechnic Institute and State University, 1999); Grace Elizabeth Hale, *Making Whiteness: The Culture of Segregation in the South, 1890–1940* (New York: Pantheon Books, 1998), 125–138; and Blair Kelley, *Right to Ride: African American Citizenship and protest in the Age of Plessy v. Ferguson* (Chapel Hill: University of North Carolina Press, forthcoming).

77. *Brown v. Memphis & Co.*, 5 Fed. 499 (1880), U.S. App. 2696.

78. Ibid.

79. Wells, *Crusade for Justice*, 18–19.

80. Wells, *The Memphis Diary*, 141.

81. Wells, *Crusade for Justice*, 9.

3. Southern White Women and the Anti-Rape Movement

1. Ann Firor Scott, *The Southern Lady: From Pedestal to Politics, 1830–1930* (Chicago: University of Chicago Press, 1970); Marjorie Spruill Wheeler, *New Women of the New South: Leaders of the Woman's Suffrage Movement in Southern States* (London: Oxford University Press, 1993); Joan Marie Johnson, *Southern Ladies, New Women: Race, Region, and Clubwomen in South Carolina, 1890–1930* (Gainesville: University Press of Florida, 2004); Judith N. McArthur, *Creating the New Woman: The Rise of Southern Women's Progressive Culture in Texas, 1893–1918* (Urbana: University of Illinois Press, 1998); Glenda Elizabeth Gilmore, *Gender and Jim Crow: Women and the Politics of White Supremacy in North Carolina, 1896–1920* (Chapel Hill: University of North Carolina Press, 1996); Elna C. Green, *Southern Strategies: Southern Women and the Woman Suffrage Question* (Chapel Hill: University of North Carolina Press, 1997); and Georgina Hickey, *Hope and Danger in the New South City: Working-Class Women and Urban Development in Atlanta, 1890–1940* (Athens: University of Georgia Press, 2003).

2. Rebecca Latimer Felton, *The Romantic Story of Georgia's Women* (Atlanta: Atlanta Georgian and Sunday American, 1930), 24.

3. Ibid.

4. LeeAnn Whites, "Rebecca Latimer Felton and the Problem of 'Protection' in the New South," in *Visible Women: New Essays on American Activism*, ed. Nancy A. Hewitt and Susan Lebsock (Chicago: University of Illinois Press, 1993), 49.

5. Robert E. Burns, *I Am a Fugitive from a Georgia Chain Gang!* (repr.; Athens: University of Georgia Press,1997); Alex Lichtenstein, "Good Roads and Chain Gangs in the Progressive South: 'The Negro Convict Is a Slave,'" *Journal of Southern History* 59 (February 1993): 85–110; Lichtenstein, *Twice the Work of Free Labor: The Political Economy of Convict Labor in the New South* (New York: Verso, 1996); Matthew Mancini, *One Dies, Get Another: Convict Leasing in the American South, 1866–1928* (Columbia: University of South Carolina Press, 1996); and John Dittmer, *Black Georgia in the Progressive Era, 1900–1920* (Urbana: University of Illinois Press, 1980), 72–88.

6. Mancini, *One Dies, Get Another*, 72–89; and C. Vann Woodward, *Tom Watson: Agrarian Rebel* (repr.; New York: Oxford University Press, 1963), 107.

7. Rebecca Latimer Felton, "The Convict System of Georgia," *Forum* 2 (January 1887): 486; and Elizabeth A. Taylor "The Abolition of the Convict Lease System in Georgia," *Georgia Historical Quarterly* 26 (1942): 273–287.

8. Felton, *Country Life in Georgia*, 155–156.

9. Felton, *The Romantic Story of Georgia's Women*, 27.

10. Rebecca Latimer Felton, *My Memoirs of Georgia Politics* (Atlanta: Index Publishing Co., 1911), 586–587.

11. Ibid., 592.

12. Ibid., 592–593.

13. Ibid.

14. Jacquelyn Dowd Hall, *Revolt against Chivalry: Jessie Daniel Ames and the Women's Campaign against Lynching*, rev. ed. (New York: Columbia University Press, 1993); Gilmore, *Gender and Jim Crow*; W. Fitzhugh Brundage, *Lynching in the New South: Georgia and Virginia, 1880–1930* (Chicago: University of Illinois Press, 1993); Tera Hunter, *To 'Joy My Freedom: Southern Black Women's Lives and Labors after the Civil War* (Cambridge, Mass.: Harvard University Press, 1997); Grace Elizabeth Hale, *Making Whiteness: The Culture of Segregation in the South, 1890–1940* (New York: Pantheon Books, 1998); George M. Fredrickson, *The Black Image in the White Mind: The Debate on Afro-American Character and Destiny, 1817–1914* (New York: Harper and Row, 1971); Joel Williamson, *The Crucible of Race: Black-White Relations in the American South since Emancipation* (New York: Oxford University Press, 1984); Deborah G. White, *Too Heavy a Load: Black Women in Defense of Themselves, 1894–1994* (New York: W. W. Norton, 1999); Evelyn Brooks Higginbotham, *Righteous Discontent: The Women's Movement in the Black Baptist Church, 1880–1920* (Cambridge, Mass.: Harvard University Press, 1993); Gail Bederman, *Manliness and Civilization: A Cultural History of Gender and Race in the United States, 1880–1917* (Chicago: University of Chicago Press, 1995); and Stephen Kantrowitz, *Ben Tillman and the Reconstruction of White Supremacy* (Chapel Hill: University of North Carolina Press, 2000).

15. Felton, *My Memoirs of Georgia Politics*, 593.

16. Felton, *Country Life in Georgia*, 156.

17. Ruth Bordin, *Women and Temperance: The Quest for Power and Liberty, 1873–1900* (Philadelphia: Temple University Press, 1981); Barbara Leslie Epstein, *The Politics of Domesticity: Women, Evangelism, and Temperance in Nineteenth-Century America* (Middletown, Conn.: Wesleyan University Press, 1981); Ian Tyrell, *Woman's World, Woman's Empire: The Woman's Christian Temperance Union in International Perspective, 1880–1930* (Chapel Hill: University of North Carolina Press, 1991); and Leslie Kathrin Dunlap, "In the Name of the Home: Temperance Women and Southern Grass-Roots Politics, 1873–1933" (Ph.D. diss., Northwestern University, 2001).

18. Peggy Pascoe, *Relations of Rescue: The Search for Female Moral Authority in the American West, 1874–1939* (New York: Oxford University Press, 1990).

19. J. J. Ansley, *History of the Georgia W.C.T.U., 1883–1907* (Columbus: Gilbert Printing Co., 1914); David M. Fahey, *Temperance and Racism: John Bull, Johnny Reb, and the Good Templars* (Lexington: University Press of Kentucky, 1996); Dunlap, "In the Name of the Home"; Nancy A. Hardesty, "'The Best Temperance Organization in the Land': Southern Methodists and the W.C.T.U. in

Georgia," *Methodist History* 28 (April 1990); Anne Firor Scott, "How Women Have Changed Georgia—and Themselves: The 1990 Elson Lecture," *Atlanta History* 34 (1990): 5–16; Elizabeth A. Taylor, "The Abolition of the Convict Lease System in Georgia," *Georgia Historical Quarterly* 26 (1942): 273–287; Elizabeth A. Taylor, "Revival and Development of the Woman Suffrage Movement in Georgia," *Georgia Historical Quarterly* 42 (1958): 339–354; Josephine Bone Floyd, "Rebecca Latimer Felton, Champion of Women's Rights," *Georgia Historical Quarterly* 30 (1946): 81–104; and Floyd, "Rebecca Latimer Felton, Political Independent," *Georgia Historical Quarterly* 30 (1946): 14–34.

20. Ansley, *History of the Georgia W.C.T.U.*

21. Frances Willard, *Do Everything: A Handbook for the World's White Ribboners* (Chicago: Ruby I. Gilbert, 1895); and Willard, *Woman and Temperance* (Chicago: Woman's Temperance Publication Association, 1886).

22. Gilmore, *Gender and Jim Crow*, 45–59; Gilmore, "'A Melting Time': Black Women, White Women, and the WCTU in North Carolina, 1880–1900," in *Hidden Histories of Women in the New South*, ed. Virginia Bernhard et al. (Columbia: University of Missouri Press, 1994), 153–172; Dunlap, "In the Name of the Home"; Anastasia Sims, "'The Sword of the Spirit': The WCTU and Moral Reform in North Carolina, 1883–1933," *North Carolina Historical Review* 64 (October 1987): 394–415; and Anastasia Sims, *The Power of Femininity in the New South: Women's Organizations and Politics in North Carolina, 1880–1930* (Columbia: University of South Carolina Press, 1997).

23. Dunlap, "In the Name of the Home," 74–75; *Union Signal*, June 10 and 17, 1886; and Ansley, *History of the Georgia WCTU*, 94.

24. *Minutes of the National Woman's Christian Temperance Union, 12 Annual Meeting* (1885), 73–74.

25. Peter W. Bardaglio, "Rape and the Law in the Old South: 'Calculated to Excite Indignation in Every Heart,'" *Journal of Southern History* 60, 4 (November 1994): 749–772; and Bardaglio, *Reconstructing the Household: Families, Sex, and the Law in the Nineteenth-Century South* (Chapel Hill: University of North Carolina Press, 1988).

26. David Pivar, *Purity Crusade: Sexual Morality and Social Control, 1868–1900* (Westport, Conn.: Greenwood Press, 1973), 142–143; Mary E. Odem, *Delinquent Daughters: Protecting and Policing Adolescent Female Sexuality in the United States, 1885–1920* (Chapel Hill: University of North Carolina Press, 1995); Linda Gordon, *Heroes of Their Own Lives: The Politics and History of Family Violence, Boston 1880–1960* (New York: Penguin, 1988), 25–58; Mary Frances Berry, "Judging Morality: Sexual Behavior and the Legal Consequences in the Late Nineteenth-Century South," *Journal of American History* 78 (1991): 835–856; John D'Emilio and Estelle Freedman, *Intimate Matters: A History of Sexuality in America* (New York: Harper and Row, 1988), 153; Joan

Brumberg, "Ruined Girls: Changing Community Responses to Illegitimacy in Upstate New York, 1890–1920," *Journal of Social History* 18 (Winter 1984): 247–272; Kathleen R. Parker, "'To Protect the Chastity of Children under Sixteen': Statutory Rape Prosecutions in a Midwest County Circuit Court, 1850–1950," *Michigan Historical Review* 20, 1 (Spring 1994): 49–79; and Dunlap, "The Reform of Rape Law and the Problem of White Men: Age-of-Consent Campaigns in the South, 1885–1910,"in *Sex, Love, Race: Crossing Boundaries in North American History*, ed. Martha Hodes (New York: New York University Press, 1999), 352–372.

27. Felton, *My Memoirs of Georgia Politics*, 581.

28. Felton, *The Romantic Story of Georgia's Women*, 26–27.

29. Ibid.

30. Felton, *Country Life in Georgia*, 284.

31. Josephine Bone Floyd, "Rebecca Latimer Felton, Political Independent," in *Georgia Historical Quarterly* 30 (1946): 29; and "Felton Scrap Book 19, (1882–1886)," Rebecca Latimer Felton Papers, University of Georgia, Hargrett Library Rare Books and Manuscript Library (GHL).

32. Rebecca Edwards, *Angels in the Machinery: Gender in American Party Politics from the Civil War to the Progressive Era* (New York: Oxford University Press, 1997); and Elizabeth Varon, *We Mean to Be Counted: White Women and Politics in Antebellum Virginia* (Chapel Hill: University of North Carolina Press, 1998).

33. Felton, *Country Life in Georgia*, 286.

34. Felton, *My Memoirs of Georgia Politics*, 602.

35. Ibid.

36. Ibid., 614.

37. John E. Talmadge, *Rebecca Latimer Felton: Nine Stormy Decades* (Athens: University of Georgia Press, 1960), 99.

38. Felton, *Country Life in Georgia*, 286.

39. Dunlap, "The Reform of Rape Law."

40. "Petition of the Woman's Christian Temperance Union for the Protection of Women," *Union Signal*, November 11, 1886.

41. Dunlap, "The Reform of Rape Law," 360.

42. *Philanthropist* 1 (October 1886).

43. D'Emilio and Freedman, *Intimate Matters*, 153; Kathy Peis, "Charity Girls and City Pleasures," in *Passion and Power: Sexuality and History*, ed. Katy Peiss and Christine Stansell (Philadelphia: Temple University Press, 1989), 57–69; Christine Stansell, *City of Women: Sex and Class in New York, 1789–1860* (Urbana: University of Illinois Press, 1982); Hickey, *Hope and Danger*; Hunter, *To 'Joy My Freedom*; Hazel Carby, "'On the Threshold of Woman's Era': Lynching, Empire, and Sexuality in Black Feminist Theory," in *"Race" Writing and Difference*, ed. Henry Louis Gates Jr. (Chicago: University of Chicago Press, 1985),

301–316; Carby, "Policing the Black Woman's Body in an Urban Context," *Critical Inquiry* 18, 4 (Summer, 1992): 738–755; and Joanne J. Meyerowitz, *Women Adrift: Independent Wage Earners in Chicago, 1880–1930* (Chicago: University of Chicago Press, 1988).

44. "The Age of Consent," *Union Signal*, June 10, 1886.

45. *Philanthropist*, 1 (October 1886): 1–2; "The Age of Consent"; and "Equal Rights in Morals," *Union Signal*, October 21, 1886.

46. Dunlap, "The Reform of Rape Law," 362–365.

47. Quoted in ibid., 360.

48. Ibid., 362.

49. Ibid. See also Lily Hardy Hammond, *Southern Women and Racial Adjustment*, 2nd ed. (N.p.: The Trustees of the John F. Slater Fund, 1917), 12.

50. Rebecca Latimer Felton, "The Rights of Children," n.d., in Rebecca Latimer Felton Papers, GHL. Felton would continue to voice complaints until 1918, when Georgia finally raised the age of consent—see Felton, "Mrs. Felton's Message to the 20th Century," in *Country Life in Georgia*, 154; and Felton, "The Country Home," May and June 1915, in Rebecca Latimer Felton Papers, GHL.

51. *Atlanta Constitution*, September 17, 1886.

52. *Union Signal*, October 7, 1886.

53. *Atlanta Constitution*, September 17, 1886.

54. Hannah Rosen, *Terror in the Heart of Freedom: Citizenship, Sexual Violence, and the Meaning of Race in the Postemancipation South* (Chapel Hill: University of North Carolina, 2008); Danielle L. McGuire, "'It Was Like All of Us Had Been Raped': Sexual Violence, Community Mobilization, and the African American Freedom Struggle," *Journal of American History* 91 (December 2004): 906–931; and White, *Too Heavy a Load*.

55. Five for rape and one for wife abuse—see Brundage, *Lynching in the New South*, chapter 3 and Appendix A.

56. *Atlanta Constitution*, September 17, 1886.

57. Ibid.

58. Ibid.

59. Ibid.

60. Dunlap, "The Reform of Rape Law," 358.

61. George Frederickson, *The Black Image in the White Mind: The Debate of Afro-American Character and Destiny, 1817–1914* (New York: Harper and Row, 1971).

62. Philip Alexander Bruce, *The Plantation Negro as a Freeman: Observations on His Character, Condition, and Prospects in Virginia* (New York: G. P. Putnam's Sons, 1889).

63. Edward Ayers, *Promise of the New South* (New York: Oxford University Press, 1984), 155–159; Leon Litwack, *Trouble on the Mind: Black Southerners in the*

Age of Jim Crow (New York: Alfred A. Knopf, 1998), 197–216; Joel Williamson, *A Rage for Order: Black-White Relations in the American South since Emancipation* (New York: Oxford University Press, 1986), 78–88; and Ray Stannard Baker, *Following the Color Line: American Negro Citizenship in the Progressive Era* (New York: Harper and Row, 1908), 178–179.

64. By 1910 all but three southern states had reformed their rape laws—Georgia was the last state to do so in 1918. See Dunlap, "The Reform of Rape Law," 357.

65. Wheeler, *New Women of the New South*, 9–11; and Green, *Southern Strategies*, 20.

66. Epstein, *The Politics of Domesticity*, 100–111; Ellen DuBois and Linda Gordon, "Seeking Ecstasy on the Battlefield: Danger and Pleasure in the Nineteenth-Century Feminist Sexual Thought," in *Pleasure and Danger: Exploring Female Sexuality*, ed. Carol S. Vance (Boston: Routledge, 1984), 34–35; and Suzanne Lebsock, "Women and American Politics, 1880–1920," in *Women, Politics, and Change*, ed. Louise A. Tilly and Patricia Gurin (New York: Russell Sage, 1990), 40.

67. Frances Willard, "Home Protection" (1876) and "Home Protection II" (1879), in Amey Rose Slagell, *A Good Woman Speaking Well: The Oratory of Frances E. Willard* (Ph.D. diss., University of Wisconsin–Madison, 1992), 184–197, 249–267.

68. Felton, *Country Life in Georgia*, 121.

69. Ibid., 292–293.

70. "From a Woman's Standpoint: Address in Favor of Prohibition." (speech delivered in Monroe, Ga., August 18, 1894). Newspaper Clippings, Rebecca Latimer Felton Papers, GHL.

71. Molly Ladd-Taylor, *Mother-Work: Women, Child Welfare, and the State, 1890–1930* (Urbana: University of Illinois Press, 1995); Gordon, *Heroes of Their Own Lives*; and Peggy Pascoe, *Relations of Rescue: The Search for Female Moral Authority in the American West, 1874–1930* (New York: Oxford University Press, 1990), 32–69.

72. Felton, *Country Life in Georgia*, 295.

73. Ibid., 294.

74. *Atlanta Constitution*, November 15, 1890.

75. Interview with Frances Willard, "The Race Problem," *The Voice*, (October 28, 1890).

76. Ibid.

77. Ibid.

78. In 1919 Jane Addams refused to allow her name to be used in connection to the National Conference on Lynching. Letter, February 14, 1919, in NAACP Papers at the Library of Congress.

79. Jane Addams, "Respect for Law," *The Independent*, January 3, 1901.

80. Rebecca Latimer Felton, "Prohibition in Georgia," n.d., and "The Rescue Work in Relation to Womanhood and Temperance" Rebecca Latimer Felton Papers, GHL.

81. Steven Hahn, *The Roots of Southern Populism: Yeoman Farmers and the Transformation of the Georgia Upcountry, 1850–1890* (New York: Oxford University Press, 1983); Matthew Hild, *Greenbackers, Knights of Labor, and Populists: Farmer-Labor Insurgency in the Late-Nineteenth-Century South* (Athens: University of Georgia Press, 2007); Barton C. Shaw, *The Wool-Hat Boys: Georgia's Populist Party* (Baton Rouge: Louisiana State University Press, 1984); C. Vann Woodward, *Tom Watson, Agrarian Rebel* (New York: Macmillan, 1938).

82. Edwards, *Angels in the Machinery*; Charles Postel, *The Populist Vision* (New York: Oxford University Press, 2007); Marion K. Barthelme, ed., *Women in the Texas Populist Movement: Letters to the Southern Mercury* (College Station: Texas A&M University Press, 1997); and Michael Lewis Goldberg, *An Army of Women: Gender and Politics in Gilded Age Kansas* (Baltimore: Johns Hopkins University Press, 1997).

83. Woodward, *Tom Watson*.

84. Felton, "Prohibition in Georgia: Morgan County" (August 1894), Rebecca Latimer Felton Papers, GHL.

85. At the same time the Democratic governor of Georgia passed an anti-lynching law in an attempt to neutralize Populists who were gaining black votes. See Donald L. Grant, *The Anti-lynching Movement, 1883–1932* (San Francisco: R and E Research Associates, 1975), 68–70; and David Fort Godshalk, *Veiled Visions: The 1906 Atlanta Race Riot and the Reshaping of American Race Relations* (Chapel Hill: University of North Carolina Press, 2005), 170–171.

4. Organizing in Defense of Black Womanhood

1. Frederick Douglass, "Address by Hon. Frederick Douglass Delivered in the Congregational Church, Washington, D.C., April 19, 1883," Daniel A. P. Murray Pamphlet Collection: African American Perspective, 1818–1907, Rare Books and Special Collections Division, Library of Congress.

2. Ida B. Wells, *The Memphis Diary of Ida B. Wells: An Intimate Portrait of the Activist as a Young Woman*, ed. Miriam Decosta-Willis (Boston: Beacon Press, 1995), 131–132.

3. Ida B. Wells, *Crusade for Justice: The Autobiography of Ida B. Wells* (Chicago: University of Chicago Press, 1970), 47–70.

4. Linda O. McMurray, *To Keep the Waters Troubled: The Life of Ida B. Wells* (New York: Oxford University Press, 1998), 130–168.

5. *Indianapolis Freeman*, March 19, 1892.

6. Wells, *Southern Horrors: Lynch Law in All Its Phases* (1892), in *On Lynchings: Southern Horrors, A Red Record, Mob Rule in New Orleans* (Salem, N.H.: Ayer Company, Publishers, 1991), 46.

7. Wells, *Crusade for Justice*, 61.

8. Ibid., 64; and Wells, *The Memphis Diary*, 131–132.

9. Quoted in *American Citizen*, July 1, 1892. This version is very close to the one in Wells's pamphlet, *Southern Horrors: Lynch Law in All Its Phrases* (1892), 12–13. The pamphlet was originally an article published in the newspaper *Free Speech*, May 21, 1892.

10. *American Citizen*, July 1, 1892.

11. Emma Lou Thornbrough, *T. Thomas Fortune: Militant Journalist* (Chicago: University of Chicago Press, 1972); and John Hope Franklin and August Meier, eds., *Black Leaders of the 20th Century* (Urbana: University of Illinois Press, 1981).

12. Wells, *Crusade for Justice*, 69.

13. Ibid., 64.

14. Wells, *Southern Horrors*.

15. Deborah G. White, *Too Heavy a Load: Black Women in Defense of Themselves, 1894–1994* (New York: W. W. Norton, 1999); Schechter, "Unsettled Business: Ida B. Wells against Lynching, or, How Anti-Lynching Got Its Gender," in *Under the Sentence of Death: Lynching in the South*, ed. W. Fitzhugh Brundage (Chapel Hill: University of North Carolina Press, 1997), 292–317; and Paula J. Giddings, *Ida: A Sword among Lions: Ida B. Wells and the Campaign against Lynching* (New York: HarperCollins, 2008), 238.

16. Wells, *Southern Horrors*, 16–27.

17. Ibid., 30; Stewart E. Tolnay and E. M. Beck, *Festival of Violence: An Analysis of Southern Lynchings, 1882–1930* (Chicago: University of Illinois Press, 1995); and W. Fitzhugh Brundage, *Lynching in the New South: Georgia and Virginia, 1880–1930* (Chicago: University of Illinois Press, 1993).

18. Wells, *A Red Record*, in *On Lynchings*, 67.

19. Ibid., 65.

20. Ibid.

21. Wells recounted the rape of black women in *A Red Record* under the heading "Color Line Justice."

22. *Daily American*, May 23 and 25, 1892, and *Nashville Banner*, May 23, 24, 26, and 28, 1892.

23. *Nashville Banner*, May 19 and 24, 1892, and *Daily American*, May 20, 21, 22, and 27, 1892.

24. *Daily American*, May 1, 2, 3, and 6, 1892, and *Nashville Banner*, April 28 and 30, May 3, 9, 11, and 20, 1892.

25. *Nashville Banner*, May 24, 1892.

26. *Nashville Banner*, May 3 and 19, June 4, 28, 29 and 30, and July 8, 1982. Italics mine.

27. *Nashville Banner*, May 24 and July 8, 1892.

28. Herbert Shapiro, *White Violence and Black Response: From Reconstruction to Montgomery* (Amherst: University of Massachusetts Press, 1988); Robin D. G. Kelley, "'We Are Not What We Seem': Rethinking Black Working-Class Opposition in the Jim Crow South," *Journal of American History* 80, 1 (June 1993): 75–112; W. Fitzhugh Brundage, "The Roar on the Other Side of Silence: Black Resistance and White Violence in the American South, 1880–1940," in Brundage, ed., *Under Sentence of Death: Lynching in the South* (Chapel Hill: University of North Carolina Press, 1997), 271; Timothy B. Tyson, *Radio Free Dixie: Robert F. Williams and the Roots of Black Power* (Chapel Hill: University of North Carolina Press, 1999); Kidada E. Williams, "'Pistols and Guns Are the Only Weapons to Stop a Mob': Rethinking African-American Responses to Racial Violence, 1890–1925" (paper presented at the annual meeting of the American Studies Association, Houston, Texas, 16 November 2002); and Kidada E. Williams, "'By Any and All Means Necessary': Black Communities in Defense of Themselves against Racial Terror, 1890–1925" (paper presented at Lynching and Racial Violence in America: Histories and Legacies conference, Emory University, Atlanta, Georgia, 4 October 2002).
29. *Nashville Banner*, May 14, 1892.
30. *Nashville Banner*, May 19, 1892.
31. *Nashville Banner*, May 19, 1892.
32. *Daily American*, May 22, 1892. Also see "Bluff by Boston Coons," *Daily American*, May 22, 1892.
33. *Daily American*, May 23, 1892.
34. *Nashville Banner*, April 28, 1892.
35. Ibid.
36. *Nashville Banner*, April 29 and 30, 1892.
37. *Nashville Banner*, April 30, 1892.
38. Ibid.
39. Ibid.
40. *Daily American*, May 1, 1892
41. *Nashville Banner*, April 30, 1892, and *Daily American*, May 1, 1892.
42. *Daily American*, May 1, 1892.
43. Ibid.
44. *Daily American*, May 22, 1892, and *Nashville Banner*, April 28, 1892.
45. *Nashville Banner*, April 28, 1892.
46. Martha Hodes, *White Women, Black Men: Illicit Sex in the 19th-Century South* (New Haven: Yale University Press, 1997); Lisa Dorr, *White Women, Rape, and the Power of Race in Virginia, 1900–1960* (Chapel Hill: University of North Carolina Press, 2003); and Diane Miller Sommerville, *Rape and Race in the Nineteenth-Century South* (Chapel Hill: University of Chapel Hill, 2004).
47. *Daily American*, May 2, 1892.

48. *Daily American* and *Nashville Banner*, May 3, 1892.

49. *Daily American*, May 1, 1892.

50. *Daily American*, May 2, 1892.

51. Brundage, *Lynching in the New South*, 86–102.

52. Tolnay and Beck, *Festival of Violence*, 51.

53. Jasper L. Watts, "Editorial," *Nashville Banner*, May 20, 1892.

54. *Nashville Banner*, May 20, 1892.

55. Watts, "Editorial," *Nashville Banner*, May 20, 1892.

56. *Daily American*, May 24, 1892.

57. *Daily American* and *Nashville Banner*, May 24, 1892.

58. Ibid.

59. *Nashville Banner*, May 24, 1892.

60. *Daily American* and *Nashville Banner*, May 24, 1892.

61. *Nashville Banner*, May 24 and 28, 1892.

62. *Nashville Banner*, May 28, 1892.

63. *Nashville Banner*, May 24, 1892.

64. Tolnay and Beck, *Festival of Violence*, 97.

65. *Nashville Banner*, June 30, 1892.

66. Brundage, *Lynching in the New South*; and Tolnay and Beck, *Festival of Violence*.

67. Gail Bederman, *Manliness and Civilization: A Cultural History of Gender and Race in the United States, 1880–1917* (Chicago: University of Chicago Press, 1995).

68. *American Citizen*, June 3, 1892.

69. *Memphis Commercial*, December 15, 1892.

70. *Cleveland Gazette*, February 11, 1893.

71. Elizabeth Fortson Arroyo, "Josephine St. Pierre Ruffin," in *Black Women in America: An Historical Encyclopedia*, ed. Darlene Clark Hine (New York: Carlson, 1993), 994–996.

72. Anna J. Cooper, *A Voice from the South: By a Black Woman of the South* (Xenia, Ohio: Aldine, 1892), 111. Emphasis in original.

73. Alexander Crummell, "The Black Woman of the South: Her Neglects and Her Needs," in *Africa and America: Addresses and Discourse* (repr.; New York: Negro Universities Press, 1969), 59–82.

74. Cooper, *A Voice from the South*, 24–25.

75. Sharon Harley, "Anna J. Cooper," in *The Afro-American Woman: Struggle and Images*, ed. Sharon Harley and Rosalyn Terborg-Penn (Port Washington, N.Y.: Kennikat Press, 1978); Glenda Elizabeth Gilmore, *Gender and Jim Crow: Women and the Politics of White Supremacy in North Carolina, 1896–1920* (Chapel Hill: University of North Carolina Press, 1996), 34–44; Kevin Gaines, *Uplifting the Race: Black Leadership, Politics, and Culture in the Twentieth Century* (Chapel Hill: University of North Carolina Press, 1996), 228–151; Patricia A. Schechter, *Ida B. Wells-Barnett and American Reform, 1880–1930* (Chapel Hill:

University of North Carolina Press, 2001), 34–37, 51–64, 81–90; Giddings, *Ida*, 271–272; White, *Too Heavy a Load*, 37–39; and Evelyn Brooks Higginbotham, *Righteous Discontent: The Women's Movement in the Black Baptist Church, 1880–1920* (Cambridge, Mass.: Harvard University Press, 1993), 67–68, 123–124.

76. Cooper, *A Voice from the South*, 32.

77. Ibid.

78. Giddings, *Ida*, 259–289.

79. Ibid.

80. Ibid., 263–264.

81. *Indianapolis Freeman*, June 8, 1893.

82. *Memphis Appeal-Avalanche*, April 23, 1893.

83. Ida B. Wells, *The Reason Why the Colored Americans Is Not in the World's Columbian Exposition* (1893), in *Selected Works of Ida B. Wells-Barnett*, compiled by Trudier Harris (New York: Oxford University Press, 1991), 46–196.

84. Wells, *Crusade for Justice*; and Henry Lewis Suggs, ed., *The Black Press in the Middle West, 1865–1985* (Westport, Conn.: Greenwood Press, 1996).

85. Quoted in McMurray, *To Keep the Waters Troubled*, 237–238.

86. McMurray, *To Keep the Waters Troubled*, 238.

87. Giddings, *Ida*, 282.

88. White, *Too Heavy a Load*, 21–55; Deborah G. White, "The Cost of Club Work, the Price of Black Feminism," in *Visible Women: New Essays on American Activism*, ed. Nancy A. Hewitt and Suzanne Lebsock (Chicago: University of Illinois Press, 1993), 247–269; Beverly Washington Jones, *Quest for Equality: The Life and Writings of Mary Eliza Church Terrell, 1863–1955* (New York: Carlson, 1990), 17–29; Stephanie Shaw, "Black Club Women and the Creation of the National Association of Colored Women," in *"We Specialize in the Wholly Impossible": A Reader in Black Women's History*, ed. Darlene Clark Hine, Wilma King, and Linda Reed (New York: Carlson, 1995), 433–447; Darlene Clark Hine, *When the Truth Is Told: A History of Black Women's Culture and Community in Indiana, 1875–1950* (Indianapolis: National Council of Negro Women, 1981); Higginbotham, *Righteous Discontent*; and Dorothy Salem, "National Association of Colored Women," in *Black Women in America: An Historical Encyclopedia*, ed. Darlene Clark Hine (New York: Carlson, 1993), 842–851.

89. Organized in 1892 by Mary Church Terrell, Anna Julia Cooper, and Mary Jane Patterson, the Women's League of Washington, D.C., was one of the first clubs to attempt to organize nationally. The Woman's Loyal Union of New York was founded by Victoria Earle Matthews and Maritcha Lyons in December 1892 after a dinner to honor and encourage Ida B. Wells in her work against lynching. Josephine St. Pierre Ruffin and her daughter Florence Ridley, who attended Wells's testimonial dinner, played central roles in establishing the Boston Woman's Era Club a few months later. They also founded the first monthly

magazine to be published by African American women—*Woman's Era*. White, *Too Heavy a Load*; Shaw, "Black Club Women"; Dorothy Salem, *To Better Our World: Black Women in Organized Reform, 1890–1920* (New York: Carlson, 1990); Darlene Clark Hine, ed., *Black Women in America: A Historical Encyclopedia*, 2 vols. (New York: Carlson, 1993); Jones, *Quest for Equality*; and Charles Harris Wesley, *The History of the National Association of Colored Women's Clubs: A Legacy of Service* (Washington, D.C.: National Association of Colored Women's Clubs, 1984).

90. Quoted in Giddings, *Ida*, 286.

91. Letter, Florida Ruffin Ridley, Corresponding Secretary of the Woman's Era Club, to Mrs. Ormiston Chant, in Wells, *Crusade for Justice*, 199–200.

92. *New York Voice*, October 23, 1890.

93. McMurray, *To Keep the Waters Troubled*, 210–216; Schechter, *Ida B. Wells-Barnett and American Reform*, 102–112; Giddings, *Ida*, 266–378; Gilmore, *Gender and Jim Crow*, 55–58; and White, *Too Heavy a Load*, 103.

94. See Willard's interview with Lady Henry Somerset in Wells, *Crusade for Justice*, 201–212.

95. Giddings, *Ida*, 308–309.

96. Letter, Ridley to Chant.

97. Quoted in (Kansas City) *American Citizen*, July 12, 1895.

98. *Woman's Era*, 2 (August 1895).

99. Mary Church Terrell, "The History of the Club Women's Movement," in *Quest for Equality*, 320; Terrell, "A Plea to the White South by a Colored Woman," in *Quest for Equality*, 70–84; Terrell, *A Colored Woman in a White World* (Washington, D.C.: Ransdell Publishing Company, 1940); Jones, *Quest for Equality*; Jones, "Mary Eliza Church Terrell," in *Black Women in America*, 1157–1159; Sharon Harley, "Mary Church Terrell: Genteel Militant," in *Black Leaders of the Nineteenth Century*, ed. Leon Litwack and August Meir (Chicago: University of Illinois Press, 1988), 307–321; and the papers of Mary Church Terrell, located at the Library of Congress and in the Moorland-Spingarn Collection at Howard University, Washington, D.C.

100. Margaret Murray Washington, "Club Work among Negro Women," in *Progress of a Race: Or the Remarkable Advancement of the Colored American*, ed. John W. Gibson (Naperville, Ill.: J. L. Nichols, 1920), 179.

101. Fannie Barrier Williams, "The Club Movement among Colored Women in America," in *A New Negro for a New Century*, ed. J. E. MacBrady (Chicago: American, 1900), 397.

102. Terrell, "The History of the Club Women's Movement," 320–321.

103. Josephine St. Pierre Ruffin, "Address of Josephine St. Pierre Ruffin to the First National Conference of Colored Women, 1898," in *Black Women in White America*, 443.

104. Ibid.

105. Quoted in McMurray, *To Keep the Waters Troubled*, 247

106. At the 1891 meeting of the National Council of Women of the United States, Frances Ellen Watkins Harper berated the federal government for failing to "protect and defend its citizens from wrong and outrages" — see *Transaction of the National Council of Women of the United States Assembled in Washington, D.C. February 22, 1891* (Philadelphia: J. B. Lippincott Co., 1891), 29. In 1892 Harper published *Iola Leroy, or Shadow Uplifted* — reprinted in *Three Classic African-American Novels*, ed. Henry Louis Gates Jr. (New York: Vintage Books, 1990) — a novel that acknowledges the increased use of lynching of African Americans in the South.

107. *Woman's Era* 2 (August 1895).

108. Wells, *Crusade for Justice*, 242.

109. Josephine St. Pierre Ruffin, "Address to the First National Conference of Colored Women, July 1895," *Woman's Era* 2, 5 (September 1895): 14.

110. Higginbotham, *Righteous Discontent*; Gaines, *Uplifting the Race*; and Gilmore, *Gender and Jim Crow*.

111. Booker T. Washington, "Cotton States and International Exposition Speech in Atlanta, September 18, 1895," in *The Booker T. Washington Papers*, vol. 3, ed. Louis R. Harlen (Urbana: University of Illinois Press, 1974), 583–587.

112. *Plessy v. Ferguson*, 163 U.S. 537 (1896).

113. Quoted in White, *Too Heavy a Load*, 70. Williams was also the Chicago reporter for the *Woman's Era* and secretary of the board of directors of the Phyllis Wheatley Home Association. See Fannie Williams, "The Intellectual Progress of the Colored Women of the United State since the Emancipation Proclamation," in *Black Women in Nineteenth Century American Life: Their Words, Their Thoughts, Their Feelings*, ed. Bert James Loewenberg and Ruth Bogin (University Park: Pennsylvania State University Press, 1977); and Williams, "The Club Movement among Colored Women," *Voice of the Negro* 1, 3 (1904): 102.

114. Mary Church Terrell, "The Duty of the National Association of Colored Women to the Race," in *Quest for Equality*, 148. Originally published in the *AME Church Review* (January 1900): 340–354.

115. Terrell, "The Duty," 148–149.

116. Higginbotham, *Righteous Discontent*, 185–229.

117. Ibid., 185–188, 211–221; and Evelyn Brooks Higginbotham, "Nannie Burroughs and the Education of Black Women," in *The Afro-American Woman: Struggles and Images*, ed. Sharon Harley and Rosalyn Terborg-Penn (Port Washington, N.Y.: Kennikat Press, 1978).

118. Terrell, "The Duty of the National Association of Colored Women," 148–149.

119. Ibid., 149.

120. Mary Church Terrell, "Lynching from a Negro's Point of View," *North American Review* 178, 571 (June 1904): 865; and Anonymous, "A Colored Woman, However Respectable, Is Lower Than the White Prostitute, 1902," in *Black Women in White America: A Documentary History*, ed. Gerda Lerner (New York: Vintage, 1992), 166–169.

121. Anonymous, "A Colored Woman," 167.

122. Felton, "The Rights of Children" (n.d., ca. 1893), Rebecca Latimer Felton Papers (Athens: University of Georgia).

123. Anastatia Sims, *The Power of Femininity in the New South: Women's Organizations and Politics in North Carolina, 1880–1930* (Columbia: University of South Carolina Press, 1997); and Schechter, *Ida B. Wells-Barnett and American Reform, 1880–1930*, 134.

124. "The Negro Problem by a Colored Woman and Two White Women," *Independent* 64 (March 17, 1904): 589.

125. Addie Hunton, "Negro Womanhood Defended," *The Voice of the Negro* 1, 7 (July 1904): 281. For more information see Gretchen E. Maclachlan, "Addie Waits Hunton," in *Black Women in America: An Historical Encyclopedia*, ed. Darlene Clark Hine (New York: Carlson Publishing, 1993), 596–597.

126. Hunton, "Negro Womanhood Defended," 282.

127. Ibid.

128. Nannie Burroughs, "Not Color but Character," *The Voice of the Negro* 1, 1 (July 1904): 277–279; Evelyn Higginbotham, "Nannie Burroughs and the Education of Black Women," in *The Afro-American Woman*; Higginbotham, "Religion, Politics, and Gender: The Leadership of Nannie Helen Burroughs," *Journal of Religious Thought* (Winter-Spring 1988); and Higginbotham, *Righteous Discontent*.

129. Anonymous Negro nurse, "More Slavery at the South," *The Independent* 72, 3295 (January 25, 1912): 197–200.

130. Cooper, *A Voice from the South*, 24.

131. Burroughs, "Not Color but Character," 277–279.

132. Thomas Nelson Page, "The Lynching of Negroes, Its Cause and Its Prevention," *North American Review* 178 (January 1904): 33–48.

133. "The Progress of Colored Women," *Voice of the Negro* (July 1904): 292–294; "The International Congress of Women," *Voice of the Negro* (December 1904): 454–461; "Service Which Should Be Rendered the South," *Voice of the Negro* (February 1905): 182–186; "The Mission of Meddlers," *Voice of the Negro* (August 1905): 566–568; "A Plea for the White South by a Coloured Woman," *Nineteenth Century* (July 1906): 70–84; "The Disbanding of the Colored Soldiers," *Voice of the Negro* (December 1906): 554–558; "What It Means to Be Colored in the Capital of the United States," *Independent* (January 24, 1907): 181–86; and "Peonage in the United States: The Convict Lease System and the Chain Gangs," *Nineteenth Century* (August 1907): 306–322.

134. Terrell, "Lynching from a Negro's Point of View," 853–854, 860–861.

135. Ibid., 865.

136. Yates to Washington, February 1906, and Yates to Washington, 16 May 1904, in Box 132, Margaret Murray Washington Papers, Hollis Burke Frissel Library, Tuskegee University.

137. Thompson, *Ida B. Wells*, 67–84; and McMurray, *To Keep the Waters Troubled*, 244–282.

138. Thomas Holt, "The Lonely Warrior: Ida B. Wells-Barnett and the Struggle for Black Leadership," in *Black Leaders of the Twentieth Century*, ed. John Hope Franklin and August Meier (Urbana: University of Illinois Press, 1982), 48–49.

139. Wells, *Crusade for Justice*, 258–261.

140. Wells, "Booker T. Washington and His Critics," *World Today* (April 1904): 518–521, as part of a symposium entitled "The Negro Problem from the Negro Point of View."

141. Wells, *Southern Horrors*, 46.

142. Lois R. Harlan, *Booker T. Washington*, vol. 1, *The Making of a Black Leader, 1856–1901* (New York: Oxford University Press, 1975); Harlan, *Booker T. Washington*, vol. 2, *The Wizard of Tuskegee, 1901–1915* (New York: Oxford University Press, 1986); W. Fitzhugh Brundage, *Booker T. Washington and Black Progress: Up from Slavery 100 Years Later* (Gainesville: University Press of Florida, 2003).

143. *Proceedings of the National Negro Conference 1909: New York May 31 and June 1* (n.p., n.d.), 174–179.

144. Quoted in McMurray, *To Keep the Waters Troubled*, 282.

145. Wells, *Crusade for Justice*, 328–329. Also see Salem, *To Better Our World*, 106; McMurray, *To Keep the Waters Troubled*, 286; and White, *Too Heavy a Load*, 84–85.

146. Gaines, *Uplifting the Race*.

147. Tuskegee Institute News Clipping File, "Lynching, 1899–1966" (Microfilm Reels 221–236); March 31, 1914 newspaper editions of *Traveler & Evening Herald* (Boston); *Plain Dealer* (Cleveland, Ohio); *Evening Telegram* (New York City); *Chronicle* (San Francisco); *Weekly News and Observer* (Raleigh, N.C.); and *Times* (Seattle, Wash.).

148. "Mob Lynches a Negress: A Special to *The New York Times*," *New York Times*, April 1, 1914, p. 3.

149. Letter, W. Scott Brown Jr. to Miss May Childs Nerney (April 16, 1914), NAACP Papers, Library of Congress Manuscripts.

150. Ibid.

151. Letter, Chapin Brinsmade to Mrs. E. W. Anderson (April 22, 1914), NAACP Papers, Library of Congress Manuscripts.

152. Letter, Jas. Harold Coleman to Miss MaBelle A. White (May 15, 1914), NAACP Papers, Library of Congress.

153. W. E. B. Du Bois, "The Cause of Lynching," *The Crisis* (July 1914): 127.

5. New Southern Women and the Triumph of White Supremacy

1. Rebecca Felton, "Women on the Farm," *Atlanta Journal*, August 12, 1897, and *Macon Telegraph*, August 18, 1897, in Rebecca Latimer Felton Papers, University of Georgia Hargrett Rare Book and Manuscript Library (GHL).

2. Rebecca Felton, "Southern Women and Farm Life," in Rebecca Latimer Felton Papers, GHL; LeeAnn Whites, "Rebecca Latimer Felton and the Wife's Farm: The Class and Racial Politics of Gender Reform," *Georgia Historical Quarterly* 76, 2 (Summer 1992); Joel Williamson, *A Rage for Order: Black-White Relations in the American South since Emancipation* (London: Oxford University Press, 1986), 95; and Glenda Elizabeth Gilmore, *Gender and Jim Crow: Women and the Politics of White Supremacy in North Carolina, 1896–1920* (Chapel Hill: University of North Carolina Press, 1996), 106.

3. Felton, "Women on the Farm."

4. Ibid.

5. "Correspondence 1897–1904," Mr. Ulla Hardiman to Rebecca Latimer Felton, December 22, 1898, in Rebecca Latimer Felton Papers, GHL.

6. "Correspondence 1897–1904," A Virginia Woman to Rebecca Latimer Felton, n.d., Rebecca Latimer Felton Papers, GHL.

7. "Correspondence 1897–1904," Mrs. Fannie H. Williams to Rebecca Latimer Felton, November 18, 1897, Rebecca Latimer Felton Papers, GHL.

8. *Northern Georgia Citizen*, August 19, 1897, Rebecca Latimer Felton Papers, Special Collections, GHL.

9. Ibid.

10. Letter to Editor of *Atlanta Journal*, June 1898, Rebecca Latimer Felton Papers, GHL.

11. *Boston Transcript*, August 17, 1897.

12. *Macon Telegraph*, August 20, 1897, Rebecca Latimer Felton Papers, GHL.

13. Ibid.

14. Ibid.

15. Glenda Gilmore, "Murder, Memory, and the Flight of the Incubus," and LeeAnn Whites, "Love, Hate, Rape, Lynching: Rebecca Latimer Felton and the Gender Politics of Racial Violence," in *Democracy Betrayed: The Wilmington Race Riot of 1898 and its Legacy*, ed. David S. Cecelski and Timothy B. Tyson (Chapel Hill: University of North Carolina Press, 1998), 73–93, 143–162.

16. Gilmore, *Gender and Jim Crow*, 105–117; David S. Cecelski and Timothy B. Tyson, eds., *Democracy Betrayed: The Wilmington Race Riot of 1898 and Its Legacy* (Chapel Hill: University of North Carolina Press, 1998).

17. Originally printed in the *Wilmington Record*, August 18, 1898 (no copies exist); it also appeared in the *Wilmington Morning Star*, August 23 and 25, 1898, and the *Raleigh News and Observer*, August 26, 1898.

18. Ibid.

19. Ibid.

20. *North Carolinian*, September 8, 1898.

21. "Mrs. Felton vs. Manly," and *Atlanta Journal*, n.d., in Rebecca Latimer Felton Papers, GHL.

22. "Newspaper clippings," *Atlanta Journal*, November 21, 1898, and *The Courant*, November 1898, Rebecca Latimer Felton Papers, GHL.

23. Ibid.

24. *Atlanta Constitution*, December 19, 1898.

25. *Atlanta Constitution*, December 19, 22, and 29, 1898; *Cincinnati Enquirer*, December 22, 1898; and *Atlanta Journal*, May 3, 1899. Original and unedited version of the letter in Rebecca Latimer Felton Papers, GHL.

26. Ibid.

27. W. Fitzhugh Brundage, *Lynching in the New South: Georgia and Virginia, 1880–1930* (Urbana: University of Illinois Press, 1993), 272–273.

28. Newman *Herald and Advertiser*, April 14, 1899; and *Atlanta Constitution*, April 13 and 14, 1899.

29. "Correspondence 1897–1904," Wells B. Whitmore to William H. Felton, April 25, 1899, in Rebecca Latimer Felton Papers, GHL.

30. *Atlanta Constitution*, April 19, 1899.

31. *Atlanta Constitution*, April 14, 1899; and *Atlanta Journal*, April 15, 1899.

32. "How Shall the Women and the Girls of the Country Districts Be Protected?" *Atlanta Constitution*, April 23, 1899.

33. Ibid.

34. Ibid.

35. Ibid.

36. Ibid.

37. Ibid.

38. Ibid.

39. Ibid.

40. Ibid.

41. Numan V. Bartley, *The Creation of Modern Georgia* (Athens: University of Georgia Press, 1990), 94–99. See Governor Northen's anti-lynching pamphlets, "The Evolution of Lawlessness and the Unchallenged Crime" (n.d., ca. 1908) and "Civic Righteousness in Georgia," which is a copy of Northen's speech to the Georgia Baptist Convention, December 2, 1908, in the William J. Northen Papers, Special Collections, University of Georgia Hargrett Library.

42. *Washington Post*, March 17, 1899.

43. E. Merton Coulter, *College Life in the Old South* (1928; Athens: University of Georgia Press, 1983); Steven R. Henderson, "Patrick Hues Mell: The Life, Character, and Influence of a Baptist King," *Viewpoints: Georgia Baptist History* 19 (2004); Spencer B. King Jr., "Patrick Hues Mell: Preacher, Pedagogue, and Parliamentarian," *Baptist History and Heritage* 5 (October 1970); P. H. Mell, *Life of Patrick Hues Mell* (1895; Harrisonburg, Va.: Gano Books, 1991); Bennie Lewis Noles Jr., "Patrick Hues Mell, 1814–1888: The Southerner as Educator" (master's thesis, University of Georgia, 1996).

44. "Correspondence 1897–1904," Letter from J. C. Clark to Mrs. W. H. Felton, May 2, 1899—letter included clipping from *Atlanta Constitution*, "A Woman's Protest," Rebecca Latimer Felton Papers, Special Collections, GHL. Clark sent Mell's protest to Felton and asked that she write a "proper rebuke."

45. Jacquelyn Dowd Hall, *Revolt against Chivalry: Jessie Daniel Ames and the Women's Campaign against Lynching*, rev. ed. (New York: Columbia University Press, 1993).

46. Grace Elizabeth Hale, *Making Whiteness: The Culture of Segregation in the South, 1890–1940* (New York: Vintage, 1999), 235.

47. Hale, *Making Whiteness*, 234–235; and Brundage, *Lynching in the New South*, 37–38.

48. Hall, *Revolt against Chivalry*, 151; and Gretta Palmer, "Lynching Women Aid the Crime They Abhor," *Washington Daily News*, December 5, 1933.

49. *Atlanta Constitution*, July 28, 1887.

50. *Savannah Morning*, November 16, 1893.

51. *Atlanta Constitution*, April 30, 1899.

52. *Scimitar* (Memphis, Tenn.), February 12, 1893; and Ida B. Wells, *A Red Record*, in *On Lynching* (Salem, N.H.: Ayer Company, Publishers, 1991), 139–141.

53. *Atlanta Constitution*, November 3 and 4, 1919.

54. *Daily Herald*, May 18 and 22, 1919; *Vicksburg Evening Post*, May 15 and 16, 1919; Chicago *Defender*, May 24, 1919.

55. *Chicago Defender*, May 24, 1919; and *Vicksburg Evening Post*, May 15, 1919.

56. Quoted in Herbert J. Seligmann, "Protecting Southern Womanhood," *The Nation*, June 14, 1919, in Tuskegee Institute News Clipping Files, "Lynching, 1899–1966" (microfilm reels 221–236).

57. *Daily Charlotte Observer*, August 10 and 12, 1897.

58. *Atlanta Constitution*, April 14 and 24, 1899; *Atlanta Journal*, April 15, 1899; *Macon Telegraph*, April 24 and 25, 1899; *Birmingham News*, April 24, 1899; and *New York Times*, April 25, 1899.

59. *Leesburg Mirror*, February 5 and 19, 1880; *Leesburg Washingtonian*, February 21, 1880; *Richmond State*, February 19, 1880; and *Baltimore Sun*, February 18 and 19, 1880.

60. *Baltimore Morning Herald*, March 28, 1900; *Washington Times*, March 27, 1900; and *American*, March 28, 1900, located in Tuskegee Institute News Clipping Files, "Lynching, 1899–1966" (microfilm reels 221–236).

61. *Baltimore Morning Herald*, March 28, 1900.

62. *Chattanooga Times*, February 14, 1918.

63. NAACP, *The Lynching of Claude Neal* (New York: NAACP, 1934); Frank Shay, *Judge Lynch: His First Hundred Years* (New York: Ives Washburn, 1938), 178–187; and James R. McGovern, *Anatomy of a Lynching: The Killing of Claude Neal* (Baton Rouge: Louisiana State University Press, 1982).

64. *Associated Negro Press*, August 31, 1922; and *Baltimore Herald*, September 6, 1922.

65. *Associated Press*, May 23, 1917.

66. *New York World*, December 7, 1899.

67. *Sea Coast Echo Bay* (Bay Saint Louis, Miss.), June 13, 1903.

68. Arthur Raper, *The Tragedy of Lynching* (1933; New York: Dover Publications, 1970), 319–355.

69. Ibid., 338–339.

70. *Without Sanctuary: Lynching Photography in America* (Santa Fe, N.M.: Twin Palms Publishers, 2000); Shawn Michelle Smith, *Photography on the Color Line* (Durham, N.C.: Duke University Press, 2004); and Dora Apel and Shawn Smith, *Lynching Photographs* (Los Angeles: University of California Press, 2008).

71. Tuskegee Institute News Clippings, "Lynching, 1899–1966," (microfilm reels 221–236).

72. *Atlanta Independent*, November 18, 1918.

73. *Atlanta Constitution*, February 10, 1920.

74. *Commercial Appeal*, February 8, 1926.

75. Frederick Douglass, "Lynch Law in the South," *North American Review* 155 (July 1892).

76. R. C. O Benjamin, *Southern Outrages: A Statistical Record of Lawless Doings* (N.p., 1894), and Wells, *The Red Record*, 137–138.

77. Benjamin, *Southern Outrages*.

78. Gail Bederman, *Manliness and Civilization: A Cultural History of Gender and Race in the United States, 1880–1917* (Chicago: University Chicago Press, 1995).

79. Tuskegee Institute News Clippings, "Lynchings, 1899–1966" (microfilm reels 221–236).

80. *Informer* (Muskogee, Oklahoma), August 9, 1916.

81. *Chicago Defender*, January 12, 1929; *Afro-American*, January 5 and 12, 1928; *New York Times*, January 1, 1929; and *Montgomery Advertiser*, January 1, 1929.

82. Francis J. Grimké, "Lynching: Its Causes—A Low State of Civilization and Race Hatred," in *The Works of Francis J. Grimké*, ed. Carter G. Woodson (Washington: Associated Publishers, 1942), 297.

83. *Houston Informer*, August 20, 1927.
84. Neil R. McMillen, *Dark Journey: Black Mississippians in the Age of Jim Crow* (Chicago: University of Illinois Press, 1989), 244–245; Jackson *Daily News*, June 21, 26, and 27, 1919; *Memphis Commercial-Picayune*, June 26 and 27, 1919; *Birmingham News*, June 27, 1919; *New Orleans Item*, June 27, 1919; and *New York Times*, June 27, 1919.
85. *Chicago Defender*, May 27, 1922.
86. *Washington Eagle*, 1921, Tuskegee Newspaper Clippings, "Lynchings, 1899–1966" (Reel 222).
87. *Arkansas Gazette*, May 5, 1927.
88. Arthur F. Raper, *The Tragedy of Lynching* (Chapel Hill: University of North Carolina Press, 1933), 326.
89. *Chicago Defender*, May 24, 1919. Also see *Herald* (Vicksburg, Miss.), May 15, 1919; and *New York Age*, June 14, 1919.
90. *Chicago Defender*, May 24, 1919.
91. Tuskegee Newspaper Clipping File, Reel 222.
92. *Memphis Commercial*, July 23, 1893; and Wells, *On Lynchings*, 128.
93. *St. Louis Argus*, September 25, 1925.
94. Ibid.
95. Ibid.
96. Christine Stansell, *American Moderns: Bohemian New York and the Creation of a New Century* (New York: Henry Holt and Company, 2000).
97. *Post Dispatch* (St. Louis, Mo.), April 4, 1920; *Examiner* (Chicago, Ill.), April 4, 1920; *Advocate* (Cleveland, Ohio), April 10, 1920; and *Courier-Journal* (Louisville, Ky.), April 3, 1920.
98. *Post Dispatch*, April 4, 1920; and *Examiner*, April 4, 1920.
99. *Advocate*, April 10, 1920.
100. Ibid.

6. The Lynching of Black and White Women

1. *Memphis Daily Appeal*, August 19, 1886.
2. Ida B. Wells, "September 4, 1886," in *The Memphis Diary of Ida B. Wells: An Intimate Portrait of the Activist as a Young Woman*, ed. Miriam Decosta-Willis (Boston: Beacon Press, 1995), 102.
3. *Memphis Daily Appeal*, August 19, 1886.
4. Ida B. Wells, *A Red Record*, in *On Lynching* (Salem, N.H.: Ayer Company, Publishers, 1991),120.
5. Ibid.
6. Ibid., 158.
7. Wells, "Lynching and the Excuses for It," *Independent*, May 16, 1901.

8. Catherine Clinton, "Bloody Terrain: Freewomen, Sexuality, and Violence during Reconstruction," *Georgia Historical Quarterly* 76 (Summer 1992): 313–332.

9. Stewart E. Tolnay and E. M. Beck, *A Festival of Violence: An Analysis of Southern Lynchings, 1882–1930* (Urbana: University of Illinois Press, 1995), 86–113.

10. *Weekly Clarion* (Mississippi), November 20, 1878. Also see *Memphis Appeal*, November 12, 1878; and *New York Times*, November 12, 1878.

11. *News and Courier* (Charleston, S.C.), December 10 and 11, 1880.

12. *New York Times*, December 12, 1880.

13. *News and Courier*, December 10 and 11, 1880.

14. Gail Bederman, *Manliness and Civilization: A Cultural History of Gender and Race in the United States, 1880–1917* (Chicago: University of Chicago Press, 1995).

15. *New York Times*, April 15, 1881.

16. *News and Courier*, April 15, 1881; and *New York Times* (Special Report from Spartanburg, S.C.), April 15, 1881.

17. *New York Times* (Special Report from Spartanburg, S.C.), April 15, 1881.

18. *Newberry Herald* (Newberry, S.C.), April 13, 1881. On April 27, 1881, the *Newberry Herald* reprinted articles from the *Abberville Press and Banner*, the *Laurensville Herald*, the *Greenville Enterprise and Mountaineer*, and the *New York Herald* denouncing the lynching of Judith Metts.

19. *Newberry Herald*, April 20, 1881.

20. *New York Times* (Special Report from Newberry, S.C.), April 18, 1881.

21. Reprinted in *Newberry Herald*, April 27, 1881.

22. *News and Courier*, April 20, 1881.

23. *New York Times*, September 30, 1885.

24. *News and Observer*, October 1, 1885.

25. *News and Observer*, July 8 and 16, 1885; and *Chatham Record*, July 16, October 1, and 8, 1885.

26. Tolnay and Beck, *Festival of Violence*,

27. *Courier-Journal* (Louisville, Ky.), May 6, 1891.

28. Glenda Elizabeth Gilmore, *Gender and Jim Crow: Women and the Politics of White Supremacy in North Carolina, 1896–1920* (Chapel Hill: University of North Carolina Press, 1996); and Tera Hunter, *To 'Joy My Freedom: Southern Black Women's Lives and Labors after the Civil War* (Cambridge, Mass.: Harvard University Press, 1997).

29. *Daily Picayune*, January 13, 1896.

30. *New York Tribune*, March 17, 1901.

31. *The State* (Columbia, S.C.), December 6, 1895.

32. Eugene D. Genovese, *Roll, Jordan, Roll: The World the Slaves Made* (New York: Vintage Books, 1976), 616.

33. Thomas Cooper and David J. McCord, eds., *Statutes at Large of South Carolina* (Columbia: South Carolina State, 1836–1841).

34. Elizabeth Fox-Genovese, *Within the Plantation Household: Black and White Women of the Old South* (Chapel Hill: University of North Carolina Press, 1988), 306–307.

35. Ida B. Wells, *Southern Horrors,* in *On Lynchings* (Salem, N.H.: Ayer Company, Publishers, 1991), 50.

36. *Richland Beacon News,* March 12, 1892; and *New York Times,* March 14, 1892.

37. *Shreveport Journal,* July 27, 1903.

38. Tuskegee Institute News Clipping Files, "Lynchings, 1899–1966" (microfilm reels 221–236): *Shreveport Times,* July 26 and 28, 1903; *Shreveport Journal,* July 27 and 28, 1903; *New York Times,* July 27, 1903; *Chicago Record-Herald,* July 27, 1903.

39. Lucrezia Borgia (1480–1519), the daughter of the notorious Pope Alexander VI, was infamous for participating in the murders carried out by her father and brother. Many believed that she had poisoned her enemies. For more information on Lucrezia Borgia, see Maria Bellonci, *The Life and Times of Lucrezia Borgia* (New York: Harcourt, Brace, 1953) and *Lucrezia Borgia* (Milan: Mondadori, 1989).

40. Edward L. Ayers, *Vengeance and Justice: Crime and Punishment in the 19th-Century American South* (New York: Oxford University Press, 1984); W. Fitzhugh Brundage, *Lynching in the New South: Georgia and Virginia, 1880–1930* (Chicago: University of Illinois Press, 1993); and Julie Saville, *The Work of Reconstruction: From Slave to Wage Laborer in South Carolina, 1860–1870* (New York: Cambridge University Press, 1994).

41. Marie Thompson of Lebanon Junction, Kentucky; Mrs. Oliver Wideman of Greenwood, South Carolina; Anne Bostwick of Pinehurst, Georgia; Mary Turner of Lowndes, Georgia; Mary Conley of Calhoun County, Georgia; and Ella Williams and Liza Lowe of Henry County, Alabama, were discharged by their employers before they were accused of murder or arson.

42. *Courier-Journal,* August 8, 1891.

43. "Last Testimony of Oliver and Emma Wideman," *Greenwood Index,* January 1, 1903.

44. *The State,* December 28 and 29, 1902; *News and Courier,* December 28, 1902; *Greenwood Index,* January 1, 1903; and *New York Times,* December 28, 1902.

45. Tuskegee Institute News Clipping Files, "Lynchings, 1899–1966" (microfilm reels 221–236): *Atlanta Constitution,* July 13, 1914; *Detroit Free Press,* July 13, 1914; *Advertiser,* July 13, 1914; *New York Times,* July 13, 1914; and San Francisco *Chronicle,* July 13, 1914.

46. *Atlanta Constitution,* July 13, 1914.

47. Tuskegee Institute News Clipping Files, "Lynchings, 1899–1966" (microfilm reels 221–236); *Sentinel,* November 27, 1914; *Nashville Banner,* November 18,

1914; *Republican*, November 26, 1914; *Star*, November 26, 1914; and *Enterprise*, November 26, 1914.

48. Saville, *The Work of Reconstruction*; Steven Hahn, *A Nation under Our Feet: Black Political Struggles in the Rural South from Slavery to the Great Migration* (Cambridge, Mass.: Harvard University Press, 2003); Hunter, *To 'Joy My Freedom*; and Laurie B. Green, *Battling the Plantation Mentality: Memphis and the Black Freedom Struggle* (Chapel Hill: University of North Carolina Press, 2007).

49. Saville, *The Work of Reconstruction*, 107.

50. Edward Ayers, *The Promise of the New South: Life after Reconstruction* (New York: Oxford University Press, 1992), 155.

51. *Courier-Journal*, June 15, 1904.

52. *Courier-Journal*, June 16, 1904.

53. Jacqueline Jones, *Labor of Love, Labor of Sorrow: Black Women, Work, and the Family from Slavery to the Present* (New York: Basic Books, 1985).

54. *The State*, February 23, 1898; *News and Courier*, February 23, 1898; *County Record*, February 24, March 3, 10, and 24, 1898.

55. U.S. Congress, *Punishment for the Crime of Lynching*, 74th Cong., 1st sess., S. 24, 14 February 1935; National Association for the Advancement of Colored People, *Thirty Years of Lynching in the United States, 1889–1918* (New York: NAACP, 1919); *The Crisis* (January, February, and September 1912); Papers of the NAACP, General Lynching Files, Manuscripts Division of the Library of Congress, Washington, D.C.

56. Laura Nelson of Okemah, Oklahoma; Hattie Bowman of Jackson, Florida; Eula and Ella Barber of Monticello, Georgia; Emma Hooper of Hammond, Louisiana; Stella Young and Mary Dennis of Newberry, Florida; Sarah and Bessie Cabaniss of Huntsville, Texas; Bertha Lowman of Aiken, South Carolina; and Mrs. Brisco of England, Arkansas, were all accused of assault or murder of a law officer.

57. *New York Times*, May 26, 1911; *The Crisis* (August and October 1911); also see Tuskegee Institute News Clipping Files, "Lynchings, 1899–1966" (microfilm reels 221–236).

58. *The Crisis* (August 1911), 153.

59. *Eatonton Messenger*, January 22, 1915. Also see *Covington News*, January 20, 1915, and *Atlanta Journal*, January 15, 1915.

60. Tuskegee Institute News Clipping Files "Lynchings, 1899–1966," reprinted in *Literary Digest*, January 30, 1915; *Cincinnati Times*, January 16, 1915; and *Brooklyn Eagle*, January 15, 1915; *New York Times*, January 17, 18, 19, 22, and February 19, 1915; and *Atlanta Constitution*, January 16, 17, and 20, 1915.

61. *Manchester Mercury*, January 26, 1912; *Columbus Enquire Sun*, January 23, 1912; *Austin Statesman*, January 23, 1912; *New York Times*, January 23, 1912; *Atlanta Constitution*, January 23, 1912; *Griffin Weekly News*, January 26, 1912; and *Mont-*

gomery Advertiser, January 23, 1912. For the House case, see *Jackson Daily News*, December 21, 1918; *New York Times*, December 21, 1918; *New York Telegram*, December 21, 1918; *The Crisis* (May 1919); and the NAACP Lynching Files.

62. Tuskegee Institute News Clipping Files, "Lynching, 1899–1966": *Traveler and Evening Herald* (Boston); *Plain Dealer* (Ohio); *Evening Telegram* (New York); *Chronicle* (San Francisco); *Weekly News and Observer* (Raleigh, N.C.); *Times* (Seattle, Wash.), March 31, 1914; and *New York Times*, April 1, 1914.

63. News clipping, October 13, 1923, Tuskegee Institute News Clipping Files, "Lynchings, 1899–1966" (reel 223).

64. *Jackson Daily News*, December 21, 1918.

65. *Daily Herald*, December 28, 1918, Tuskegee Institute News Clipping Files, "Lynchings, 1899–1996."

66. *The Crisis* (October 1911).

67. *Chicago Defender*, December 18, 1915.

68. Frank Shay, *Judge Lynch: His First Hundred Years* (New York: Ives Washburn, 1938), 98.

69. *Vicksburg Evening Post*, February 13, 1904, quoted in Walter White, *Rope and Faggot: A Biography of Judge Lynch* (repr.; Notre Dame, Ind.: University of Notre Dame Press, 2001), 35–36.

70. *The Crisis* 16, 2 (September 1918): 55.

71. *Voice of the Negro* 2, 2 (February 1905): 106–107.

72. Jacquelyn Down Hall, *Revolt against Chivalry: Jessie Daniel Ames and the Women's Campaign against Lynching*, rev. ed. (New York: Columbia University, 1992); and Hall, "'The Mind That Burns in Each Body': Women, Rape, and Racial Violence," in *Powers of Desire: The Politics of Sexuality*, ed. Amy Snitow, Christine Stansell, and Sharon Thompson (New York: Monthly Review Press, 1983), 328–349.

73. Grace Elizabeth Hale, *Making Whiteness: The Culture of Segregation in the South, 1890–1940* (New York: Pantheon Books, 1998), 234.

74. Georgina Hickey, *Hope and Danger in the New South City: Working-Class Women and Urban Development in Atlanta, 1890–1940* (Athens: University of Georgia Press, 2003); Jacquelyn Dowd Hall, "Disorderly Women: Gender and Labor Militancy in the Appalachian South," in *Unequal Sisters: A Multicultural Reader*, ed. Ellen Carol DuBois and Vicki L. Ruis (New York: Routledge, 1990): 298–312; Hall, "O. Delight Smith's Progressive Era: Labor, Feminism, and Reform in the Urban South," in *Visible Women: New Essays on American Activism*, ed. Nancy A. Hewitt and Suzanne Lebsock (Urbana: University of Illinois Press, 1993), 166–198; and Hall, "Private Eyes, Public Women: Images of Class and Sex in the Urban South, Atlanta, Georgia, 1913–1915," in *Work Engendered: Toward a New History of American Labor*, ed. Ava Baron (Ithaca:

Cornell University Press, 1991), 243–272; Nancy MacLean, *Behind the Mask of Chivalry: The Making of the Second Ku Klux Klan* (New York: Greenwood Press, 1989); and MacLean, "The Leo Frank Case Reconsidered: Gender and Sexual Politics in the Making of Reactionary Populism," *Journal of American History* 78 (December 1991): 917–948.

75. Victoria E. Bynum, *Unruly Women: The Politics of Social and Sexual Control in the Old South* (Chapel Hill: University of North Carolina Press, 1992); and Kathleen M. Brown, *Good Wives, Nasty Wenches, and Anxious Patriarchs* (Chapel Hill: University of North Carolina Press, 1996).

76. Leslie Dunlap, "The Reform of Rape Law and the Problem of White Men," in *Sex, Love, Race: Crossing Boundaries in North American History*, ed. Martha Hodes (New York: New York University Press, 1999), 360–361; Lisa Dorr, *White Women, Rape, and the Power of Race in Virginia, 1900–1960* (Chapel Hill: University of North Carolina Press, 2003); Mary Frances Berry, "Judging Morality: Sexual Behavior and Legal Consequences in the Late Nineteenth-Century South," *Journal of American History* 78 (1991): 835–856; and Laura Edwards, *Gendered Strife and Confusion: The Political Culture of Reconstruction* (Urbana: University of Illinois Press, 1997). Also see Joan Hoff, *Law, Gender, and Injustice: A Legal History of U.S. Women* (New York: New York University Press, 1991), 151–180.

77. Drew Faust, *Mothers of Invention: Women of the Slaveholding South in the American Civil War* (Chapel Hill: University of North Carolina Press, 1996); and Catherine Clinton and Nina Silber, eds., *Divided Houses: Gender and the Civil War* (New York: Oxford University Press, 1992).

78. Martha Hodes, "Sexualization of Reconstruction Politics: White Women and Black Men in the South after the Civil War," *Journal of the History of Sexuality* (January 1993): 402–417.

79. Martha Hodes suggests that white fears of black male sexual threats did not pervade the antebellum or even the war years. See Hodes, "Wartime Dialogues on Illicit Sex: White Women and Black Men," in *Divided Houses*, 239; and Hodes, *White Women, Black Men: Illicit Sex in the 19th-Century South* (New Haven: Yale University Press, 1997). In Diane Miller Sommerville's study of rape in the antebellum South, she argues that even in cases of alleged rape by a black man it was difficult for white women, especially lower-class white women, to prove themselves worthy of protection. See Sommerville, "The Rape Myth in the Old South Reconsidered," *Journal of Southern History* 61, 3 (August 1995): 514–515.

80. *New York Times*, April 27, 1903.

81. Bynum, *Unruly Women*; Brown, *Good Wives, Nasty Wenches*; Alice Morse Earle, *Curious Punishments of Bygone Days* (Chicago: Herbert S. Stone &

Company, 1896); and Peter Laslett, Karen Oosterveen, and Richard M. Smith, eds., *Bastardy and Its Comparative History: Studies in the History of Illegitimacy and Marital Nonconformism in Britain, France, Germany, Sweden, North America, Jamaica, and Japan* (Cambridge, Mass.: Harvard University Press, 1980). On witches, see Carol Kalson, *Devil in the Shape of a Woman: Witchcraft in Colonial New England* (New York: Vintage Books, 1987).

82. Hall, "O. Delight"; Nancy Maclean, "Leo Case Reconsidered"; Hickey, *Hope and Danger;* Cliff Kuhn, *Contesting the New South Order: The 1914–1915 Strike at Atlanta's Fulton Mills* (Chapel Hill: University of North Carolina Press, 2000); and Susan Cahn, *Sexual Reckonings: Southern Girls in a Troubling Age* (Cambridge, Mass.: Harvard University, 2007).

83. Jacquelyn Hall et al., *Like a Family: The Making of a Cotton Mill World* (Chapel Hill: University of North Carolina Press, 1987).

84. Ruth Rosen, *Lost Sisterhood: Prostitution in America, 1900–1918* (Baltimore: Johns Hopkins University Press, 1982); Timothy J. Gilfoyle, *City of Eros: New York City, Prostitution, and the Commercialization of Sex, 1790–1920* (New York: W. W. Norton, 1992); and Barbara Meil Hobson, *Uneasy Virtue: The Politics of Prostitution and the American Reform Tradition* (New York: Basic Books, 1987).

85. Elizabeth Lunbeck, *The Psychiatric Persuasion: Knowledge, Gender, and Power in Modern America* (Princeton: Princeton University Press, 1994).

86. Steven Schlossman and Stephanie Wallach, "The Crime of Precocious Sexuality: Female Juvenile Delinquency in the Progressive Era," *Harvard Educational Review* 48 (1978): 65–94; Kathy Peiss, "'Charity Girl' and City Pleasures: Historical Notes on Working Class Sexuality, 1880–1920," in *Powers of Desire: The Politics of Sexuality,* ed. Ann Snitow, Christine Stansell, and Sharon Thompson (New York: Monthly Review Press, 1983); Mary Odem, *Delinquent Daughters: Protection and Policing Adolescent Female Sexuality in the United States, 1885–1920* (Chapel Hill: University of North Carolina Press, 1995).

87. Anastatia Sims, *The Power of Femininity in the New South: Women's Organizations and Politics in North Carolina, 1880–1930* (Columbia: University of South Carolina Press, 1997), 74–75.

88. Anastatia Sims argues that after 1900 the King's Daughters, the Florence Crittenten League, and the WCTU of North Carolina had abandoned most of their attempts to rehabilitate prostitutes and were turning to the government to take action to stop prostitution. In *The Power of Femininity in the New South,* she explained, "White organized women increasingly adopted a coercive approach toward moral reform" and "became more interested in enforcing their moral code than in reclaiming lost souls who strayed from the straight and narrow" (p. 75). In *Gender and Jim Crow,* Glenda Gilmore highlights the efforts of late nineteenth-century citizens of New Bern, North Carolina, to police lower-class

white women's behavior when the city council passed the following ordinance: "Any lewd woman who shall be found on the streets or alleys soliciting male persons, drinking, sitting on the streets in front of or lounging about bar rooms, or conducting herself in a forward or improper manner shall be deemed guilty of a nuisance . . . and fined." Gilmore, *Gender and Jim Crow*, 73.

89. *Dalton Argus*, August 22, 1885; *Calhoun Times*, August 27, 1885; and *Atlanta Constitution*, August 21, 22, and 23, 1885.

90. *Calhoun Times*, June 6, 1889.

91. Ibid.

92. W. J. Wright, "Pound, Virginia," in *Our Appalachia: An Oral History*, ed. Laurel Shackelford and Bill Weinberg (New York: Hill and Wang, 1977), 58–9.

93. William F. Holmes, "Whitecapping in Georgia: Carroll and Houston Counties, 1893," *Georgia Historical Quarterly* 64 (1980): 388–404; Holmes, "Moonshining and Collective Violence: Georgia, 1889–1895," *Journal of American History* 67 (1980): 489–611; Holmes, "Whitecapping: Agrarian Violence in Mississippi, 1902–1906," *Journal of Southern History* 35 (May 1969): 165–185; Ayers, *Vengeance and Justice*, 255–261; Richard Maxwell Brown, "Historical Patterns of Violence in America," in *History of Violence in America: Historical and Comparative Perspectives*, ed. Hugh Davis Graham and Ted Robert Gurr (New York: Bantam, 1969), 70–71; James O. Nall, *The Tobacco Night-Riders of Kentucky and Tennessee, 1905–1909* (Louisville, 1939); and E. W. Crozier, *The White-Caps: A History of the Organization in Sevier County* (1899; n.p., 1963).

94. At least five white women were lynched outside the South between 1880 and 1900.

95. The most notorious lynchings of women were the 1851 lynching of Juanita (a Mexican woman) in California, the 1885 lynching of Elizabeth Taylor (white) in Nebraska, and the 1889 lynching of "Cattle Kate" (Ella Watson) (white) in Wyoming. All took place in the western region of the United States. See William B. Secrest, *The Only Woman Lynched in the Gold Rush Days* (Fresno, Calif.: Saga-West, 1967); Jean Williams, *The Lynching of Elizabeth Taylor* (Santa Fe, N.M.: The Press of the Territorian, n.d.); and George Hufsmith, *The Wyoming Lynching of Cattle Kate, 1889* (Glendo, Wyo.: High Plains Press, 1993).

96. *Courier-Journal*, December 30, 1895.

97. Ibid.

98. "Resolution," published in the *Courier-Journal*, December 31, 1895.

99. *Courier-Journal*, December 31, 1895; and *New York Times*, December 31, 1895.

100. *The State*, November 27, 1901.

101. *Courier-Journal*, December 30, 1895.

102. *Atlanta Constitution*, October 22, 1884; and *Walker County Messenger* (Lafayette, Ga.), October 30, 1884. Also see *Calhoun Times*, October 30, 1884.

103. *Courier-Journal*, July 2, 1895.

104. *Dallas Morning News*, July 21, 1895.

7. Equal Rights for Southern Women

1. W. E. B. Du Bois, *The Souls of Black Folk: Authoritative Text, Contexts, Criticism*, ed. Henry Louis Gates Jr. and Terri Hume Oliver (New York: W. W. Norton, 1999).

2. Rebecca Latimer Felton, "Woman's Suffrage," *Woman's World*, n.d., Rebecca Latimer Felton Papers, Rare Book and Manuscript Library (GHL).

3. Rebecca Latimer Felton, "Education Is Not a Success, and Unfits the Negro for Anything," n.p., 1901, Rebecca Latimer Felton Papers, GHL.

4. Ibid.

5. Ibid.

6. Ibid.

7. Letter, Rebecca Lattimer Felton to the *Atlanta Journal* [1905], clipping, "Race Problems Folder," Felton Papers.

8. W. Fitzhugh Brundage, *Lynching in the New South: Georgia and Virginia, 1880–1930* (Chicago: University of Illinois Press, 1993); and Christopher Waldrep, *The Many Faces of Judge Lynch: Extralegal Violence and Punishment in America* (New York: Palgrave Macmillan Press, 2002).

9. Grace Elizabeth Hale, *Making Whiteness: The Culture of Segregation in the South, 1890–1940* (New York: Pantheon Books, 1998), 209–215.

10. *Atlanta Constitution*, April 2 and 3, 1902.

11. Ray Stannard Baker, "What Is Lynching? A Study of Mob Justice South and North," *McClure's Magazine* 24 (January 1905): 299–430.

12. Joel Williamson, *The Crucible of Race: Black-White Relations in the American South since Emancipation* (New York: University of Oxford Press, 1984), 115–117, 140–141, 169–176, 183–189, 306–310; Nell Irvin Painter, *Standing at Armageddon: The United States, 1877–1919* (New York: W. W. Norton, 1987), 219–220; Glenda Elizabeth Gilmore, *Gender and Jim Crow: Women and the Politics of White Supremacy in North Carolina, 1896–1920* (Chapel Hill: University of North Carolina Press, 1996), 135–138; Daniel Levering Lewis, *W. E. B. Du Bois: Biography of a Race, 1868–1919* (New York: Henry Holt, 1993), 506–509; Michael Rogin, "'The Sword Became a Flashing Vision': D. W. Griffith's *The Birth of a Nation*," *Representations* no. 9 (Winter 1985): 150–195; David Fort Godshalk, *Veiled Visions: The 1906 Atlanta Race Riot and the Reshaping of American Race Relations* (Chapel Hill: University of North Carolina Press, 2005), 36, 143; Hale, *Making Whiteness*, 233; Tera Hunter, *To 'Joy My Freedom: Southern Black*

Women's Lives and Labors after the Civil War (Cambridge, Mass.: Harvard University Press, 1997), 161; and John Dittmer, *Black Georgia in the Progressive Era, 1900–1920* (Urbana: University of Illinois Press, 1980), 66–67.

13. Ibid.

14. Rebecca Latimer Felton, "Sober Thoughts about 'The Clansman,'" *Atlanta Journal*, n.d., Rebecca Latimer Felton Papers, GHL.

15. "Dixon's Play Stirs Wrath of Columbia," *Atlanta Constitution*, October 19, 1905. See John Inscoe, "*The Clansman* on Stage and Screen," *North Carolina Historical Review* 64 (April 1987): 139–161.

16. James B. Heyward, "The Hissing of the 'Clansman,'" *Atlanta Constitution*, October 22, 1905.

17. Ibid.

18. Tomas Dixon, "Tom Dixon Talks of the Clansman," *Atlanta Constitution*, October 29, 1905.

19. Ibid.

20. Len Broughton, "Dr. Broughton Talks of Dixon," *Atlanta Constitution*, November 6, 1905.

21. Ibid.

22. Godshalk, *Veiled Visions*, 9–21.

23. Ibid.; Georgina Hickey, *Hope and Danger in the New South City: Working-Class Women and Urban Development in Atlanta, 1890–1940* (Athens: University of Georgia Press, 2003); Hunter, *To 'Joy My Freedom*; and Gregory Lamont Mixon, *The Atlanta Riot: Race, Class, and Violence in a New South City* (Gainesville: University Press of Florida, 2005).

24. Godshalk, Veiled Vision.

25. *Atlanta Journal*, August 1, 1906.

26. Goldshalk, *Veiled Vision*, 50–54; Painter, *Standing at Armageddon*, 221; C. Vann Woodward, *The Origins of the New South, 1877–1913* (Baton Rouge: Louisiana State University Press, 1951), 330–333, 345; C. Vann Woodward, *Tom Watson: Agrarian Rebel* (repr.; New York: Oxford University Press, 1963), 379; and Dittmer, *Black Georgia*, 94–104.

27. *Atlanta Georgian*, August 21, 1906.

28. W. H. Felton, "In Regard to 'Negro' Disfranchisement," *Atlanta Constitution*, August 19, 1906.

29. Mixon, *The Atlanta Race Riot*; and Godshalk, *Unveiled Visions*.

30. *Atlanta Constitution*, September 23, 1906.

31. Godshalk, *Veiled Visions*, 85–114.

32. Ibid., 54; and Leslie Kathrin Dunlap, "In the Name of Home: Temperance Women and Southern Grass-Roots Politics, 1873–1933" (Ph.D. diss., Northwestern University, 2001), 164–170.

33. *Atlanta Georgian*, September 1, 1906.

34. Carole A. Stevens, "The Road Is Still Rough: The Contribution of the Latimer Sisters to Georgia's Temperance and Suffrage Work, 1880–1921" (master's thesis, Georgia State University, 1994); A. Elizabeth Taylor, "The Last Phase of the Woman Suffrage Movement in Georgia," *Georgia Historical Quarterly* 43 (1959); A. Elizabeth Taylor, "The Origin of the Woman Suffrage Movement in Georgia," *Georgia Historical Quarterly* 28 (1944); A. Elizabeth Taylor, "Revival and Development of the Woman Suffrage Movement in Georgia," *Georgia Historical Quarterly* 42 (1958); and A. Elizabeth Taylor, "Woman Suffrage Activities in Atlanta," *Atlanta Historical Journal* 23 (1979–80).

35. *Atlanta Georgian*, September 8 1906; and Godshalk, *Veiled Visions*, 54–55.

36. *Atlanta Constitution*, September 27, 1906.

37. Rebecca Latimer Felton, "Mrs. Felton Denounces the Dispensary System," *Atlanta Constitution*, October 14, 1906 (emphasis in the original).

38. Godshalk, *Veiled Visions*, 144.

39. *Atlanta Constitution*, September 27 and 29, 1906.

40. Godshalk, *Veiled Visions*.

41. Marjorie Spruill Wheeler, *New Women of the New South: The Leaders of the Woman Suffrage Movement in the Southern States* (New York: Oxford University Press, 1993), 102.

42. Wheeler, *New Women of the New South*, 113–114; and A. Elizabeth Taylor, "The Woman Suffrage Movement in Mississippi, 1890–1920," *Journal of Mississippi History* 30 (February 1968): 207–210.

43. Kate Gordon to Laura Clay, May 30, 1907, Clay Papers, quoted in Wheeler, *New Women of the New South*, 100.

44. Belle Kearney, "The South and Woman Suffrage," *Woman's Journal*, April 4, 1903, reprinted in *Up from the Pedestal: Selected Writings in the History of American Feminism*, ed. Aileen S. Kraditor (Chicago: Quadrangle Books, 1968), 262–265; Wheeler, *New Women of the New South*; Elna Green, *Southern Strategies: Southern Women and the Woman Suffrage Question* (Chapel Hill: University of North Carolina Press, 1997); and Gilmore, *Gender and Jim Crow*.

45. Wheeler, *New Women of the New South*, 125–132; and Sims, *The Power of Femininity in the New South: Women's Organizations and Politics in North Carolina, 1880–1930* (Columbia: University of South Carolina Press, 1997), 170–180; Gilmore, *Gender and Jim Crow*, 203–224; Suzanne Lebsock, "Woman Suffrage and White Supremacy: Virginia Case Study," in *Visible Women: New Essays on American Activism* (Urbana: University of Illinois Press, 1993); Green, *Southern Strategies*; and Sarah Wilkerson-Freeman, "The Second Battle for Woman Suffrage: Alabama White Women, the Poll Tax, and V. O. Key's Master Narrative of Southern Politics," *Journal of Southern History* 68 (2002).

46. Rebecca Latimer Felton, "Woman's Suffrage," *Woman's World* and Felton, *The Subjection of Women and the Enfranchisement of Women*, Rebecca Latimer Felton Papers, GHL.

47. Rebecca Latimer Felton, "Southern Congressman Opposing Equal Suffrage," n.d., Rebecca Latimer Felton Papers, GHL.

48. *Atlanta Constitution*, July 8, 1914.

49. Felton, *The Subjection of Women*.

50. Ibid., 8.

51. Ibid., 12.

52. Rebecca Latimer Felton, "Making Slaves of Their Wives," *Atlanta Journal Semi-weekly*, January 27, 1914, Rebecca Latimer Felton Papers, GHL.

53. Rebecca Latimer Felton, "The Murder of Wives Getting Intolerable," *Atlanta Journal Semi-weekly*, May 19, 1925, Rebecca Latimer Felton Papers, GHL.

54. Rebecca Latimer Felton, "Out to Be Lynched," *Atlanta Journal Semi-weekly*, n.d., Rebecca Latimer Felton Papers, GHL.

55. Rebecca Latimer Felton, "Lynching in Georgia," *Timely Topics by Mrs. Felton*, n.d., Rebecca Latimer Felton Papers, GHL.

56. *Atlanta Journal*, May 5, 1913, Rebecca Latimer Felton Papers.

57. John E. Talmadge, *Rebecca Latimer Felton: Nine Stormy Decades* (Athens: University of Georgia Press, 1960), 118.

58. "Crime of Mob Violence Unpunished in Georgia, Declares Mrs. Felton," *Atlanta Constitution*, January 13, 1920.

59. Ibid.

60. Ibid.

61. Letter, "Editor of the Tuskegee Student to Mrs. W. H. Felton," January 17, 1920, Rebecca Latimer Felton Papers, GHL.

62. Letter, C. M. Battey to Mrs. W. H. Felton, January 13, 1920, Felton Papers.

63. Letter, "Lynward F. Cole to Mrs. W. H. Felton," January 21, 1920, Rebecca Latimer Felton Papers, GHL.

64. Dunlap, "In the Name of Home," 162–163; and *Georgia Bulletin*, January 1920, 3.

65. Rebecca Latimer Felton, "Where Is the Remedy?" *Atlanta Journal Semi-weekly*, October 6, 1925, Rebecca Latimer Felton Papers, GHL.

66. *Atlanta Constitution*, January 5, 19, and 30, 1921; February 6, 1921.

67. Excerpts from the *Dalton Citizen* and *Cordele Dispatch* appeared in the *Chatsworth Times*, January 27, 1921.

68. *New York Times*, November 19, 1922.

69. Nancy MacLean, "The Leo Frank Case Reconsidered: Gender and Sexual Politics in the Making of Reactionary Populism," *Journal of American History* 78 (1991): 917–948; Leonard Dinnerstein, *The Leo Frank Case* (repr.; Athens: University of Georgia Press, 1987); Albert S. Lindemann, *The Jew Accused: Three*

Anti-Semitic Affairs (Dreyfus, Beilis, Frank), 1894–1915 (Cambridge: Cambridge University Press, 1991); Steve Oney, *And the Dead Shall Rise: The Murder of Mary Phagan and the Lynching of Leo Frank* (New York: Pantheon Books, 2003).

70. Woodward, *Tom Watson*; Walter J. Brown, *J. J. Brown and Thomas E. Watson: Georgia Politics, 1912–1928* (Macon, Ga.: Mercer University Press, 1989); G. Jack Gravlee, "Tom Watson: Disciple of 'Jeffersonian Democracy,'" in *The Oratory of Southern Demagogues*, ed. Cal M. Logue and Howard Dorgan (Baton Rouge: Louisiana State University Press, 1981), 85–108; Richard Nelson, "The Cultural Contradictions of Populism: Tom Watson's Tragic Vision of Power, Politics, and History," *Georgia Historical Quarterly* 72 (Spring 1988): 1–29; and Fred D. Ragan, "Obscenity or Politics? Tom Watson, Anti-Catholicism, and the Department of Justice," *Georgia Historical Quarterly* 70 (Spring 1986): 17–46.

71. "Watson of Georgia Dies in Washington," *New York Times*, September 27, 1922.

72. Dewey W. Grantham Jr., ed., "Some Letters from Thomas W. Hardwick to Tom Watson Concerning the Georgia Gubernatorial Campaign of 1906," *Georgia Historical Quarterly* 34 (December 1950): 328–340; and Josephine Mellichamp, "Thomas W. Hardwick," in *Senators from Georgia* (Huntsville: Strode Publishers, 1976), 212–214.

73. Eleanor G. Hirsch, "Grandma Felton and the U.S. Senate," *Mankind* 4 (April 1974): 44–57; and Mellichamp, *Senators from Georgia*, 224–229.

74. Rebecca Latimer Felton, *The Romantic Story of Georgia's Women* (Atlanta: Atlanta Georgian & Sunday American, 1930), 44.

75. Charles E. Hall, "Has Mrs. Felton Changed Her Opinion on Lynching Negroes?" *New York Age*, October 14, 1922; and Nick Chiles, "Sounds Mrs. Felton on Lynching Evil in South," *Topeka Plaindealer*, November 10, 1922.

76. John E. Talmadge, "Rebecca Latimer Felton," in *Georgians in Profile: Historical Essays in Honor of Ellis Merton Coulter*, ed. Horace Montgomery (Athens: University of Georgia Press, 1958), 277–302; Talmadge, *Rebecca Latimer Felton*; Talmadge, "Rebecca Latimer Felton, Georgian," *Georgia Review* 9 (Spring 1955): 65–73; Talmadge, "The Seating of the First Woman in the United States Senate," *Georgia Review* 10 (Summer 1956): 168–174; LeeAnn Whites, "The De Graffenried Controversy: Class, Race, and Gender in the New South," *Journal of Southern History* 54, 3 (August 1988): 449–478; Whites, "Rebecca Latimer Felton and the Wife's Farm: The Class and Racial Politics of Gender Reform," *Georgia Historical Quarterly* 76 (Summer 1992): 354–372; Whites, "Love, Hate, Rape, Lynching: Rebecca Latimer Felton and the Gender Politics of Racial Violence," in *Democracy Betrayed: The Wilmington Race Riot and Its Legacy*, ed. David S. Cecelski and Timothy B. Tyson (Chapel Hill: University of North Carolina Press, 1998): 143–162; Josephine

Bone Floyd, "Rebecca Latimer Felton, Champion of Women's Rights," *Georgia Historical Quarterly* 30 (June 1946): 81–104; Floyd, "Rebecca Latimer Felton, Political Independent," *Georgia Historical Quarterly* 30 (March 1946): 14–34; Hirsch, "Grandma Felton and the U.S. Senate," 52–57; Josephine Mellichamp, "Rebecca Latimer Felton," in *Senators from Georgia*, 224–229; Joan Conerly Hunter, "Rebecca Latimer Felton" (master's thesis, University of Georgia, 1944); and Henry Y. Warnock, "Andrew Sledd, Southern Methodists, and the Negro: A Case History," *Journal of Southern History* 31, 3 (August 1965): 251–271.

77. Article II, section 3 of the Constitution gives the president power to "on extraordinary Occasions, convene both Houses, or either of them." Presidents, before the adoption of the Twentieth Amendment, often used this power to call the Senate alone into special session. Despite the phrase "extraordinary Occasions" in the enabling clause of the Constitution, most special sessions of the Senate were rather routine: it was common practice for the president of an outgoing administration to call the Senate of the incoming Congress into special session on March 4 of the odd-numbered year so that it could "advise and consent" to any executive and ministerial nominations made by the new president as soon as possible after the incoming administration was sworn in that March 4.

78. Letter, "Warren G. Harding to R. L. Felton," November 16, 1922, quoted in Talmadge, *Rebecca Latimer Felton*, 142.

79. Josephine Mellichamp, "Walter F. George," in *Senators from Georgia*, 230–239; and Luther Harmon Zeigler Jr., "Senator Walter George's 1938 Campaign," *Georgia Historical Quarterly* 43 (December 1959): 333–352.

80. "Will Wage Senate Campaign against Anti-Lynching Law," *New York Times*, October 29, 1922.

81. Felton, *The Romantic Story of Georgia's Women*, 44.

82. Ibid., 25.

83. Nancy MacLean, *Behind the Mask of Chivalry: The Making of the Second Ku Klux Klan* (New York: Oxford University Press, 1994).

8. The Gender and Racial Politics of the Anti-Lynching Movement

1. "Anti-Lynching Delegation to President Harding, August 14, 1922," *The Crisis* (October 1922), 260. The delegates were Mrs. Ida Brown, New Jersey; Miss Mary B. Jackson, Rhode Island; Mrs. Ida Wells-Barnett, Illinois; Mrs. Mary Parrish, Kentucky; Miss Hallie Q. Brown, Ohio; Mrs. Minnie Scott, Ohio; Mrs. Cora Horne, New York; Mrs. Estelle Davis, Ohio; Mrs. E. G. Rose, Delaware; Mrs. Lethia Fleming, Ohio; Mrs. Ida Posties, Michigan; Mrs. Pearl Winters,

California; Mrs. Myrtle F. Cook, Missouri; Mrs. C. Chiles, Kansas; and Mrs. Ruth Bennett, Pennsylvania.

2. Mary Church Terrell, "What Role Is the Educated Negro Woman to Play in the Uplifting of Her Race?" in *Twentieth Century Negro Literature, or A Cyclopedia of Thought on the Vital Topics Relating to the American Negro*, ed. D. W. Culp (Atlanta: J. L. Nichols & Co., 1902), 177.

3. For a discussion of how World War I radicalized African Americans, see Adriane Lentz-Smith, *Freedom Struggles: African Americans and World War I* (Cambridge, Mass.: Harvard University Press, 2009).

4. Ida B. Wells, "How Enfranchisement Stops Lynching," *Original Rights Magazine* (June 1910): 42–53. Nannie Bourroughs argued that female suffrage would ensure the passage of legislation to win legal protection against rape. See Evelyn Brooks Barnett, "Nannie Burroughs and the Education of Black Women," in *The Afro-American Woman: Struggles and Images*, ed. Sharon Harley and Rosayln Terborg-Penn (Baltimore: Black Classic Press, 1978), 97–108; and Rosalyn Terborg-Penn, "Woman Suffrage: 'First because We Are Women and Second because We Are Colored Women,'" *Truth: Newsletter of the Association of Black Women Historians* (April 1985): 9.

5. James L. Crouthamel, "The Springfield Race Riot of 1908," *Journal of Negro History* (July 1960): 164–181.

6. Ida B. Wells, *Crusade for Justice: The Autobiography of Ida B. Wells*, ed. Alfeda M. Duster (Chicago: University of Chicago Press, 1970), 298–301.

7. Quote in Paula J. Giddings, *Ida: A Sword among Lions: Ida B. Wells and the Campaign against Lynching* (New York: HarperCollins, 2008), 483.

8. Wells, *Crusade for Justice*, 311.

9. Giddings, *Ida*, 481–487.

10. Ida B. Wells-Barnett, "How Enfranchisement Stops Lynchings," *Original Rights Magazine* (June 1910): 42–53.

11. Ibid.

12. Giddings, *Ida*, 515–519.

13. *Chicago Defender*, March 8, 1913.

14. *Chicago Defender*, April 5 and 19, 1913.

15. Wells, *Crusade for Justice*, 346.

16. Wells, *Crusade for Justice*, 342–344; and Giddings, *Ida*, 350.

17. *Chicago Broad Ax*, October 27, 1917.

18. Nell Irvin Painter, *Standing at Armageddon: The United States, 1877–1919* (New York: W. W. Norton, 1987).

19. Memorandum, "Walter F. White to Governor Dorsey," July 10, 1918. NAACP Papers, Manuscripts Collection Library of Congress.

20. Meta Vaux Warrick Fuller's *Mary Turner (A Silent Protest)* is on display at the Boston Museum of Afro-American History.

21. Northeastern Federation of Women's Clubs, *Propaganda Campaign, 1926–1927* (Anti-lynching Department, New York) in NAACP Papers, Manuscripts Collection, Library of Congress.

22. Evelyn Brooks Higginbotham, *Righteous Discontent: The Women's Movement in the Black Baptist Church, 1880–1920* (Cambridge, Mass.: Harvard University Press, 1993), 222–224.

23. Northeastern Federation of Women's Clubs, "Propaganda Campaign, 1926–1927."

24. Claudine Ferrell, *Nightmare and Dream: Anti-lynching in Congress, 1911–1922* (New York: Garland, 1986); Robert Zangrando, *The NAACP Crusade against Lynching, 1909–1950* (Philadelphia: Temple University Press, 1980); George C. Rable, "The South and the Politics of Antilynching Legislation, 1920–1940," *Journal of Southern History* 51, 2 (May 1985): 201–220; Donald Grant, *The Anti-lynching Movement, 1883–1932* (San Francisco: R & R Research Associates, 1975); and William B. Hixson Jr., "Moorfield Storey and the Defense of the Dyer Anti-Lynching Bill," *New England Quarterly* 42, 1 (March 1969): 65–81.

25. Anti-Lynching Bill, 1918, 67th Cong., 2d sess., 1921–22, S. Rept. 7951, 2: 33–34.

26. William M. Tuttle Jr., *Race Riot: Chicago in the Red Summer of 1919* (Urbana: University of Illinois Press, 1996); Robert J. Booker, *The Heat of a Red Summer: Race Mixing, Race Rioting in 1919 Knoxville* (Danbury, Conn.: Rutledge Books, 2001); Shelia Smith McKoy, *When Whites Riot: Writing Race and Violence in American and South African Culture* (Madison: University of Wisconsin Press, 2001); Arthur M. Waskow, *From Race Riot to Sit-in: 1919 and the 1960s. A Study in the Connections between Conflict and Violence* (New York: Doubleday, 1960); and Lee E. Williams, *Anatomy of Four Race Riots: Racial Conflict in Knoxville, Elaine, Tulsa, and Chicago, 1919–1921* (Jackson: University of Mississippi Press, 1972).

27. James Weldon Johnson, *Along This Way: The Autobiography of James Weldon Johnson* (New York: Viking Press, 1933); Kenneth M. Price, *Critical Essays on James Weldon Johnson* (Woodbridge, Conn.: Twayne Publishers, 1997); Eugene Levy, *James Weldon Johnson: Black Leader, Black Voice* (Chicago: University of Chicago Press, 1973); Higginbotham, *Righteous Discontent*, 221–229; Kevin Gaines, *Uplifting the Race: Black Leadership, Politics, and Culture in the Twentieth Century* (Chapel Hill: University of North Carolina Press, 1996), 216–217; Glenda Elizabeth Gilmore, *Gender and Jim Crow: Women and the Politics of White Supremacy in North Carolina, 1896–1920* (Chapel Hill: University of North Carolina Press, 1996), 195–202; Tera Hunter, *To 'Joy My Freedom: Southern Black Women's Lives and Labor after the Civil War* (Cambridge, Mass.: Harvard University Press, 1997), 222–238; Deborah Gray White, *Too Heavy a Load: Black Women in Defense of Themselves, 1894–1994* (New York: W. W. Norton, 1999), 114–115; Painter, *Standing at Armageddon*, 344–380.

28. Jacquelyn Dowd Hall, *Revolt against Chivalry: Jessie Daniel Ames and the Women's Campaign against Lynching*, rev. ed. (New York: Columbia University, 1992); Mary Jane Brown, *Eradicating This Evil: Women in the American Anti-Lynching Movement, 1892–1940* (New York: Garland Press, 2000); and Rosalyn Terborg-Penn, "African-American Women's Networks in the Anti-lynching Crusade," in *Gender, Class, Race and Reform in the Progressive Era,* ed. Noralee Frankel and Nancy S. Dye (Kentucky: University of Kentucky Press, 1991); Higginbotham, *Righteous Discontent;* White, *Too Heavy a Load;* Ida B. Wells, "The Race Conflict in Arkansas," *The Survey* (December 13, 1919): 233–234; and NAACP, *Thirty Years of Lynching, 1889–1918* (New York: NAACP, 1919). The NAACP also published *Burning at the Stake in the US* (1919) and *The Fight against Lynching* (1919). For coverage of the NAACP coming out to support the Dyer Bill, see "The National Conference on Lynching," *New York Times,* May 6, 1919, p. 15; Press Service of the NAACP, Press Release: "Senator France, Representative Dyer to Urge Federal Anti-Lynching [Law]," November 29, 1920, NAACP Papers; "The Shame of America," *New York Times,* November 23, 1922; and "A Terrible Blot on American Civilization," NAACP Papers, Manuscripts Collection, Library of Congress.

29. Craig Sautter and Edward M. Burke, *Inside the Wigwam: Chicago Presidential Conventions, 1860–1996* (Chicago: Wild Onion Books, an imprint of Loyola Press, 1996); Paul F. Boller Jr., *Presidential Campaigns,* rev. ed. (New York: Oxford University Press, 1996); Keith Mellder, *Hail to the Candidate: Presidential Campaigns for Banners to Broadcasts* (Washington, D.C.: Smithsonian Institution Press, 1992); Letter, "Warren Harding to James Weldon Johnson," June 18, 1921, Warren Harding Papers, Library of Congress; Letter, Warren Harding's Secretary to James Weldon Johnson, December 8, 1922, NAACP Papers; and Richard B. Sherman, "The Harding Administration and the Negro: An Opportunity Lost," *Journal of Negro History* 49, 3 (July 1964): 151–168.

30. January 26, 1922, *Congressional Record,* 67th Cong., 2d sess., 1795–1796.

31. *New York Times,* July 9, 1922, p. 33.

32. Ida B. Wells, *A Red Record,* in *On Lynchings* (Salem, N.H.: Ayer Company, Publishers, 1991), 154–155; *New York Times,* September 11, 1894; and McMurry, *To Keep the Waters Troubled: The Life of Ida B. Wells* (New York: Oxford University Press, 1998), 230.

33. Wells, *Crusade for Justice,* 252–254; and Wells, "Letter from Ida B. Wells to William McKinley, 1898," accessed May 2008 at www.digitalhistory.uh.edu/learning_history/lynching/wells3.cfm. For negative press, see *Indianapolis Freeman,* March 5, 1898; *Colored American,* April 16, 1898; and *Cleveland Gazette,* April 16, 1898.

34. W. Fitzhugh Brundage, *Lynching in the New South: Georgia and Virginia, 1880–1930* (Chicago: University of Illinois Press, 1993); W. Fitzhugh Brundage, "The

Roar on the Other Side of Silence: Black Resistance and White Violence in the American South, 1880–1940," in *Under the Sentence of Death: Lynching in the South*, ed. W. Fitzhugh Brundage (Chapel Hill: University of Chapel Hill, 1997), 271–291; Hall, *Revolt against Chivalry*; and Zangrando, *The NAACP Crusade against Lynching*.

35. Patricia A. Schechter, *Ida B. Wells-Barnett and American Reform, 1880–1930* (Chapel Hill: University of North Carolina Press, 2001), 165–168; and Schechter, "Unsettled Business: Ida B. Wells against Lynching, or, How Anti-lynching Got Its Gender," in *Under the Sentence of Death*, 292–317; and Brown, *Eradicating This Evil*.

36. *Senate Reports*, 67th Cong., 2d sess., 1921–1922, 2.

37. Wells, *Crusade for Justice*, 328–229; Schechter, *Ida B. Wells-Barnett*, 144–145; White, *Too Heavy a Load*, 106; and Dorothy Salem, *To Better Our World: Black Women in Organized Reform, 1890–1920* (New York: Carlson, 1990), 106.

38. National Association of Colored Women, "Program and Minutes, 13th Biennial Session National Association of Colored Women: Dedication of Frederick Douglass Home (Ebenezer Baptist Church, Richmond, Virginia, August 6–12, 1922)," NACW Papers, Manuscripts Collection, Library of Congress.

39. Ibid., 33.

40. Ibid., 38.

41. Anti-Lynching Crusaders, *A Million Women United to Suppress Lynching* (Buffalo, N.Y.: Office of National Director, 1922); "The Anti-Lynching Crusaders," *Crisis* 24 (November 1922): 8; *Woman's Voice* 4 (January 1923); Mary B. Talbert et al., "Minutes of the Executive Committee of the Anti-Lynching Crusaders" [1922], NAACP Papers; "The Anti-Lynching Crusaders: The Lynching of Women," [1922], NAACP Papers; "Plan Organization of 1,000,000 Women to Stop Lynching in United States," [1922], NAACP Papers; "Agreement between the Anti-Lynching Crusaders and the N.A.A.C.P.," [1922], NAACP Papers; and "Why the Million Dollars?" [Editorial], *Pittsburgh Courier*, October 28, 1922, NAACP Papers. For a discussion of the Anti-Lynching Crusaders, see Terborg-Penn, "African-American Women's Networks in the Anti-lynching Crusade," 154–156; Hall, *Revolt against Chivalry*, 165–166; Gerda Lerner, ed., *Black Women in White America: A Documentary History* (New York: Vintage Books, 1972), 211–214; Schechter, *Ida B. Wells-Barnett*, 165–168; and Schechter, "Unsettled Business," 309.

42. NACW, "Program and Minutes," p. 38.

43. Gidding, *Ida*, 628.

44. Jessie Fauset, "The 13th Biennial of the NACW," *Crisis* 24 (October 1922): 260.

45. *New York Times*, August 15, 1922, p. 10.

46. "Petition to President Harding on Dyer Bill," *Union* 17, 34 (August 30, 1922): 2.

47. Quoted in Giddings, *Ida*, 626–631.

48. Anti-Lynching Crusaders, "A Million Women United to Suppress Lynching."

49. National Baptist Convention, *Thirteenth Annual Report of the Executive Board and Corresponding Secretary of the Women's Convention* (Nashville: National Baptist Convention, 1913), 31–32.

50. "The Colored Women's Statement to the Women's Missionary Council, American Missionary Association, 1919," in *Black Women in White America*, 461. The letter was signed by Charlotte Hawkins Brown, president of the North Carolina Federation of Colored Women; Marion B. Wilkinson, president of the South Carolina Federation of Colored Women; Lucy C. Laney, president of the Georgia Federation of Colored Women; Mary J. McCrovey, Charlotte Branch YWCA; Janie P. Barret, president of the Virginia Federation of Colored Women; Mrs. Booker T. Washington, president of the National Association of Colored Women's Club; Mrs. R. R. Moton, Tuskegee Institute; Mrs. John Hope, National Federation of Colored Women's Clubs; Mrs. M. L. Crostwait; and Mary McLeod Bethune, president of the Southern Eastern Federation of Colored Women.

51. "The Colored Women's Statement."

52. Charlotte Hawkins Brown, "Speaking Up for the Race at Memphis, Tennessee, October 8, 1920," in Lerner, *Black Women in White America*, 471. For more information about Charlotte Hawkins Brown, see Tera Hunter, "The Correct Thing: Charlotte Hawkins Brown and the Palmer Institute," *Southern Exposure* 11, 15 (September/October 1983) 37–43; Sandra N. and Earle H. West, "Charlotte Hawkins Brown," in Lerner, *Black Women in White America*, 172–174; Gilmore, *Gender and Jim Crow*; and Charlotte Hawkins Brown Papers at the Arthur and Elizabeth Schlesinger Library at Radcliffe College, Cambridge, Massachusetts.

53. Charlotte Hawkins Brown, "Speaking up for the Race at Memphis," in *Black Women in American History*, 467–472.

54. Commission on Interracial Cooperation, "Southern Women and Race Cooperation: A Story of the Memphis Conference, October Sixth and Seventh, Nineteen Hundred and Twenty," The Commission 1921, North Carolina Collection, University of North Carolina at Chapel Hill.

55. "The Anti-Lynching Crusaders," 8.

56. Rosalyn Terborg-Penn, "African-American Women's Networks in the Anti-lynching Crusade," 154–156.

57. Margaret Murray Washington, "Club Work among Negro Women," in *Progress of a Race*, ed. J. L. Nichols and William Crogam rev. ed. (Atlanta: J. L. Nichols Co., 1929), 209.

58. *Congressional Record*, 67th Cong., 3d sess., 1922, 63, pt. 1: 14.

59. Ibid., 23.

60. *New York Times*, November 23, 1922.

61. Mary Garrett Hay, president of the Women's City Club of New York; Mary Austin, novelist; Janet Simmons Harris of the National Council of Women; Mrs. Frederic C. Howe, wife of the former Commissioner of Immigration; Belle Caldwell Culbertson, president of the Woman's Inter-denominational Missionary Union; Ethel Stover, mayor of Cokeville, Wyoming; Mrs. Cyrus Beard, widow of the late Chief Justice of the Supreme Court of Memphis, Tennessee; and Winnifred L. Chappell of the Methodist Federation for Social Service. "Women of America Respond to Call of Anti-Lynching Crusaders" and "Mary Garrett Hay Joins Anti-Lynching Crusaders," November 24, 1922, NAACP Papers.

62. "Women Back Dyer Bill," *New York Times*, December 5, 1922; and "Democratic Women Protest Dyer Bill Filibuster," NAACP Press Release, December 4, 1922, NAACP Papers, Manuscripts Collection, Library of Congress.

63. "Southern Women Oppose Lynching," *New York Evening Post*, December 15, 1922.

64. *New York Times*, December 12, 1922.

65. "Methodist Women South Open War on Lynching," Commission on Interracial Cooperation Press Release, April 17, 1923, NAACP Papers; and Letter to the Editor of the *Globe* from James Weldon Johnson, April 17, 1923, NAACP Papers, Manuscripts Collection, Library of Congress.

66. "Louisiana Women Join Good Will Movement," Commission on Interracial Cooperation press release, April 1923, NAACP Papers.

67. Brown, *Eradicating This Evil*.

68. Hall, *Revolt against Chivalry*.

69. Brown, *Eradicating This Evil*, 174.

70. ASWPL, *A New Public Opinion on Lynching: A Declaration and a Pledge* (Georgia: ASWPL, 1932).

71. *Atlanta Constitution*, January 26, 1930.

72. S. Res. 39 [109]: Lynching Victims Senate Apology Resolution, 109th Cong., 1st sess., S. Res. 39.

ACKNOWLEDGMENTS

Mary Church Terrell once said, "In myself I am nothing, but with the loyal support of conscientious, capable women, all things are possible." The completion of *Southern Horrors* would not have been possible without the support and guidance of so many brilliant women. First and foremost, I must thank Nell Irvin Painter, my constant advisor, friend, and inspiration. Her commitment to writing "southern history across the color line" gave me the courage to write this book.

When I began writing *Southern Horrors* I was teaching at Boston College, and with the support of my colleagues in the history department I was able to make tremendous progress. I am especially grateful to Virginia Reinburg, Karen Miller, Robin Fleming, Ellen Friedman, Carol Green, Peter Weiler, Cynthia Lyerly, Deborah Levenson-Estrada, Davarian Baldwin, Marilynn Johnson, Stephanie Leone, Todd Romero, and Ed Rugmer. During the 2002–2003 academic year I was a visiting scholar at the American Academy of Arts and Sciences and had the privilege of sharing and discussing ideas with Leslie Berlowitz, James Carroll, Ann Mikkelson, Eileen Babbitt, Robert Chodat, Jonathan Hansen, Matthew Lindsay, Adam Webb, and Jerrold Meinwald. In 2006 I joined the history department at UNC–Chapel Hill, where I have had the benefit of working with wonderful colleagues. I am especially grateful to Lloyd Kramer, Jacquelyn Dowd Hall, Jerma Jackson, Heather Williams, Genna Rae McNeil, Kathleen Duval, Chad Byrant, Michelle King, Brett Whalen, Fitzhugh Brundage, Harry Watson, William Ferris, Miles Fletcher, John Kasson, John Sweet, Jim Leloudis, Bob Korstad, Karen Hagemann, Donald Raleigh, Louise McReynolds, Malinda Maynor Lowery, Nadine Kinsey, LaTissa Davis, Kelly Morrow, Katy Smith, Julie Reed, Jennifer Dixon, and Joey Fink. I could not have asked for better research assistants than Sarah Rosen, Emily Byrne, David Pedulla, and Nicolette Hylan. After the birth of my son, I was able to carve out time to write only with the help of fabulous childcare provided by Laura Blum Smith, Katy Smith, Stan Cho-jnacki, Nicolette Hylan, Nate Ginedele, Kelly Lowe, Wanda Weaver, and Giomaris Boyd.

I am especially grateful for the many people who read and commented on the book at different stages; they listened patiently, made observations, and raised objections that have found their way into the text. Jacquelyn Dowd Hall, Glenda Gilmore, and Christine Stansell went over the whole manuscript with an affectionate care others save for their own work. Jacquelyn's support has been unwavering, and her pathbreaking work on Jessie Daniel Ames inspired me to write *Southern Horrors*. Elizabeth Lunbeck, Joan Scott, and Tera Hunter shared insights that helped define what the book would become. Drew Faust, Darlene Clark Hine, Charles Payne, Sylvia Frye, Fitzhugh Brundage, Barbara Savage, Linda Reed, Elsa B. Brown, and Barbara Ransby provided constructive feedback on conference papers that emerged out of this project. My writing group—Cheryl Hicks, Deborah Thomas, Ginetta Candelario, and Mary Lui—was invaluable. An array of friends and colleagues deserve singular thanks and gratitude: Barbara Sicherman, Adriane Lentz-Smith, Katherine Charron, Dylan Pennigroth, Jane Daily, Laura Edwards, Hannah Rosen, Timothy Tyson, Steven Kantrowitz, Marjorie Spruill, Patricia Schechter, Daniel Sharfstein, Anore Horton, Samuel Roberts, Kenneth Mack, David Gordon, Evan Hafeli, Leslie Harris, Clayborne Carson, Claire Nee Nelson, Lawrence Blum, Tuire Vallkeakari, Anastasia Curwood, Vanessa Kubach, and Lauren Tallevi.

The research and writing could not have been completed without the generous financial support I received from Yale University, Boston College, the University of North Carolina at Chapel Hill, the Ford Foundation, the North Caroliniana Society, the American Association of University Women Educational Foundation, and the American Academy of Arts and Sciences. Of course, there would be no book without the folks at Harvard University Press. My editor, Joyce Seltzer, believed in my work and insisted on its completion. Jeannette Estruth managed the details with charm, and the production team was fabulous. I am grateful to the two anonymous readers who suggested revisions that improved the book.

While many wonderful people have made the research, writing, and completion of *Southern Horrors* possible, I owe much to my dearest friends, who have kept me sane, intellectually inspired, and socially committed. Ginny Reinburg has taught me much about being an engaged scholar and a devoted friend. On her keen perception, her critical intelligence, and her good judgment, as well as on her friendship, I relied without reservation—I owe her more than I can ever repay. Judith Smith is a constant reminder of the kind of colleague, intellectual, mother, and friend that I strive to be. Ann Trapasso has never let me forget what is most important. Marcella and Michael Bungay Stanier have not only made me a better Scrabble player, but have also exposed me to worlds (as well as words) I could never have imagined. Erica Armstrong Dunbar has been with me every step of the way—from our summer in Palo Alto to the birth of our sons. Ann Mikkelsen, Jennifer Tucker, Karen Miller, Annie Reinhart, Kim Holshouser, Stanley Chojnacki, Anna Frazer, Angela Gantt Holliday, Patricia Turner, Victoria Klein, Sherrie Hartsoe Sigmon, Carolyn Cannon, Margo MacIntyre, and Paul Miller have all in their individual ways contributed to this project I call my life—and for their friendships and support I am extremely grateful.

I cannot measure the debt of gratitude that I owe Deborah Greenman for her invaluable insight, never-failing encouragement, and unwavering support as I made the final push to complete the manuscript. I am forever grateful to Barbara Harris. Her extraordinary commitment to my academic career and to my personal well-being over the past fifteen years has made all the difference.

I want to thank my mother, Nettie Johnson, for never letting me give up on my dreams and inspiring me to always stand up for what I believe. From the moment I was born, I had an ally and friend in my sister, Andrea Feimster. Quentin Johnson, Marie Cowan, Betty and Aldine Cloud, Hugh Cowan, Mozetta Dobbins, Barbara Botsman, Lyn and Andrew, Tarita and Jose, and Peter and Cat have proven that with the support of family anything is possible.

Finally, my most profound gratitude is reserved for Dani Botsman. As a constant source of inspiration and encouragement, Dani has contributed to this work in more ways than I can enumerate. His genius inspires me to think more broadly, to write better, and to read more. As I made the intellectual journey to write *Southern Horrors*, Dani's love and devotion, as a husband and father, confirmed my belief in the power of interracial alliances to heal wounds of the past and inspire hope for the future. Thus, it is to him and our son, Charles Peter Botsman, that I dedicate this book.

INDEX